The Relationship Between State and Individual Responsibility for International Crimes

The Relationship Between State and Individual Responsibility for International Crimes

By

Beatrice I. Bonafè

MARTINUS
NIJHOFF
PUBLISHERS

LEIDEN • BOSTON
2009

On the cover: Public Announcement of the Establishment of the Studium Iuris in Macerata in 1920 (detail). Fresco by Giulio Rolland, XIX Century. University of Macerata, Aula Magna.

This book is printed on acid-free paper.

Library of Congress Cataloging-in-Publication Data

Bonafe, Beatrice I.
The relationship between state and individual responsibility for international crimes / by Beatrice I. Bonafe.
p. cm.
Includes bibliographical references and index.
ISBN 978-90-04-17331-6 (hardback : alk. paper)
1. Criminal liability (International law) 2. International offenses. 3. Government liability. 4. Administrative responsibility. 5. Superior orders (Criminal law) I. Title.
K5301.B66 2009
345'.04—dc22

2008051891

ISBN: 978 90 04 17331 6

PRINTED IN THE NETHERLANDS

Contents

Acknowledgments

I would like to thank my family, my friends and the members of the Institute of International and European Law of the University of Macerata for their constant support and encouragement.

I would furthermore like to express my profound gratitude to Professor Philip Alston, Professor Antonio Cassese, Professor Pierre-Marie Dupuy, Professor Giorgio Gaja, Professor Paolo Palchetti, Guido Acquaviva, Mel Marquis, and last but not least Marco Maria Sigiani. Without them this book would never have seen the light of day.

Special thanks are due to Professor Enzo Cannizzaro for his precious guidance throughout the preparation of this book.

Needless to say, I bear sole responsibility for any errors or omissions.

List of Abbreviations

AD	Annual Digest and Reports of Public International Law Cases
AFDI	Annuaire français de droit international
AJIL	American Journal of International Law
AJPIL	Austrian Journal Public International Law
AVR	Archiv des Völkerrechts
BYIL	British Yearbook of International Law
Calif. L. Rev.	California Law Review
Colum. L. Rev.	Columbia Law Review
Comun. e Stud.	Comunicazioni e studi
Comunità Internaz.	La Comunità internazionale
Den. J. Int'l L. & Pol'y	Denver Journal of International Law and Policy
EJIL	European Journal of International Law
GYIL	German Yearbook of International Law
Hastings Int'l & Comp. L. Rev.	Hastings International and Comparative Law Review
HRLJ	Human Rights Law Journal
ICLQ	International and Comparative Law Quarterly
ILR	International Law Reports (formerly, "Annual Digest")
JACL	Journal of Armed Conflict Law
JDI	Journal du droit international
JICJ	Journal of International Criminal Justice
Max Planck Y. UN L.	Max Planck Yearbook of United Nations Law
Mich. J. Int'l L.	Michigan Journal of International Law
NILR	Netherlands International Law Review
Nord. J. Int'l L.	Nordic Journal of International Law
NYIL	Netherlands Yearbook of International Law
NYU J. Int'l L. Pol.	New York University Journal of International Law and Politics
RBDI	Revue belge de droit international
RCADI	Recueil des Cours de l'Académie de Droit International de La Haye
Riv. Dir. Int.	Rivista di diritto internazionale
RDISDP	Revue de droit international et des sciences diplomatiques et politiques

RGDIP	Revue générale de droit international public
Va. J. Int'l L.	Virginia Journal of International Law
YILC	Yearbook of the International Law Commission
Yale J. Int'l L.	Yale Journal of International Law
ZaöRV	Zeitschrift für ausländisches öffentliches Recht und Völkerrecht
AC	Appeals Chamber
ICC	International Criminal Court
ICJ	International Court of Justice
ILC	International Law Commission
ICTR	International Criminal Tribunal for Rwanda
ICTR St.	Statute of the International Criminal Tribunal for Rwanda
ICTY	International Criminal Tribunal for Former Yugoslavia
ICTY St.	Statute of the International Criminal Tribunal for Former Yugoslavia
IMT	International Military Tribunal (Nuremberg)
IMTFE	International Military Tribunal for the Far East (Tokyo)
GA	General Assembly of the United Nations
PCIJ	Permanent Court of International Justice
PrepCom	ICC Preparatory Commission
SC	Security Council of the United Nations
SWGCA	ICC Special Working Group on the Crime of Aggression
TC	Trial Chamber
UN	United Nations

Introduction

It is a settled principle that states incur international responsibility when they breach international obligations, and all the more so when these breaches are particularly serious, that is, when they amount to international crimes. On the other hand, today it is undisputed that international law provides for the criminal responsibility of those individuals who commit international crimes. What is much more uncertain is the relationship between these two regimes of international responsibility, that is, the connections between state and individual responsibility when the same or analogous conduct, performed respectively by individuals and by states, gives rise to both individual and state crimes.

A recent case decided by the International Court of Justice (ICJ), the *Genocide* case,[1] provides a good example of the kind of problems that may arise from the uncertainty concerning the relationship between state and individual responsibility for international crimes.

In this case, the ICJ was asked to ascertain whether genocide was in fact carried out in Bosnia against the Muslim population in the mid-1990s, and whether Serbia was internationally responsible for that international crime. The same conduct falls under the jurisdiction of the international criminal tribunal established in 1993 and charged with the prosecution of individuals who have committed international crimes in the former Yugoslavia (ICTY). Before the ICJ decided the merits of the *Genocide* case, the ICTY had already had the occasion to try individuals charged with genocide in connection with the facts subsequently brought before the ICJ.[2] When the same facts are at the origin of both individual and state responsibility, and two different courts have to pronounce on these facts, although they are framed in two different legal regimes, the question of the relationship between individual and state responsibility is almost inevitable. Indeed, the ICJ was confronted with

---

[1] ICJ, *Case Concerning the Application of the Convention on the Prevention and Punishment of the Crime of Genocide* (Bosnia and Herzegovina v. Yugoslavia), *Preliminary Objections*, Judgment, 11 July 1996, *ICJ Reports* 1996, p. 595 et seq.; ICJ, *Application for the Revision of the Judgment of 11 July 1996 in the Case Concerning the Application of the Convention on the Prevention and Punishment of the Crime of Genocide* (Yugoslavia v. Bosnia and Herzegovina), *Preliminary Objections*, Judgment, 3 February 2003, *ICJ Reports* 2003, p. 7 et seq.; ICJ, *Case Concerning the Application of the Convention on the Prevention and Punishment of the Crime of Genocide* (Bosnia and Herzegovina v. Serbia and Montenegro), *Merits*, Judgment, 26 February 2007, <www.icj-cij.org>.

[2] *See* ICTY, *Prosecutor v. Krstić*, TC, Judgment, 2 August 2001, and AC, Judgment, 19 April 2004; ICTY, *Prosecutor v. Blagojević and Jokić*, TC, Judgment, 17 January 2005.

several problems of this kind. At the stage of preliminary issues, it was uncertain whether the ICJ could make a finding of genocide by a state in the absence of a prior assessment of individual criminal responsibility. Another issue concerned the standard of proof: could the ICJ rely on the relevant findings of fact made by the ICTY at trial? Questions regarding the relationship between state and individual responsibility for genocide also arose in connection with the core issue brought before the Court, that is, the establishment of Serbia's responsibility for genocide. For example, it was unclear whether the material breach entailing state responsibility for genocide had to be established in the same way as the *actus reus* entailing individual responsibility under international criminal law. Likewise, the parties to the dispute debated the question of whether the requirement of state fault necessary to establish state responsibility for genocide in fact corresponds to the *mens rea* necessary to find an accused liable for the same crime under international criminal law.

This is just one example of the kind of issues raised by the relationship between state and individual responsibility for international crimes. Today, the number of similar cases is increasing, together with the rapid development at the international level of international criminal law enforcement mechanisms, and the growing reliance on international (political and judicial) bodies to address situations in which states are responsible for international crimes. Thus, for example, the 1998 NATO bombing campaign against the former Yugoslavia has given rise to claims of both state responsibility before the ICJ,[3] and of individual criminal liability before the

[3] Serbia and Montenegro instituted proceedings before the ICJ against ten NATO Member States. However, the Court found that it lacked jurisdiction. *See* ICJ, *Case concerning Legality of Use of Force* (Serbia and Montenegro v. Belgium), *Preliminary Objections*, Judgment, 15 December 2004, *ICJ Reports* 2004, p. 279 et seq.; ICJ, *Case concerning Legality of Use of Force* (Serbia and Montenegro v. Canada), *Preliminary Objections*, Judgment, 15 December 2004, *ICJ Reports* 2004, p. 429 et seq.; ICJ, *Case concerning Legality of Use of Force* (Serbia and Montenegro v. France), *Preliminary Objections*, Judgment, 15 December 2004, *ICJ Reports* 2004, p. 575 et seq.; ICJ, *Case concerning Legality of Use of Force* (Serbia and Montenegro v. Germany), *Preliminary Objections*, Judgment, 15 December 2004, *ICJ Reports* 2004, p. 720 et seq.; ICJ, *Case concerning Legality of Use of Force* (Serbia and Montenegro v. Italy), *Preliminary Objections*, Judgment, 15 December 2004, *ICJ Reports* 2004, p. 865 et seq.; ICJ, *Case concerning Legality of Use of Force* (Serbia and Montenegro v. Netherlands), *Preliminary Objections*, Judgment, 15 December 2004, *ICJ Reports* 2004, p. 1101 et seq.; ICJ, *Case concerning Legality of Use of Force* (Serbia and Montenegro v. Portugal), *Preliminary Objections*, Judgment, 15 December 2004, *ICJ Reports* 2004, p. 1160 et seq.; ICJ, *Case concerning Legality of Use of Force* (Serbia and Montenegro v. United Kingdom), *Preliminary Objections*, Judgment, 15 December 2004, *ICJ Reports* 2004, p. 1307 et seq.; ICJ, *Case concerning Legality of Use of Force* (Yugoslavia v. Spain), *Request for the Indication of Provisional Measures*, Order, 2 June 1999, *ICJ Reports* 1999, p. 761 et seq.; ICJ, *Case concerning Legality of Use of Force* (Yugoslavia v. United States of America), *Request for the Indication of Provisional Measures*, Order, 2 June 1999, *ICJ Reports* 1999, p. 916 et seq.

ICTY.[4] Among other cases, one may recall the situation in Darfur, which has led the Security Council (SC) to adopt measures with respect to both Sudan[5] and the individuals liable for the international crimes committed there, triggering for the first time the jurisdiction of the International Criminal Court (ICC) under Article 13 (b).[6] Moreover, there are cases in which the lawfulness of conduct amounting to international crimes was assessed under either state responsibility, for instance before the Inter-American Court of Human Rights (IACHR),[7] or international criminal law, for instance before the International Criminal Tribunal for Rwanda (ICTR),[8] but in each case the assessment could have been made under the other regime of international responsibility. There are even cases in which this dual responsibility has been explicitly acknowledged by international courts and tribunals. Apart from the *Genocide* case,[9] one may recall the *Furundžija* case in which the ICTY made a distinction between state and individual responsibility for torture.[10]

Questions arising from the relationship between state and individual responsibility for international crimes have also started attracting the attention of international law scholars. On the one hand, it was occasionally pointed out that the scope of

[4] The ICTY "Final Report to the Prosecutor by the Committee Established to Review the NATO Bombing Campaign Against the Federal Republic of Yugoslavia" (13 June 2000), which recommended that no investigation be commenced before the ICTY, is available at <www.un.org/icty/pressreal/ nato061300.htm>.

[5] *See* SC Resolutions 1547(2004), 1556(2004), 1564(2004), 1574(2004), 1585(2005), 1588(2005), 1590(2005), 1591(2005), 1593(2005), 1627(2005), 1651(2005), 1663(2006), 1665(2006), 1672(2006), 1679(2006), 1706(2006), 1709(2006), 1713(2006), and 1714(2006), <www.un.org/Docs/sc>. This case is further discussed in Chapter 7.

[6] SC Resolution 1593(2005) of 31 March 2005, <www.un.org/Docs/sc>.

[7] See, for example, the IACHR, *Velásquez Rodriguez* Case, Judgment, 29 July 1988, *Annual Report of the Inter-American Court of Human Rights*, Series C No. 4, 1988, and more recently, the IACHR, *Myrna Mack Chang* Case, Judgment, 25 November 2003, *Annual Report of the Inter-American Court of Human Rights*, Series C No. 101, 2003.

[8] In a landmark decision, the ICTR took judicial notice of the Rwandan genocide as a "fact of common knowledge", thus relieving the Prosecutor of the obligation to demonstrate in each case the existence of the genocidal campaign (ICTR, *Prosecutor v. Karemera et al.*, AC, Decision on Prosecutor's Interlocutory Appeal of Decision on Judicial Notice, 16 June 2006). This case is further discussed in Chapter 3.

[9] Although the main focus of the Genocide Convention is on individual criminal liability, the ICJ has pointed out that it "does not exclude any form of State responsibility". ICJ, *Case Concerning the Application of the Convention on the Prevention and Punishment of Genocide* (Bosnia and Herzegovina v. Yugoslavia), *Preliminary Objections*, Judgment, 11 July 1996, supra note 1, para. 32.

[10] "Under current international humanitarian law, in addition to individual criminal liability, State responsibility may ensue as a result of State officials engaging in torture or failing to prevent torture or to punish torturers. If carried out as an extensive practice of State officials, torture amounts to a serious breach on a widespread scale of an international obligation of essential importance for safeguarding the human being, thus constituting a particularly grave wrongful act generating State responsibility." ICTY, *Prosecutor v. Furundžija*, TC, Judgment, 10 December 1998, para. 142.

the overlap between state and individual responsibility for international crimes is not entirely clear,[11] in particular as regards the distinction between the elements of crimes entailing individual criminal liability and the elements of serious wrongful acts entailing state responsibility.[12] On the other hand, specific questions concerning the relationship between state and individual responsibility for international crimes have been addressed, such as the possibility for the punishment of state organs who have committed international crimes to exhaust state responsibility,[13] or the existence of elements differentiating between state and individual responsibility[14] and the growing autonomy of the latter,[15] or finally the impact that individual criminal liability can have on both the establishment and the basic principles of state responsibility.[16]

In the end, the question raised in international cases and by international law scholars is whether state and individual responsibility for international crimes are simply two different sides of the same regime of international responsibility, whether they are two completely different and separate regimes of international responsibility, or finally whether certain links can indeed be established between these two regimes under international law.[17]

---

11 M. Spinedi, 'International Crimes of State. The Legislative History', in J.H.H. Weiler *et al.* (eds.), *International Crimes of State. A Critical Analysis of the ILC's Draft Article 19 on State Responsibility* (Berlin, De Gruyter, 1989), p. 138, points out that the ILC seems to consider these notions to be linked but does not clarify the elements of such a relationship.

12 M.C. Bassiouni, 'The Sources and Content of International Criminal Law: A Theoretical Framework', in M.C. Bassiouni (ed.), *International Criminal Law*, vol. I (Ardsley, Transnational Publishers, 1999), pp. 29–30, doubts that state responsibility for international crimes can be established without first determining the individual criminal liability of decision-makers and principal offenders for the same facts. Similarly, Rosenne raises the question of the possibility of establishing state responsibility by relying on the previous establishment of State organs' criminal liability: S. Rosenne, 'State Responsibility and International Crimes: Further Reflections on Article 19 of the Draft Articles on State Responsibility', 30 *NYU J. Int'l L. Pol.* (1997–1998), pp. 161–162.

13 M.D. Evans, 'International Wrongs and National Jurisdiction', in M.D. Evans (ed.), *Remedies in International Law: The Institutional Dilemma* (Oxford, Hart Publishing, 1998), pp. 173–190; S. Rosenne, supra note 12, pp. 163–164.

14 A. Cassese, *International Law* (Oxford, Oxford University Press, 2001), p. 271.

15 P.-M. Dupuy, 'International Criminal Responsibility of the Individual and International Responsibility of the State', in A. Cassese *et al.* (eds.), *The Rome Statute of the International Criminal Court. A Commentary*, vol. II (Oxford, Oxford University Press, 2002), pp. 1091–1099; P. Gaeta, 'On What Conditions Can a State Be Held Responsible for Genocide?', 18 *EJIL* (2007), pp. 631–648.

16 A. Bos, 'Crimes of State: In Need of Legal Rules?', in G. Kreijen (ed.), *State, Sovereignty, and International Governance* (Oxford, Oxford University Press, 2002), pp. 221–237; A. Nollkaemper, 'Concurrence between Individual Responsibility and State Responsibility in International Law', 52 *ICLQ* (2003), pp. 615–640; A. Cassese, 'On the Use of Criminal Law Notions in Determining State Responsibility for Genocide', 5 *JICJ* (2007), pp. 875–887.

17 For a survey of the problems connected to the relationship between state and individual responsibility, *see* B.I. Bonafè, 'Responsabilità dello Stato per fatti illeciti particolarmente gravi e responsa-

The following analysis will address this crucial issue. The story of the relationship between state and individual responsibility for international crimes is of great interest. Although the existence of a system of dual responsibility is widely acknowledged, there are hardly any theoretical inquiries shedding light on their mutual relationship. An investigation of the *relationship between state and individual responsibility for international crimes* requires a patient and systematic analysis of international practice in order to isolate and evaluate the points of contact between state and individual responsibility for international crimes. The purpose of this work is to put together the results of the analysis and provide as coherent a theoretical framework as possible in which to locate and solve the numerous problems raised by this relationship.

Difficult as this task may be, three main reasons justify such an inquiry. First, this relationship raises a number of specific legal questions of practical interest for the daily application of and compliance with international norms. These concern, for instance, the possibility to prosecute state organs notwithstanding the immunity to which they might be entitled, or the possibility to recognize different degrees of culpability for state organs according to the position they hold in the state apparatus. More generally, it is uncertain whether the same or different elements of international crimes are to be proved to establish state and individual responsibility arising out the same facts. From a different perspective, one may also wonder whether state responsibility has a role in the establishment of individual liability for international crimes, and, conversely, whether individual criminal

---

bilità penale dell'individuo: due approcci a confronto', in M. Spinedi *et al.* (eds.), *La codificazione della responsabilità degli Stati alla prova dei fatti* (Milano, Giuffré, 2006), pp. 501–517. *See* also C. Dominicé, 'La question de la double responsabilité de l'Etat et de son agent', in E. Yakpo and T. Boumedra (eds.), *Liber Amicorum Judge Mohammed Bedjaoui* (The Hague, Kluwer Law International, 1999), pp. 143–157; M. Kamto, 'Responsabilité de l'Etat et responsabilité de l'individu pour crime de génocide. Quels mécanismes de mise en œuvre?', in K. Boustany and D. Dormoy (eds.), *Génocide(s)* (Bruxelles, Bruylant, 1999), pp. 487–511; H. Gros Espiell, 'International Responsibility of the State and Individual Criminal Responsibility in the International Protection of Human Rights', in M. Ragazzi (ed.), *International Responsibility Today: Essays in Memory of Oscar Schachter* (Leiden, Boston, M. Nijhoff, 2005), pp. 151–160; L. Condorelli, 'Responsabilité Etatique et Responsabilité Individuelle pour Violations Graves du Droit International Humanitaire', in L.C. Vohrah *et al.* (eds.), *Man's Inhumanity to Man. Essays on International Law in Honour of Antonio Cassese* (The Hague, M. Nijhoff, 2003), pp. 211–219; P.-M. Dupuy, 'States Sponsor of Terrorism: Issues of International Responsibility', in A. Bianchi (ed.), *Enforcing International Law Norms Against Terrorism* (Oxford, Hart Publishing, 2004), pp. 3–16; V.D. Degan, 'Responsibility of States and Individuals for International Crimes', in S. Yee and W. Tieya (eds.), *International Law in the Post-Cold War World: Essay in Memory of Li Haopei* (London, New York, Routledge, 2001), pp. 202–223; A.A. Cançado Trinidade, 'Complementarity between State Responsibility and Individual Responsibility for Grave Violations of Human Rights: The Crime of State Revisited', in M. Ragazzi (ed.), *International Responsibility Today: Essays in Memory of Oscar Schachter* (Leiden, Boston, M. Nijhoff, 2005), pp. 253–270.

liability has a role in the establishment of state responsibility for international crimes. International jurisdictions are increasingly confronted by such problems. At present, international case law has provided for *ad hoc* solutions to some of these issues. Yet the increasing complexity that characterizes new cases tends to show the inappropriateness of such a case-by-case approach. A general theoretical framework is therefore indispensable for addressing the various problems raised by the relationship between state and individual responsibility for international crimes in a systematic and consistent manner.

Second, the relationship between state and individual responsibility for international crimes strikingly has not yet been the object of systematic theoretical inquiry. While much attention has been drawn to state responsibility and to international criminal law, the relatively new phenomenon of the relationship between state and individual responsibility for international crimes has rarely been addressed. Thus, the aim of the present analysis is to systematize the relationship between state and individual responsibility and to provide a clear theoretical framework capable of shedding light on the overall picture of these two regimes of international responsibility for international crimes, as well as the nexus between them. This work represents only a tentative effort aimed at filling this gap. It has been written in the hope that further reflection, different ideas and an increased awareness will emerge to enrich the debate on this subject.

Last but not least, identifying the precise relationship between state and individual responsibility for international crimes is highly stimulating from a theoretical point of view. It requires an analysis of some basic principles of international law and of different conceptions of the international legal order. Understanding the relationship in question thus provides a privileged viewpoint from which to examine conflicting conceptions of the international legal order and to evaluate the radical changes international law has undergone in the last 60 years. A rigorous legal analysis of this relationship can be useful for understanding the broader phenomenon of universal recognition of the most important obligations owed to the international community as a whole and its possible legal consequences.

General Plan

From a methodological point of view, the present inquiry into the relationship between state and individual responsibility for international crimes will be carried out on the basis of a three-step analysis.

Part I will deal with the way in which this relationship can be ideally conceived of from a pure theoretical viewpoint. First, some preliminary notions are set forth in order to illustrate the legal framework in which the inquiry will be developed. These notions include the basic features of the two regimes of international responsibility, their overlap as far as international crimes are concerned, and the way in which their relationship has been treated by the International Law Commission (ILC) in the codification of both state responsibility and international criminal law. Second, the works of international law scholars will be taken into account. Neither a systematic analysis of the relationship between state and individual responsibility entailed by the commission of international crimes nor a general theory of this relationship is to be found in the international law literature. However, international law scholars have expressed a number of views on specific issues raised by this relationship. These can be used as a starting point from which to identify the conceptual schemes that can be relied upon to explain the relationship between state and individual responsibility. According to an 'individual-oriented' scheme, international criminal law is separate and independent from aggravated state responsibility. Exceptionally, international law imposes legal obligations directly upon individuals (providing for the criminal liability of those who do not comply with such obligations), but this has nothing to do with the traditional regime of state responsibility. According to a 'state-oriented' scheme rooted in the traditional conception of the international legal order, states are the only subjects of international law and international responsibility can only concern state conduct. Therefore, individual liability for international crimes can only be conceived of as a particular form of reaction against the responsible state. These two ideal approaches are difficult to reconcile, and they lead to diverging solutions when applied to practical problems that arise from the relationship between state and individual responsibility.

Part II will then turn to a systematic analysis of international practice, and some particularly problematic aspects of the relationship between state and individual responsibility for international crimes. Inevitably, this part presents a selection of the most significant problems entailed by the relationship between these regimes. In particular, these regard the overlapping elements of state and individual responsibility for international crimes, and the parallel establishment of state and individual responsibility for the same crime. These problems are addressed separately, but following the same methodology, that is, first using the conceptual schemes identified in Part I as terms of comparison in order to illustrate the solutions which could abstractly be given to these practical problems, and then examining in detail the relevant cases in international practice in order to see how these issues have actually been addressed and solved.

Finally, Part III will address the basic question set out at the beginning of this introduction, that is, the existence of a relationship between state and individual responsibility for international crimes. First, the results emerging from the analysis of international practice will be discussed and examined from a more general viewpoint, that of the identification of a general legal framework explaining this relationship. Second, the general conceptual schemes developed in Part I will be taken into account and evaluated in light of the results of the analysis of international practice. Since the various connections between state and individual responsibility for international crimes revealed by the study of international practice show a certain complementarity between these regimes, an attempt will be made to explain their relationship according to a comprehensive framework capable of securing a more effective co-ordination between them.

Part I

General Approaches to the Relationship Between State and Individual Responsibility for International Crimes

Chapter 1

The General Framework of the Relationship Between State and Individual Responsibility for International Crimes

1. *Clarifying Some Basic Concepts*

The present work has the limited purpose of examining the relationship between aggravated state responsibility and individual criminal liability for international crimes. The use of the expression 'international crimes', referring to both state and individual responsibility, may need some preliminary clarification.

First, *international crimes* is a very short and clear expression that will be employed here – for the sake of simplicity – to refer to those very serious breaches of customary international law rules entailing both state responsibility and individual criminal liability. In no way is this intended to suggest that, when referring to breaches entailing state responsibility, international law provides for a criminal regime of state responsibility.[1]

Second, only international crimes prohibited under *customary international law* will be taken into account. Focusing on the so-called 'core crimes' has the advantage of limiting the analysis to a relatively small number of well-established

---

[1] The ILC has used this expression for years in connection with state responsibility, and in particular in the attempt to codify special consequences to attach to very serious breaches of international obligations. From the very beginning, the ILC has made it plain that referring to international crimes did not imply the establishment of a criminal regime of state responsibility under international law (*see* the ILC commentary on Article 19, ILC, 'Report of the ILC on the Work of its 28th Session', *YILC* (1976), vol. II(2), pp. 104, and 119). Nonetheless, the use of this expression raised some concern, because it could suggest the development of such a regime (*see* the general commentary on Articles 40 and 41, ILC, 'Report of the ILC on the Work of its 53rd Session', *YILC* (2001), vol. II(2), p. 111, paras. 5–6). Thus, the ILC decided to abandon this terminology in favour of a more neutral one (*see* J. Crawford, 'First Report on State Responsibility', UN Doc. A/CN.4/490/Add.1, para. 60, and UN Doc. A/CN.4/490/Add.2, paras. 68–71; J. Crawford, 'Third Report on State Responsibility', UN Doc. A/CN.4/507, para. 9, and A/CN.4/507/Add.4, para. 407; J. Crawford, 'Fourth Report on State Responsibility', UN Doc. A/CN.4/517, paras. 48–9). This aspect is examined in detail infra in Chapter 8.

international rules which respond to the needs of the international community as a whole, and which establish binding obligations on all the members of the international community.[2]

Third, the present analysis concentrates on the particular consequences that the international legal order attaches to the commission of international crimes either by states or by individuals. Accordingly, it will essentially focus on the relationship between aggravated state responsibility and individual criminal liability under international law.[3] As will be discussed below, these regimes originate from the breach of primary norms aimed at safeguarding the same collective interests of the international community and can be compared quite easily. The main characteristics of these regimes are briefly described here, in order to set out the general framework in which the following analysis will be developed.

A. *Individual Criminal Responsibility*

With respect to *individual criminal liability*, it is beyond question that today serious breaches of certain obligations owed to the international community as a whole entail individual criminal liability.[4] In other words, customary international law

[2] The categories of international crimes entailing state and individual responsibility under customary international law are examined infra in this Chapter.

[3] This means that the present analysis essentially deals with international crimes committed by, on the one hand, individuals (acting both in their private capacity and on behalf of a state, that is, as state organs), and, on the other hand, by states (that is, independent and stable political entities exercising effective authority over a human community living in a given territory, to use the definition adopted by A. Cassese, *International Law* (Oxford, Oxford University Press, 2001), pp. 46–48). Thus, the relationship with other regimes of international responsibility (for example, that concerning international organizations) will not be taken into account.

[4] *See*, in particular, M.C. Bassiouni, 'The Sources and Content of International Criminal Law: A Theoretical Framework', in M.C. Bassiouni (ed.), *International Criminal Law*, vol. I (Ardsley, Transnational Publishers, 1999), p. 21; F. Malekian, 'International Criminal Responsibility', in M.C. Bassiouni (ed.), *International Criminal Law*, vol. I (Ardsley, Transnational Publishers, 1999), p. 157; K. Ambos, 'Article 25', in Triffterer O. (ed.), *Commentary on the Rome Statute of the International Criminal Court* (Baden-Baden, Nomos, 1999), pp. 475–492; K. Ambos, 'Individual Criminal Responsibility in International Criminal Law: A Jurisprudential Analysis – From Nuremberg to The Hague', in G. Kirk McDonald and O. Swaak-Goldman (eds.), *Substantive and Procedural Aspects of International Criminal Law*, vol. I (The Hague, Kluwer Law International, 2000), p. 6; P. Saland, 'International Criminal Law Principles', in R.S. Lee (ed.), *The International Criminal Court. The Making of the Rome Statute. Issues, Negotiations, Results* (The Hague, Kluwer, 1999), pp. 189–216; S. Lamb, '*Nullum crimen, nulla poena sine lege* in International Criminal Law', in A. Cassese et al (eds.), *The Rome Statute of the International Criminal Court. A Commentary*, vol. I (Oxford, Oxford University Press, 2002), pp. 733–766; A. Cassese, *International Criminal Law* (Oxford, Oxford University Press, 2003), p. 136. The principle of individual criminal liability is recognized in both international documents of a universal character (*see* the London Charter of 8 August 1945 establishing the International Military Tribunal; GA Resolution 95/I of 11 December

provides for a regime of criminal responsibility with respect to individuals who commit certain international offences considered by the international community to be serious violations of its most important rules.[5] Accordingly, individuals are brought to trial before national and international criminal courts and, if their responsibility is proved, they will face criminal punishment. Thus, international individual responsibility is a traditional regime of criminal liability providing for the punishment of individuals who have perpetrated international crimes.

As for the offences entailing individual criminal liability, there is general agreement over the recognition of the existence of at least three categories of customary international crimes, namely, the so-called Nuremberg crimes: crimes of aggression, war crimes, and crimes against humanity.[6] As will be discussed below, it is possible

---

1946 affirming "the principles of international law recognized by the Charter of the Nuremberg Tribunal and the Judgment of the Tribunal"; SC Resolution 827(1993) establishing the International Criminal Tribunal for former Yugoslavia; SC Resolution 935(1994) establishing the International Criminal Tribunal for Rwanda; Draft Code of Crimes against the Peace and Security of Mankind adopted by the ILC in 1996; Statute of the International Criminal Court adopted in 1998 at the Rome Conference) and in specific conventions (Convention on the Prevention and Punishment of the Crime of Genocide of 1948; Four Geneva Conventions of 1949 and the Additional Protocols of 1977; International Convention on the Suppression and Punishment of the Crime of Apartheid of 1974; Convention against Torture and other Cruel, Inhuman or Degrading Treatment or Punishment of 1984). Moreover, states have expressed indisputable support for the principle of individual criminal liability under international law. *See*, in particular, the states' comments on the Draft Articles on State Responsibility, UN Doc. A/CN.4/488, and UN Doc. A/CN.4/515.

[5] It has been pointed out that "*[dans le] domaine de la responsabilité internationale de l'individu, nous nous apercevons que les termes de la nouvelle relation juridique qui s'établit sont l'individu (en tant qu'auteur du fait illicite) et l'ensemble des Etats qui constituent la communauté internationale (en tant que sujet subissant le préjudice). Cette notion introduit, comme donnée nouvelle dans le cadre du droit international, le lien juridique entre l'individu et la communauté internationale*" (V. Abellán Honrubia, 'La responsabilité internationale de l'individu', 280 *RCADI* (1999), p. 205). *See*, in general, S. Glaser, *Introduction à l'étude du droit international pénal* (Bruxelles, Bruylant, 1954), p. 11; A. Cassese, supra note 4, pp. 3–6; D. Thiam, 'First Report on the Draft Code of Crimes against the Peace and Security of Mankind', *YILC* (1983), vol. II(1), p. 148; D. Thiam, 'Second Report on the Draft Code of Crimes against the Peace and Security of Mankind', *YILC* (1984), vol. II(1), p. 94; D. Thiam, 'Thirteenth Report on the Draft Code of Crimes against the Peace and Security of Mankind, *YILC* (1995), vol. II(1), p. 33; S. Szurek, 'Historique. La formation du droit international pénal', in H. Ascensio *et al.* (eds.), *Droit international pénal* (Paris, Pedone, 2000), p. 8.

[6] S. Plawski, *Etude des principes fondamentaux du droit international pénal* (Paris, LGDJ, 1972); L.S. Sunga, *The Emerging System of International Criminal Law* (The Hague, Kluwer Law International, 1997); M.C. Bassiouni (ed.), *International Criminal Law* (Ardsley, Transnational Publishers, 1999); V. Abellán Honrubia, supra note 5, p. 135; J. Barboza, 'International Criminal Law', 278 *RCADI* (1999), pp. 9–199; H. Ascensio *et al.* (eds.), *Droit international pénal* (Paris, Pedone, 2000); G. Kirk McDonald and O. Swaak-Goldman (eds.), *Substantive and Procedural Aspects of International Criminal Law* (The Hague, Kluwer Law International, 2000); K. Kittichaisaree, *International*

to ask whether two additional categories of international crimes, namely, genocide and torture, can now be listed among those offences entailing individual criminal liability under customary international law.[7]

As for the elements of international crimes entailing individual liability under international law, the following analysis will essentially consider three of them. The first is the 'subjective' element, which concerns the subjects who can commit the international offences. Individuals are certainly among the subjects that can commit international crimes. But for purposes of the present work, what is important to stress is that international criminal law applies only to individuals and not to juridical persons, at least at its present stage of development.[8]

The second is the 'material' (or 'objective') element, which consists of the description of the prohibited conduct. If we take torture, for example, as a crime against humanity in the ICC Statute, its material element listed by the PrepCom indicates that: (1) the perpetrator inflicted severe physical or mental pain or suffering upon one or more persons; (2) such person or persons were in the custody or under the control of the perpetrator; (3) such pain or suffering did not arise only from, and was not inherent in or incidental to, lawful sanctions; and (4) the conduct was committed as part of a widespread or systematic attack directed against a civil-

Criminal Law (Oxford, Oxford University Press, 2001); A. Cassese, supra note 4. *See* Articles 16 (aggression), 18 (crimes against humanity), and 20 (war crimes) of the Draft Code of Crimes against the Peace and Security of Mankind, ILC, 'Report on the Work of its 48th Session', *YILC* (1996), vol. II(2), pp. 44, 49, 56; Article 5 of the ICC Statute listing crimes against humanity, war crimes, and the crime of aggression, UN Doc. A/CONF.183/9, <untreaty.un.org/cod/icc/index.html>.

7 The developments concerning these crimes are illustrated infra in this Chapter.

8 For example, the Rome Statute explicitly gives the ICC jurisdiction only over natural persons. Article 25 reads: "1. The Court shall have jurisdiction over natural persons pursuant to this Statute. 2. A person who commits a crime within the jurisdiction of the Court shall be individually responsible and liable for punishment in accordance with this Statute.... 4. No provision in this Statute relating to individual criminal responsibility shall affect the responsibility of States under international law" (A/CONF.183/9, < untreaty.un.org/cod/icc/index.html>). For general comments on this provision, *see* K. Ambos, 'Article 25', supra note 4, p. 475; A. Eser, 'Individual Criminal Responsibility', in A. Cassese *et al.* (eds.), *The Rome Statute of the International Criminal Court. A Commentary*, vol. I (Oxford, Oxford University Press, 2002), pp. 767–822. *See* also Article 1 of the ICTY Statute (SC Res. 827(1993)), and Article 1 of the ICTR Statute (SC Res. 955 (1994)). It can at least be said that in the establishment of the existing international criminal courts and tribunals a clear choice has been made not to include legal persons in their jurisdiction (*see* infra Chapter 2, note 85). While the existence of such a limited scope of criminal law may be fairly clear in many national legal orders, at the international level it plays an important role: it draws a clear borderline between individual and state responsibility. What lies between – the question of liability for legal persons or associations – will be conceived not in terms of corporate or group liability as such, but rather as individual or state responsibility. This gives rise to interesting problems of co-ordination between the two regimes of international responsibility in question (*see* infra Chapter 6).

ian population.[9] This immediately highlights a particular feature of international crimes. War crimes, crimes against humanity, genocide, etc. are broad categories covering specific sub-categories of prohibited conduct. Accordingly, the material element of international crimes can be considered as formed by, on the one hand, *specific elements* of the offence (murder, torture, etc.) and, on the other, *general pre-requisites* (nexus with an armed conflict, systematic attack against the civilian population, etc.) allowing the specific offence to be listed in one of the broader categories of international crimes. Thus, the perpetration of murder in the context of and linked to an armed conflict will constitute a *war crime*, while murder committed as a part of a systematic attack on the civilian population will constitute a *crime against humanity*. From the comparative viewpoint of the present analysis, these general pre-requisites are very important, as they can be regarded as the normative devices transforming domestic offences, such as murder or rape, into international crimes, such as war crimes or crimes against humanity. Moreover, these general pre-requisites define the general context in which international crimes are carried out, and they are therefore crucial to establishing a link between state responsibility and individual criminal liability.[10]

The third is the 'psychological' element (*mens rea*): the intention to produce the consequences of the prohibited act,[11] which is a distinctive element of crimes in all criminal systems. Accordingly, international criminal law not only requires that some subjective and material elements be met, but also requires proof of the existence of the psychological participation of the alleged perpetrator in carrying out the offence in order to sustain a conviction for international crimes. Taking the same example as above, with respect to torture as a crime against humanity, the PrepCom for the ICC adds to the material element a further point (5): "the perpetrator knew that the conduct was part of or intended the conduct to be part of a widespread or systematic attack directed against a civilian population". It is important to take the existence of such a distinguishing feature into account when establishing the relationship between individual and state responsibility, since the need for a psychological element has long been a highly controversial issue with respect to the latter.[12]

The establishment of individual criminal responsibility for international crimes and the punishment of the offenders are the tasks of competent criminal tribunals. Since international crimes are among the most serious breaches of obligations of concern to the entire international community, one would expect the competent criminal tribunals to have been established directly by the entire international

---

[9] UN Doc. PCNICC/2000/1/Add.2, p. 12, <untreaty.un.org/cod/icc/ index.html>.

[10] *See* infra Chapter 3.

[11] A. Cassese, supra note 4, p. 57.

[12] *See* infra Chapter 4.

community and to have jurisdiction over international crimes committed in every part of the world. The enforcement mechanism of international criminal law has not reached such a stage of development. What we have today is a more complicated system, a patchwork of international *ad hoc* tribunals dealing with crimes committed in specific areas of the globe,[13] an ICC established by treaty and binding upon the states parties only,[14] mixed tribunals operating at the domestic level but with the participation of international resources,[15] and national criminal tribunals.[16] Put simply, there is a mixture of international and domestic criminal courts. The international legal order thus secures the prosecution of international crimes by way of both institutionalization and 'decentralization'.[17] Despite this complexity,

[13] The ICTY was established by SC Resolution 827 (1993), and the ICTR was established by SC Resolution 955 (1994), <www.un.org/Docs/sc>.

[14] The ICC was established by the Rome Treaty, adopted on 17 July 1998 and entering into force on 1 July 2002 (UN Doc. A/CONF/183/9, <untreaty.un.org/cod/icc/index.html>). As of June 2008, 106 states have become parties to the ICC Statute (*see* <www.icc-cpi.int>).

[15] These include the so-called mixed or internationalized tribunals in Sierra Leone, Kosovo, East Timor, and Cambodia. *See* in general C.P. Romano *et al.* (eds.), *Internationalized Criminal Courts: Sierra Leone, East Timor, Kosovo, and Cambodia* (Oxford, Oxford University Press, 2004); and D. Shraga, 'The Second Generation UN-Based Tribunals: A Diversity of Mixed Jurisdictions', in E. Skaar *et al.* (eds.), *Roads to Reconciliation* (Lanham, Lexington Books, 2005), pp. 55–79.

[16] States have been punishing international criminals through national tribunals since the end of World War I. For a study of the relevant practice, *see* R.S. Clark and M. Sann (eds.), *The Prosecution of International Crimes* (New Brunswick, London, Transaction Publishers, 1996); M.C. Bassiouni (ed.), supra note 6; G. Kirk McDonald and O. Swaak-Goldman (eds.), supra note 6; H. Fischer *et al.* (eds.), *International and National Prosecution of Crimes under International Law: Current Developments* (Berlin, Spitz, 2001); A. Cassese and M. Delmas-Marty (eds.), *Juridictions nationales et crimes internationaux* (Paris, PUF, 2002); A. Cassese, supra note 4, pp. 277–326.

[17] In particular, the punishment of individual crimes started with the use of the *aut dedere aut judicare* clause in international conventions and then developed into a customary rule allowing the exercise of universal jurisdiction over international crimes. *See* L.C. Green, 'International Crimes and the Legal Process', 20 *ICLQ* (1980), pp. 567–584; F. Weiss, 'Time Limits for the Prosecution of Crimes against International Law', 53 *BYIL* (1982), pp. 163–196; B. Graefrath, 'Universal Criminal Jurisdiction and an International Criminal Court', 1 *EJIL* (1990), pp. 67–88; B. Stern, 'La compétence universelle en France: les cas des crimes commis en ex-Yougoslavie et au Rwanda', 40 *GYIL* (1997), pp. 280–299; M. Henzelin, *Le principe de l'universalité en droit pénal international. Droit et obligation pour les Etats de poursuivre et juger selon le principe de l'universalité* (Bâle, Genève, Munich, Helbing & Lichtenhahn, 2000); L. Reydams, *Universal Jurisdiction. International and Municipal Legal Perspectives* (Oxford, Oxford University Press, 2003). The debate has essentially concerned the precise definition of the 'universality principle' applied by domestic criminal courts, and in particular whether reliance on this principle is dependent on the existence of some links between the offence and the domestic legal order. As recently pointed out, the requirement of a link with the forum state is simply a matter for domestic law, and must not be confused with the option of every state under international law to prosecute those responsible for international crimes (R. O'Keefe, 'Universal Jurisdiction. Clarifying Basic Concepts', 2 *JICJ* (2004), pp. 754–759). *See* also H. Donnedieu de Vabres, *Les principes modernes du droit pénal international* (Paris, Recueil

two general features can be pointed out. On the one hand, it is on behalf of the entire international community that the punishment of international crimes is secured.[18] On the other hand, individual criminal liability is generally established by bodies different from those dealing with state responsibility.

B. *Aggravated State Responsibility*

Turning to state conduct, states too incur international responsibility when they commit international crimes. More precisely, customary international law provides for a particular regime of *aggravated state responsibility* when the wrongful state act amounts to a serious breach of obligations owed to the international community as a whole.[19] Thus, individual liability for international crimes overlaps, most of the time,

---

Sirey, 1928), pp. 142–143; G. Werle, *Principles of International Criminal Law* (The Hague, TMC Asser Press, 2005), p. 59; K.C. Randall, 'Universal Jurisdiction Under International Law', 66 *Texas Law Review* (1987–1988), pp. 810–815; M.C. Bassiouni, 'Universal Jurisdiction for International Crimes: Historical Perspectives and Contemporary Practice', 42 *Va. J. Int'l L.* (2001–2002), p. 81; C. Tomuschat, 'The Duty to Prosecute International Crimes Committed by Individuals', in H.-J. Cremer *et al.* (eds.), *Tradition und Weltoffenheit des Rechts. Festschriff für Helmut Steinberger* (Berlin, Springer, 2002), pp. 315–350; D. Vandermeersch, 'La compétence universelle', in A. Cassese and M. Delmas-Marty (eds.), *Juridictions nationales et crimes internationaux* (Paris, PUF, 2002), pp. 589–611; P. Gaeta, 'Il diritto internazionale e la competenza giurisdizionale degli Stati per crimini internazionali', in A. Cassese *et al.* (eds.), *Problemi attuali della giustizia penale internazionale* (Torino, Giappichelli, 2005), pp. 497–511; S. Zappalà, 'L'universalità della giurisdizione e la Corte penale internazionale', in A. Cassese *et al.* (eds.), *Problemi attuali della giustizia penale internazionale* (Torino, Giappichelli, 2005), pp. 549–559; and the various contributions in 1 *JICJ* (2003), p. 580 et seq.

18 This is what emerges from the case law of the domestic criminal courts that have relied on the universality principle to prosecute international crimes. *See*, in particular, Israeli Supreme Court, *Eichmann* case, 29 May 1962, 36 *ILR* (1968), p. 277; US Court of Appeals, Sixth Circuit, *Demjanjuk* case, 31 October 1985, 776 F.2d 571; House of Lords, *Regina v. Bartle and the Commissioner of Police for the Metropolis and others EX Parte Pinochet* (*Pinochet I*), 25 November 1998, 19 *HRLJ* (1998), p. 419; House of Lords, *Regina v. Bartle and the Commissioner of Police for the Metropolis and others EX Parte Pinochet* (*Pinochet II*), 24 March 1999, 20 *HRLJ* (1999), p. 61; Federal Supreme Court, *Sokolovic* case, 21 February 2001, BGHSt. 46, p. 292; Assize Court of Bruxelles, *Butare Four* case, Verdict of 8 June 2001, <asf.be>; Audiencia Nacional, *Scilingo case*, Decisions of 25 March 1998, 11 May 1998, 4 November 1998, and 27 June 2003, and Judgment of 19 April 2005, <www.derechos.org>; Audiencia Nacional, *Cavallo* case, Decision of 12 September 2000, and Mexico Supreme Court, Decision of 11 June 2003, <www.derechos.org>; House of Lords, *Jones* case, Judgment of 29 March 2006, <www.publications.parliament.uk/pa/ld200506/ldjudgmt/jd060329/ jones.pdf>.

19 *See* R. Ago, 'Eighth Report on State Responsibility', *YILC* (1979), vol. II(1), p. 43; R. Ago, 'Obligations *Erga Omnes* and the International Community', in J.H.H. Weiler *et al.* (eds.), *International Crimes of State. A Critical Analysis of the ILC's Draft Article 19 on State Responsibility* (Berlin, De Gruyter, 1989), pp. 237–239; M. Spinedi, 'From One Codification to Another: Bilateralism and Multilateralism in the Genesis of the Codification of the Law of Treaties and the Law of State

with aggravated state responsibility. Accordingly, in order to study the relationship between state and individual responsibility for international crimes, the following analysis will essentially focus on this specific regime of state responsibility.

Aggravated state responsibility has emerged under customary international law for the purpose of providing for more effective means to react against particularly serious breaches of international obligations aimed at the protection of collective interests of the entire international community. Today, aggravated state responsibility is supported by international practice and has been codified by the ILC.

To be more precise, it was in reliance on the developments of international practice that Special Rapporteur Ago proposed, in the 1970s, that the ILC should codify the distinction between ordinary and aggravated state responsibility.[20] Indeed, in a significant number of cases states not injured by the wrongful act had felt empowered to react against the breach of certain fundamental obligations on behalf the entire international community. The ILC accepted such a distinction and included Article 19 (on international crimes of states) in its first draft on state responsibility. International crimes were defined as wrongful acts resulting "from the breach by a state of an international obligation so essential for the protection of fundamental interests of the international community that its breach is recognized as a crime by that community as a whole".[21] As examples of international crimes of

---

Responsibility', 13 *EJIL* (2002), pp. 1116–8; C. Annacker, 'The Legal Régime of *Erga Omnes* Obligations in International Law', 46 *AJPIL* (1994), pp. 131–166; A. Cassese, supra note 3, pp. 200–1; P. Picone, 'Obblighi *erga omnes* e codificazione della responsabilità degli Stati', 88 *Riv. Dir. Int.* (2005), pp. 893–954; S. Villalpando, *L'émergence de la communauté internationale dans la responsabilité des Etats* (Paris, PUF, 2005). *See* also C.T. Eustathiades, 'Les sujets du droit international et la responsabilité internationale. Nouvelles tendances', 84 *RCADI* (1953), p. 534.

20 R. Ago, 'Fifth Report on State Responsibility', *YILC* (1976), vol. II(1), p. 24 et seq.

21 This definition recalls the circular definition of *jus cogens* included a few years before in the Vienna Convention on the Law of Treaties: "a norm accepted and recognized by the international community of states as a whole as a norm from which non derogation is possible" (Article 53). Arguably, the Special Rapporteur had in mind a close connection between the notion of *jus cogens* and international crimes of states. The basic idea was that some international obligations are so important for the entire international community that their breach is particularly repugnant, and consequently that a special, different, and particularly serious set of consequences must be attached to their breach. Relying on the notion of *jus cogens*, inevitably the selection of the most important international obligations should have led to the establishment of very severe consequences arising out the commission of international crimes by states. This recalls a quasi-criminal regime of state responsibility (for a discussion of previous proposals on state criminal responsibility put forward at the beginning of the twentieth century *see* infra in this Chapter), and Ago was arguably aiming for a quasi-criminal regime of state responsibility for international crimes (*see*, in particular, R. Ago, 'Le délit international', 68 *RCADI* (1939), pp. 415–554; R. Ago, 'La colpa nell'illecito internazionale', in *Scritti giuridici in onore di Santi Romano*, vol. III (Padova, Cedam, 1940), pp. 177–206).

states, the ILC cited: aggression, self-determination of peoples, slavery, genocide, apartheid, and massive pollution of the atmosphere or of the seas.

Today, there is an ever-increasing practice regarding measures taken to safeguard the most important interests of the international community as a whole.[22] In 2001, the ILC at second reading adopted the Articles on State Responsibility. The expression 'international crimes' has disappeared, but there is a specific chapter dedicated to aggravated state responsibility (Articles 40 and 41) for breaches such as aggression, slave trade, genocide, apartheid, torture, basic principles of international humanitarian law, and the right of self-determination of peoples.[23]

The main characteristic of aggravated state responsibility is that it has developed around the concept of obligations owed to the international community as a whole. For years, the ILC has strived to find an agreement on both the definition of the most important obligations whose breach would amount to an international crime, and the definition of the most serious consequences that would attach to the commission of international crimes by states. In the end, the ILC realized that it had to adopt a different approach more in line with international practice. Leaving aside those controversial 'substantive' aspects, it focused instead on 'procedural' aspects, that is, explaining which subjects are entitled to react against serious breaches of obligations owed to the entire international community. Thus, it concentrated on a particular category of international norms, *i.e.*, obligations owed to the international community as a whole. Accordingly, aggravated state responsibility originates from the breach of obligations characterized by a particular structure. Contrary to most international norms which establish bilateral relations between states, the legal relation[24] underlying such obligations is between a state and the entire international community. Therefore, when such obligations are violated, the injured party is the international community, which is also the party entitled to react against such breaches.

Surprisingly,[25] the final text refers to peremptory norms, and this can be misleading. However, it must be pointed out that the ILC tends to blur the distinction

---

[22] *See* infra notes 31–34 and accompanying text.

[23] ILC commentary on Article 40, ILC, 'Report on the Work of its 53rd Session', *YILC* (2001), vol. II(2), pp. 112–113, paras. 4–5.

[24] P. Allott, *Eunomia. New Order for a New World* (Oxford, Oxford University Press, 1990) p. 156, para. 10.32.

[25] The ILC had always referred to obligations owed to the international community as a whole until the provisional draft adopted in 2000 (*see* Article 41 of the Draft Articles on State Responsibility provisionally adopted by the Drafting Committee on second reading, UN Doc. A/CN.4/L 600). All of a sudden a year later, the final version of Article 40 emerged, referring to "serious breaches of peremptory norms of general international law" (ILC, 'Report on the Work of its 53rd Session', *YILC* (2001), vol. II(2), p. 112). According to E. Wyler, 'From 'State Crime' to Responsibility for 'Serious Breaches of Obligations under Peremptory Norms of General International Law', 13

between peremptory norms and obligations owed to the entire international community, and conceives of these two categories of international obligations as substantially overlapping.[26] As a matter of fact, over the decades the ILC has always referred to the same examples of breaches entailing aggravated state responsibility. On the other hand, too much weight must not be given to the formal expression finally inserted in Article 40. One should rather take into account the kind of regime codified in Article 41 and the consequences of serious breaches listed therein.

Article 41 lists four types of consequences to be attached to serious breaches within the meaning of Article 40: 1) a duty of co-operation to bring to an end the serious breach; 2) a duty not to recognize as lawful a serious breach, and not to render aid or assistance in maintaining the situation created by a serious breach; 3) 'ordinary' consequences entailed by every wrongful state act; 4) further consequences that may be provided for under customary international law.[27]

EJIL (2002), p. 1159, the substitution of 'crimes' with 'serious breaches' "has been nothing more than a 'cosmetic' change in the law of responsibility".

26 In the general commentary on Articles 40 and 41 the ILC explains that: "Whether or not peremptory norms of general international law and obligations to the international community as a whole are aspects of a single basic idea, there is at the very least substantial overlap between them. The examples which the International Court has given of obligations towards the international community as a whole all concern obligations which, it is generally accepted, arise under peremptory norms of general international law. Likewise the examples of peremptory norms given by the Commission in its commentary to what became article 53 of the Vienna Convention involve obligations to the international community as a whole. But there is at least a difference in emphasis. While peremptory norms of general international law focus on the scope and priority to be given to a certain number of fundamental obligations, the focus of obligations to the international community as a whole is essentially on the legal interest of all States in compliance – *i.e.*, in terms of the present Articles, in being entitled to invoke the responsibility of any State in breach" (ILC, 'Report on the Work of its 53rd Session', *YILC* (2001), vol. II(2), pp. 111–112, para. 7).

27 One can doubt whether Articles 48 and 54 should be included among the consequences of aggravated state responsibility. These provisions refer to obligations owed to the international community as a whole, but arguably do not codify a reaction by or on behalf of the international community as a whole. Requests of reparation can be made or 'lawful measures' can be adopted only on behalf of the beneficiaries of the obligations breached. This means that the underlying idea is to 'bilateralize' the legal relation turning the obligation owed to the entire international community into an obligation entailing a bilateral relation between the author state and the state that decides to act on behalf of the victim (*see* B. Simma, 'From Bilateralism to Community Interest in International Law', 250 *RCADI* (1994), pp. 314–8; P.-M. Dupuy, 'A General Stocktaking of the Connections between the Multilateral Dimension of Obligations and Codification of the Law of Responsibility', 13 *EJIL* (2002), p. 1069; I. Scobbie, 'The Invocation of Responsibility for the Breach of 'Obligations under Peremptory Norms of General International Law", 13 *EJIL* (2002), p. 1205). It seems more appropriate to say that it is Article 41 which allows states to act on behalf of the international community as a whole. In any case, and independently of the provision referred to, international law scholars agree that the main feature of the regime of aggravated state responsibility is to permit a collective reaction against the breaches of obligations owed to the international community as a whole (*see* infra notes 31–34).

These consequences are important to point out that, first, aggravated state responsibility has been elaborated not as a set of completely new secondary rules but rather as additional consequences to 'ordinary' secondary rules (this is the so-called '*délit plus*' approach).[28] This means that ordinary secondary rules apply to every wrongful state act, including serious breaches of obligations owed to the international community as a whole. Second, what differentiates aggravated state responsibility from ordinary state responsibility is not the material content of the consequences but the subjects entitled to react against serious breaches. The basic idea is that the reaction against serious breaches must come from the entire international community. According to the ILC, the sense of the additional consequences listed in Article 41, and in particular of the duty of co-operation, is to state clearly that "what is called for in the face of serious breaches is a joint and coordinated effort by all states to counteract the effects of these breaches".[29] It does not matter whether this co-operation takes institutionalized or decentralized forms.[30] What counts is that the international community adopts an appropriate response to those serious breaches.

International practice shows that a regime of aggravated state responsibility is developing under customary law.[31] International law scholars point out that there

---

[28] J. Crawford, 'First Report on State Responsibility', UN Doc. A/CN.4/490/Add.2, para. 73.

[29] ILC commentary to Article 41, ILC, 'Report on the Work of its 53rd Session', *YILC* (2001), vol. II(2), p. 114, para. 3.

[30] Accordingly, the ILC leaves open one of the most controversial issues connected to the codification of aggravated state responsibility, that is, the precise identification of the ways in which the international community can react against the breach of its most important obligations. This has been a matter of significant concern to States (*see*, in particular, the comments on the Draft Articles on State Responsibility by Austria, France, Germany, and Ireland, UN Doc. A/CN.4/488). Similarly, it gave rise to a wide debate among international law scholars. *See* the positions expressed by Dupuy, Sinclair, Condorelli, Spinedi, McCaffrey, Ago, Graefrath, Dominicé, and Simma in J.H.H. Weiler *et al.* (eds.), *International Crimes of State. A Critical Analysis of the ILC's Draft Article 19 on State Responsibility* (Berlin, De Gruyter, 1989).

[31] It goes beyond the scope of the present discussion to develop a systematic analysis of international practice on that particular issue. *See* P.-M. Dupuy, 'Observations sur la pratique récente des 'sanctions' de l'illicite', 87 *RGDIP* (1983), pp. 505–548; J.I. Charney, 'Third States Remedies in International Law', 10 *Mich. J. Int'l L.* (1989), pp. 57–101; L. Condorelli, 'Measures Available to Third States Reacting to Crimes of State', in J.H.H. Weiler *et al.* (eds.), *International Crimes of State. A Critical Analysis of the ILC's Draft Article 19 on State Responsibility* (Berlin, De Gruyter, 1989), pp. 264–266; L.-A. Sicilianos, *Les réactions décentralisées à l'illicite. Des contre-mesures à la légitime défense* (Paris, LGDJ, 1990); K. Hailbronner, 'Sanctions and Third Parties and the Concept of International Public Order', 30 *AVR* (1992), pp. 2–15; J. Delbrück (ed.), *The Future of International Law Enforcement. New Scenarios – New Law?* (Berlin, Duncker & Humblot, 1993); J.A. Frowein, 'Reactions by Not Directly Affected States to Breaches of Public International Law', 248 *RCADI* (1994), pp. 345–437; M. Iovane, *La tutela dei valori fondamentali nel diritto internazionale* (Napoli, Editoriale scientifica, 2000), pp. 194–318; D. Alland, 'Countermeasures of General Interest', 13 *EJIL* (2002), pp. 1221–1239.

is an increasing number of cases in which it is possible to say that the international community was able to "speak with one voice"[32] and to react against breaches of its fundamental obligations.[33] This is not to play down the fact that the non-institutionalized nature of the international community may give rise to serious questions when trying to identify concrete ways in which the international community can react against the breach of community obligations.[34] Nonetheless, from the viewpoint of the present analysis, another aspect is crucial, that is, the assessment of aggravated state responsibility. Although there are increasing attempts to seek universal condemnations of breaches of community obligations, the assessment of aggravated state responsibility is still normally left to the traditional mechanisms of state disputes settlement. Accordingly, aggravated state responsibility is likely to be addressed by international organizations, arbitral tribunals, international courts, and so on, in other words, through mechanisms which are normally different from those used to establish individual liability for international crimes.

Finally, it must be recalled that not all breaches of community obligations but only those breaches that reach a certain threshold of seriousness entail aggravated state responsibility.[35] Thus, there may be cases in which the wrongful act does not reach the threshold of seriousness necessary to entail aggravated state responsibility, and therefore the regime of individual liability for international crimes overlaps

[32] N.H.B. Jørgensen, *The Responsibility of States for International Crimes* (Oxford, Oxford University Press, 2000) p. 244, considering that examples in which the international community as a whole may be considered to have collectively reacted against breaches of community obligations are the Gulf crisis, the South Africa regime of apartheid, and interventions in Kosovo and Afghanistan.

[33] M. Iovane, supra note 31, p. 379, referring to generalized countermeasures against the USSR (for the invasion of Afghanistan), South Africa, Iraq and the former Yugoslavia (for gross violations of human rights in Kosovo). Interestingly, G. Perrin, 'La détermination de l'Etat lésé. Les régimes dissociables et les régimes indissociables', in J. Makarczyk (ed.), *Theory of International Law at the Threshold of the 21st Century. Essays in Honour of K. Skubiszewski* (The Hague, Kluwer Law International, 1996), pp. 243–247, notes that "*[l]orsque certains Etats occidentaux ont pris des mesures à l'encontre de pays qui avaient commis des agressions ou avaient très gravement violé les droits de l'homme, ils semblent s'être considérés comme agissant au nom de la légalité internationale et n'ont jamais invoqué une atteinte à leur droit subjectif au respect des règles en cause*" (p. 245). For an evaluation of measures aimed at protecting 'absolute obligations', *see* E. Cannizzaro, *Il principio della proporzionalità nell'ordinamento internazionale* (Milano, Giuffré, 2000), pp. 409–14.

[34] Criticism on the ILC's 'empty' codification of state aggravated responsibility has been expressed by P.-M. Dupuy, 'Quarante ans de codification de la responsabilité internationale des Etats. Un bilan', 107 *RGDIP* (2003), pp. 321 and 343 ("*le régime institué se solde par une absence véritable de différenciation entre la responsabilité de l'Etat pour la violation des normes impératives et celle qu'il encourt à raison de la méconnaissance de ses obligations 'ordinaires'*"); A. Gattini, 'A Return Ticket to "Communitarisme", Please', 13 *EJIL* (2002), pp. 1181–1199; C.J. Tams, 'All's Well That Ends Well. Comments on the ILC's Articles on State Responsibility', 62 *ZaöRV* (2002), pp. 759–808; C.J. Tams, 'Do Serious Breaches Give Rise to Any Specific Obligations of the Responsible State?', 13 *EJIL* (2002), pp. 1161–1180.

[35] The seriousness requirement will be examined infra in Chapter 3.

with the traditional regime of ordinary state responsibility. For example, if a state organ perpetrates an isolated war crime, this conduct 'only' entails ordinary state responsibility. While the present analysis will mainly focus on serious breaches entailing aggravated state responsibility, crimes entailing an overlap between ordinary state responsibility and individual criminal liability will be taken into account as far as they are capable of revealing particular aspects of the relationship between state and individual responsibility.[36]

2. *The Overlap Between State and Individual Responsibility for International Crimes*

If it is undeniable that the commission of international crimes entails a dual responsibility (of states and individuals) under contemporary international law, the present analysis cannot start but from the overlap between these regimes. This overlap is the source of the questions about the kind of relationship existing between state and individual responsibility for international crimes. Two aspects must be considered to define this overlap with more precision.

First, aggravated state responsibility and individual criminal liability have a common origin. They both stem from the serious breach of obligations owed to the international community as a whole.[37] Thus, the starting point of the present

---

[36] *See* infra Chapters 5 and 8.

[37] The concept of *erga omnes* obligations has been the object of numerous works by international law scholars. *See*, in general, P. Picone, 'Obblighi reciproci ed obblighi *erga omnes* nel campo della protezione internazionale dell'ambiente marino dall'inquinamento', in V. Starace (ed.), *Diritto internazionale e protezione dell'ambiente marino* (Milano, Giuffré, 1983), pp. 15–135; A. De Hoogh, *Obligations* Erga Omnes *and International Crimes. A Theoretical Inquiry into the Implementation and Enforcement of the International Responsibility of States* (The Hague, Kluwer, 1996); M. Ragazzi, *The Concept of International Obligations Erga Omnes* (Oxford, Oxford University Press, 1997); C.J. Tams, *Enforcing Obligations* Erga Omnes *in International Law* (Cambridge, Cambridge University Press, 2005). In the framework of state responsibility, different expressions have also been used to refer to more or less the same phenomenon. Cassese refers to 'community obligations' (A. Cassese, supra note 3, p. 15), while Dupuy speaks of '*normes communautaires*' (P.-M. Dupuy, supra note 31, pp. 536–9). However, there are two ways in which *erga omnes* obligations have been conceived of, namely, either as obligations towards *all* states or as obligations towards the international community as a whole. From the viewpoint of state responsibility, this distinction implies that the holder of the corresponding right of reaction is either *any* state or the international community as a whole. International law scholars are divided on the matter. Some seem to support a 'bilateralized' conception of *erga omnes* obligations (*see*, for example, F. Lattanzi, *Garanzie dei diritti dell'uomo nel diritto internazionale generale* (Milano, Giuffré, 1983), pp. 123–8; A. Daví, *Comunità europee e sanzioni economiche* (Napoli, Jovene, 1993), pp. 9 (note 7), 46 (note 22), 137 (note 156), and 254; M. Byers, 'Conceptualising the Relationship between *Jus Cogens* and *Erga Omnes* Obligations', 66 *Nord. J. Int'l L.* (1997), p. 232), while others adopt a 'communitarian' conception of such obligations (*see*, for example, M. Iovane, supra note 31,

analysis is that the international legal order provides for two sets of consequences (with respect to states and individuals) when the same type of international obligations is not complied with.[38] In other words, the relationship between state and individual responsibility for international crimes is characterized by a certain unity as far as primary norms[39] are concerned.

This unity does not necessarily mean that primary norms entailing aggravated state responsibility are identical to primary norms entailing individual criminal responsibility under international law. What can be legitimately assumed at this preliminary stage is that the unity of state and individual responsibility at the level of primary norms means that both these regimes originate from the breach of primary norms aiming at the protection of the same collective interests of the entire international community, and having the same structure, that is, establishing a legal relation between the state or the individual and the international community as a whole.

The fact is that this unity apparently breaks down at the stage of secondary norms. It seems undeniable that there are two regimes of responsibility entailed by the commission of international crimes under international law, that is, aggravated state responsibility and individual criminal liability. Arguably, this is due to the particular structure of obligations owed to international community as a whole. The holder of the corresponding right, *i.e.*, the international community as a whole, can react against the commission of international crimes by taking measures towards either the responsible state or the responsible individual. And it can do so either in an

pp. 140–1, and 155; A. Bos, 'Crimes of State: In Need of Legal Rules?', in G. Kreijen (ed.), *State, Sovereignty, and International Governance* (Oxford, Oxford University Press, 2002), pp. 231–2; A. Cassese, *Diritto internazionale* (Bologna, Il Mulino, 2006), pp. 24–26; P. Picone, 'La distinzione tra norme internazionali di *jus cogens* e norme che producono obblighi *erga omnes*', 91 *Riv. Dir. Int.* (2008), pp. 5–38).

[38] A. Nollkaemper, 'Concurrence between Individual Responsibility and State Responsibility in International Law', 52 *ICLQ* (2003), p. 627 ("Both individual and State responsibility are consequences of breaches of fundamental norms of concern to the international community"); P. Fois, 'Sul rapporto tra i crimini internazionali dello Stato e i crimini internazionali dell'individuo', 87 *Riv. Dir. Int.* (2004), pp. 929–954.

[39] The distinction between primary and secondary norms was proposed as a general criterion to codify the law of state responsibility by Special Rapporteur Ago in his 'Second Report on State Responsibility', *YILC* (1970), vol. II, p. 179. Primary norms are obligations under international law. Secondary norms are the legal consequences attached to the violations of primary obligations. This distinction allowed the ILC to set aside the definition of primary obligations entailing aggravated state responsibility, so that the codification of state responsibility can concentrate on the consequences entailed by the breach of such obligations. *See* also J. Combacau and D. Alland, 'Primary and Secondary Rules in the Law of State Responsibility: Categorising International Obligations', 16 *NYIL* (1985), pp. 81–109; J. Crawford, 'First Report on State Responsibility', UN Doc. A/CN.4/490, paras. 12–18; P.-M. Dupuy, supra note 27, p. 1059. For a broader conception of secondary rules, *see*, H.L.A. Hart, *The Concept of Law* (Oxford, Clarendon Press, 1994), pp. 79–99 (originally published in 1961).

institutionalized manner or in a decentralized manner. However, this explanation provides no direct answer to the crucial issues raised by the relationship between state and individual responsibility, that is, whether the primary norms concerning international crimes are identical, and (if so) whether a unity at the level of secondary norms can be recomposed.

Second, the overlap between state and individual responsibility must be identified with respect to specific categories of international crimes. It seems appropriate to start by drawing a comparison between the list of wrongful acts entailing both aggravated state responsibility and individual criminal liability under international law. In particular, to sustain such a dual responsibility at least two conditions must be fulfilled: 1) the overlap between the material (or objective) elements of breaches entailing state and individual responsibility; and 2) the overlap between their subjective elements, that is, the prohibited conduct must be attributable both to an individual and to a state. What follows is an examination of the relevant categories of international crimes from this perspective.[40]

A. *Aggression*

The crime of aggression represents one of the most if not the most serious breach of fundamental rules of the international community. The process leading to the elaboration of mechanisms capable of guaranteeing, at least to a certain extent, international peace and security has been described as a "long journey"[41] fraught with obstacles. While the attainment of peace and security has been the primary

[40] Breaches of the right to self-determination of peoples and of the prohibition of apartheid will not be taken into account. While these are generally regarded as *erga omnes* obligations (*see* ICJ, *Case concerning East Timor (Portugal v. Australia)*, Judgment, 30 June 1995, *ICJ Reports* 1995, p. 102, para. 29, and the ILC commentary on Article 40 on State Responsibility, ILC, 'Report on the Work of its 53rd Session', *YILC* (2001), vol. II(2), p. 112, para. 5) whose breach entails aggravated state responsibility, it is difficult to maintain that a corresponding crime entails individual criminal liability under customary international law: the ILC has decided not to include the crime of colonial domination in the Draft Code of Crimes against the Peace and Security of Mankind (ILC, 'Report on the Work of its 47th Session', *YILC* (1995), vol. II(2), p. 23, para. 77), and notwithstanding the fact that the crime of apartheid is explicitly prohibited by the 1973 Convention on the Elimination and Punishment of the Crime of Apartheid (GA Resolution 3068(XXVIII)), the Convention has never been applied and arguably does not codify customary international law (*see* J. Dugard, 'L'apartheid', in H. Ascensio *et al.* (eds.), *Droit international pénal* (Paris, Pedone, 2000), pp. 349–360). Likewise, piracy cannot give rise to dual responsibility under international law: the very definition of piracy rules out conduct committed with a public purpose, and consequently piracy only entails individual liability under international law (*see* A. Cassese, supra note 4, p. 24; A. Cassese, 'When May Senior State Officials Be Tried for International Crimes? Some Comments on the *Congo v. Belgium* Case', 13 *EJIL* (2002), pp. 857–8, and infra Chapter 3).

[41] G. Gaja, 'The Long Journey towards Repressing Aggression', in A. Cassese *et al.* (eds.), *The Rome Statute of the International Criminal Court. A Commentary*, vol. I (Oxford, Oxford University Press, 2002), pp. 427–441.

objective of the international community for centuries, it is a relatively new fact (but at present well established) that the international legal order prohibits the use of force in international relations, and that in particular it prohibits aggression. According to the UN Charter,[42] the practice of the SC,[43] the ICJ case law,[44] and the 1974 UN Definition of aggression,[45] it seems undeniable that today states committing a very serious violation of international peace trigger an aggravated regime of international responsibility.[46]

On the other hand, the *Nuremberg* trial recognized that the commission of crimes against peace, *i.e.*, crimes of aggression, entails individual criminal liability under international law. Although there have been no convictions since then, individual liability for such crimes is confirmed in the codification of the ILC,[47] in the Rome Statute for the ICC,[48] and by domestic case law.[49]

---

[42] *See* Article 2 para. 4 of the UN Charter, and GA Resolution 2625(XXV), Declaration on Principles of International Law concerning Friendly Relations and Co-operation among States in accordance with the Charter of the United Nations, adopted on 24 October 1970.

[43] For SC resolutions explicitly dealing with acts of aggression, *see* Resolutions 83(1950), 326(1973), 386(1976), 387(1976), 405(1977), 411(1977), 418(1977), 419(1977), 424(1978), 445(1979), 455(1979), 496(1981), 507(1982), 527(1982), 546(1984), 568(1985), 571(1985), 572(1985), 573(1985), 580(1985), 581(1986), 611(1988), and 667(1990), <www.un.org/Docs/sc>.

[44] *See*, in particular, ICJ, *Case Concerning Military and Paramilitary Activities in and against Nicaragua* (Nicaragua v. USA), *Merits*, Judgment, 27 June 1986, ICJ *Reports* 1986, p. 14 et seq.; ICJ, *Legality of the Threat or Use of Nuclear Weapons*, Advisory Opinion, 8 July 1996, ICJ *Reports* 1996, p. 226 et seq.; ICJ, *Case Concerning Oil Platforms* (Iran v. USA), Judgment, 6 November 2003, *ICJ Reports* 2003, p. 161 et seq.; ICJ, *Legal Consequences of the Construction of a Wall in the Occupied Palestinian Territory*, Advisory Opinion, 9 July 2004, *ICJ Reports* 2004, p. 136 et seq.; ICJ, *Case Concerning Armed Activities on the Territory of the Congo* (Democratic Republic of the Congo v. Uganda), Judgment, 19 December 2005, <www.icj-cij.org>.

[45] GA Resolution 3314 (XXIX), adopted on 14 December 1974.

[46] *See*, in general, the ILC Commentary on Article 19 (ILC, 'Report on the Work of its 28th Session', *YILC* (1976), vol. II(2), p. 95 et seq.) and to Article 40 of the Draft Articles on State Responsibility (ILC, 'Report on the Work of its 53rd Session', *YILC* (2001), vol. II(2), p. 112).

[47] *See* Article 16 of the Draft Code of Crimes (ILC, 'Report on the Work of its 48th Session', *YILC* (1996), vol. II(2), pp. 44–45), which reads: "An individual who, as leader or organizer, actively participates in or orders the planning, preparation, initiation or waging of aggression committed by a State shall be responsible for a crime of aggression".

[48] Article 5 of the Rome Statute provides that "1. The jurisdiction of the Court shall be limited to the most serious crimes of concern to the international community as a whole. The Court has jurisdiction in accordance with this Statute with respect to the following crimes: (a) The crime of genocide; (b) Crimes against humanity; (c) War crimes; (d) The crime of aggression. 2. The Court shall exercise jurisdiction over the crime of aggression once a provision is adopted in accordance with articles 121 and 123 defining the crime and setting out the conditions under which the Court shall exercise jurisdiction with respect to this crime. Such a provision shall be consistent with the relevant provisions of the Charter of the United Nations" (A/CONF.183/9, <untreaty.un.org/cod/icc/index.html>).

[49] For a recent case, *see* House of Lords, *Jones* case, supra note 18.

With respect to this crime, the overlap between aggravated state responsibility and individual criminal liability is due to the fact that, under international law, acts of aggression always entail a dual responsibility. As concerns the material element, only acts involving the use of armed force by states amount to aggression and give rise to state and individual responsibility under international law.[50] As concerns the subjective element, the crime of aggression entails both the responsibility of the author state, and the criminal liability of the political and military leaders of the state who have planned, prepared, initiated, or waged a war of aggression.[51]

B. *War Crimes*

War crimes are probably the most classic example of offences under international law. The prohibition of certain conduct in wartime was recognized long before WWII.[52] Even at a time in which waging war was considered to be lawful, international law already provided for rules that aimed to humanize warfare. Not only were states held responsible in the case of violation of the laws and customs of war,[53] but individual liability was also clearly affirmed.[54] Consequently, when the *Nuremberg* trial was held, criminal liability of individuals for war crimes was not a controversial issue.

After World War II, the importance of international humanitarian law was reaffirmed, together with the complete ban on the use of force in international relations. While the 1949 Geneva Conventions and the 1977 Protocols provided explicitly for the punishment of persons committing 'grave breaches', state responsibility for the same war crimes was regarded as corresponding to customary international law. Due to the 'intransgressible' character of the basic rules of international humanitarian

---

50 The material element of the crime of aggression is discussed at length below (*see* infra Chapter 3).

51 *See* infra Chapter 4.

52 The Hague regulations on the laws of war date back to the 19th Century. *See* in general J.W. Garner, 'Punishment of Offenders against the Laws and Customs of War', 14 *AJIL* (1920), pp. 70–94, and T.L.H. McCormack and G.J. Simpson (eds.), *The Law of War Crimes: National and International Approaches* (The Hague, Kluwer Law International, 1997).

53 State responsibility was explicitly recognized, for the first time, in Article 3 of the Fourth Convention respecting the Laws and Customs of War, adopted in 1907. More generally, the ILC has recognized aggravated state responsibility for breaches of "the basic rules of international humanitarian law applicable in armed conflict" (Commentary on Article 40, ILC, 'Report on the Work of its 53rd Session', *YILC* (2001), vol. II(2), p. 113, para. 5).

54 Individual responsibility for war crimes was first affirmed in the Versailles Treaty at the end of WWI, and then established during the Leipzig trials (W.A. Schabas, 'International Sentencing: From Leipzig (1923) to Arusha (1996)', in M.C. Bassiouni (ed.), *International Criminal Law*, vol. III (Ardsley, Transnational Publishers, 1999), pp. 171–193). The first international convention providing an international obligation of states to prosecute those responsible for war crimes was the 1929 Geneva Convention for the Amelioration of the Condition of the Wounded and Sick in Armies in the Field.

law,[55] their violation is viewed as entailing an aggravated state responsibility.[56] In particular, aggravated state responsibility was derived, on the one hand, from the conduct of state organs committing such crimes and, on the other, from the violation of specific obligations concerning the punishment of perpetrators. As a result, a dual responsibility for war crimes was, and still is, well-established under international law.[57]

However, the overlap between state and individual responsibility for the breach of such community obligations is not complete. The scope of this overlap is different with respect to the subjective and material elements of war crimes. As to the former, the overlap between state and individual responsibility is dictated by the requirements of state responsibility, as individual war crimes can be committed by all individuals – both private individuals and state organs. Such an overlap is therefore limited to war crimes committed by state organs.[58] This means that there may be war crimes committed by private individuals which only entail individual criminal liability and do not lead to an overlap between state and individual responsibility. Conversely, with respect to the material element, the overlap between these regimes is limited to customary offences entailing individual criminal liability.[59] Abstractly, state responsibility has a broader scope than individual criminal liability. For example, there may be war crimes not amounting to 'grave breaches' of the Geneva Conventions which only entail state responsibility and do not give rise to an overlap between state and individual responsibility under customary international law.

C. *Crimes against Humanity*

The third category of the so-called Nuremberg crimes, *i.e.*, crimes against humanity,[60] also gives rise to a dual responsibility under international law. Both states and

---

55 ICJ, *Legality of the Threat or Use of Nuclear Weapons*, Advisory Opinion, 8 July 1996, *ICJ Reports* 1996, p. 257, para. 79.

56 ILC commentary on Article 40, ILC, 'Report on the Work of its 53rd Session', *YILC* (2001), vol. II(2), p. 113, para. 5.

57 In particular, aggravated state responsibility is explicitly recognized under the 1977 Protocol I (*see* Article 89). *See*, in general, H. Lauterpacht, 'The Law of Nations and the Punishment of War Crimes', 21 *BYIL* (1944), p. 65.

58 Over the last few decades the scope of the breaches considered to be war crimes has evolved, and therefore the violations entailing individual and state responsibility under international law have widened, particularly as regards the criminalization of war crimes committed in internal armed conflicts. This reduces the overlap between state and individual responsibility even more for war crimes committed by armed opposition groups. *See*, in general, L. Zegveld, *The Accountability of Armed Opposition Groups in International Law* (Cambridge, Cambridge University Press, 2002).

59 ICTY, *Prosecutor v. Tadić*, AC, Decision on the Defence Motion for Interlocutory Appeal on Jurisdiction, 2 October 1995, paras. 94–99.

60 E. Schwelb, 'Crimes against Humanity', 23 *BYIL* (1946), pp. 178–226; J. Graven, 'Les crimes contre l'humanité', 76 *RCADI* (1950), pp. 433–607; R.S. Clark, 'Crimes against Humanity', in

individuals can incur international liability if they commit such serious breaches of community obligations. Indeed, it is generally acknowledged that the universal recognition of the need to protect human rights at the international level has led to the agreement of the international community with respect to the *erga omnes* nature of the most fundamental human rights and, accordingly, to the affirmation of international rules on the aggravated regime of responsibility applicable to states – and on the criminal responsibility applicable to individuals – in the case of their violation.[61] This is confirmed, on the one hand, in national and international case law and, on the other, in various international documents embodying rules of customary law.[62] Regarding the precise scope of the overlap, its limits are very similar to those identified with respect to war crimes. In other words, the overlap between state and individual responsibility is limited to offences constituting crimes against humanity and entailing individual responsibility under customary law when such crimes are committed by state organs.

D. *Genocide and Torture*

In light of the developments that international criminal law has undergone in the last fifty years, two further categories have emerged as autonomous international crimes giving rise to a dual responsibility under customary international law,

G. Ginsburg, and V.N. Kudriavtsev (eds.), *The Nuremberg Trial and International Law* (Dordrecht, M. Nijhoff, 1990), pp. 177–199; E. Zoller, 'La définition des crimes contre l'humanité', *JDI* (1993), pp. 549–568; L. Mansfield, 'Crimes against Humanity: Reflections on the Fiftieth Anniversary of Nuremberg and a Forgotten Legacy', 64 *Nord. J. Int'l L.* (1995), pp. 293–341; Y. Dinstein, 'Crimes against Humanity', in J. Makarczyk (ed.), *Theory of International Law at the Threshold of the 21st Century. Essays in Honour of K. Skubiszewski* (The Hague, Kluwer Law International, 1996), pp. 891–908; M.C. Bassiouni, *Crimes against Humanity in International Criminal Law* (The Hague, Kluwer Law International, 1999); M. Bettati, 'Le crime contre l'humanité', in H. Ascensio *et al.* (eds.), *Droit international pénal* (Paris, Pedone, 2000), pp. 293–317; O. Swaak-Goldman, 'Crimes against Humanity', in G. Kirk McDonald and O. Swaak-Goldman (eds.), *Substantive and Procedural Aspects of International Criminal Law*, vol. I (The Hague, Kluwer Law International, 2000), pp. 141–168; K. Kittichaisaree, supra note 6, p. 85; A. Cassese, 'Crimes against Humanity', in A. Cassese *et al.* (eds.), *The Rome Statute of the International Criminal Court. A Commentary*, vol. I (Oxford, Oxford University Press, 2002), p. 353; A. Cassese, supra note 4, pp. 64–95.

61 *See* J. Graven, supra note 60; M.C. Bassiouni, 'The Normative Framework of International Humanitarian Law: Overlaps, Gaps and Ambiguities', in M.C. Bassiouni (ed.), *International Criminal Law*, vol. I (Ardsley, Transnational Publishers, 1999), pp. 617–642.

62 Individual responsibility for crimes against humanity is provided for under Article 18 of the Draft Code of Crimes against the Peace and Security of Mankind (ILC, 'Report on the Work of its 48th Session', *YILC* (1996), vol. II(2), p. 49), Article 5 of the ICTY Statute (SC Resolution 827(1993)), Article 3 of the ICTR Statute (SC Resolution 955 (1994)), and Article 7 of the ICC Statute (<www.icc-cpi.int>). Aggravated state responsibility for crimes against humanity has been recognized by the ILC with respect to both 'old' Article 19 (ILC, 'Report on the Work of its 28th Session', *YILC* (1976), vol. II(2), para. 70) and 'new' Article 40 (ILC, 'Report on the Work of its 53rd Session', *YILC* (2001), vol. II(2), p. 112, para. 4).

namely, genocide[63] and torture.[64] These crimes can be regarded as originating from the broader category of crimes against humanity, but they are generally regarded as autonomous crimes characterized by their own definition and requirements. The existence of important conventions on the prohibition of genocide and torture, ratified by a large number of states, has undoubtedly played a significant role in the emergence of these crimes as separate from other crimes against humanity.[65]

With respect to genocide, this offence is now included as an independent international crime in the most important documents of the last decade, such as the ICTY Statute, the ICTR Statute, the Draft Code of Crimes and the Rome

[63] R. Lemkin, *Axis Rule in Occupied Europe* (Washington, Carnegie Endowment for International Peace, 1944); J. Graven, supra note 60; M.N. Shaw, 'Genocide and International Law', in Y. Dinstein and M. Tabory (eds.), *International Law at a Time of Perplexity. Essays in Honour of Shabtai Rosenne* (Dordrecht, M. Nijhoff, 1989), pp. 797–820; A. Cassese, 'La communauté internationale et le génocide', in *Mélanges Michel Virally. Le droit international au service de la paix de la justice et du développement* (Paris, Pedone, 1991), p. 183; J. Verhoeven, 'Le crime de génocide. Originalité et ambiguïté', 24 *RBDI* (1991), pp. 5–26; M. Steinberg, 'Le génocide au XXe siècle: lecture juridique ou historique?', in A. Destexhe and M. Foret (eds.), *Justice internationale. De Nuremberg à La Haye et Arusha* (Bruxelles, Bruylant, 1997), pp. 49–64; L.S. Sunga, supra note 6, p. 105; J. Verhoeven, 'La spécificité du crime de génocide', in A. Destexhe and M. Foret (eds.), *Justice internationale. De Nuremberg à La Haye et Arusha* (Bruxelles, Bruylant, 1997), p. 39–47; M. Lippman, 'Genocide', in M.C. Bassiouni (ed.), *International Criminal Law*, vol. I (Ardsley, Transnational Publishers, 1999), pp. 589–613; V. Morris and M.P. Scharf, *The International Criminal Tribunal for Rwanda* (Irvington-on-Hudson, Transnational Publishers, 1998), p. 163; K. Boustany and D. Dormoy (eds.), *Génocide(s)* (Bruxelles, Bruylant, 1999); R. Maison, 'Le crime de génocide dans les premiers jugements du Tribunal Pénal international pour le Rwanda', 103 *RGDIP* (1999), pp. 129–145; W.A. Schabas, 'Article 6', in O. Triffterer (ed.), *Commentary on the Rome Statute of the International Criminal Court* (Baden-Baden, Nomos, 1999), pp. 107–116; D.D. Ntanda Nsereko, 'Genocide: A Crime against Mankind', in G. Kirk McDonald and O. Swaak-Goldman (eds.), *Substantive and Procedural Aspects of International Criminal Law*, vol. I (The Hague, Kluwer Law International, 2000), pp. 113–140; W.A. Schabas, *Genocide in International Law. The Crime of Crimes* (Cambridge, Cambridge University Press, 2000); K. Kittichaisaree, supra note 6, p. 67; A. Cassese, 'Genocide', in A. Cassese *et al.* (eds.), *The Rome Statute of the International Criminal Court. A Commentary*, vol. I (Oxford, Oxford University Press, 2002), p. 335.

[64] Z. Haquani, 'La Convention des Nations Unies contre la torture', 90 *RGDIP* (1986), p. 127; J.H. Burgers and H. Danelius, *The United Nations Convention against Torture* (Dordrecht, M. Nijhoff, 1988); R.St.J. Macdonald, 'International Prohibitions Against Torture and Other Forms of Similar Treatment or Punishment', in Y. Dinstein and M. Tabory (eds.), *International Law at a Time of Perplexity. Essays in Honour of Shabtai Rosenne* (Dordrecht, M. Nijhoff, 1989), p. 385; D.H. Derby, 'Torture', in M.C. Bassiouni (ed.), *International Criminal Law*, vol. I (Ardsley, Transnational Publishers, 1999), p. 705; E. Delaplace, 'Torture', in H. Ascensio *et al.* (eds.), *Droit international pénal* (Paris, Pedone, 2000), p. 369; A. Cassese, supra note 4, pp. 117–120.

[65] Convention on the Prevention and Punishment of the Crime of Genocide, adopted by GA Resolution 260(III) A of 9 December 1948, and Convention against Torture and Other Cruel, Inhuman or Degrading Treatment or Punishment, adopted by GA Resolution 39/46 of 10 December 1984.

Statute.[66] International case law confirms that both states and individuals can be held responsible for genocide.[67] With respect to the autonomous crime of torture, the expression 'official torture' is generally used to distinguish this autonomous crime from torture as one of the offences regarded as a crime against humanity, and despite the fact that official torture gives rise to a separate claim, it continues to be considered a crime against humanity. Admittedly, international practice concerning official torture is not abundant, but international scholarship and jurisprudence seem to agree that two different crimes, with different definitions and requirements, now co-exist in international criminal law.[68]

The definition of these crimes, provided for under the two conventions and corresponding to customary international law, makes it much easier to identify the overlap between state and individual responsibility. With respect to genocide, the overlap is limited to criminal acts perpetrated by state organs. Indeed, genocide can in principle be committed by private individuals, in which case there is no overlap between state and individual responsibility. With respect to torture, there is an overlap from the viewpoint of the subjective element, as the definition of 'official torture' establishes that only state organs can commit such a crime. But the overlap is limited from the viewpoint of the material element, as aggravated state responsibility is established only if the act of official torture reaches a certain degree of seriousness.[69]

To sum up, there is undoubtedly an overlap between aggravated state responsibility and individual criminal liability with respect to the following international crimes: aggression, war crimes, crimes against humanity, genocide and torture. Thus, the carrying out of such prohibited conduct gives rise to a dual responsibility under international law. While the overlap between state and individual responsibility for these crimes is not always complete, most of the time the commission of international crimes raises the question of the relationship between state and individual responsibility under international law.

---

66 These are Article 4 of the ICTY Statute (SC Resolution 827(1993)), Article 2 of the ICTR Statute (SC Resolution 955(1994)), Article 17 of the Draft Code of Crimes against the Peace and Security of Mankind (ILC; 'Report on the Work of its 48th Session', *YILC* (1996), vol. II(2), p. 46), and Article 6 of the ICC Statute (<www.icc-cpi.int>).

67 The analysis of the relevant practice is examined in detail below in Part II.

68 *See*, in general, A. Cassese, supra note 4, pp. 117–119. With respect to international case law, *see* in particular ICTY, *Prosecutor v. Furundžija*, TC, Judgment, 10 December 1998; with respect to national case law, *see* in particular *Pinochet I*, and *Pinochet II*, supra note 18.

69 On this particular aspect, *see* infra Chapter 3.

3. *The Relationship Between State and Individual Responsibility for International Crimes in the Works of the ILC*

The ILC has worked for many years both on the codification of state responsibility and on a code of crimes entailing individual criminal liability. Thus, one might expect to find in its works a position on the link or connection between these two regimes of international responsibility. However, the ILC has not adopted an explicit position on the matter.

The ILC has been entrusted with the task of studying and codifying separately state responsibility and individual criminal liability under international law. Its work has led to the adoption of two separate proposals, one in 1996 (Draft Code of Crimes against the Peace and Security of Mankind), and one in 2001 (Draft Articles on State Responsibility). However, there have been, at least to a certain extent, some points of contact between these two codification projects.

As concerns the Draft Code of Crimes against the Peace and Security of Mankind, Special Rapporteur Thiam proposed to establish a very close link with the codification of aggravated state responsibility. The works of the ILC on this matter were interrupted in the 1950s and resumed in the early 1980s after international crimes of state (former Article 19) had been adopted in the framework of the codification of state responsibility. Thus, the new Rapporteur on the Draft Code of Crimes proposed to link individual criminal liability to state responsibility by codifying only those international crimes that also amounted to an international crime of state according to former Article 19.[70] According to the Rapporteur, individual criminal liability should arise under international law only for crimes carried out by state organs and entailing aggravated state responsibility.[71] However, this proposal was highly controversial, and the members of the Commission decided in the end to reject it, leaving aside the co-ordination between the Draft Code of Crimes and the Draft Articles on State responsibility.[72] The Commission considered that:

---

[70] In his First Report, Special Rapporteur Thiam deals with the scope of the Draft Code, which according to him should only deal with crimes committed by states or with the state complicity. Accordingly, he proposed that the Draft Code should address the entire issue of international responsibility for international crimes, that is, both state and individual responsibility (*see* D. Thiam, 'First Report on the Draft Code of Crimes against the Peace and Security of Mankind', *YILC* (1983), vol. II(1), pp. 143–157).

[71] In his Third Report, Special Rapporteur Thiam explicitly affirmed that international crimes can only be committed by state organs, and he proposed a definition of 'crimes against the peace and security of mankind' based on Article 19 concerning international crimes of states. This provision was considered to be the general definition which should inspire both state and individual responsibility for international crimes (*see* D. Thiam, 'Third Report on the Draft Code of Crimes against the Peace and Security of Mankind', *YILC* (1985), vol. II(1), pp. 64–70).

[72] The ILC first declined to codify a regime of international criminal responsibility of states in the Draft Code alongside the regime of individual criminal liability for international crimes. State

> the criminal responsibility of individuals does not eliminate the international responsibility of States for the consequences of acts committed by persons acting as organs or agents of the State. But such responsibility is of a different nature and falls within the traditional concept of State responsibility. The criminal responsibility of the State cannot be governed by the same regime as the criminal responsibility of individuals.[73]

On the other hand, with respect to the codification of state responsibility, a major point of contact between state and individual responsibility has been taken into account at various stages, namely, the possibility of considering the punishment of state organs for international crimes to be a special consequence under the regime of aggravated state responsibility.

A proposal in that sense was put forward by Special Rapporteur García-Amador at the very beginning of the ILC's codification work on state responsibility.[74] In his view, international law at that time included a criminal regime of state responsibility applying to those states that breach certain international obligations, such as aggression, genocide, and crimes against humanity. In order to overcome the objections according to which criminal sanctions cannot be imposed on a state and that, even if it were possible, it would not be fair to sanction the entire population for the crimes committed at the state level, García-Amador put forward a simple solution: the content of criminal state responsibility should be co-extensive with the punishment of those state organs responsible for international crimes.[75] Accordingly, individual criminal liability for international crimes was explicitly conceived of as effectively defining the content of criminal state responsibility.

Some years later, Special Rapporteur Ago rejected such an approach. In proposing to the Commission a distinction between ordinary and aggravated state responsibility, he touched upon the question of the role that individual criminal liability can play under the aggravated regime of state responsibility. Ago strongly relied on the fact that international law provides for the criminal liability of state organs who have committed international crimes to show that a new category of

---

responsibility for international crime should exclusively be a matter of concern for the Draft Articles on State Responsibility (ILC, 'Report on the Work of its 35th Session', *YILC* (1983), vol. II(2), pp. 13–15). Thus, the Draft Code "should be devoted exclusively to the criminal responsibility of *individuals*" (ILC, 'Report on the Work of its 36th Session', *YILC* (1984), vol. II(2), p. 11). Second, the Commission refused to codify the definition of crimes against the peace and security of mankind grounded on Article 19 (ILC, 'Report on the Work of its 37th Session', *YILC* (1985), vol. II(2), pp. 13–14). Therefore, the Special Rapporteur proposed a different and neutral definition of the crimes to be included in the Code (*see* D. Thiam, 'Fourth Report on the Draft Code of Crimes against the Peace and Security of Mankind', *YILC* (1986), vol. II(1), pp. 82–83).

[73] ILC, 'Report on the Work of its 36th Session', *YILC* (1984), vol. II(2), p. 11.

[74] *See* F.V. García-Amador, 'Rapport sur la Responsabilité des Etats', *YILC* (1956), vol. II, pp. 181–213.

[75] *Ibid.*, pp. 212–213.

international obligations of exceptional importance has emerged in customary international law. However, he pointed out that

> it would be a mistake to assimilate the right or duty accorded to certain States to punish individuals who have committed such crimes to the 'special form' of international responsibility applicable to the State in such cases... Punishment of those in charge of the State machinery who have unleashed a war of aggression or organized an act of genocide does not *per se* release the State itself from its own international responsibility for such acts.[76]

The issue emerged again when the ILC proceeded with the elaboration of the consequences of wrongful state acts. Special Rapporteur Arangio-Ruiz did not hide a certain support for a punitive connotation of international responsibility, and he proposed to list the punishment of state organs among the special sanctions to be directed at the state responsible for international crimes.[77] Nonetheless, he had to acknowledge the firm intention of the ILC to keep separate the codification of international 'civil' responsibility in the Draft Articles on State Responsibility, and of international 'criminal' responsibility in the Draft Code of Crimes against the Peace and Security of Mankind.[78]

Thus, while the ILC could not entirely avoid the question of the relationship between state and individual responsibility for the serious breaches of obligations owed to the international community as a whole, it was not able to agree on a legal framework explaining the connection between these two regimes. In the end, it opted for the insertion of two 'without prejudice' clauses in the 1996 Draft Code of Crimes against the Peace and Security of Mankind: "The fact that the present Code provides for the responsibility of individuals for crimes against the peace and security of mankind is without prejudice to any question of the responsibility of States under international law";[79] and in the 2001 Draft Articles on State Responsibility: "These articles are without prejudice to any question of the individual responsibility under international law of any person acting on behalf of a State."[80]

These provisions are very important because they constitute a further acknowledgment of the existence of problems concerning the relationship between state and individual responsibility for international crimes. They tend to presume a separation of secondary rules arising out international crimes committed by states and individuals respectively, that is, they presume the independence of these two

---

[76] *See* R. Ago, 'Fifth Report on State Responsibility', *YILC* (1976), vol. II(1), para. 101.

[77] *See* G. Arangio-Ruiz, 'Fifth Report on State Responsibility', *YILC* (1993), vol. II(1), pp. 51–58, and in particular paras. 233–234.

[78] *Ibid.*, pp. 54–55.

[79] Article 4 of the Draft Code of Crimes against Peace and Security of Mankind (ILC, 'Report on the Work of its 48th Session', *YILC* (1996), vol. II(2), p. 23).

[80] Article 58 of the Draft Articles on State Responsibility, ILC, 'Report on the Work of its 53rd Session', *YILC* (2001), vol. II(2), p. 142.

regimes.[81] Indeed, these have been codified in two separate documents and generally treated as concerning two separate branches of international law. By the same token, the two 'without prejudice' clauses embodied in the Draft Code of Crimes and in the Draft Articles on State Responsibility show that the ILC assumes that state and individual responsibility for international crimes are not mutually exclusive. Unfortunately, this presumption is not definitive, and these articles are silent regarding the precise relationship between state and individual responsibility. In the end, the ILC leaves the definition of the relationship in question to future developments under customary international law.

4. *Historical Overview*

The separation that, according to the ILC, characterizes the relationship between state and individual responsibility was not so clear-cut in the past. In the less recent scholarship, the two regimes of international responsibility were viewed as closely connected to each other. However, a gradual process of separation took place until the rapid development of international criminal law in the 1990s brought to the surface various practical issues concerning their relationship.

The idea of a 'higher international justice' with respect to both states and individuals dates back to the beginning of the 20th Century. The Versailles Treaty represents the first attempt to impose punishment on individuals for the commission of a category of international crimes, namely, war crimes, which traditionally entailed only state responsibility. The Leipzig trials in particular cannot be regarded as a successful example of justice as regards individual liability.[82] However, the atrocities of World War I and the emergence of a closer international community of states led, on the one hand, to the establishment of the League of Nations[83] and,

[81] *See* Commentary on Part Two, Chapter III of the Draft Articles on State Responsibility (*ibid.*, p. 110). *See* C.J. Tams, 'Do Serious Breaches Give Rise to Any Specific Obligations of the Responsible State?', supra note 34, pp. 1173–4, and P. De Sena, 'Immunità dell'individuo-organo dalla giurisdizione e responsabilità dello Stato: rapporti e problemi di coordinamento', in M. Spinedi *et al.* (eds.), *La codificazione della responsabilità degli Stati alla prova dei fatti* (Milano, Giuffré, 2006), p. 467.

[82] The Versailles Treaty recognized the individual criminal liability of both the German Emperor responsible for "a supreme offence against international morality and the sanctity of treaties" (Article 227) and the persons responsible for war crimes (Article 228). Although the Netherlands refused to extradite the German Emperor, and while the 'special international tribunal' charged with trying him was therefore never established, the trial of war criminals was left to German domestic courts. The Leipzig trials revealed the punishment of war criminals to be totally ineffective when decided by domestic courts. *See* A. Cassese, supra note 4, pp. 327–9.

[83] Particularly relevant in this context were Articles 10, 11, 12 and 16 (of the League of Nations Covenant) on the use of force. *See* I. Brownlie, *International Law and the Use of Force by States* (Oxford, Clarendon Press, 1963).

on the other, to an attempt to draw up guidelines for a normative evolution of international law and to the first attempts to elaborate universal frameworks for the punishment of international crimes, regardless of whether these were committed by states or individuals.[84]

It was at this time that international law scholars started setting out their proposals to criminalize what were perceived as the most serious international wrongful acts.[85] Accordingly, alongside states individuals should also be recognized as bearing criminal responsibility for the commission of international crimes. For example, one proposal aimed at establishing a single institutional mechanism for the punishment of both state and individual international crimes: focusing substantially on aggression and war crimes, states and individuals together were to have been held responsible by the PCIJ or a separate criminal Chamber and to face a series of international sanctions.[86]

After World War II, the new international community showed its definite willingness to respect some fundamental rules of the international legal order, in particular, peace and basic human rights.[87] These were embodied in the UN Charter, the General Assembly (GA) Declaration on the Nuremberg Principles, the Universal Declaration on Human Rights, etc.[88] In addition, the UN embraced the elaboration of aggravated state responsibility and individual criminal liability as regimes providing for special consequences for the violation of such fundamental rules. With respect to the former, the UN Charter provided for a collective mechanism of reaction against states breaching the most important international obligations, *i.e.*, threat to peace, breach of the peace and aggression.[89] With respect to individual

---

[84] For an overview of early proposals concerning international criminal law, *see* D. Thiam, 'First Report on the Draft Code of Crimes against the Peace and Security of Mankind', *YILC* (1983), vol. II(1), pp. 144–146.

[85] *See*, for example, V.V. Pella, *La criminalité collective des Etats et le droit pénal de l'avenir* (Bucharest, State Printing Office, 1926); Q. Saldaña, 'La justice pénale internationale', 10 *RCADI* (1925), p. 223; H. Donnedieu de Vabres, supra note 17.

[86] *See* V.V. Pella, supra note 85, pp. 331–333. An interesting comparison could be made between these provisions and the modifications added by Pella to his proposal immediately after WWII. *See* V.V. Pella, *La guerre-crime et les criminels de guerre* (Neuchâtel, La Baconnière, 1964), pp. 116–123. State responsibility is proposed with respect to aggression, violations of the Hague law, crimes against humanity and terrorism. Individual liability for such international crimes is limited to state organs. Individual criminal liability of both state organs and private individuals is proposed with respect to violations of the Geneva law, indirect aggression and other offences endangering international peace. The overlap clearly concerns typical state crimes, and state organs' individual responsibility is apparently aimed at guaranteeing an effective reaction against collective criminality.

[87] P.-M. Dupuy, 'L'unité de l'ordre juridique international', 297 *RCADI* (2002), pp. 9–489.

[88] P. Alston and H.J. Steiner, *Human Rights in Context. Law, Politics, Morals. Text and Materials* (Oxford, Clarendon Press, 1996).

[89] *See*, in general, B. Conforti, *Le Nazioni unite* (7th edn, Padova, Cedam, 2005), pp. 175–222.

responsibility, the *Nuremberg* trial[90] established the fundamental precedent for the subsequent development of international criminal law,[91] which was perceived, at least at the beginning, as an accessory or even alien branch of international law.

The Nuremberg revolution – that is, the affirmation of individual criminal liability under international law – is often summarized with the famous quotation from the IMT judgment: "Crimes against international law are committed by men, not by abstract entities, and only by punishing individuals who commit such crimes can the provisions of international law be enforced."

However, liability of individuals for international crimes was not completely detached from state responsibility. Indeed, the trial of the major Nazi war criminals was intended to serve some functions that state responsibility could not reach at that time, for instance, the effective punishment of perpetrators of international crimes and the judicial establishment of the involvement of the Third Reich in the commission of heinous international crimes, thereby (it was hoped) deterring states from future violations. The close link between state and individual responsibility is exemplified by, among others, the crime of membership, according to which members of groups or organizations could face trial simply on the ground of the previous establishment by the IMT of the (entire) group's criminality.

Thus, without downplaying the importance of the *Nuremberg* judgment, it is possible to say that, from a historical point of view, this was only the starting point from which individual criminal liability was able to evolve as a regime of international responsibility increasingly independent from state responsibility, and as a regime applicable to all individuals, state organs included.

The subsequent efforts were mainly directed towards the affirmation, through the establishment of legal rules, of fundamental principles of international criminal law. While trials essentially concentrated on the crimes perpetrated by the Axis Powers, efforts concentrated on a significant work of codification. In that connection, the UN GA rapidly adopted a resolution on the Nuremberg Principles;[92] the ILC started working on the establishment of an International Criminal Jurisdiction[93]

---

[90] International Military Tribunal, *Nuremberg* Judgment, 1 October 1946, 41 *AJIL* (1947), pp. 172–333 ('IMT Judgment').

[91] According to some, this is a natural development of every legal order which sooner or later has to abandon mechanisms of collective responsibility and adopt a concept of individual criminality in which fault and perpetrator match perfectly. *See* I. Caracciolo, *Dal diritto penale internazionale al diritto internazionale penale* (Napoli, Editoriale Scientifica, 2000), p. 3; E. Van Sliedregt, *The Criminal Responsibility of Individuals for Violations of International Humanitarian Law* (The Hague, TMC Asser Press, 2003), p. 344. *See* also A.G.D. Levy, 'Criminal Responsibility of Individuals and International Law', 12 *The University of Chicago Law Review* (1945), p. 313.

[92] GA Resolution 96(I), UN Doc. A/64/Add.1 (1946).

[93] *See* Report of the Committee on International Criminal Jurisdiction, 1951, UN Doc. A/2136 (*Official Records of the General Assembly*, 7th Session, Supplement N. 11), and Report of the

and on the Draft Code of Crimes against the Peace and Security of Mankind;[94] and treaties were concluded on international crimes in the immediate aftermath of WWII: the Genocide Convention and the Geneva Conventions. Interestingly, these efforts mainly focused on individual criminal liability. For example, the reports on the establishment of an International Criminal Jurisdiction limited its subject matter jurisdiction to natural persons only. Similarly, during the drafting of the Genocide Convention, a proposal aimed at extending criminal responsibility to states was rejected.[95]

In the meantime, the ILC had started a massive project of codification concerning state responsibility. In 1954, the ILC decided to postpone its work on individual criminal liability pending the adoption of the Declaration on the definition of aggression.[96] Thus, despite new occasions to address the problems of the relationship between state and individual responsibility for international crimes, these regimes were simply treated separately. While the 1974 Declaration on the definition of aggression seems to implicitly accept the principle of a dual responsibility under international law,[97] it essentially focused on state conduct. Other treaties adopted in that period maintained a similar separation between state and individual responsibility for international crimes, like for example the 1973 Apartheid Convention, the 1977 Protocols to the Geneva Conventions, and the 1984 Torture Convention. As already noted, the ILC did not elaborate on the relationship between these regimes and refused to establish any explicit connection between state responsibility and individual criminal liability either in the Draft Articles on State Responsibility[98] or in the Draft Code of Crimes Against the Peace and Security on Mankind, whose preparation was resumed in the early 1980s.[99]

As a result, state and individual responsibility for international crimes have been carefully kept separate. On the one hand, there are the rules governing aggravated state responsibility, the assessment of which is left to the traditional mechanisms of dispute settlement. On the other hand, under international criminal law, the prosecution of individuals is left to international and domestic criminal courts. This situation might be explained by the exceptional application of international

Committee on International Criminal Jurisdiction, 1953, UN Doc. A/2645 (*Official Records of the General Assembly*, 9th Session, Supplement N. 12).

[94] *See* ILC, 'Report on the Work of its 6th Session', *YILC* (1954), vol. II, p. 140.

[95] *See* N. Ruhashyankiko, 'Study of the Question of the Prevention and Punishment of the Crime of Genocide', UN Doc. E/CN.4/Sub.2/416 of 4 July 1978, paras. 127–135.

[96] *See* GA Resolution 897(IX) adopted on 4 December 1954.

[97] *See* infra Chapter 3.

[98] *See* the ILC Commentary on Article 19, ILC, 'Report on the Work of its 28th Session', *YILC* (1976), vol. II(2), pp. 96 and 110.

[99] *See* the proposal advanced by Special Rapporteur Thiam, 'First Report on the Draft Code of Crimes against the Peace and Security of Mankind', *YILC* (1983), vol. II(2), p. 16.

criminal law during this period. After the post-WWII trials, prosecution for international crimes lay dormant for decades. Thus, the question of the relationship between state and individual responsibility for international crimes could be quite easily set aside.

The present situation is completely different. The rapid development of international criminal law since the 1990s is well known: the establishment of the ICTY and ICTR,[100] the adoption of the Draft Code of Crimes,[101] the adoption of the Rome Statute,[102] an ever-increasing domestic case law, and the establishment of the so-called 'mixed tribunals'.[103] Great efforts have been made to codify aggravated state responsibility and to entrust the assessment of state responsibility issues to international third-party organs.[104] In recent practice, the SC – the body whose primary responsibility is the maintenance of international peace and security – has not hesitated to adopt measures against both states and individuals for the breach of community obligations, as will be discussed below.[105] Therefore, it is recent practice which reveals a growing number of cases in which the relationship between state and individual responsibility for international crimes is potentially problematic. In particular, it is mainly from the viewpoint of individual criminal liability that domestic and international courts have gradually been confronted by practical questions arising from this relationship.

These problems are likely to increase with the policies recently adopted by international criminal tribunals. Reliance is now constantly professed on the following scheme: international prosecution should focus on those major responsible for international crimes, while minor players should be left to domestic courts.[106] This scheme has taken various forms. For example, it was the background political justification for the selection of the defendants brought before the *ad hoc* tribunals

---

[100] *See* supra note 13.

[101] The text was adopted by the Commission at its 48th session, in 1996, and submitted to the GA as part of the Commission's report covering the work of that session. The report (A/48/10), which also contains commentaries on the draft articles, is published in *YILC* (1996), vol. II(2).

[102] *See* supra note 14.

[103] *See* supra note 15.

[104] As for the attempts to codify an institutional mechanism for the assessment of aggravated state responsibility *see* G. Arangio-Ruiz, 'Fifth Report on State Responsibility', *YILC* (1993), vol. II(1), p. 1. However, the ILC decided not to include this proposal in the final text adopted in 2001. With respect to state responsibility in general, one may recall the mechanisms established in the fields of human rights law, international trade law, international investments law, the law of the sea, and so on, as more successful examples of institutionalized third-party adjudication systems.

[105] *See* infra Chapter 7.

[106] A. Cassese, supra note 4, p. 353, uses the expression: 'Nuremberg scheme'.

set up at the end of WWII.[107] It now explicitly governs the completion strategies of the ICTY[108] and ICTR.[109] It has also been adopted to co-ordinate the jurisdiction of the ICC with that of domestic courts.[110] Such a division of labour between domestic and international criminal courts will inevitably lead the latter courts to concentrate on the criminal liability of state leaders,[111] thus focusing on international crimes that automatically entail a dual responsibility under international law. This is not to say that the relationship between state and individual responsibility is limited to international crimes committed by state leaders. But these policies, together with the recent development of international criminal law, will produce an ever-increasing number of cases raising the question of the relationship between state and individual responsibility for international crimes.

Thus, when the same conduct is capable of entailing a dual responsibility – of states and individuals – under international law, several questions arise concerning the mutual relationship between these two regimes. For example, one may doubt whether states can be held responsible for international crimes when no state organ has previously been convicted for the same offence. Conversely, it is possible to wonder whether the establishment of individual criminal liability requires a previous finding of state responsibility. More generally, the question can be raised as to whether the elements of individual liability for international crimes are the same as the elements of aggravated state responsibility. To cite a more specific example, it is uncertain whether circumstances precluding state responsibility can likewise

---

107 While the IMT had jurisdiction over "the *major* war criminals of the European Axis" (Article 1), Control Council Law N. 10 established "a uniform legal basis in Germany for the prosecution of war criminals and other similar offenders, *other* than those dealt with by the International Military Tribunal" (Article 1). Similarly, under Article 1 the IMTFE had jurisdiction over "the *major* war criminals in the Far East".

108 Despite its initial purpose to deal with all sorts of perpetrators, at the request of the SC (*see* Resolutions 1329(2000), 1503(2003), and 1534(2004) and the statements of the SC President S/PRST/2002/21, and S/PRST/2004/28, <www.un.org/Docs/sc>), the ICTY had to elaborate a 'completion strategy' (Report on the Judicial Status of the International Criminal Tribunal for the Former Yugoslavia and the Prospects for Referring Certain Cases to National Courts, June 2002, annexed to UN Doc. S/2002/678) and decided that all its activity would be concentrated "on holding a very limited number of *particularly exemplary trials*" (*ibid.*, para. 27, emphasis added). For the considerable shift in prosecutorial policy entailed by this strategy, *see* D. Raab, 'Evaluating the ICTY and its Completion Strategy', 3 *JICJ* (2005), pp. 82–102.

109 The ICTR Prosecutor made it plain from the beginning that it would be almost impossible for the Tribunal to try all those allegedly responsible for the Rwanda genocide, and that it would focus on major responsible leaving minor players to domestic courts (UN Doc. E/CN.4/1996/7, 28 June 1995).

110 ICC, 'Paper on some policy issues before the Office of the Prosecutor' (ICC Policy Paper), September 2003, pp. 6–7 (<www.icc-cpi.int>).

111 C. Del Ponte, 'Prosecuting the Individuals Bearing the Highest Level of Responsibility', 2 *JICJ* (2004), pp. 515–519.

be invoked before criminal courts to exclude individual liability for international crimes. And the list of unresolved issues could be much longer.

These problems have generally arisen before international criminal tribunals, and most of the time they have been solved on a case-by-case basis.[112] The solutions that have been adopted in practice will be examined in detail below. Two points must be stressed here. First, in light of the increasing complexity of the relevant issues, it is doubtful that this casuistic approach is still adequate, if certainty and consistency in the application of state and individual responsibility for international crimes are to be secured. Second, in order to understand the problems arising from this dual responsibility for international crimes, it is important to carry out a preliminary inquiry into the way in which the relationship between these regimes can be conceived of from a pure theoretical standpoint. The next chapter is devoted to the identification of the alternative theoretical approaches that can be adopted to explain the relationship between state and individual responsibility for international crimes.

---

112 *See* A. Cassese and M. Delmas-Marty (eds.), *Crimes internationaux et juridictions internationales* (Paris, PUF, 2002).

Chapter 2

Theoretical Approaches to the Relationship Between State and Individual Responsibility for International Crimes

1. *Dual Responsibility for International Crimes*

An inquiry into the theoretical approaches to the relationship between state and individual responsibility for international crimes must necessarily start from the development of the principle of individual criminal responsibility under international law. It is the emergence of this principle that raised the question of the identification of a general legal framework which could explain a dual responsibility under international law.

The principle of individual criminal liability and, as a consequence, the issue of a dual responsibility of states and individuals for international crimes have recently attracted the attention of international law scholars. From different perspectives, they have addressed some of the questions raised by the relationship between state and individual responsibility. These are, for example, the risks of an increasing focus on individual responsibility at the detriment of state responsibility for the same acts[1] or more generally of a compartmentalized conception of state and individual responsibility under international law,[2] the question of whether the establishment of state organs' liability for international crimes also entails state responsibility,[3] the

---

[1] M.D. Evans, 'International Wrongs and National Jurisdiction', in M.D. Evans (ed.), *Remedies in International Law: The Institutional Dilemma* (Oxford, Hart Publishing, 1998), pp. 173–190; A. Pellet, 'La responsabilité pénale individuelle, alternative aux sanctions collectives?', in V. Gowlland-Debbas (ed.), *United Nations Sanctions and International Law* (The Hague, Kluwer Law International, 2001), pp. 105–116.

[2] A.A. Cançado Trinidade, 'Complementarity between State Responsibility and Individual Responsibility for Grave Violations of Human Rights: The Crime of State Revisited', in M. Ragazzi (ed.), *International Responsibility Today: Essays in Memory of Oscar Schachter* (Leiden, Boston, M. Nijhoff, 2005), pp. 253–270.

[3] C. Dominicé, 'La question de la double responsabilité de l'Etat et de son agent', in E. Yakpo and T. Boumedra (eds.), *Liber Amicorum Judge Mohammed Bedjaoui* (The Hague, Kluwer Law International, 1999), pp. 143–157.

different degrees of the relationship between state and individual responsibility,[4] the underdevelopment of aggravated state responsibility for international crimes when compared to individual criminal liability,[5] the impact of the development of international criminal law on state responsibility,[6] and the question of the application of similar defences under both state and individual responsibility for international crimes.[7]

However, these works address isolated issues and do not aim at elaborating a comprehensive theoretical framework which could explain the various connections between state and individual responsibility. They rely on implicit assumptions concerning the origin of this relationship which are seldom explicitly set out. But at least they seem to point to the same direction with respect to certain main characteristics of this relationship.[8] The first is dual attribution, as there are certain acts which are attributable both to states and individuals and entail a dual responsibility under international law. The second is complementarity: individual and state responsibility for international crimes are viewed as complementary regimes, and the emphasis is generally on the fact that individual criminal responsibility cannot exhaust state responsibility for the same serious wrongful acts.

---

[4] P.-M. Dupuy, 'International Criminal Responsibility of the Individual and International Responsibility of the State', in A. Cassese *et al.* (eds.), *The Rome Statute of the International Criminal Court. A Commentary*, vol. II (Oxford, Oxford University Press, 2002), pp. 1085–1099.

[5] A. Bos, 'Crimes of State: In Need of Legal Rules?', in G. Kreijen (ed.), *State, Sovereignty, and International Governance* (Oxford, Oxford University Press, 2002), pp. 221–237.

[6] A. Nollkaemper, 'Concurrence between Individual Responsibility and State Responsibility in International Law', 52 *ICLQ* (2003), pp. 615–640.

[7] L. Condorelli, 'Responsabilité Etatique et Responsabilité Individuelle pour Violations Graves du Droit International Humanitaire', in L.C. Vohrah *et al.* (eds.), *Man's Inhumanity to Man. Essays on International Law in Honour of Antonio Cassese* (The Hague, M. Nijhoff, 2003), pp. 211–219.

[8] These points are made not only by the authors just cited (supra notes 1–7), but also by other international law scholars, in particular, S. Rosenne, 'State Responsibility and International Crimes: Further Reflections on Article 19 of the Draft Articles on State Responsibility', 30 *NYU J. Int'l L. Pol.* (1997–1998), pp. 145–166; M. Kamto, 'Responsabilité de l'Etat et responsabilité de l'individu pour crime de génocide. Quels mécanismes de mise en œuvre?', in K. Boustany and D. Dormoy (eds.), *Génocide(s)* (Bruxelles, Bruylant, 1999), pp. 487–511; V.D. Degan, 'Responsibility of States and Individuals for International Crimes', in S. Yee and W. Tieya (eds.), *International Law in the Post-Cold War World: Essay in Memory of Li Haopei* (London, New York, Routledge, 2001), pp. 202–223; P. Fois, 'Sul rapporto tra i crimini internazionali dello Stato e i crimini internazionali dell'individuo', 87 *Riv. Dir. Int.* (2004), pp. 929–954; D. Caron, 'State Crimes: Looking at Municipal Experience with Organizational Crime', in M. Ragazzi (ed.), *International Responsibility Today: Essays in Memory of Oscar Schachter* (Leiden, Boston, M. Nijhoff, 2005), pp. 23–30; P.S. Rao, 'International Crimes and State Responsibility', in M. Ragazzi (ed.), *International Responsibility Today: Essays in Memory of Oscar Schachter* (Leiden, Boston, M. Nijhoff, 2005), pp. 63–80; H. Gros Espiell, 'International Responsibility of the State and Individual Criminal Responsibility in the International Protection of Human Rights', in M. Ragazzi (ed.), *International Responsibility Today: Essays in Memory of Oscar Schachter* (Leiden, Boston, M. Nijhoff, 2005), pp. 151–160.

These main characteristics correspond to the conception of the ILC underlying the separate codification of state and individual responsibility as witnessed by the two 'without prejudice' clauses examined above. As already noted, these general statements are not enough to explain the relationship between state and individual responsibility for international crimes.

In addition, these works contain what may at first appear to be diverging views. The clearest example concerns the alternative between exhaustion and no exhaustion, that is, whether there are cases in which individual responsibility can exhaust state responsibility. Although in principle it is affirmed that individual criminal liability is not a substitute for state responsibility, particular circumstances are examined which seem to justify a different conclusion. For example, it is maintained that, in the case of international crimes committed by isolated state organs, "there may be good reasons to allocate responsibility exclusively to individuals",[9] or that the punishment of those state organs can be regarded as a remedy under the law of state responsibility.[10]

The question that naturally arises is whether these exceptional circumstances can be reconciled with the general statement concerning the complementarity of state and individual responsibility for international crimes. In order to fully appreciate and inquire further into this issue (and more generally into the problems resulting from the relationship between state and individual responsibility for international crimes), it is of fundamental importance to identify and set out explicitly the various theoretical approaches by which this relationship can be understood. Coming back to our example, if exhaustion is *a priori* excluded, this may imply that individual and state responsibility are governed by totally different international norms. On the other hand, if the possibility of exhaustion is accepted, this means that there is an overlap between secondary norms, because individual responsibility can be part of the remedies provided for under state responsibility.

The next section contains an overview of the works of international law scholars that can be used as a starting point in extrapolating the theoretical approaches underlying the conception of the relationship between state and individual responsibility for international crimes.

2. *Diverging Approaches to the Relationship Between State and Individual Responsibility for International Crimes*

Identifying the general approaches to the relationship between state and individual responsibility is not an easy task. Essentially, the literature on this issue is

[9] A. Nollkaemper, supra note 6, p. 622.

[10] S. Rosenne, supra note 8, p. 163.

fragmentary, international law scholars have very different conceptions of the international legal order, and their views on this relationship have generally been expressed in relation to specific contexts. What follows is an attempt to identify more general lines of reasoning as far as the relationship between state and individual responsibility is concerned.

On the one hand, there is today the tendency to emphasize the difference between state and individual responsibility for international crimes and to stress the peculiarities of international criminal law. On the other hand, more traditional views insist on the primary role played by states under international law and try to bring individual criminal liability back within the framework of state responsibility as a special consequence for the commission of international crimes by state organs.

A. *The Separation of State and Individual Responsibility*

A first approach that can be traced back in the works of international law scholars essentially focuses on the differences between state and individual responsibility for international crimes. While no explicit theory on the relationship between state and individual responsibility for international crimes is put forward, this approach responds to the concrete need to prosecute those responsible for international crimes and to develop, both logically and practically, a regime of individual criminal liability separate and independent from state responsibility.

In the aftermath of WWII, some authors welcomed the attribution to individuals of a certain role in international law and focused essentially on the newborn individual liability for international crimes. They seemed to take for granted, at least to a certain extent, the independence of international criminal law from state responsibility.[11]

---

[11] *See*, in particular, H. Donnedieu de Vabres, 'La théorie des délits de droit des gens en droit pénal interétatique', 28 *RDISDP* (1950), p. 159; J. Graven, 'Principes fondamentaux d'un code répressif des crimes contre la paix et la sécurité de l'humanité', 28 *RDISDP* (1950), p. 173; C.T. Eustathiades, 'Les sujets du droit international et la responsabilité internationale. Nouvelles tendances', 84 *RCADI* (1953), p. 397; S. Glaser, 'Culpabilité en droit international pénal', 99 *RCADI* (1960), p. 467. The evolution of Lauterpacht's position on the subject is well known: in the sixth edition of *Oppenheim's International Law* (London, Longmans, 1940), he recognized the existence under customary international law of the principle of individual criminal liability. Generally, the debate arising from the affirmation of individual criminal liability under international law has focused on whether individuals can be regarded as international subjects (*see*, in particular, I. Brownlie, *Principles of Public International Law* (6th edn, Oxford, Oxford University Press, 2003), pp. 561–564, and 580–581; C.G. Tornaritis, 'The Individual as a Subject of International Law and International Criminal Responsibility', in M.C. Bassiouni and V.P. Nanda (eds.), *A Treatise on International Criminal Law* (Springfield, Thomas, 1973), pp. 103–121; J.A. Barberis, 'Nouvelles questions concernant la personnalité juridique internationale', 179 *RCADI* (1983), p. 181; C. Dominicé, *L'ordre juridique international entre tradition et innovation. Recueil d'études* (Paris, PUF, 1997), pp. 121–122; F. Malekian, 'International Criminal Responsibility', in M.C. Bassiouni

More recently, the works of some international law scholars who have addressed the question of the relationship between state and individual responsibility for international crimes seem to agree that it is crucial to dissociate the conduct of the state from that of its organs.[12] Dupuy points out that the *Nuremberg* judgment consisted of a twofold revolution:

> *a) du point de vue de la responsabilité internationale, l'affirmation de celle de l'individu-organe apparaît en rupture avec les règles classiques de la responsabilité de l'Etat, puisqu'en principe, les agissements illicites de l'agent de l'Etat ayant agi comme tel restent imputés à l'Etat pour le compte duquel il a exercé ses fonctions. Pour autant, le fait que ces individus-organes soient déclarés personnellement responsables n'exonère pas l'Etat concerné de sa propre responsabilité en droit international…*
>
> *b) du point de vue du droit pénal international, l'Accord de Londres du 8 août 1945 portant statut du TMI introduisait une autre innovation majeure. Jusque-là, en effet, le droit international pénal ne concernait que les infractions commises par les individus à titre privé,… et non les infractions commises en tant qu'agent étatique, en raison même du jeu des règles d'imputation rappelées ci-dessus.*[13]

In other words, while in traditional international law there were only a very few cases of private individuals' responsibility, after 1945 the dissociation led to the establishment of a general principle of individual responsibility for breaches of international obligations, whether committed by private individuals or by state organs.

(ed.), *International Criminal Law*, vol. I (Ardsley, Transnational Publishers, 1999), p. 153; L.S. Sunga, *Individual Responsibility in International Law for Serious Human Rights Violations* (Dordrecht, M. Nijhoff, 1992), p. 139; F.A. Satchivi, *Les sujets de droit. Contribution à l'étude de la reconnaissance de l'individu comme sujet direct du droit international* (Paris-Montréal, L'Harmattan, 1999), p. 78; T. Scovazzi, *Corso di diritto internazionale, Parte I*, (Milano, Giuffré, 2000), pp. 76–77; B. Conforti, *Diritto internazionale* (7th edn, Napoli, Editoriale Scientifica, 2006), pp. 19–21). An inquiry into the legal *status* of individuals under international law goes beyond the scope of the present analysis. In addition, this question does not *per se* provide any clarification on the relationship between state and individual responsibility for international crimes. Here, it will simply be assumed that today certain obligations are directed at individuals under international law.

12 *See* L.S. Sunga, supra note 11, p. 48 ("The Nuremberg trials also demonstrate that international resolve can be sufficiently compelling in modern times to result in the prosecution and punishment of individuals for the systematic commission of gross violations of human rights. This was a complete rejection of the extreme positivist assertion that the State, supreme within its own sphere, sovereign and equal to other States in international law, shields its officials from international sanctions by virtue of State privileges and immunities. The political resolve of the international community to punish individuals responsible for crimes committed in World War II translated into penal sanctions. These sanctions were enforced notwithstanding that the acts in question were committed pursuant to official orders backed by the full legal authority of the State. Moreover, the Nuremberg trials symbolized the possibility that such a trial might be carried out in future."); S. Rosenne, supra note 8, p. 156; A. Cassese, *International Law* (Oxford, Oxford University Press, 2001), p. 271.

13 P.-M. Dupuy, *Droit international public* (7th edn, Paris, Dalloz, 2004), p. 523.

Moreover, as regards the relationship between state and individual responsibility for international crimes, such an assumption inevitably leads to the conclusion that individual criminal liability is distinct from state responsibility.[14]

Explicitly dealing with the question of the "relationship between State responsibility in the classic sense and individual responsibility for acts that are themselves violations of international law",[15] Rosenne starts his analysis from the general assumption concerning the "dissociation of international criminal law from the law of international responsibility".[16] The validity of such an assumption is then demonstrated by both international documents and case law:[17] reference is made to the two 'without prejudice' clauses incorporated in the ILC Draft Code of Crimes and Draft Articles on State Responsibility,[18] and to the case law of the ICJ[19] and of the ICTY.[20] Accordingly, Rosenne assumes that international crimes of the individual "stand on their own and are not necessarily attributable to a State in a manner which would implicate the law of State responsibility."[21] In other words, the dissociation in question gives rise to a dual responsibility at the international level – of the state and of the individual – and these regimes of responsibility for international crimes must be considered to be mutually independent.

Similarly, the importance of taking into account the dissociation described above as a basic assumption when establishing the relationship between state and

---

14 *Ibid.*, pp. 523, and 527. In particular, Dupuy refers to the 1996 decision of the ICJ in the *Case Concerning the Application of the Convention on the Prevention and Punishment of the Crime of Genocide* (Bosnia and Herzegovina v. Yugoslavia), *Preliminary Objections*, Judgment, 11 July 1996, *ICJ Reports* 1996, p. 595 et seq. *See* also P.-M. Dupuy, supra note 4, p. 1091 ("Identifying the international individual responsibility of natural persons who have committed crimes in international law... leads to a responsibility system where everything leads one to believe, in the state of incompleteness and of evolution that the matter finds itself in, that it will end by increasingly dissociating the respective responsibility systems for the individual and the State.").

15 S. Rosenne, supra note 8, p. 156.

16 *Ibid.*, p. 164.

17 *Ibid.*, pp. 159–160.

18 *See* supra the Introduction.

19 ICJ, *Case Concerning the Application of the Convention on the Prevention and Punishment of the Crime of Genocide* (Bosnia-Herzegovina v. Yugoslavia), supra note 14, para. 32. S. Rosenne, supra note 8, p. 159 ("an individual can be tried and punished for an act which is a crime according to international law even if the impugned act cannot be attributed to a State or entity such as to engage its international responsibility").

20 ICTY, *Prosecutor v. Tadić*, TC, Judgment, 7 May 1997, para. 606. S. Rosenne, supra note 8, p. 160 ("the obligations of individuals under international humanitarian law are independent and apply without prejudice to any questions of State responsibility under international law").

21 S. Rosenne, supra note 8, p. 157. *See* also S. Rosenne, 'War Crimes and State Responsibility', in Y. Dinstein and M. Tabory (eds.), *War Crimes in International Law* (The Hague, M. Nijhoff, 1996), pp. 65–106.

individual responsibility is acknowledged by Cassese.[22] Thus, the main reason for considering individual criminal liability as something separate from state responsibility lies in the basic assumption regarding the dissociation between the conduct of the state and that of its organs.[23] This dissociation may seem to be an abstract concept. However, in concrete terms it implies that when a state organ is on trial, it is not normally perceived so much as the state but as an individual. If a member of the government is charged with persecution, for example, what is ascertained is the prohibited personal conduct of the accused amounting to a crime against humanity, not the state policy or the general organization according to which crimes have been committed and in which the accused may have had a greater or lesser role.

The dissociation between the conduct of the state and that of its organs is a fundamental element to be taken into account when examining the relationship between state and individual responsibility under international law. If rejected, international crimes committed by state organs can only be regarded as conduct attributable to a state.[24] On the contrary, if accepted, the dissociation between the conduct of the state and that of its organs entails the possibility of affirming a general principle of criminal liability of all individuals under international law, regardless of whether they are private individuals or state organs.

Another consideration helps to understand the way in which the relationship between state and individual responsibility for international crimes is conceived of by a part of international law scholars. This concerns the emphasis put on the specific features of international criminal law. International criminal law focuses only on the conduct of natural persons,[25] and it is governed by the principle of personal guilt.[26] Therefore, it concentrates on the establishment of very personal

---

[22] A. Cassese, supra note 12, p. 271: "Individuals behaving contrary to the most fundamental legal standards may be held criminally responsible regardless of whether they have acted in an official capacity, that is, both when they were State organs and when they acted as private individuals; their link with a State may be relevant (in the case of genocide, aggression, or crimes against humanity, when normally their action tends to be promoted, supported, acquiesced in, or condoned, by State authorities); *legally, however, this link is not indispensable.*" (emphasis added).

[23] Even if the dissociation in question is not explicitly demonstrated, many scholars seem to assume it to be the basic reason for the strict separation between state and individual responsibility under international law. *See*, for example, L.S. Sunga, supra note 11, pp. 132–133; C. Dominicé, supra note 3, p. 144; B. Conforti, supra note 11, p. 189; T. Scovazzi, supra note 11, p. 77.

[24] *See* infra in this Chapter.

[25] *See* supra Chapter 1, note 8.

[26] A. Cassese, *International Criminal Law* (Oxford, Oxford University Press, 2003), pp. 136–137, and 159–178; K. Ambos, 'Individual Criminal Responsibility in International Criminal Law: A Jurisprudential Analysis – From Nuremberg to The Hague', in G. Kirk McDonald and O. Swaak-Goldman (eds.), *Substantive and Procedural Aspects of International Criminal Law*, vol. I (The Hague, Kluwer Law International, 2000), pp. 8, 14, 21, and 28.

requirements, such as the *actus reus* and the *mens rea* of the accused, and it results in the punishment of the culprit independently of his position in the state apparatus.[27] When all these elements are collectively taken into account, international criminal law may naturally appear as a regime completely independent from state responsibility.

In the infrequent works on international criminal law that have addressed the question of the relationship between state and individual responsibility for international crimes, at least two general points are explicitly made. First, individual criminal liability and aggravated state responsibility are *separate*.[28] This 'separation' is not investigated any further, but it seems naturally connected to or inferred from the second point explicitly made, that is, that the two regimes of international responsibility in question are *different*. In particular, these regimes differ with respect to: the subjects which can commit international crimes; the contents of the responsibility implied by the commission of international crimes; and the enforcement mechanism which should guarantee compliance with primary international rules.[29]

International criminal law is conceived of as a special branch of international law which prohibits certain conduct in order to protect some fundamental collective interests of the international community, and which establishes a direct legal relationship between the international community as a whole and all individuals. This cosmopolitan perspective has been expressed as follows:

> It seems unquestionable that in recent times a number of international rules have come into being that directly impose *obligations* upon individuals.... Thus individuals are at

[27] Individual criminal liability can in no way be inferred merely from the position of the accused in the state apparatus. In addition, the *ad hoc* tribunals have rejected the view according to which sentencing must reflect the higher or lower position of the accused in the state hierarchy (ICTY, *Prosecutor v. Delalić et al.*, AC, Judgment, 20 February 2001, para. 847).

[28] *See*, in particular, S. Plawski, *Etude des principes fondamentaux du droit international pénal* (Paris, LGDJ, 1972), p. 64; M.C. Bassiouni, 'The Sources and Content of International Criminal Law: A Theoretical Framework', in M.C. Bassiouni (ed.), *International Criminal Law*, vol. I (Ardsley, Transnational Publishers, 1999), p. 19; I. Caracciolo, *Dal diritto penale internazionale al diritto internazionale penale* (Napoli, Editoriale Scientifica, 2000), pp. 130, 222, and 225.

[29] M. Kamto, supra note 8, p. 490, puts the question in analogous terms, although his analysis is limited to the crime of genocide ("*Théoriquement, responsabilité pénale de l'individu et responsabilité pénale de l'Etat pour crime de génocide peuvent être envisagées de façon autonome. D'abord, il existe une différence de nature entre les deux sujets dont la responsabilité peut ainsi être engagée. Ensuite la mise en œuvre de cette responsabilité obéit à des règles différentes. Enfin, les conséquences juridiques de cette responsabilité ne sont pas les mêmes pour l'un et l'autre sujet.*"). *See* also P. Gaeta, 'On What Conditions Can a State Be Held Responsible for Genocide?', 18 *EJIL* (2007), p. 643. For a similar view expressed in more general terms, *see* P.-M. Dupuy, supra note 4; A. Cassese, supra note 12, pp. 271–272; and G. Werle, *Principles of International Criminal Law* (The Hague, TMC Asser Press, 2005), pp. 35–36.

> present under many international obligations, some solely relating to armed conflict, others (those on crimes against humanity, genocide, aggression, terrorism, torture) also concerning peacetime. These obligations are incumbent upon *all individuals of the world*: they are all obliged to refrain from breaching the aforementioned rules; if they do not do so, they are accountable for their transgression. This is so regardless of whether the national legal system within which individuals live contains a similar or the same obligation (translated into national legislation). In other words, this is an area where the international legal system enters into direct contact, as it were, with individuals, without the medium of national legal systems.[30]

The main feature of such an approach is that it completely removes the relationship between state and individual responsibility for international crimes. Legally, there is no link between these regimes.[31] The major development international criminal law has undergone since the *Nuremberg* judgment is that it can now apply to all individuals, in particular because it recognizes that core crimes can also be perpetrated by private individuals independently of any connection with state responsibility.[32]

General statements on the difference and separateness of state and individual responsibility for international crimes do not provide a clear picture of the relationship between these two regimes. To say that these regimes are different and separate might not exclude some kind of relationship between them, but at the same time it does not reveal which are the characteristics of such a relationship, if any.

Sometimes, international law scholars have also advanced more explicit views on this issue. In a recent comment to the *Genocide* case, Gaeta deals with this issue, and maintains that primary norms entailing individual criminal liability for genocide or war crimes are different from the primary norms entailing aggravated

---

30 A. Cassese, supra note 12, p. 79 (emphasis added).

31 *Ibid.*, p. 271.

32 According to J. Graven, 'Les crimes contre l'humanité', 76 *RCADI* (1950), p. 566: "*C'est une singulière erreur de perspective et un rétrécissement regrettable de la notion juridique, d'affirmer et vouloir faire admettre que l'Etat seul peut être l'auteur de ce crime du droit des gens parce que celui-ci serait le résultat d'un « acte de souveraineté criminel » ou parce que le crime ne se concevrait pas sans « un ordre ou une tolérance étatique », comme la doctrine a eu tendance à l'admettre au début, ou encore, selon la thèse française officielle, parce qu' « aux gouvernants seuls remontent l'initiative et la décision de l'entreprise criminelle », les exécutants n'étant « que de vulgaires meurtriers et assassins, gouvernés par le droit commun » et ne relevant pas du droit international. En effet, cette initiative, cette décision, cet ordre ou cette tolérance n'existent pas nécessairement toujours. Des crimes contre l'humanité peuvent fort bien être commis indépendamment de la volonté de l'Etat ou même contre elle, par l'effet de haines raciales, politiques ou religieuses latentes, éclatant à la suite de quelque incident, d'une propagande murmurée, d'une action secrète ou d'une provocation privée, et la triste et longue histoire des pogroms et des lynchages, parallèle à celle des déportations et des exterminations étatiques, en fournirait maints exemples. Il faut définitivement sortir de la notion du « complot » ou « plan étatique » introduite dans le statut de Nuremberg et qui, plus ou moins toujours présente à l'arrière-plan des constructions juridiques, en gêne et fausse le juste développement.*"

state responsibility for 'similar' serious breaches.[33] Therefore, "the two forms of responsibility are *fully independent of each other* from the start".[34] A similar, more nuanced position is taken by Pellet, who admits the possibility that, "*sauf pour le crime d'agression, les définitions que donne des différents crimes contre la paix et la sécurité de l'humanité... ne renvoient pas nécessairement à un crime correspondant de l'Etat.*"[35]

B. *Individual Criminal Responsibility as Part of State Responsibility*

A careful review of the literature reveals an alternative approach to the relationship between state and individual responsibility for international crimes. In fact, there are international law scholars who have explicitly dealt with this issue. The common element of these works is that they focus on the close connection between state and individual responsibility for international crimes, and try to recompose a unity at the level of secondary norms concerning the breach of the most important obligations owed to the international community as a whole.

In the aftermath of WWII, international law scholars were confronted, for the first time, with a development of the highest importance, namely, the affirmation of the principle of individual criminal liability under international law. There was an urgent need to explain why and how international rules were suddenly also being applied to individuals. Some of these authors appraised the emergence of individual criminal liability under international law according to the available conceptual framework, but abstained, at least in the beginning, from calling the familiar conceptual categories into question. They used the traditional approach at their disposal: a state-oriented conception of the international legal order.

These few attempts generally ended up considering individual criminal liability to be part of the regime of aggravated state responsibility, that is, as a special sanction[36]

---

33 P. Gaeta, supra note 29, pp. 631–648.

34 *Ibid.*, p. 641. See also, A. Cassese, *International Criminal Law* (2nd edn, Oxford, Oxford University Press, 2008), pp. 129–130.

35 A. Pellet, 'La responsabilité des dirigeants pour crime international de l'Etat. Quelques remarques sommaires au point de vue du droit international', in G. Doucet (ed.), Terrorisme, victimes et responsabilité pénale internationale (Paris, Calmann-Lévy, 2003), p. 207.

36 The term 'sanction' is used here simply to put the emphasis on the punitive function which generally applied to individual criminal liability when regarded as a particular consequence of wrongful state acts. For a general analysis of the subject, *see* M.L. Forlati Picchio, *La sanzione nel diritto internazionale* (Padova, Cedam, 1974); G. Abi-Saab, 'De la sanction en droit international. Essai de clarification', in J. Makarczyk (ed.), *Theory of International Law at the Threshold of the 21st Century. Essays in Honour of K. Skubiszewski* (The Hague, Kluwer Law International, 1996), p. 61; E. Cannizzaro, *Il principio della proporzionalità nell'ordinamento internazionale* (Milano, Giuffré, 2000), p. 384; M. Spinedi, 'La responsabilité de l'État pour 'crime': une responsabilité pénale?', in H. Ascensio *et al.* (eds.), *Droit international pénal* (Paris, Pedone, 2000), pp. 103–113.

for the responsible state.[37] This is because, as a general assumption, this approach presumes that only states can commit international crimes. Traditionally, only states were regarded as international subjects. While it was not possible to deny that individuals were actually prosecuted for the commission of international crimes, individual criminal liability was nonetheless viewed as a reaction against the responsible state. Thus, individual accountability was simply conceived of as one of the consequences attached to the commission of wrongful acts by states.

According to Sperduti, the prosecution of state organs for war crimes was conceived of as a reprisal against the state responsible for these violations of fundamental international obligations.[38] This 'specific reprisal' was only possible, according to Sperduti, as a reaction against particularly grave breaches of international law. It was thus considered to be a form of aggravated state responsibility, *i.e.*, an otherwise unlawful reaction by the injured state, authorized on an exceptional basis by international law because it constituted a reaction to a breach of a fundamental obligation owed to the international community as a whole.[39]

The origin of aggravated state responsibility is – as it is normally affirmed – the violation of an obligation owed to the international community as a whole. However, while Sperduti identifies the source of this special regime of international responsibility as the breach of 'community' obligations, he confines its implementation to a strictly bilateral framework.[40] Thus, individual liability for international crimes is a specific reprisal directed against the state responsible for the violation of the most important obligations arising under international law, a reprisal consisting of the punishment of its organs. From this perspective, only the injured state is entitled to adopt such an exceptional countermeasure. Individual criminal liability is thereby brought back into the traditional framework of bilateral state responsibility. Sperduti

---

[37] The origins of this traditional approach can be traced back to the works of Anzilotti. *See* D. Anzilotti, *Corso di diritto internazionale* (Roma, Athenaeum, 1923); and G. Arangio-Ruiz, *Diritto internazionale e personalità giuridica* (Bologna, Cooperativa libraria universitaria, 1972). For a somewhat different conception of the phenomenon, *see* G. Carella, *La responsabilità dello stato per crimini internazionali* (Napoli, Jovene, 1985); G. Carella, 'Il Tribunale penale internazionale per la ex Iugoslavia', in P. Picone (ed.), *Interventi delle Nazioni Unite e diritto internazionale* (Padova, Cedam, 1995), p. 463 et seq. Starting from a number of widely shared assumptions – that the breach of community obligations are international wrongful acts, that individual criminal liability is provided under a set of international secondary rules, and that the punishment of individuals is not a sanction for state crimes – she concludes that individual accountability for international crimes is only a matter of domestic law, and that *no relationship* exists between the responsibility of states at the international level and the criminal liability of individuals at the domestic level. The punishment of individuals is the object of an international obligation addressed to the states only, and it must be carried out within their domestic legal orders.

[38] G. Sperduti, *L'individuo nel diritto internazionale* (Milano, Giuffré, 1950), pp. 175–6.

[39] *Ibid.*, p. 173.

[40] *Ibid.*, pp. 173–4.

denies any relation established under international law between the individual and the entire international community: the breach is always a wrongful state act and the reaction is strictly directed against the responsible state. Individuals completely disappear from the analysis.[41]

From this early perspective, the power to punish individuals, even foreign state organs, derives from state sovereignty and criminal law is the province of domestic legal orders, not international law. The limited role of international law, according to Sperduti, is to provide for a justification[42] when exercising national criminal jurisdiction would otherwise be in breach of customary rules on immunity. On this view, when state organs are charged with international crimes before foreign national courts, international law allows the judge to disregard the customary protection to which *states* are entitled. Indeed, Sperduti regards organs' exemption from jurisdiction as being directly derived from the attribution of their behaviour to the state.[43] Under this approach, state organs are merely instruments for state activities. Since, according to Sperduti, a general principle of international law provides for the obligation to respect state organization, organs' activities must be considered to be state activities and cannot be attributed to the individual. Accordingly, state activities are completely out of the reach of foreign jurisdictions. When a grave breach is committed by a state, international law exceptionally allows the injured state to exercise criminal jurisdiction over foreign organs by means of reprisal.

Thus, in Sperduti's conception, individual liability for international crimes is transposed into the framework of a bilateral relationship between states – the injured state and the responsible state. All in all, in the traditional view, international law was strictly confined to the regulation of reciprocal state behaviour. It may have seemed natural, therefore, to frame this new phenomenon (individual criminal liability) according to the existing conception of international law. Thus, Sperduti proposed to conceive of individual liability for international crimes (*i.e.*, the attribution of state activities directly to state organs in breach of the obligation to attribute such behaviour to the state) as a special form of state responsibility.

A systematic analysis of the international literature shows that a similar view – sometimes designated as the 'privative sanction' or 'privative guarantee' theory[44] – has

---

41 *Ibid.*, p. 187.

42 The term 'justification' is used here to indicate the legal requirement which under international law transforms a wrongful act into a countermeasure characterized by its "*légalité globale*" (D. Alland, *Justice privée et ordre juridique international. Etude théorique des contre-mesures en droit international public* (Paris, Pedone, 1994), pp. 59–60).

43 G. Sperduti, 'Sull'esenzione degli Stati stranieri dalla giurisdizione', 27 *Giurisprudenza completa della Corte suprema di cassazione. Sezioni civili* (1948), p. 593.

44 This particular expression is used to refer to sanctions consisting of the possibility for the injured state to lawfully suspend the binding force of a legal norm attributing a subjective right to the responsible state. That is why the sanction results in being 'privative'.

been subscribed to by other scholars.[45] Moreover, this theory has also been adopted by some scholars who explicitly relied upon it to affirm the criminal responsibility of states under international law. It has been held that, while states cannot bear criminal sanctions, states' criminal behaviour can be sanctioned by punishing the responsible organs. Individual criminal liability under international law can be conceived of as a special sanction for grave state violations. In particular, international criminal law supplies state responsibility with a regime of criminal responsibility which could not be elaborated with respect to states. The mechanism allowing for the conception of individual punishment as a sanction against the criminal state is the one described above: the perpetration of the state crime allows the injured state to exercise its criminal jurisdiction over the responsible organs, disregarding the right of the responsible state to have its effective organization respected.

According to García-Amador, state responsibility under modern international law is no longer confined to a regime of civil responsibility, as it can also have a criminal character.[46] In particular, the most important consequence of this new kind of state responsibility is the punishment of those state organs responsible for the breach of fundamental international obligations.

The origin of this new regime of criminal responsibility of states corresponds to the one identified by Sperduti: the importance of the international obligation which has been breached.[47] The difference between the two approaches lies in the fact that the latter considers the consequences of such violations, *i.e.*, individual criminal liability, to be a "*sanction pénale*" against the responsible state or, better yet, a substitute for criminal sanctions, which can hardly be applicable to states.[48]

---

[45] *See* M.L. Forlati Picchio, supra note 36, p. 41 (note 72), and pp. 257–258 (note 184). According to Wengler, the victim state or third states can punish foreign state organs who have committed genocide, war crimes or the crime of aggression, notwithstanding the fact that they were acting in their official capacity, because in such cases "the suspension of the immunity rule is itself a legal sanction provided for in international law" (W. Wengler, 'Public International Law. Paradoxes of a Legal Order', 158 *RCADI* (1977), p. 25). A similar view has been expressed with respect to the punishment of war criminals before WWI by G. Schwarzenberger, *International Law as Applied by International Courts and Tribunals* (London, Stevens & Sons Limited, 1968), pp. 453–4.

[46] F.V. García-Amador, 'Rapport sur la Responsabilité des Etats', *YILC*, vol. II, 1956, p. 180. *See* the analysis of García-Amador's position by G. Nolte, 'From Dionisio Anzilotti to Roberto Ago: The Classical International Law of State Responsibility and the Traditional Primacy of a Bilateral Conception of Inter-state Relations', 13 *EJIL* (2002), p. 1096.

[47] F.V. García-Amador, 'Rapport sur la Responsabilité des Etats', *YILC*, vol. II, 1956, p. 184. In particular, the examples he gives all concern the traditional categories of the most serious breaches of international law – crimes against humanity, genocide, aggression – giving rise to both aggravated state responsibility and individual criminal liability.

[48] "*[C]ette nouvelle conception aurait le grand avantage de vaincre la répugnance parfaitement justifiée que l'on éprouvait à imposer des sanctions à une collectivité nationale toute entière, absolument étrangère à l'acte punissable. D'autre part, le châtiment du coupable ne serait pas en soi incompatible avec la conception traditionnelle, selon laquelle ce châtiment est un des éléments de la « satisfaction ». A cet égard,*

Thus, except for the particular aim of affirming state criminal responsibility, García-Amador reaches the same conclusion as Sperduti, *i.e.*, that international criminal responsibility of state organs ("*les auteurs d'actes illicites qui engagent la responsabilité civile de l'Etat*") is an exception, provided for by international law, to the general principle protecting states from external interference. What is slightly different is the principle invoked thereto. Sperduti's obligation to respect state organization is replaced by the duty of non-interference. However, both principles can be regarded as corollaries of the more general rule on sovereign equality of states.

A very similar approach was put forward by Drost.[49] Starting from the assumption that states can commit international crimes but that criminal law cannot be applied to states, he reached the conclusion that state criminal responsibility overlaps with the criminal responsibility of its organs.[50] Thus, the prosecution of state organs charged with international crimes by foreign tribunals becomes possible through an exception to the principle regarding diplomatic immunity.[51]

After these first attempts aiming to bring back the newly established regime of international criminal law into the framework of traditional bilateral state responsibility, an analogous conception of the relationship between state and individual responsibility can still be found in more recent works of international law scholars.

Modern commentators take into account important developments that have occurred in international law in the last decades. These include, first of all, the universal recognition of the category of obligations owed to the international com-

l'innovation porterait plus sur la forme que sur le fond. Un autre argument serait décisif: cette solution serait entièrement conforme à la pratique des accords internationaux qui définissent et règlementent la répression des delicta juris gentium, *accords en vertu desquels l'Etat s'engage à punir ses propres ressortissants; elle serait conforme également au système inauguré par la Convention sur le génocide à propos des « crimes contre la paix et la sécurité de l'humanité ». On ne pourrait donc faire valoir qu'une seule objection contre la suggestion de Lauterpacht: la solution qu'il envisage suppose une ingérence dans les affaires qui relèvent exclusivement de la compétence nationale de l'Etat. Pour répondre à cette nouvelle objection, aussi valable que celle que l'on a fait valoir contre l'idée d'infliger des sanctions à l'Etat, on pourrait exiger* que le fait « punissable » soit punissable en vertu du droit international. *En réalité, à partir du moment où l'on admet la notion de responsabilité* pénale *de l'individu, on ne peut contester qu'il y ait lieu de punir les auteurs d'actes illicites qui engagent la responsabilité* civile *de l'Etat, si ces actes constituent de véritables délits internationaux*" (*ibid.*, pp. 212–213, emphasis added).

49 P.N. Drost, *Humanicide. International Governmental Crime Against Individual Human Rights* (Leiden, Sythoff, 1959).

50 "[C]ollective crime is essentially a combination of individual crimes to be repressed by the judicial establishment of numerous cases of individual liability to personal punishment. . . . The criminality of a human group dissolves into the criminality of its human members since there exists neither a group's body nor a group's mind to be held criminally responsible for the incriminated deeds performed in concerted action by the combined members of the group." (*ibid.*, pp. 295, and 297).

51 *Ibid.*, p. 311.

munity as a whole. The affirmation of *jus cogens* and *erga omnes* obligations had a deep impact on international law, and in particular on the law of state responsibility.[52] Thus, the protection of fundamental values of international law could no longer be confined to the strait-jacket of a bilateral regime of responsibility. A mechanism of reaction against serious breaches of the most important international obligations became an urgent need. This led to the elaboration of the doctrine of aggravated state responsibility. On the other hand, international criminal law was regarded as aiming at the protection of fundamental values belonging to the international community as a whole. International rules providing for individual criminal liability were therefore listed among *erga omnes* obligations, and even *jus cogens*.[53] Consequently, the conceptual framework under examination had to be adapted to such new circumstances in order to maintain its cogency. Thus, the fundamental change in more recent contributions does not concern the basic mechanism of the 'specific reprisal', but the fact that individual criminal liability becomes one of the consequences (if not the sole consequence) of aggravated state responsibility.

Lattanzi essentially adheres to the conception of individual criminal liability as a form of aggravated responsibility of states, and refers to the same mechanism as the one Sperduti had affirmed decades before.[54] However, this mechanism is adapted to the new conceptual framework. The indication of serious breaches giving rise to special consequences turns here into an explicit reference to *jus cogens* norms.[55] Particularly, *delicta juris gentium* – crimes against peace, war crimes and crimes against humanity – are listed among the most important international rules protecting the fundamental values of the international community as a whole and therefore giving rise to an aggravated regime of state responsibility, where the

---

[52] *See* supra the Introduction. Such developments have been welcomed by many, but they have also been the subject of strong criticism. *See*, in particular, P. Weil, 'Towards Relative Normativity in International Law', 77 *AJIL* (1983), p. 413.

[53] *See*, for example, ICTY, *Prosecutor v. Furundžija*, TC, Judgment, 10 December 1998, paras. 151–7; House of Lords, *Pinochet II*, supra Chapter 1, note 18, p. 88; M.C. Bassiouni, *Le fonti e il contenuto del diritto penale internazionale. Un quadro teorico* (Milano, Giuffré, 1999), p. 65.

[54] F. Lattanzi, *Garanzie dei diritti dell'uomo nel diritto internazionale generale* (Milano, Giuffré, 1983), p. 357. *See* also F. Lattanzi, 'Riflessioni sulla competenza di una Corte penale internazionale', 76 *Riv. Dir. Int.* (1993), p. 661. First, the general assumption is that individuals have no international legal personality (F. Lattanzi, *Garanzie dei diritti dell'uomo nel diritto internazionale generale*, p. 354, note 4). Second, the repression of individual crimes is exclusively attributed to domestic legal systems (*ibid.*, pp. 353–4). Therefore, no individual criminal liability is provided for under international law (*ibid.*). The punishment of state organs is strictly derived from the commission by states of particularly serious breaches of international obligations. International crimes – war crimes, crimes against humanity and crimes against peace – are particularly serious wrongful state acts, and only entail individual liability if they are perpetrated by states. Consequently, the sanction provided for by international law is directed against the responsible state, *i.e.*, its organization.

[55] *Ibid.*, p. 352.

criminal liability of state organs represents only one of the possible special consequences for the commission of state crimes.[56] In other words, the punishment of state organs finds its place among the special consequences of 'international crimes' as codified by the ILC in Article 19 of the Draft Articles on State Responsibility adopted in 1976.[57]

Furthermore, the general framework of the relationship between state and individual responsibility for international crimes is no longer the strictly bilateral regime of ordinary state responsibility, but the new regime of aggravated state responsibility, which entails a relationship between the author state and the international community as a whole. The punishment of state organs by a foreign tribunal is no longer a 'specific reprisal' of the injured state. It becomes a measure that every state can adopt on behalf of the entire international community, that is, a decentralized sanction by an implicitly delegated agent. Indeed, since the regime of aggravated state responsibility lacks an institutional mechanism of reaction against the breach of obligation owed to the international community as a whole, Lattanzi maintains that under international law every state has a subjective right to react against such serious breaches.[58]

More recently, a similar theory has been advocated by Maison, who has taken into account a further evolution of the international community, that is, the process of institutionalization of international criminal law,[59] in particular, international criminal tribunals.[60] While Maison excludes, on the one hand, that "*l'individu – en tant que tel – se trouve directement obligé par le droit international*",[61] and, on the other, that international tribunals' power to prosecute individuals for international

---

[56] *Ibid.*, pp. 419–422.

[57] *Ibid.*, p. 533.

[58] In particular, the decentralized sanction against international crimes consists of the fact that the author state is no longer protected under international law, and that the other states can accordingly prosecute its organs (*ibid.*, p. 419). With respect to 'other states', she specifies that general international law allows *any* state to punish those responsible for international crimes (*ibid.*, p. 417).

[59] R. Maison, *La responsabilité individuelle pour crime de l'Etat en droit international public* (Bruxelles, Bruylant, 2004). Maison starts from the assumption that international crimes are prohibited by peremptory norms of international law (*ibid.*, pp. 11–17). Therefore, it is their special nature that justifies an aggravated regime of state responsibility and, in particular, a centralized reaction of the international community towards the responsible state (*ibid.*, pp. 18–19). Crimes against peace, crimes against humanity and war crimes are regarded as collective criminal phenomena, that is, essentially state crimes (*ibid.*, p. 28). Individual accountability of state organs is accordingly simply an indirect sanction for the responsible state. The legal relation which is taken into account is that between the international community as a whole and the responsible state.

[60] The international courts she takes into account are essentially the IMT, the IMTFE, the ICTY, the ICTR, and the ICC.

[61] R. Maison, supra note 59, p. 3. Thus, individual criminal liability cannot be regarded as a separate regime under international law.

crimes is simply carried out "*au nom commun des différents Etats y participant*",[62] she concludes that institutional repression of international crimes is a special sanction of the international community against the author state.[63] Thus, the new element consists of the fact that the punishment of state organs is considered to be a direct and centralized reaction of the international community as a whole.

What is the nature of this reaction? As the legal relation arising from the commission of an international crime is no longer considered to be a bilateral relation between the injured state and the responsible state, the mechanism of the 'specific reprisal' seems to be unworkable. Maison holds that this reaction consists of a different mechanism, namely, the breach of the international customary obligation which prohibits every state from exercising its jurisdiction over a foreign state.[64] The sanction for the commission of international crimes is therefore the imposition of compulsory jurisdiction over the author state, since such a compulsory jurisdiction is normally illegal under customary international law.[65] After all, such a mechanism is not so different from the 'specific reprisal' examined above. Certainly, it focuses on jurisdiction rather than immunity. However, the breach – by the injured state or the international community – concerns the 'respect of state internal organization' or the principle *par in parem non habet jurisdictionem*, which is a corollary of sovereignty. Thus, the commission of state crimes allows, as a sanction, a certain degree of intrusion into state sovereignty. This actually would consist of the fact that international tribunals have to assess the requirements of state responsibility for

---

[62] *Ibid.*, pp. 10–11.

[63] *See* also R. Maison, 'Les poursuites pénales internationales comme modalité de réparation du crime d'Etat', in *Studi di diritto internazionale in onore di Gaetano Arangio-Ruiz*, vol. I (Napoli, Editoriale Scientifica, 2004), p. 808 et seq. For a similar view, *see* M. Iovane, *La tutela dei valori fondamentali nel diritto internazionale* (Napoli, Editoriale scientifica, 2000), pp. 542–564, affirming that the establishment of the ICTY is a centralized sanction of the international community against the responsible state. By contrast, he maintains that the establishment of the ICTR could not be explained in the same manner (*ibid.*, pp. 564–566).

[64] R. Maison, supra note 59, pp. 407–8 ("*Cette théorie des représailles, formulée dans le cadre de la poursuite d'agents étrangers devant le juge interne, ne peut être appliquée telle quelle à l'institution de poursuites internationales. En effet, on a constaté que le juge pénal international n'est jamais tenu de respecter les règles immunitaires classiques. La 'sanction' de l'illicite étatique ne consiste donc pas dans la levée au cas par cas de l'immunité d'actes de fonction mais dans l'institution même d'une juridiction internationale obligatoire, dont le principe est exceptionnel. Imposer à un Etat le jugement de ses actes par l'intermédiaire de l'accusation pénale de ses agents peut sans doute être appréhendé comme une mesure de représailles, au sens où cette imposition constitue un acte normalement illicite, qui tire sa validité de la perpétration par cet Etat d'une infraction internationale. Cependant, le caractère centralisé de la décision d'instituer un tribunal* ad hoc *ou de saisir la nouvelle juridiction permanente d'actes d'un Etat non partie à son Statut correspond mal à la notion juridique de représailles fréquemment attachée à une relation non institutionnalisée. Une telle décision s'intègre plus évidemment au régime de responsabilité découlant du crime d'Etat.*").

[65] *Ibid.*, pp. 417–419.

international crimes, since international crimes are collective criminal phenomena and they can only prosecute state organs.[66]

Similar views seem to be shared by other international law scholars who have indirectly dealt with more specific questions raised by the relationship between state and individual responsibility for international crimes.

A certain tendency to conceive of individual liability for international crimes as a part of the wider legal framework of interstate responsibility for breaches of *erga omnes* obligations can be perceived in the work of Picone. It is well known that this author is among those who developed the idea that breaches of *erga omnes* obligations entail a decentralized reaction performed by states acting on behalf of the international community as a whole.[67] It is in the frame of this sophisticated theory that he has also addressed the specific question of the legal foundations of the establishment of the ICTY.[68] In particular, the prosecution of state organs by the *ad hoc* tribunal is seen as a specific sanction adopted by the SC on behalf of the international community as a whole against states that have committed atrocities – *i.e.*, serious breaches of *erga omnes* obligations – during the conflict in the Bal-

[66] Unfortunately, when attempts are made to locate such a sanction in the regime of aggravated state responsibility, individual criminal liability is vaguely associated with a very broad concept of reparation for wrongful acts: "*[elle] trouve sa place dans un régime* sui generis *de* réparation *du crime d'Etat. Alors seulement, elle est amenée à remplir sa fonction principale de* satisfaction, *tandis qu'associée à d'autres mesures contraignantes elle garantit également la* non-répétition *de l'illicite, en laissant subsister, lorsqu'elle peut être mise en œuvre, une obligation collective de* restitution *ou de* compensation *des dommages créés par l'illicite*" (*ibid.*, p. 510, emphasis added).

[67] *See* P. Picone, *Comunità internazionale e obblighi erga omnes: studi critici di diritto internazionale* (Napoli, Jovene, 2006).

[68] *See* P. Picone, 'Sul fondamento giuridico del Tribunale penale internazionale per la ex Iugoslavia', 51 *Comunità Internaz.* (1996), p. 3 et seq. The legal basis of the establishment of the ICTY by the SC has been identified by international law scholars either in the UN Charter or in customary international law. There have also been authors pronouncing against its legitimacy. *See*, in general, A. Bernardini, 'Il Tribunale penale internazionale per la (ex) Iugoslavia: considerazioni giuridiche', 4 *I diritti dell'uomo, cronache e battaglie* (1993), pp. 15–25; A. Pellet, 'Le Tribunal criminel international pour l'ex Yougoslavie', 98 *RGDIP* (1994), pp. 7–60; C. Tomuschat, ‚Ein internationales Strafgerichtshof als Element einer Weltfriedensordnunng', 49 *Europa Archiv* (1994), pp. 61–70; G. Carella, 'Il Tribunale penale internazionale per la ex Iugoslavia', supra note 37; F.L. Kirgis, 'The Security Council's First Fifty Years', 89 *AJIL* (1995), p. 506–539; G. Arangio-Ruiz, 'The Establishment of the International Criminal Tribunal for the Former Territory of Yugoslavia and the Doctrine of Implied Powers of the United Nations', in F. Lattanti and E. Sciso (eds.), *Dai Tribunali penali internazionali ad hoc a una Corte permanente* (Napoli, Editoriale Scientifica, 1996), pp. 31–45; T. Christakis, *L'ONU, le Chapitre VII et la crise Yougoslave* (Paris, Montchrestien, 1996), pp. 187–204; P. Palchetti, 'Il potere del Consiglio di sicurezza di istituire tribunali penali internazionali', 79 *Riv. Dir. Int.* (1996), p. 413; D. Shraga and R. Zacklin, 'The International Criminal Tribunal for Rwanda', 7 *EJIL* (1996), pp. 501–518; M.C. Vitucci, *Il Tribunale ad hoc per la ex Iugoslavia e il consenso degli Stati* (Milano, Giuffré, 1998); B. Conforti, *Le Nazioni unite* (7th edn, Padova, Cedam, 2005), pp. 219–222.

kans.[69] The emphasis is put on the role of the SC as a 'material organ' of the entire international community, and on the power it has under customary law to adopt punitive measures against those states seriously breaching *erga omnes* obligations. The establishment of the ICTY and the punishment of state organs (who have committed international crimes) appears to be conceived of as a sanction imposed on the wrongful state and not on the individual.[70] International crimes are committed by states,[71] and the establishment of the ICTY can be seen as an interstate measure essentially aiming at sanctioning the author state or states.[72]

In his book on the immunity of state organs under international law, De Sena addresses the problem of the punishment of state organs who have committed international crimes.[73] In principle, he rejects the existence of a general rule establishing the immunity *ratione materiae* of state organs under customary law,[74] and accordingly he accepts that both international tribunals and domestic courts can prosecute those organs charged with international crimes without breaching the rules on functional immunity. Therefore, the punishment of state organs should not be regarded as specific countermeasures against the responsible state.[75] However, when state organs are accused of crimes committed by the entire state apparatus, they are responsible for conduct which is substantially attributable to the state. To be more precise, with respect to 'state crimes' the punishment of state organs by the competent tribunal must be based on the preliminary finding that a serious breach of community obligations has been committed by the state.[76] Only states can commit such crimes, and state organs are punished on behalf of the author state.[77] On the other hand, state organs *can* be prosecuted before international tribunals for 'state crimes' since this can be regarded as a special centralized sanc-

[69] P. Picone, 'Interventi delle Nazioni Unite e obblighi *erga omnes*', in P. Picone (ed.), *Interventi delle Nazioni Unite e diritto internazionale* (Padova, Cedam, 1995), p. 551 (note 116); P. Picone, supra note 68, p. 12.

[70] P. Picone, supra note 68, p. 8.

[71] *Ibid.*, p. 16.

[72] *Ibid.*, p. 15.

[73] P. De Sena, *Diritto internazionale e immunità funzionale degli organi statali* (Milano, Giuffré, 1996).

[74] *Ibid.*, p. xviii. The traditional approach is to recognize a certain immunity on the part of state organs acting in their official capacity. *See*, in general, A. Cassese, supra note 12, pp. 90, and 93–97. On the particular question concerning the prosecution of state organs for international crimes, and the way in which the lifting of this immunity can be justified under international law in this particular case, *see* infra Chapter 8, note 1.

[75] P. De Sena, supra note 73, p. 184.

[76] *Ibid.*, p. 186.

[77] Therefore, he admits that the immunity of the state itself can (exceptionally) shield those state organs who are responsible for 'state crimes' from prosecution before domestic courts of other countries (*ibid.*, pp. xix, 176, and 178).

tion adopted by the entire international community against the wrongful state, and not the individual.[78]

Finally, a more recent analysis is carried out by May, who nonetheless limits his theoretical inquiry to crimes against humanity.[79] He starts his analysis from the assumption that states must protect a basic minimum of individual rights. Thus, sovereignty can legitimately be breached by the entire international community if states commit international crimes, since these crimes are violations of this minimum protection provided under peremptory international law.[80] According to what he calls the 'international harm' principle,[81] the international community has a legal interest to react against crimes committed by states or targeting a whole social group. In particular, when such crimes are committed by states, sovereignty dissolves, and state organs can be prosecuted. Thus, international criminal tribunals must first demonstrate the special interest of the international community before establishing individual criminal liability. Accordingly, they must focus on the most serious international crimes only and exclude from prosecution individually-oriented crimes.[82] In particular, a link must always be established between the individual conduct of the accused and the collective criminal context. This should in principle exclude the responsibility of non-state organs and of minor players who are not sufficiently linked to the larger criminal policy of the state. Prosecution should concentrate on state leaders, that is, those persons who have devised the state criminal policy and have ordered the carrying out of international crimes.[83]

---

[78] *Ibid.*, pp. 185 and 187 (note 105). It must be noted that De Sena distinguishes two different categories of international crimes. On the one hand, there are typical 'individual crimes' which entail a form of individual criminal liability that is completely independent from state responsibility. This is the case, for instance, of certain war crimes and of the crime of 'official torture'. On the other hand, there are 'state crimes', namely, what De Sena calls crimes attributable "to the entire state organization" (*ibid.*, pp. 149–166). And the typical state-oriented scheme displayed by this author is limited to this latter category of international crimes. For example, the IMT and the prosecution of Nazi criminals is considered to be one of the various measures taken at the end of WWII to secure the "systematic dismantlement of the entire German *state* organization" (*ibid.*, p. 185, emphasis added). Similarly, the establishment of the ICTY is better understood as a sanction adopted by the international community as a whole – through the Security Council – against those states taking part in the Balkan conflict, rather than a form of punishment of those individuals responsible for the international crimes committed in such a context (*ibid.*, p. 187, note 105).

[79] L. May, *Crimes Against Humanity: A Normative Account* (Cambridge, Cambridge University Press, 2005).

[80] *Ibid.*, pp. 68–71.

[81] *Ibid.*, pp. 80–95.

[82] *Ibid.*, pp. 115–138.

[83] *Ibid.*, pp. 139–156. Inevitably, May is particularly unsatisfied with existing elements of crimes against humanity (and genocide) which do not manifest the collective nature of this international crime (*ibid.*, pp. 157–176). While command responsibility is proposed as the ideal form of individual criminal liability for the purpose of prosecuting state leaders, he pleads for an extended conception of defences in order to shield minor players from punishment (*ibid.*, pp. 179–200).

3. *The Individual-Oriented and State-Oriented Conceptual Schemes*

It is important to point out that it is difficult to generalize as regards the positions of the international law scholars examined above. These views are not only very different, but they have also been elaborated in the framework of very different conceptions of the international legal order. However, it seems possible to use these views as a valid starting point from which to identify the conceptual schemes that can abstractly order the relationship between state and individual responsibility for international crimes. Indeed, the purpose of this section is to understand, from a purely theoretical viewpoint, the range of (extreme) conceptions of this relationship. This inquiry into the theoretical schemes that can govern the relationship between state and individual responsibility for international crimes is essential because it provides for the general framework in which to locate and discuss the practical problems concerning this relationship.

Ideally, two opposed conceptual schemes can be applied to the relationship between state and individual responsibility for international crimes. At one end of the spectrum, there is a conception grounded on the complete separation of these regimes and putting the emphasis on their mutual differences. At the other hand, by contrast, there is a conception which focuses on the close connections between these regimes and considers them to be the two parts of a unitary system of consequences to be attached to the most serious breaches of community obligations.

A. *Individual-Oriented Conceptual Scheme*

What may be called an 'individual-oriented conceptual scheme' starts from the basic assumption concerning the *dissociation* between the conduct of the state and that of its organs. It takes into account the particular characteristics of international criminal law which are regarded as completely different from those of state responsibility, and it leads to the conclusion that individual accountability for international crimes is totally independent of aggravated state responsibility.

This individual-oriented scheme essentially focuses on the autonomy of individual criminal liability. International crimes of individuals can be committed, established and punished independently of the attribution of state responsibility for the same wrongful acts. State and individual responsibility are totally independent because they are governed by different primary and secondary norms under international law. Individual criminal liability for international crimes is established having regard only to very personal elements, such as the *actus reus* and the *mens rea* of the accused, and not because of the particular position in state hierarchy or because of the contribution to a broader criminal activity carried out at the state level. While aggravated state responsibility is a collective responsibility to be attributed to a collective entity, individual criminal liability is a personal responsibility to be attributed individually to any offender.

On the other hand, the individual-oriented scheme does not deny the parallel existence of an aggravated regime of state responsibility for international crimes. In order for such a terminology not to be misleading, it must be clarified that this approach does not exclude the possibility of an overlap between state and individual responsibility, in the sense that certain wrongful acts may give rise to a dual responsibility under international law. However, this overlap has no legal effect in the establishment of individual criminal liability, which is completely separate from that of state responsibility.

It is from this point of view that, in its more radical version, the individual-oriented scheme denies any relationship between state and individual responsibility for international crimes. They both deal with the commission of international crimes, and both states and individuals are responsible under international law, but no connection or link can be established between the rules governing aggravated state responsibility and individual criminal liability respectively. Accordingly, the problems that may be associated with such a relationship should be solved in different ways from the standpoint of individual criminal liability and from that of aggravated state responsibility respectively, since the overlap between these regimes is legally irrelevant. To be more precise, the mere idea of a relationship is abstractly unacceptable, because (by definition) there can be no relationship between two completely separate regimes.

This conceptual scheme essentially focuses on international criminal law, its basic assumption and its main features which profoundly differentiate it from state responsibility. State and individual responsibility for international crimes stem from different sets of international law rules, and therefore are established by different bodies, according to different rules, different requirements, different purposes, and give rise to different consequences for the responsible subject. The fact that the same serious breach of community obligations can also give rise to aggravated state responsibility is generally considered, from this point of view, to be *irrelevant*. In the end, this approach leads to the conclusion that *no relationship* between state and individual responsibility needs to be taken into account.

B. *State-Oriented Conceptual Scheme*

From an opposite perspective, the relationship between state and individual responsibility for international crimes tends to fade out in a scheme which is totally state-oriented. International crimes are committed by states, and individual criminal liability for serious breaches of obligations owed to the international community as a whole is understood as a form of aggravated state responsibility.

What may be called a 'state-oriented conceptual scheme' relies on a basic assumption positing the *identity* between the state conduct amounting to an international crime and that of its organs. This assumption implies that there is only one subject responsible under international law: the state. Private individuals cannot be held responsible for international crimes, nor can state organs be held responsible when acting in their private capacity. State organs can only be punished when their conduct is attributable to the state. Indeed, under this basic (fictive) assumption there is only one wrongful act: that of the author state. This has a significant consequence: individuals cannot be prosecuted for crimes not reaching the threshold of serious breaches of obligations owed to the international community as a whole entailing aggravated state responsibility.

Therefore, individual criminal liability should depend on the establishment of a generalized context of state criminality, *i.e.*, the serious breach giving rise to the international responsibility of the author state. Individual and state responsibility are so closely connected that the same requirements must be met. If the criteria for establishing individual criminal liability and aggravated state responsibility are the same, this also means that state organs should be punished according to their participation in this broad context, and according to their official position in the state apparatus. Indeed, the assumption of identical criteria implies that state leaders should bear greater responsibility than low-ranking offenders. This can be problematic from the standpoint of international criminal law, because individual liability can turn into a form of vicarious responsibility.

In addition, the basic assumption of the identity between the conduct of the state and that of its organs implies that, under international law, there is only one set of consequences attached to the serious breach of community obligations, that is, aggravated state responsibility. In particular, this regime provides for the possibility to breach state organs' immunity or to impose a compulsory jurisdiction over the responsible state by prosecuting its organs. This is regarded as a special sanction because these acts would otherwise be prohibited under international law. Individual criminal liability does not give rise to a separate regime of international responsibility. Individuals, or rather state organs, are currently prosecuted for international crimes, but this should not be regarded as an emerging form of international criminal law. It is simply an indirect and specific expression of state responsibility.

According to this conceptual scheme, individual criminal liability is a special secondary rule provided for under the regime of aggravated state responsibility. The commission of international crimes consequently gives rise to a particular relationship between the author state and the entire international community. Thus, the punishment of the responsible state organs is considered to be a centralized reaction by the international community against the author state. Most importantly, the establishment of individual criminal liability implies the assessment of the requisites of aggravated state responsibility, since the punishment of individuals strictly depends upon their participation in the wider context of state criminality. The unity posited with respect to the subjects of international law is maintained until the end, at the stage of the establishment of international responsibility: the same sets, not only of primary norms but also of secondary norms, govern both state and individual responsibility.

It is from this point of view that, in its more radical version, the state-oriented scheme denies any relationship between state and individual responsibility for international crimes. The regime of international responsibility arising out of the breach of obligations owed to the international community as a whole is conceived of by means of a single theoretical perspective: there is one subject, one wrongful act, one set of consequences. Therefore, there is only one international responsibility regime: aggravated state responsibility. This is because individual responsibility is brought back into the framework of aggravated state responsibility. State organs are prosecuted but this is merely a special consequence of state crimes. Individual criminal liability is a *metaphor*, in the literal sense of this word. In reality, when organs face trial for international crimes, a sanction is imposed on their state.

4. *Concluding Observations*

The theoretical schemes identified above represent two ideal paradigms for the relationship between state and individual responsibility for international crimes. As such, they can hardly be sustained in their theoretical comprehensiveness, and rather more nuanced views can be envisaged. However, this effort of conceptualization is important because it reveals the basic underlying assumptions as well as the pros and the cons of the two opposite perspectives of the relationship between state and individual responsibility.

The individual-oriented scheme takes into account recent developments of international criminal law and puts the emphasis on the fact that the two regimes of international responsibility for core crimes serve parallel functions within their respective spheres. Accordingly, the problems that may be entailed by the relationship between international criminal law can receive totally different solutions, and the latter can develop its own rules in perfect independence from the former.

On the other hand, the state-oriented scheme focuses on the close connections that may link state and individual responsibility for international crimes. In particular, it has the advantage of recomposing the normative unity of the regime concerning international crimes at the stage of secondary rules, even though this is only a relative unity.[84] Therefore, the problems emerging from the relationship between state and individual responsibility can consistently be solved according to the principles governing state responsibility.

---

[84] The price to be paid is that crimes committed by individuals in their private capacity – whether private individuals or state organs – are totally disregarded. Therefore, a separate regime of criminal liability must be established in domestic legal orders to deal with the latter class of crimes.

However, both these conceptual schemes have in common a major drawback. While the individual-oriented scheme *a priori* denies any relationship between state and individual responsibility for international crimes, the state-oriented scheme ends up nullifying this relationship, as it is completely 'internalized' in the regime of aggravated state responsibility. In both cases, the result is that, in fact, *no relationship* between state and individual responsibility needs to be taken into account.

It will be shown and discussed in due course that these radical views of the relationship between state and individual responsibility for international crimes are not reflected in international practice, which seems more complex and multifaceted by far, and which pays more attention to the points of contact between these regimes. To give an example, while international law finally seems prepared to take into account individuals, international practice shows that its present challenge is to find ways to deal efficiently with collective criminality. Unlike municipal law,[85] international criminal law contemplates only individuals as perpetrators. However, it focuses most of the time on crimes committed at the collective level, and international jurisprudence shows that it is developing specific tools to address this kind of collective crimes. From a comparative perspective this may be problematic, since the theoretical schemes described above do not allow the particular features of crimes committed by, for instance, members of criminal organizations, corporations or military and paramilitary groups, to be duly taken into account. Organized criminal phenomena are difficult to appraise with the tools of individual criminal liability, and they cannot necessarily be framed in terms of state action. Thus, it may be extremely difficult to establish either individual or state responsibility for crimes committed by perpetrators who have participated in a collective criminal enterprise, and who share with many other perpetrators the criminal intent.[86]

---

[85] Domestic case law displays different approaches with respect to collective responsibility for international crimes. At present, legal entities cannot be held *criminally* liable under international criminal law, but US courts, for example, have recognized that not only natural persons but also legal entities can face *civil* liability when they are found to have committed international crimes (*see* US District Court, *Doe v. Unocal*, 963 F. Supp. 880, pp. 890–892; US District Court, *Tachiona v. Mugabe*, 169 F. Supp. 2d 259, pp. 309–316). Thus, "non-state entities should be deemed individuals for the purposes of effectively applying statutes like the ATCA and the TVPA" (*ibid.*, p. 313). Most interestingly, reference is made to the development of international law in the area of human rights in order to justify the imposition of liability (provided for under domestic law) on organized non-state actors (responsible for crimes provided under international law). The view has been expressed that domestic case law already shows a tendency to recognize the liability of legal entities for international crimes, and that a similar development at the international level cannot be excluded in the future. *See* G. Acquaviva, 'Verso una responsabilità delle multinazionali per gravi violazioni dei diritti umani? Note in margine a *Doe v. Unocal*', 57 *Comunità Internaz.* (2002), pp. 593–611, and references therein.

[86] *See* infra Chapters 3 and 4, and, more generally, Chapter 6.

Thus, the next step is to leave in the background these conceptual schemes. The following analysis will concentrate instead on the points of contact between state and individual responsibility for international crimes, and on the connections between them which increasingly emerge in international practice.

Part II

The Overlap Between State and Individual Responsibility for International Crimes in International Practice

Chapter 3

The Overlap of the Material Element: The Seriousness Requirement

International practice shows that international crimes are most of the time carried out with the substantial involvement of states.[1] International crimes are offences which require to be carried out on such a large scale that the participation or at least the support of the state apparatus has often been present. Thus, the material element – that is, the conduct amounting to an international crime – represents the most important point of contact between state and individual responsibility for international crimes.

This is also reflected in the definition of international crimes provided under customary international law. On the one hand, aggravated state responsibility requires the wrongful act to be serious. On the other hand, individual liability arises under customary international law for criminal conduct mostly carried out in a widespread or systematic manner. In particular, some international crimes demonstrate by definition a general pre-requisite concerning the seriousness of the offence.

Therefore, it becomes very important to see how this seriousness requirement is capable of establishing a relationship between state and individual responsibility. In particular, the present inquiry must focus on the way in which the general pattern of state criminality is actually taken into account when establishing individual criminal liability. This question is crucial to determine whether individuals are internationally responsible only for crimes committed in such a widespread and systematic manner as to require the involvement of the entire state apparatus. If so, it remains to be established whether international criminal tribunals first assess aggravated state responsibility or at least a state policy in carrying out international crimes before convicting the responsible state organs. Otherwise, the question concerns the extent to which the broader criminal context can play a role in holding individuals accountable for international crimes.

---

1 *See* E. Van Sliedregt, *The Criminal Responsibility of Individuals for Violations of International Humanitarian Law* (The Hague, TMC Asser Press, 2003), pp. 4–5.

Before trying to answer these questions, the notion of seriousness requires some preliminary clarification. Two different concepts of seriousness are generally used with respect to international crimes, and a clear distinction between the two needs to be made.

1. *Two Different Concepts of Seriousness*

From a very general point of view, all international crimes – no matter whether they entail aggravated state responsibility or individual criminal liability – can be considered the most serious breaches of fundamental international obligations owed to the international community as a whole. At first, gravity is associated with the importance of the international obligation breached. From this point of view, gravity is a characteristic pertaining to the nature of the primary norm. This undoubtedly reveals a point of contact between state and individual responsibility.

Indeed, it was in accordance with this general conception of gravity that Article 19 on state crimes was drafted.[2] Only breaches of the most important primary rules should entail a special regime of state responsibility.[3] International crimes are therefore breaches of a selected group of international rules, which are *per se* of fundamental importance. The prohibition of aggression, colonial domination, genocide, apartheid and so on are *per se* fundamental obligations of the international legal order. In Ago's conception, the breach of one of these obligations is *per se* an international crime, and does not need to fulfil any further requirement to lead to aggravated state responsibility.[4]

---

2 *See* supra the Introduction.

3 In his Fifth Report, Special Rapporteur Ago made it extremely clear that: "it seems undeniable that today, for the international community as a whole, such acts violate principles formally embodied in the Charter, and even if the Charter is not taken into account, principles which are now so deeply embedded in the consciousness of mankind that they have become particularly important rules of general international law. It also seems undeniable that world opinion regards the acts in question as genuine 'crimes', *i.e.*, wrongful acts which are more serious than others, and that they must therefore entail more serious legal consequences... This is a substantive distinction, related to the difference in the content of international obligations and to the fact that, while all of them are important and while respect for all of them must be ensured, some of them are recognized today as being of more fundamental value than others for inter-State society as a whole, and observance of these must therefore be guaranteed by laying a heavier responsibility on those infringing them." (R. Ago, 'Fifth Report on State Responsibility', *YILC* (1976), vol. II(1), pp. 39 and 50).

4 In Article 19, drafted by Ago, the word 'serious' only appears in paragraph 3, giving some examples of international crimes of state. In the commentary on Article 19, such a requirement is considered by the ILC to be implicit in all the examples of paragraph 3, except for the "breach of an international obligation of essential importance for safeguarding the human being". In this case, an additional requirement must be met for the breach to constitute an international crime. Moreover, it must be carried out on a widespread scale, that is, the breach "it must take the form

Accordingly, the general definition of international crimes of state did not refer to concrete standards of seriousness, but to a general criterion making it possible to shortlist certain international primary norms essential for safeguarding community interests. This criterion is the particular importance attached to certain obligations by the international community as a whole. Article 19 (2), provided for the following definition of state crimes: "An internationally wrongful act which results from the breach by a State of an international obligation so essential for the protection of fundamental interests of the international community that its breach is recognized as a crime by that community as a whole constitutes an international crime".[5]

In other words, the general criterion of gravity results in a selection made by the international community as whole among international obligations aimed at safeguarding its fundamental interests. As already discussed, aggravated state responsibility arises as a result of the breach of the most important obligations owed to the entire international community.[6]

The same is true with respect to international criminal responsibility of individuals. It only arises out of the breach of the most important obligations owed to the international community as a whole. At the beginning of the 1980s, when the ILC resumed its work on the Draft Code of Crimes against the Peace and Security of Mankind, it referred to the same general criterion of gravity adopted in the Draft Articles on State Responsibility in selecting international crimes giving rise to individual criminal liability.[7] In more general terms, it is possible to say that individual liability for international crimes is limited to the perpetration of the most grave violations of international community obligations. Thus, in order to establish the existence under customary law of a war crime entailing individual criminal liability, the ICTY required (*inter alia*) the violation to be serious, "that is to say, it must constitute a breach of a rule protecting important values".[8]

On the one hand, gravity is a criterion used for selecting primary norms whose breach will give rise to a particular regime of individual or state responsibility.

---

of a large-scale or systematic practice adopted in contempt of the rights and dignity of the human being" (ILC, 'Report on the Work of its 28th Session', *YILC* (1976), vol. II(2), p. 121).

[5] *Ibid.*, p. 89. For a similar opinion, according to which the gravity requirement was implicit in international crimes of states, *see* G. Carella, *La responsabilità dello stato per crimini internazionali* (Napoli, Jovene, 1985), p. 249.

[6] *See* supra Chapter 1.

[7] D. Thiam, 'First Report on the Draft Code of Crimes against the peace and Security of Mankind', *YILC* (1983), vol. II(1), p. 137. *See* also the discussion of the members of the ILC on the issue, *YILC* (1983), vol. I, p. 2 et seq.

[8] ICTY, *Prosecutor v. Tadić*, AC, Decision on the Defence Motion for Interlocutory Appeal on Jurisdiction, 2 October 1995, para. 94. *See* also ICTY, *Prosecutor v. Martić*, TC, Review of the Indictment pursuant to Rule 61, 8 March 1996, para. 19; ICTY, *Prosecutor v. Galić*, TC, Judgment, 5 December 2003, paras. 106–112.

Moreover, it highlights the fact that aggravated state responsibility and individual criminal liability share the same normative source, *i.e.*, the category of obligations owed to the international community as a whole.[9] However, such a general criterion is not very useful in establishing the material relationship between state and individual responsibility for international crimes. Despite the fact that these regimes derive from the breaches of the same kind of international obligations, it does not necessarily follow that they are governed by the same principles or that they serve the same purposes.

On the other hand, seriousness is an operational criterion embodying concrete standards which permit the identification of those international wrongful acts giving rise to either aggravated state responsibility or individual criminal liability. From this point of view, seriousness is a requirement provided under a regime of international responsibility, that is, secondary norms, in order to attach particular consequences to certain (serious) wrongful acts.[10]

In the context of an inquiry into the relationship between state and individual responsibility, it is very important to keep these two concepts separate.[11] The first

---

9 *See* supra Chapter 1.

10 Interestingly, the distinction between these two different conceptions of seriousness were pointed out by the Czech Republic in its Comment on the Draft Articles on State Responsibility, suggesting that a regime of aggravated state responsibility should be grounded on the second conception of seriousness (UN Doc. A/CN.4/488, p. 134). *See* also P.-M. Dupuy, 'L'unité de l'ordre juridique international', 297 *RCADI* (2002), p. 365; and S. Villalpando, *L'émergence de la communauté internationale dans la responsabilité des Etats* (Paris, PUF, 2005), pp. 246–259.

11 To give an example, Article 89 of the 1977 Additional Protocol I to the Geneva Conventions speaks of 'serious violations', and this raises doubts about the difference between 'grave breaches' and 'serious violations' (T. Meron, '*Lex Lata*: Is there already a Differentiated Regime of State Responsibility in the Geneva Conventions?', in J.H.H. Weiler *et al.* (eds.), *International Crimes of State. A Critical Analysis of the ILC's Draft Article 19 on State Responsibility* (Berlin, De Gruyter, 1989), p. 231; L. Condorelli, 'The Continuity between Certain Principles of Humanitarian Law and the Concept of Crimes of States', in J.H.H. Weiler *et al.* (eds.), *International Crimes of State. A Critical Analysis of the ILC's Draft Article 19 on State Responsibility* (Berlin, De Gruyter, 1989), p. 236). 'Grave breaches' are *selected* breaches of the Geneva Conventions and the Additional Protocols entailing individual criminal liability under international law (according to Article 85 of Protocol I, they "shall be regarded as war crimes"). Thus, the term 'grave' refers to the importance of certain primary norms and is used to select those breaches that will give rise to a particular regime of individual liability (with respect to breaches of Common Article 3 *see*, ICTR, *Prosecutor v. Kamuhanda*, TC, Judgment, 22 January 2004, para. 73). On the other hand, the term 'serious' is used to refer to a characteristic of the wrongful act and consequently to establish a threshold (within the regime of state responsibility) beyond which certain consequences can be attached to the serious violation ("the High Contracting Parties undertake to act, jointly or individually, in co-operation with the United Nations and in conformity with the United Nations Charter"). The importance of the distinction between these two concepts of seriousness was pointed out by the United Kingdom and France in their comments to the Draft Articles on State Responsibility (UN Doc. A/CN.4/488).

one pertains to the nature of certain primary norms, and is essential to acknowledge a common origin of both aggravated state responsibility and individual criminal liability. The second one fundamentally is an operational criterion provided for under secondary norms, and according to which certain prohibited conduct can trigger international responsibility. When this threshold is crossed, state and individual responsibility are generally established with respect to the same facts, and making a distinction between the two can become very difficult. It is on this second concept of seriousness that the following pages will mainly focus.

A. *The Seriousness Requirement under Aggravated State Responsibility*

Aggravated state responsibility differs from ordinary state responsibility because it requires that the breach of an obligation owed to the international community as a whole be serious.[12] According to Article 40 (2) of the Draft Articles on State Responsibility: "A breach of such an obligation is serious if it involves a gross or systematic failure by the responsible State to fulfil the obligation".

This additional requirement was not present in the former Article 19, except for paragraph 3 (c). Indeed, in 1976, seriousness was limited to human rights breaches. Accordingly, in order to constitute an international crime, the "breach of an international obligation of essential importance for safeguarding the human being" should be carried out "on a widespread scale". In particular, the ILC explained in the Commentary that this additional requirement was necessary to avoid the broadening of the concept of international crimes beyond the actual scope of customary international law.[13] Thus, only gross violations of human rights would entail aggravated state responsibility, while isolated violations would give rise to ordinary state responsibility.

On the other hand, it seemed obvious that all other breaches listed in paragraph 3 constituted *per se* international crimes.[14] No further requirement was needed to consider aggression, establishment or maintenance by force of colonial domination, slavery, genocide and apartheid as international crimes of state. Indeed, these breaches have traditionally been considered typical state crimes, in the sense that they have historically been perpetrated on a very large scale and with the indispensable involvement of the state apparatus.

---

[12] N.H.B. Jørgensen, *The Responsibility of States for International Crimes* (Oxford, Oxford University Press, 2000), pp. 106–116; C.J. Tams, 'All's Well That Ends Well. Comments on the ILC's Articles on State Responsibility', 62 *ZaöRV* (2002), p. 773.

[13] ILC, 'Report on the Work of its 28th Session', *YILC* (1976), vol. II(2), p. 121.

[14] Due to their controversial status under customary law, breaches of international obligations "of essential importance for the safeguarding and preservation of the human environment, such as those prohibiting massive pollution of the atmosphere or of the seas" will not be dealt with here. *See* J. Crawford, 'First Report on State Responsibility', UN Doc. A/CN.4/490/Add.1, para. 49.

A seriousness requirement extending to all breaches of obligations "owed to the international community as a whole and essential for the protection of its fundamental interests" appears in the draft articles provisionally adopted by the Drafting Committee in 2000.[15] At that time, the ILC was revising the Draft Articles on State Responsibility in order to have them adopted at second reading by 2001. In particular, the ILC had to deal with the strong criticism aimed at international crimes of state. Thus, in redrafting Article 19, the Commission was inevitably faced with a different panorama. International criminal law had undergone some major developments and had increasingly become emancipated from state responsibility. In 2000, the Draft Code of Crimes had been adopted, international *ad hoc* tribunals had been established, the ICC statute had been signed, the *Nuremberg* judgment was no longer an isolated international judicial precedent, an increasingly extensive international and national case law had applied and clarified a wide range of fundamental rules of international criminal law, and a whole set of principles had been recognized as the core legal ground for this relatively new field of international law.

Therefore, in revising the Draft Articles, the ILC had to deal somehow with the problem of the relationship between aggravated state responsibility and individual criminal liability. While the ILC essentially avoided addressing this problem, the seriousness requirement can be regarded as a useful means to reach indirectly such an end. The seriousness requirement can be seen as a link between aggravated state responsibility and individual criminal liability. Crimes entailing individual criminal liability under international law can also give rise to aggravated state responsibility if they are committed by state organs, and if they reach a certain threshold of seriousness.

However, in its Commentary the ILC did not explicitly justify the generalization of the seriousness requirement to all categories of international crimes entailing aggravated state responsibility. The Commission carefully made clear that no criminal responsibility of states is provided for under customary law; that only individuals can be held criminally accountable for international crimes; and that the codification of aggravated state responsibility must therefore be strictly limited to breaches of an uncontroversial category of international obligations and to serious breaches. Arguably, the generalization of the seriousness requirement offered an additional safeguard against the criticism concerning this part of its work. In practice, the seriousness requirement tends to narrow down the class of wrongful acts triggering aggravated state responsibility.[16]

---

[15] UN Doc. A/CN.4/L.600, 21 August 2000, Article 41.

[16] The same rationale seems to lie at the basis of the resolution adopted in 2005 by the Institute of International Law on 'Obligations *erga omnes* in International Law' (71 *Annuaire de l'Institut de Droit International* (2005), pp. 287–289). According to Article 5 of the resolution, only "widely

The main problem with that requirement is to identify its precise contents in the framework of aggravated state responsibility. As pointed out above, the ILC explained in 1976 that violations of human rights would entail aggravated state responsibility only if carried out as a "large scale or systematic practice". Although it recalled a wording familiar to international criminal law provisions, the Commission put the emphasis on the 'practice' element. A similar view can be found in the commentary on Article 40 of the Draft Articles finally adopted in 2001.[17]

It must be noted that in establishing this general requirement of seriousness, the Commission maintained that certain breaches are *per se* serious and by their very nature entail aggravated state responsibility. According to the Commission, an operational criterion of seriousness is already provided for under certain primary norms, such as the prohibition of aggression or genocide. In other words, the material element of breaches such as aggression and genocide by definition require a gross or systematic violation of fundamental international rules.[18] Therefore, these primary norms are characterized by their particular importance for the protection of community interests and by a definition which already includes an operational criterion of seriousness.

With respect to other breaches of obligations owed to the entire international community, an additional requirement of seriousness must be fulfilled in order to trigger aggravated state responsibility. The contents of this seriousness requirement corresponds, according to the ILC commentary, to a certain degree of state involvement. Although the Commission puts a certain emphasis on the intent of the responsible state as an *indicium* of seriousness, the analysis of this aspect can be postponed until the next chapter. It is important here to concentrate on

acknowledged grave breaches of an *erga omnes* obligation" can trigger special consequences under international law.

17 "The word 'serious' signifies that a certain order of magnitude of violation is necessary in order not to trivialize the breach and it is not intended to suggest that any violation of these obligations is not serious or is somehow excusable. But relatively less serious cases of breach of peremptory norms can be envisaged, and it is necessary to limit the scope of this chapter to the more serious or systematic breaches. Some such limitation is supported by State practice.... To be regarded as systematic, a violation would have to be carried out in an *organized* and deliberate way. In contrast, the term 'gross' refers to the intensity of the violation or its effects; it denotes violations of a flagrant nature, amounting to a direct and outright assault on the values protected by the rule. The terms are not of course mutually exclusive; serious breaches will usually be both systematic and gross. Factors which may establish the seriousness of a violation would include the intent to violate the norm; the scope and number of *individual violations*, and the gravity of their consequences for the victims" (ILC, 'Report on the Work of its 53rd Session', *YILC* (2001), vol. II(2), p. 113, paras. 7 and 8, emphasis added).

18 *Ibid.*, para. 8 ("It must also be borne in mind that some of the peremptory norms in question, most notably the prohibitions of aggression and genocide, by their very nature require an intentional violation on a large scale"). For a more detailed analysis of these crimes, *see* infra in this Chapter.

operational criteria permitting us to establish when wrongful acts amount to 'serious breaches'. While the Commission intends to exclude isolated breaches from conduct giving rise to aggravated state responsibility, it puts the emphasis on the pattern of violations that may occur and on their magnitude. This points to the need for a sum of prohibited conduct to be planned or actually carried out at the state level. Thus, the seriousness requirement results not merely in a collection of wrongful acts but in a systematic infringement of fundamental community obligations. This is something more than the collective perpetration of an international crime. The seriousness requirement involves a significant participation of the state in the breach of the most important obligations owed to the international community as a whole. Some commentators refer to breaches committed by the state as a whole or by the whole state system.[19] When serious breaches are carried out as an extensive practice of state organs so as to show a general involvement of the state apparatus, then aggravated state responsibility applies.

An analysis of the relevant international practice confirms this interpretation of the seriousness requirement under state responsibility. The *Velásquez* case[20] represents a significant example of the way in which the seriousness requirement has actually been established by the IACHR. In particular, the case is important because it shows how a practice of wrongful acts can concretely be taken into account to establish a serious breach entailing aggravated state responsibility. The case originated in a petition against Honduras, which was supposedly responsible for the violation of the American Convention on Human Rights and, in particular, for the disappearance of Manfredo Velásquez. While focusing on a single disappearance, the case is noteworthy because the Court accepted a particular approach of the Commission in proving the facts underlying the petition. This approach relied on the existence of a practice of disappearances supported or tolerated by the Government of Honduras. The Court accepted that: "If it can be shown that there was an official practice of disappearances in Honduras, carried out by the Government or at least tolerated by it, and if the disappearance of Manfredo Velásquez can be linked to that practice, the Commission's allegations will have been proven to the Court's satisfaction".[21]

---

[19] Some scholars even advocate the need to revisit the rules on attribution as far as aggravated state responsibility is concerned. *See* A. Bos, 'Crimes of State: In Need of Legal Rules?', in G. Kreijen (ed.), *State, Sovereignty, and International Governance* (Oxford, Oxford University Press, 2002), pp. 234–237; A. Nollkaemper, 'Concurrence between Individual Responsibility and State Responsibility in International Law', 52 *ICLQ* (2003), p. 632; D. Caron, 'State Crimes: Looking at Municipal Experience with Organizational Crime', in M. Ragazzi (ed.), *International Responsibility Today: Essays in Memory of Oscar Schachter* (Leiden, Boston, M. Nijhoff, 2005), p. 30.

[20] IACHR, *Velásquez Rodriguez case*, supra the Introduction, note 7.

[21] *Ibid.*, p. 60. A similar approach was followed by the Commission and accepted by the Court in the *Godinez Cruz* case (IACHR, *Godinez Cruz*, Judgment, 20 January 1989, *Annual Report of the Inter-American Court of Human Rights*, Ser. C, No. 5 (1989)).

Consequently, the decision concentrated on the existence of such a state practice. In particular, the Court relied on precise elements to establish that the practice of disappearances had been proven. These were the number of disappearances during a limited period of time; the fact that those disappearances followed a similar pattern; the fact that it was public and notorious knowledge in Honduras that the kidnappings were carried out by military personnel or the police, or persons acting under their orders; and the fact that the disappearances were carried out in a systematic manner. Finally, the Court found that "the kidnapping and disappearance of Manfredo Velásquez falls within the systematic practice of disappearances referred to by the facts".[22]

Interestingly, this approach shows how state involvement in gross violations of human rights can be proven. In particular, the Court relied on the general context in which the events took place, and on the cumulative effect of various facts put together. Accordingly, it based its judgment not only on the systematic practice of disappearances, but also on the complete failure of the judicial system and of the executive branch to carry out serious investigations and punish those responsible. Thus, the Court was able to recognize that Honduras had been involved in the violation of the Convention.[23]

In *Velásquez*, the Court was not asked in principle to establish aggravated state responsibility, but in the end it indirectly found that a serious breach had been committed by a state. Thus, this case shows how the seriousness requirement can be applied. While the circumstances of specific events can be controversial, an extensive practice of disappearances and omissions by a substantial part of the state apparatus can lead to a showing that organized violations of a flagrant nature, amounting to a direct and outright assault on the values protected by human rights obligations – in the words of the ILC – have taken place. In other words, the seriousness requirement of aggravated state responsibility emerges when taking into account not particular conduct but a general pattern of events. The Court has adopted the same approach in more recent cases in which it has ascertained the commission of patterns of state serious breaches giving rise to aggravated state responsibility.[24]

---

[22] IACHR, *Velásquez Rodriguez case*, supra the Introduction, note 7, p. 65.

[23] *Ibid.*, pp. 72–73 ("not all levels of the Government of Honduras were necessarily aware of those acts, nor is there any evidence that such acts were the result of official orders. Nevertheless, those circumstances are irrelevant for the purpose of establishing whether Honduras is responsible under international law for the violations of human rights perpetrated within the practice of disappearances.").

[24] *See* IACHR, *Case of Myrna Mack-Chang v. Guatemala*, supra the Introduction, note 7, and *Case of the Plan de Sánchez Massacre v. Guatemala*, Judgment of 29 April 2004, *Annual Report of the Inter-American Court of Human Rights*, Series C No. 105 (2004). For a similar view, *see* P. Gaeta, 'On What Conditions Can a State Be Held Responsible for Genocide?', 18 *EJIL* (2007), pp. 635–637.

Another example is provided by the Report of the International Commission of Inquiry on Darfur.[25] It is true that the Commission narrowly defined its mandate, and in principle only dealt with individuals' liability for international crimes committed in Darfur between 2003 and 2005.[26] However, in the light of the cumulative effect of the widespread breaches committed at the state level, the report clearly points to the existence of Sudan's aggravated responsibility for gross violations of human rights committed in Darfur.[27]

Finally, the recent Opinion of the ICJ on the *Israeli Wall*[28] can be briefly taken into account. Arguably, this is the first time the Court has dealt with the consequences of the regime of aggravated state responsibility. The Court did not mention Articles 40 and 41 of the ILC codification work but indirectly referred to them when coming to the examination of the "legal consequences of the internationally wrongful acts flowing from Israel's construction of the wall as regards *other States*".[29] Indeed, since Israel had seriously breached obligations owed to the international community as a whole, "all other States are under an obligation not to recognize the illegal situation resulting from the construction of the wall in the Occupied Palestinian Territory, including in and around East Jerusalem. They are also under an obligation not to render aid or assistance in maintaining the situation created by such construction."[30]

These are the special consequences provided for under Article 41. Therefore, such consequences can only be entailed by a serious wrongful act as defined in Article 40. On the one hand, the conduct of Israel amounted to a violation of an *erga omnes* obligation and thus met the first meaning of gravity, that referring to the importance of the primary norms breached.[31] On the other hand, the conduct

---

[25] 'Report of the International Commission of Inquiry on Darfur to the United Nations Secretary-General pursuant to Security Council Resolution 1564 of 18 September 2004', Geneva, 25 January 2005, </www.un.org/News/dh/sudan/com_inq_darfur.pdf>.

[26] SC Resolution 1564(2004) requested the Secretary General to investigate "reports of violations of international humanitarian law and human rights law in Darfur *by all parties*". However, the Commission limited its mandate to the establishment of violations committed by natural persons, thus excluding issues of state responsibility (*ibid.*, paras. 2–11).

[27] The Commission found that the consistent pattern of indiscriminate attacks against the civilian population was substantially carried out by state *de jure* or *de facto* organs of Sudan (*ibid.*, paras. 185–186, 240, 332, 406–407). Moreover, the Commission found that the police and the judiciary of Sudan took no action to prevent or punish the crimes against humanity committed in Darfur (*ibid.*, paras. 419–455). Other official bodies took inappropriate action to that effect (*ibid.*, paras. 456–487).

[28] ICJ, *Legal Consequences of the Construction of a Wall in the Occupied Palestinian Territory*, supra Chapter 1, note 44.

[29] *Ibid.*, para. 154 (emphasis added).

[30] *Ibid.*, para. 159. For the Court, such special consequences are due to "the character and the importance of the rights and obligations involved".

[31] *Ibid.*, paras. 155–157.

of Israel also represented a serious breach in terms of its magnitude: it was a serious breach of the self-determination principle,[32] of international humanitarian law and human rights law.[33] The Court repeatedly underscored the widespread effects of the wrongful act on the Palestinian population. In particular, the Court explained, the construction of the wall will have a tremendous impact on the Palestinian population because it is "tantamount to *de facto* annexation";[34] it has led to the destruction or requisition of properties; it imposes substantial restrictions on the freedom of movement of the inhabitants of the Occupied Palestinian Territory; and it impedes the exercise by the persons concerned of the right to work, to health, to education and to an adequate standard of living.[35] As with the *Velásquez* case, the seriousness requirement of aggravated state responsibility emerges when taking into account not particular conduct but a general pattern of events.

So understood, the seriousness requirement constitutes a clear dividing line between ordinary and aggravated state responsibility. On the one hand, there are crimes in whose respect a seriousness requirement is directly provided for under primary norms. These are breaches that *per se* entail aggravated state responsibility. On the other hand, there are crimes that need not be serious by definition. While isolated breaches of such crimes can give rise to ordinary state responsibility, a practice of serious breaches will give rise to aggravated state responsibility.

B. *The Seriousness Requirement under International Criminal Law*

International crimes generally entail a widespread and systematic violation. They are planned, prepared, organized, and executed by a multiplicity of offenders. Such criminal policies could hardly have been successful without the substantial involvement of a state apparatus. Their characteristic feature is not only the violation of universal principles of fundamental importance, but also the magnitude of their effects. As the War Crimes Commission put it at the end of WWII:

> Only crimes which either by their magnitude and savagery or by their large number or by the fact that a similar pattern was applied at different times and places, endangered the international community or shocked the conscience of mankind, warranted intervention by States other than that on whose territory the crimes had been committed, or whose subjects had become their victims.[36]

---

32 *Ibid.*, para. 122.

33 *Ibid.*, para. 137.

34 *Ibid.*, para. 121.

35 *Ibid.*, paras. 132–134.

36 UNWCC, *History of the United Nations War Crimes Commission and the Development of the Laws of War* (London, H.M. Stationery Office, 1948), p. 179.

However, not all crimes need be carried out in a 'serious' manner to entail individual criminal liability. One must look at primary norms prohibiting international crimes to see whether they require a certain degree of seriousness to be met.

The elements of international crimes are defined under customary international law. These elements differ with respect to the various categories of international crimes. Some international crimes – in order to establish individual criminal liability – require a general pre-condition regarding the magnitude of the prohibited conduct to be met.[37] Others do not, and may be perpetrated by single individuals in perfect isolation. Thus, the seriousness requirement may or may not be a point of contact between aggravated state responsibility and individual criminal liability. Accordingly, the relationship between state and individual responsibility as far as the seriousness requirement is concerned must be established on a case-by-case basis, having regard to each specific category of international crimes.

The definition of 'official torture' does require a certain link with state responsibility: only state organs can commit this international crime.[38] However, no seriousness requirement must be fulfilled for an act of torture to give rise to individual criminal liability under international law.[39] As the ICTY clearly acknowledged in *Furundžija*,[40] conduct amounting to official torture would normally only entail individual criminal liability. However, when "carried out as an extensive practice of State officials", individual criminal liability cumulates with aggravated state responsibility. Thus, although torture is necessarily committed by "person[s] acting in an official capacity", it is nonetheless true that this crime can be carried out in perfect isolation and on an individual basis by persons acting on their own initiative.[41] Therefore, individual criminal liability for torture is independent of aggravated state responsibility for the same conduct. Indeed, this is the classic example of an international crime which, being committed by individual state organs, does not necessarily also entail aggravated state responsibility. For example, while the ECHR in the *Selmouni* case[42] recognized that a French policeman was responsible

[37] *See* supra the Introduction.

[38] *Ibid.*

[39] Article 1, para. 1, of the Torture Convention reads: "For the purposes of this Convention, the term 'torture' means any act by which severe pain or suffering, whether physical or mental, is intentionally inflicted on a person for such purposes as obtaining from him or a third person information or a confession, punishing him for an act he or a third person has committed or is suspected of having committed, or intimidating or coercing him or a third person, or for any reason based on discrimination of any kind, when such pain or suffering is inflicted by or at the instigation of or with the consent or acquiescence of a public official or other person acting in an official capacity. It does not include pain or suffering arising only from, inherent in or incidental to lawful sanctions." *See* ICTY, *Prosecutor v. Furundžija*, TC, Judgment, 10 December 1998, paras. 134–165.

[40] *Ibid.*, para. 142.

[41] A. Cassese, *International Criminal Law* (Oxford, Oxford University Press, 2003), p. 118.

[42] ECHR, *Selmouni v. France*, Judgment, 28 July 1999, <www.echr.coe.int/ECHR>.

for torture, this is not sufficient to attribute aggravated responsibility to France: the wrongful act must be 'gross or systematic' in order to entail aggravated state responsibility.[43] At any rate, it must be noted that the absence of a seriousness requirement does not exclude the fact that single acts of torture as defined by the Convention can well entail ordinary state responsibility alongside individual criminal liability.

A similar conclusion can be reached with respect to war crimes, that is, another category of international crimes generally regarded as individual crimes.[44] The *actus reus* of war crimes not only consists of specific prohibited acts, but also includes a general pre-requisite, namely, a nexus with an armed conflict, be it international or internal.[45] It will be inquired below whether and to what extent that general pre-requisite – as applied in international case law – establishes a connection between state and individual responsibility for war crimes. However, the definition of war crimes does not provide for any seriousness requirement as understood in aggravated state responsibility. A single act of rape committed in perfect isolation can, for example, amount to a war crime. The concept of seriousness underlying some war

---

[43] A. Nollkaemper, supra note 19, p. 623 ("the threshold 'serious' in Article 40 serves precisely to exclude breaches that are not 'gross' or 'systematic'. The acts therefore would fall under the normal reparatory scheme of the law of state responsibility").

[44] P. De Sena, *Diritto internazionale e immunità funzionale degli organi statali* (Milano, Giuffrè, 1996), p. 157; M.C. Bassiouni, *Crimes against Humanity in International Criminal Law* (The Hague, Kluwer Law International, 1999), p. 85; P.-M. Dupuy, 'International Criminal Responsibility of the Individual and International Responsibility of the State', in A. Cassese *et al.* (eds.), *The Rome Statute of the International Criminal Court. A Commentary*, vol. II (Oxford, Oxford University Press, 2002), p. 1088.

[45] ICTY, *Prosecutor v. Delalić et al.*, TC, Judgment, 16 November 1998, para. 193; ICTY, *Prosecutor v. Aleksovski*, TC, Judgment, 25 June 1999, paras. 42–45; ICTY, *Prosecutor v. Tadić*, AC, Judgment, 15 July 1999, para. 251; ICTY, *Prosecutor v. Blaškić*, TC, Judgment, 3 March 2000, paras. 69–70; ICTY, *Prosecutor v. Kunarac et al.*, TC, Judgment, 22 February 2001, paras. 402 and 407; ICTY, *Prosecutor v. Kordić and Čerkez*, TC, Judgment, 26 February 2001, paras. 32–33; ICTY, *Prosecutor v. Krnojelac*, TC, Judgment, 15 March 2002, para. 51; ICTY, *Prosecutor v. Vasiljević*, TC, Judgment, 29 November 2002, paras. 32–38; ICTY, *Prosecutor v. Naletilić and Martinović*, TC, Judgment, 31 March 2003, paras. 176–180; ICTY, *Prosecutor v. Stakić*, TC, Judgment, 31 July 2003, paras. 569–570, 575–576; ICTY, *Prosecutor v. Simić et al.*, TC, Judgment, 17 October 2003, paras. 105–106. Similarly, the nexus between the armed conflict and the alleged war crimes has been considered an essential requirement in the ICTR case law (ICTR, *Prosecutor v. Akayesu*, TC, Judgment, 2 September 1998, paras. 640–641; ICTR, *Prosecutor v. Kayishema and Ruzindana*, TC, Judgment, 21 May 1999, paras. 185–189, 601–615; ICTR, *Prosecutor v. Rutaganda*, TC, Judgment, 6 December 1999, paras. 104–105; ICTR, *Prosecutor v. Musema*, TC, Judgment, 27 January 2000, paras. 259–262, and 973; ICTR, *Prosecutor v. Bagilishema*, TC, Judgment, 7 June 2001, paras. 105–106; ICTR, *Prosecutor v. Elizaphan and Gerard Ntakirutimana*, TC, Judgment, 21 February 2003, paras. 859–861; ICTR, *Prosecutor v. Kamuhanda*, TC, Judgment, 22 January 2004, paras. 733–744); however, the existence of such a nexus has been established only once (ICTR, *Prosecutor v. Semanza*, TC, Judgment, 15 May 2003, paras. 368–369, and 516–522).

crimes, namely those defined as 'grave breaches', is not an operational standard but a characteristic pertaining to the nature of the primary norm.[46] Grave breaches are selected offences considered to be violations of norms so important for the international community as a whole that they give rise to individual criminal liability.[47] Thus, a distinction can be made between grave breaches and other breaches entailing 'only' state responsibility.[48] Moreover, in the *Nuremberg* judgment, war crimes were simply regarded as international offences, that is, prohibited actions under international law implying the criminal liability of the offender.[49] Accordingly, no reference to a 'widespread or systematic' requirement is made either in the ICTY Statute[50] or in the ICTR Statute,[51] and no further requirement of seriousness is required for war crimes in the ICTY and ICTR case law.[52]

It must be added that other elements of international practice seem to assign a certain role to the seriousness requirement with respect to war crimes. Article 20 of the 1996 Draft Code explicitly limits war crimes to acts "committed in a systematic manner or on a large scale".[53] Thus, the seriousness requirement is generally required under the Draft Code to punish individuals for war crimes. Does this correspond to a new development in international criminal law? According to the ILC's commentary on Article 20, this further requirement does not correspond to the customary definition of war crimes, and was added with the specific aim of

---

46 For a discussion on the meaning of grave breaches *see* H. Fischer, 'Grave Breaches of the 1949 Geneva Conventions', in G. Kirk McDonald and O. Swaak-Goldman (eds.), *Substantive and Procedural Aspects of International Criminal Law*, vol. I (The Hague, Kluwer Law International, 2000), pp. 70–72; G. Abi-Saab and R.-M. Abi-Saab, 'Les crimes de guerre', in H. Ascensio *et al.* (eds.), *Droit international pénal* (Paris, Pedone, 2000), pp. 280–281.

47 ICTY, *Prosecutor v. Tadić*, AC, Decision on the Defence Motion for Interlocutory Appeal on Jurisdiction, 2 October 1995, para. 94.

48 *See* supra note 11.

49 *See* Article 6 of the London Charter and the IMT Judgment, supra Chapter 1, note 90, pp. 221, and 248.

50 *See* Article 2 and 3 of the ICTY Statute (SC Res. 827(1993)).

51 *See* Article 4 of the ICTR Statute (SC Res. 955 (1994)).

52 ICTY, *Prosecutor v. Tadić*, TC, Judgment, 7 May 1997, para. 573; ICTY, *Prosecutor v. Delalić et al.*, TC, Judgment, 16 November 1998, para. 195; ICTY, *Prosecutor v. Blaškić*, TC, Judgment, 3 March 2000, para. 70; ICTY, *Prosecutor v. Naletilić and Martinović*, TC, Judgment, 31 March 2003, para. 225, note 600. *See*, in particular, Y. Dinstein, 'Crimes against Humanity', in J. Makarczyk (ed.), *Theory of International Law at the Threshold of the 21st Century. Essays in Honour of K. Skubiszewski* (The Hague, Kluwer Law International, 1996), p. 891; and S.R. Ratner and J.S. Abrams, *Accountability for Human Rights Atrocities in International Law* (Oxford, Oxford University Press, 2001), p. 88.

53 ILC, 'Report on the Work of its 48th Session', *YILC* (1996), vol. II(2), p. 56.

narrowing the scope of the Draft Code, which focuses only on crimes against the peace and security of mankind characterized by a certain level of seriousness.[54]

The conclusion that international criminal law does not require a further element of seriousness in the case of war crimes is consonant with Article 8 (1) of the 1998 ICC Statute. The *chapeau* of the article reads as follows: "The Court shall have jurisdiction in respect of war crimes *in particular* when committed as part of a plan or policy or as part of a large scale commission of such crimes".[55] In principle, the Court has jurisdiction over all the violations of the laws and customs of war listed in the following paragraphs of Article 8, even in the case of isolated breaches. However, this provision draws the attention of the Court to the most serious war crimes, those committed in accordance with a state policy or on a large scale. Abstractly speaking, the *chapeau* Article 8 does not establish an additional requirement to hold individuals criminally liable for war crimes under international law. Indeed, scholars seem to agree that a seriousness requirement is not necessary to implement individual accountability for war crimes under international law, and that Article 8 of the ICC Statute does not provide for such further requirement.[56] In practice, however, this provision can have the effect of narrowing the jurisdiction of the ICC.[57] While asking the ICC to focus on particularly 'serious' war crimes does not modify the legal elements of this category of international crimes, it can actually have an impact on the prosecution policy and lead the Court to substantially limit its jurisdiction over war crimes.[58]

Crimes against humanity are international crimes requiring by definition a certain threshold of seriousness to be met. Their constitutive elements include a general pre-requisite concerning the magnitude of the criminal offence to be demonstrated beyond any reasonable doubt in order to convict the accused for such crimes. Today, it is well established that they must be carried out in a 'widespread or systematic'

[54] *Ibid.*, p. 57, para. 5, "These general criteria for war crimes under the Code are based on the view that crimes against the peace and security of mankind are the most serious on the scale of international offences and that, in order for an offence to be regarded as a crime against the peace and security of mankind, it must meet certain *additional* criteria which raises its level of seriousness. These general criteria are provided in the chapeau of the article: the crimes in question must have been committed in a systematic manner or on a large scale" (emphasis added).

[55] A/CONF.183/9, <www.icc-cpi.int> (emphasis added).

[56] *See*, in general, H. Fischer, supra note 46, p. 83; for an isolated opinion expressing the opposite point of view, *see* J. Barboza, 'International Criminal Law', 278 *RCADI* (1999), p. 158.

[57] *See* infra note 76, as far as the war crime of plunder is concerned. It is to that very effect that the USA proposed to amend Article 8. *See* M.P. Scharf, 'Results of the Rome Conference for an International Criminal Court', *ASIL Insights*, August 1998, <www.asil.org>.

[58] *See* supra the Introduction.

manner.[59] Article 3 of the ICTR Statute,[60] Article 18 of the 1996 Draft Code,[61] and Article 7 of the 1998 ICC Statute[62] are all explicit with regard to the need for such a condition to be met.[63] Moreover, even if Article 5 of the ICTY Statute[64]

---

[59] R. Dixon, 'Article 7 – Chapeau', in O. Triffterer (ed.), *Commentary on the Rome Statute of the International Criminal Court* (Baden-Baden, Nomos, 1999), p. 126; M. Bettati, 'Le crime contre l'humanité', in H. Ascensio *et al.* (eds.), *Droit international pénal* (Paris, Pedone, 2000), p. 297; O. Swaak-Goldman, 'Crimes against Humanity', in G. Kirk McDonald and O. Swaak-Goldman (eds.), *Substantive and Procedural Aspects of International Criminal Law*, vol. I (The Hague, Kluwer Law International, 2000), p. 157; S.R. Ratner and J.S. Abrams, supra note 52, p. 58; K. Kittichaisaree, *International Criminal Law* (Oxford, Oxford University Press, 2001), pp. 96–97; A. Cassese, 'Crimes against Humanity', in A. Cassese *et al.* (eds.), *The Rome Statute of the International Criminal Court. A Commentary*, vol. I (Oxford, Oxford University Press, 2002), pp. 356–360; Y. Jurovics, *Réflexions sur la spécificité du crime contre l'humanité* (Paris, LGDJ, 2002), p. 274; A. Cassese, supra note 41, p. 64.

[60] Article 3 reads: "The International Tribunal for Rwanda shall have the power to prosecute persons responsible for the following crimes when committed as part of a *widespread or systematic* attack against the civilian population on national, political, ethnic, racial or religious grounds: a) murder; b) extermination; c) enslavement; d) deportation; e) imprisonment; f) torture; g) rape; h) persecutions on political, racial and religious grounds; i) other inhumane acts" (SC Res. 955 (1994), emphasis added).

[61] Article 18 reads: "A crime against humanity means any of the following acts, when committed in a *systematic manner* or on a *large scale* and instigated or directed by a Government or by any organization or group: a) murder; b) extermination; c) torture; d) enslavement; e) persecution on political, racial, religious or ethnic grounds; f) institutionalized discrimination on racial, ethnic or religious grounds involving the violation of fundamental human rights and freedoms and resulting in seriously disadvantaging a part of the population; g) arbitrary deportation or forcible transfer of population; h) arbitrary imprisonment; i) forced disappearance of persons; j) rape, enforced prostitution and other forms of sexual abuse; k) other inhumane acts which severely damage physical or mental integrity, health or human dignity, such as mutilation and severe bodily harm" (ILC, 'Report on the Work of its 48th Session', *YILC* (1996), vol. II(2), p. 47, emphasis added).

[62] Article 7, para. 1 reads: "For the purpose of this Statute, 'crime against humanity' means any of the following acts when committed as part of a *widespread or systematic* attack directed against any civilian population, with knowledge of the attack: a) murder; b) extermination; c) enslavement; d) deportation or forcible transfer of population; e) imprisonment or other severe deprivation of physical liberty in violation of fundamental rules of international law; f) torture; g) rape, sexual slavery, enforced prostitution, forced pregnancy, enforced sterilisation, or any other form of sexual violence of comparable gravity; h) persecution against any identifiable group or collectivity on political, racial, national, ethnic, cultural, religious, gender as defined in paragraph 3, or other grounds that are universally recognized as impermissible under international law, in connection with any act referred to in this paragraph or any crime within the jurisdiction of the Court; i) enforced disappearance of persons; j) the crime of apartheid; k) other inhumane acts of a similar character intentionally causing great suffering, or serious injury to body or to mental or physical health" (A/CONF.183/9, <www.icc-cpi.int>, emphasis added).

[63] Although this further element was not present in the Nuremberg Charter, the IMT placed emphasis on the Nazi policy lying behind the commission of crimes against humanity (*see* IMT Judgment, supra Chapter 1, note 90, pp. 224–225, and 243–246).

[64] Article 5 reads: "The International Tribunal shall have the power to prosecute persons responsible for the following crimes when committed in armed conflict, whether international or internal in

does not explicitly require seriousness, a well-established judicial interpretation given to the term 'population' implies that the criminal act should be committed systematically or on a large scale before individual criminal liability can apply.[65] The rationale underlying such a general pre-requisite of crimes against humanity is to exclude individual criminal liability for isolated or random acts.[66] Thus, in order to hold an individual accountable for crimes against humanity, an international tribunal or a domestic court will have to establish beyond any reasonable doubt that the prohibited conduct was either widespread or systematic.

With respect to the crime of genocide, things are a little bit more complicated. No reference is made in the definition of this crime to the systematic or widespread quality of the prohibited conduct.[67] However, in order to be held accountable under international criminal law, the accused charged with genocide must have carried out the *actus reus* with the special intent to destroy the protected group, and this special intent can be inferred from the fact that genocide has been carried out according to a preconceived plan or policy.[68] Thus, a seriousness element is inherent in the crime of genocide, even if in a very peculiar way. Indeed, it is only

character, and directed against any civilian population: a) murder; b) extermination; c) enslavement; d) deportation; e) imprisonment; f) torture; g) rape; h) persecutions on political, racial and religious grounds; i) other inhumane acts" (SC Res. 827(1993)).

65 ICTY, *Prosecutor v. Tadić*, TC, Judgment, 7 May 1997, para. 644.

66 Commentary on Article 18 of the Draft Code of Crimes, ILC, 'Report on the Work of its 48th Session', *YILC* (1996), vol. II(2), pp. 49–50, paras. 3 to 5. *See* also ICTY, *Prosecutor v. Kunarac et al.*, AC, Judgment, 12 June 2002, para. 93; ICTY, *Prosecutor v. Kordić and Čerkez*, TC, Judgment, 26 February 2001, paras. 174 and 179; ICTY, *Prosecutor v. Vasiljević*, TC, Judgment, 29 November 2002, para. 35.

67 When taking into account the definitions of genocide, it emerges that they all reproduce the definition embodied in the Genocide Convention ("genocide means any of the following acts committed with the intent to destroy, in whole or in part, a national, ethnical, racial or religious group, as such: a) killing members of the group; b) causing serious bodily or mental harm to the members of the group; c) deliberately inflicting on the group conditions of life calculated to bring about its physical destruction in whole or in part; d) imposing measures intended to prevent births within the group; e) forcibly transferring children of the group to another group"). *See* Article 4 of the ICTY statute (SC Res. 827(1993)), Article 2 of the ICTR statute (SC Res. 955(1994)), Article 6 of the ICC statute (A/CONF.183/9, <www.icc-cpi.int>), and Article 17 of the Draft Code of Crimes (ILC; 'Report on the Work of its 48th Session', *YILC* (1996), vol. II(2), p. 46). *See* E. Zoller, 'La définition des crimes contre l'humanité', *JDI* (1993), p. 549.

68 *See* Israeli District Court, *Enigster Case*, 4 January 1952, 18 *ILR* (1951), p. 542; M.C. Bassiouni, *Crimes against Humanity in International Criminal Law* (Dordrecht, M. Nijhoff, 1992); W.A. Schabas, 'Le génocide', in H. Ascensio *et al.* (eds.), *Droit international pénal* (Paris, Pedone, 2000), p. 319; D.D. Ntanda Nsereko, 'Genocide: A Crime against Mankind', in G. Kirk McDonald and O. Swaak-Goldman (eds.), *Substantive and Procedural Aspects of International Criminal Law*, vol. I (The Hague, Kluwer Law International, 2000), p. 127; S.R. Ratner and J.S. Abrams, supra note 52, p. 37; Y. Jurovics, supra note 59, pp. 316–319.

indirectly that the existence of a criminal plan or policy will be useful to prove the *mens rea* of the accused.[69]

Finally, a seriousness requirement is implicit in the definition of the crime of aggression. Although this definition does not explicitly include a seriousness requirement, the material element of the crime of aggression entailing individual criminal liability is the state act of aggression. And, as already noted, aggression is generally considered *per se* to be a 'serious' breach. This special relationship between state and individual responsibility will be examined in some detail below.

2. *Theoretical Approaches to the Seriousness Requirement*

The seriousness requirement is one of the most significant points of contact between aggravated state responsibility and individual criminal liability for international crimes. If we take, for example, a general practice of deportation carried out by state organs reaching the threshold of seriousness described above, this wrongful act can entail aggravated state responsibility. With respect to the same conduct, single state organs can be held accountable for crimes against humanity. But the collective criminal phenomenon seems to have paramount importance also in the establishment of individual criminal responsibility. Indeed, state organs' responsibility can only be established in connection with the broader criminal context: crimes against humanity require the 'widespread or systematic' character of the offence to be proven.

While seriousness is a general requirement under aggravated state responsibility, as far as individual criminal liability is concerned a similar element can only be identified having a look at specific primary norms prohibiting international crimes. This diversity raises various questions concerning the relationship between state and individual responsibility for the same serious wrongful acts. In particular, it is unclear whether the same conduct is capable of entailing both state and individual responsibility. One may doubt whether state and individual responsibility can still be regarded as completely independent. Does the establishment of the general pre-requisites necessary to hold individuals accountable for certain international crimes amount to an establishment of aggravated state responsibility for the same serious wrongful act? In other words, the question is whether the contents of these general pre-requisites under international criminal law and of the seriousness requirement in aggravated state responsibility is identical.

If we refer back to the general conceptual schemes elaborated in Part I, two diverging approaches can be adopted. According to the state-oriented scheme, that is, assuming that international crimes can only be committed by states, the

[69] *See* infra Chapter 4.

punishment of state organs merely is an indirect consequence of aggravated state responsibility.[70] Accordingly, only with respect to breaches committed with the involvement of the state apparatus can state organs be held accountable on behalf of the state. Therefore, the link between individual action and state action must be so close that the general pre-requisites under international criminal law must correspond to the seriousness requirement under aggravated state responsibility.[71] International prosecution should only focus on state-sponsored crimes and not on individualized international crimes.[72]

By contrast, the individual-oriented scheme relies on the assumption of a dissociation between the conduct of the state and that of its organs. While international law provides for a twofold attribution of international crimes to states and individuals, individual liability and state responsibility are regarded as independent regimes. Under international criminal law, individuals are directly accountable for the crimes they have personally perpetrated: criminal liability is a personal liability which must be established according to the personal and intentional participation of the accused in the criminal act. Accordingly, the general pre-requisites under certain categories of international crimes should essentially be assessed having regard to the personal conduct of the accused. This does not preclude elements of the general criminal context from being taken into account, but they may be considered only to the extent that they can be useful to the establishment of the criminal liability of the accused. The focus should be on individuals' conduct, not on state action. The criminal liability of single state organs must be assessed having regard to the specific elements of each international crime as provided for under international criminal law. Therefore, the general pre-requisites under international criminal

70 *See* supra Chapter 2.

71 L. May, *Crimes Against Humanity: A Normative Account* (Cambridge, Cambridge University Press, 2005), p. 115 and, more generally, Chapters 7 and 8. The author is very critical even with respect to the "three uncontroversial elements of crimes against humanity [1) directed against a civilian population, 2) part of a State or group policy, and 3) systematic or widespread]", which allegedly do not link "the acts of an individual to the collective crime in a way that will support prosecution of that individual" (*ibid.*, p. 120). Apart from the fact that international tribunals have explicitly denied that the state policy is an element of crimes against humanity (*see* infra in the main text), May claims that a much closer connection between state and individual responsibility must be taken into account by international tribunals.

72 *Ibid.*, p. 82. Ideally, May argues, state organs can only be prosecuted when the crime is state-sponsored and when there is a group-based harm (p. 90). For example, with respect to rape, he finds it difficult to justify convictions for rape as a war crime, while state organs can properly be held accountable for rape as a crime against humanity – and in particular – persecution since this is clearly a group-based crime constituting an assault on the international community (pp. 96–113). *See* also R. Maison, *La responsabilité individuelle pour crime de l'Etat en droit international public* (Bruxelles, Bruylant, 2004), pp. 245–246, who, faced with an international case law prepared to deal with all international crimes (including individualized crimes), can only criticize the absence of a sufficiently close link between individual action and state criminal policy.

law and the seriousness requirement under aggravated state responsibility can be conceived of in different ways, and individual criminal liability can be established totally independently from aggravated state responsibility for the same crime.

These approaches lead to two different notions of the seriousness requirement: either the same requirement applies to both state and individual responsibility for international crimes, or two different notions of seriousness are applicable in these regimes. The following analysis will concentrate on the way in which the seriousness requirement has actually been applied in international case law and international practice to evaluate whether a connection between state and individual responsibility has somehow been taken into account.

3. *The Seriousness Requirement as Applied in International Case Law*

In examining the relationship between the seriousness requirement under aggravated state responsibility and the general pre-requisites under international criminal law, it is opportune to treat the various categories of international crimes separately.

A. *War Crimes*

As already noted, the definition of war crimes includes, as a general pre-requisite, the condition that these crimes must be perpetrated in connection with an international or internal armed conflict. However, a finding that certain prohibited conduct is related to an armed conflict does not amount to a finding that the seriousness requirement (as defined in aggravated state responsibility) has been fulfilled. In the words of the ICTY,

> nor is it necessary that the crime alleged... be part of a policy or of a practice officially endorsed or tolerated by one of the parties to the conflict, or that the act be in actual furtherance of a policy associated with the conduct of war or in the actual interest of a party to the conflict; *the obligations of individuals under international humanitarian law are independent and apply without prejudice to any questions of the responsibility of States under international law.* The only question, to be determined in the circumstances of each individual case, is whether the offences were closely related to the armed conflict as a whole.[73]

The ICTY seems thus to conceive of war crimes as theoretically and practically independent from aggravated state responsibility for the same conduct. The seriousness requirement as provided for under aggravated state responsibility needs not

[73] ICTY, *Prosecutor v. Tadić*, TC, Judgment, 7 May 1997, para. 573 (emphasis added); ICTY, *Prosecutor v. Delalić et al.*, TC, Judgment, 16 November 1998, para. 195; ICTY, *Prosecutor v. Blaškić*, TC, Judgment, 3 March 2000, para. 70; ICTY, *Prosecutor v. Naletilić and Martinović*, TC, Judgment, 31 March 2003, para. 225, note 600.

be fulfilled to hold individuals accountable for war crimes. International case law requires war crimes to be committed in connection with military activity, in the framework of the broader criminal context represented by international or internal armed conflicts. However, war crimes need not be planned or executed on a large scale at the state level to give rise to individual criminal liability. Thus, no link is required with aggravated state responsibility.

Interestingly, the same is true with respect to customary war crimes not explicitly listed in the ICTY Statute but which can nevertheless entail individual criminal liability. The Appeals Chamber of the *ad hoc* Tribunal in *Tadić* identified four conditions for an offence to be subject to prosecution before the ICTY under Article 3. In particular, according to the third condition, "the violation must be 'serious', that is to say, it must constitute a breach of a rule protecting important values, and the breach must involve grave consequences for the victim".[74] This apparently deals both with the importance of the primary rule breached (the first concept of seriousness) and with an operational requirement on the magnitude of effects of the criminal conduct (the second concept of seriousness). However, this third condition has been applied as essentially requiring the conduct to be in breach of an obligation of particular importance for the international community. Although in its subsequent case law the ICTY has not examined the third *Tadić* condition in much detail,[75] it seems that the Tribunal has never required war crimes to be carried out according to a state policy or in a widespread and systematic manner.[76]

---

[74] ICTY, *Prosecutor v. Tadić*, AC, Decision on the Defence Motion for Interlocutory Appeal on Jurisdiction, 2 October 1995, para. 94.

[75] *See*, in particular, ICTY, *Prosecutor v. Galić*, TC, Judgment, 5 December 2003, paras. 106–112.

[76] While prosecution under Article 3 certainly does not depend on the fulfilment of a seriousness requirement such as that provided for under aggravated state responsibility, it is more doubtful whether the third *Tadić* condition requires the damage of the victim to be extensive. With respect to the war crime 'attack on civilians', for instance, no such multiplicity of victims is required. *See* ICTY, *Prosecutor v. Strugar*, TC, Judgment, 31 January 2005, para. 289, where the attack resulted in the death of two civilians. *See* also ICTY, *Prosecutor v. Blaškić*, TC, Judgment, 3 March 2000, para. 180, *Prosecutor v. Kordić and Čerkez*, TC, Judgment, 26 February 2001, para. 328. On the other hand, with respect to the war crime 'attack on civilian objects', the ICTY seems to require the damage to be extensive. *See* ICTY, *Prosecutor v. Strugar*, TC, Judgment, 31 January 2005, para. 280. *See* also ICTY, *Prosecutor v. Kordić and Čerkez*, AC, Judgment, 17 December 2004, paras. 40–68. With respect to plunder as a war crime, a different approach has been taken. While the definition of this crime under customary international law does not include such a seriousness threshold that must be met, the ICTY requires a certain 'seriousness' to be demonstrated because Article 1 of the ICTY Statute limits the jurisdiction of the Tribunal to "persons responsible for *serious* violations of international humanitarian law" (emphasis added). *See* ICTY, *Prosecutor v. Naletilić and Martinović*, TC, Judgment of 31 March 2003, paras. 612–614. On this particular issue, *see* G. Acquaviva, 'Unlawful Transfer, Unlawful Labour, Plunder, and Persecution: The State of the Law in *Prosecutor v. Naletilic and Martinovic*', 3 *The Global Community Yearbook of International Law & Jurisprudence* (2003), pp. 152–154.

While war crimes do not require a general seriousness pre-requisite to be met, a particular connection between state and individual responsibility can nonetheless exist with respect to certain war crimes. For example, employing poisonous weapons or other weapons calculated to cause unnecessary suffering or bombarding undefended towns, villages, dwellings, or buildings[77] are war crimes which seem to presuppose the existence of a regular army having at its disposal a significant arsenal, and which imply a certain preconceived method of warfare.[78] Or, to give a different example, one may think of the war crime prohibiting "the passing of sentences and the carrying out of executions without previous judgment pronounced by a regularly constituted court, affording all judicial guarantees which are generally recognized as indispensable".[79] More generally, alongside typical individual war crimes (such as killing a combatant who has surrendered or raping a civilian), there are certain categories of war crimes which are peculiar to the state military apparatus. The latter apparently need to be carefully planned and organized in advance; they involve questions of state military strategy or presuppose the existence of a state apparatus; and they should be carried out in a precise and organized manner by the army. In particular, conduct during hostilities is carefully decided, prepared, and organized at the highest levels of the military hierarchy.

Thus, doubts can be raised about the existence of a closer relationship between individual and state responsibility with respect to similar war crimes and, in particular, the violations of international obligations regulating the conduct of warfare. For example, the so-called 'Hague law' was drafted having essentially in mind the conduct of states, and not of individuals. Early conventions on international humanitarian law[80] established bilateral obligations between the Contracting Parties, their implementation resting upon the instructions of Commanders-in-Chief of the belligerent armies. An obligation to adopt 'or recommend' national criminal

---

[77] *See* Articles 23 and 25 of the 1899 Hague Convention (II) with respect to the Laws and Customs of War on Land as well as Articles 23 and 25 of the 1907 Hague Convention (IV) respecting the Laws and Customs of War on Land.

[78] Interestingly, such war crimes are not listed among the "serious violations of the laws and customs of war applicable in armed conflicts not of an international character" in the ICC Statute (*see* Article 8, para. 2 (e), A/CONF.183/9, <www.icc-cpi.int>). For a critical position on this point, *see* A. Cassese, supra note 41, pp. 61–62.

[79] Article 8 (2) (c) (iv) of the ICC Statute (A/CONF.183/9, <www.icc-cpi.int>).

[80] This reference is to agreements preceding the 1949 Geneva Conventions, such as the 1864 Geneva Convention for the Amelioration of the Condition of the Wounded in Armies in the Field, the 1899 Hague Convention (II) with respect to the Laws and Customs of War on Land, the 1906 Geneva Convention for the Amelioration of the Condition of the Wounded and Sick in Armies in the Field, the 1907 Hague Convention (IV) respecting the Laws and Customs of War on Land, the 1929 Geneva Convention on the Amelioration of the Condition of the Wounded and Sick in Armies in the Field, and the 1929 Geneva Convention relative to the Treatment of Prisoners of War.

legislation to deter violations of these Conventions first appeared in 1906,[81] their breach entailing only (ordinary) state responsibility.[82] For these reasons, it is generally recognized that obligations arising under these instruments were chiefly aimed at state conduct,[83] and individual criminal liability for these particular war crimes seemed to be closely linked to aggravated state responsibility.

War crimes have mainly been dealt with by the ICTY. In particular, individuals have generally been found guilty of individual war crimes such as wilful killing, torture or inhumane treatment, wilfully causing great suffering or serious injury to body and health, and other grave breaches under Article 2 of the ICTY Statute.

On very few occasions have individuals been charged with war crimes involving (by definition) a broader criminal context. The relevant case-law[84] shows that international tribunals, when convicting the defendant on trial, had to rely considerably on the general context in which these particular war crimes were carried out. Individuals have rarely been found guilty of war crimes such as "attack on civilian population".[85] The defendants were all political or military leaders charged with widespread notorious crimes committed during the Balkan conflict against the civilian population, namely, ethnic cleansing in the Laška Valley, the siege of Sarajevo, the attack on Dubrovnik, and the Zagreb bombing. To establish their criminal liability, the ICTY largely relied on notorious facts, the general context in which the crimes were perpetrated, and in particular the *de jure* position of these accused. However, it must be stressed that, in *Kordić*, the Appeals Chamber adopted a rigorous approach and excluded the responsibility of the appellants for

---

[81] Only in 1929 was an explicit obligation to prosecute those responsible for breaches of humanitarian law enshrined in Article 29 of the Convention For the Amelioration of the Condition of the Wounded and Sick in Armies in the Field.

[82] *See* Article 3 of the IV Convention respecting the Laws and Customs of War, 1907. Individual criminal liability for 'grave breaches' of humanitarian law was explicitly established for the first time in the four 1949 Geneva Conventions (Articles 49–50 of Convention I and II, Articles 129–130 of Convention III, and Articles 146–147 of Convention IV).

[83] *See*, in general, P. Fois, 'Sul rapporto tra i crimini internazionali dello Stato e i crimini internazionali dell'individuo', 87 *Riv. Dir. Int.* (2004), pp. 936–937.

[84] For an example of a case in which this type of war crimes has been unsuccessfully pleaded by the Prosecution, *see* the *Blaškić* case (ICTY, *Prosecutor v. Blaškić*, TC, Judgment, 3 March 2000, paras. 661–678). The accused was charged with the bombing of the town of Zenica. When coming to deal with typical military facts, such as the kind of weapons used, the location of troops, and the weapons actually at the disposal of the parties, the establishment of individual participation and thus responsibility proved very difficult and the accused was acquitted.

[85] ICTY, *Prosecutor v. Kordić and Čerkez*, TC, Judgment, 26 February 2001; ICTY, *Prosecutor v. Galić*, TC, Judgment, 5 December 2003; ICTY, *Prosecutor v. Strugar*, TC, Judgment, 31 May 2005; ICTY, *Prosecutor v. Martić*, TC, Judgment, 12 June 2007.

a number of attacks considered to be legitimate military targets or in which no targeting of civilians could be established beyond doubt.[86]

Judicial practice is too scarce to draw general consequences. Most of these cases have focused essentially on attacks on the civilian population or civilian objects, while other more significant war crimes, such as crimes concerning the methods of warfare, have so far not been the object of international proceedings. However, these few cases are interesting because they at least show that the broader context of state criminality can have a crucial role in the establishment of individual liability for certain categories of war crimes.

B. *Crimes against Humanity*

As illustrated above, crimes against humanity are predicated on the 'widespread or systematic' character of the criminal conduct to be demonstrated. It is now well established in legal scholarship and jurisprudence that these conditions are not cumulative.[87] The following discussion thus deals with them separately.

It is generally considered that a criminal act is widespread when there is a multiplicity of victims.[88] The widespread character of the criminal act therefore pertains to the magnitude of the event giving rise to individual criminal liability. Even a single

[86] ICTY, *Prosecutor v. Kordić and Čerkez*, AC, Judgment, 17 December 2004. The convictions of Galić and Strugar have been confirmed on appeal (ICTY, *Prosecutor v. Galić*, AC, Judgment, 30 November 2006, and ICTY, *Prosecutor v. Strugar*, AC, Judgment, 17 July 2008).

[87] The fact that these are alternative conditions has been regularly pointed out in the international case law. *See*, in particular, ICTY, *Prosecutor v. Tadić*, TC, Judgment, 7 May 1997, paras. 646–647; ICTY, *Prosecutor v. Blaškić*, TC, Judgment, 3 March 2000, para. 207; ICTY, *Prosecutor v. Stakić*, TC, Judgment, 31 July 2003, para. 628; ICTR, *Prosecutor v. Akayesu*, TC, Judgment, 2 September 1998, paras. 578–579; ICTR, *Prosecutor v. Kayishema and Ruzindana*, TC, Judgment, 21 May 1999, para. 123; ICTR, *Prosecutor v. Musema*, TC, Judgment, 27 January 2000, para. 203; ICTR, *Prosecutor v. Bagilishema*, TC, Judgment, 7 June 2001, para. 77. The point is normally considered uncontroversial in the works of international law scholars. *See* D. Robinson, 'Defining 'Crimes against Humanity' at the Rome Conference', 93 *AJIL* (1999), p. 47; O. Swaak-Goldman, supra note 59, p. 157; D. Robinson, 'The Context of Crimes against Humanity', in R.S. Lee (ed.), *The International Criminal Court. Elements of Crimes and Rules of Procedure and Evidence* (Ardsley, Transnational Publishers, 2001), pp. 62 and 72; A. Cassese, supra note 59, p. 366; Y. Jurovics, supra note 59, p. 279.

[88] R. Dixon, supra note 59, p. 126; M. Bettati, supra note 59, p. 298; O. Swaak-Goldman, supra note 59, p. 158; D. Robinson, 'The Context of Crimes against Humanity', supra note 87, p. 63; K. Kittichaisaree, supra note 59, p. 96; Y. Jurovics, supra note 59, p. 280. *See* also ICTR, *Prosecutor v. Akayesu*, TC, Judgment, 2 September 1998, para. 580; ICTR, *Prosecutor v. Kayishema and Ruzindana*, TC, Judgment, 21 May 1999, para. 123; ICTR, *Prosecutor v. Rutaganda*, TC, Judgment, 6 December 1999, para. 69; ICTY, *Prosecutor v. Kunarac et al.*, TC, Judgment, 22 February 2001, para. 428; ICTY, *Prosecutor v. Vasiljević*, TC, Judgment, 29 November 2002, para. 35.

instance of criminal conduct might reach such a threshold of magnitude.[89] Thus, this specific condition does not necessarily establish a close connection between individual and state responsibility, since crimes against humanity of a certain magnitude can be committed not only by private individuals but also outside of a preconceived state policy.

A much closer link with aggravated state responsibility can exist when crimes against humanity are perpetrated in a systematic way. Indeed, it is generally understood that the systematic character of crimes against humanity can be inferred from a similar pattern of prohibited conduct that is carried out according to a methodical plan or policy.[90] In other words, the commission of inhumane acts must be repeated or continuous. This necessarily requires a relatively broad number of persons to be involved in the perpetration of the criminal act. Accordingly, the connection with aggravated state responsibility is due to the fact that individual liability attaches to crimes carried out at the state level. However, recent case law seems to hold the view that under international criminal law:

> neither the attack nor the acts of the accused need to be supported by any form of 'policy' or 'plan'. There is nothing under customary international law which requires the imposition of an additional requirement that the acts be connected to a policy or plan. At most, the existence of a policy or plan may be evidentially relevant, but it is not a legal element of the crime.[91]

---

[89] Commentary on Article 18 of the Draft Code of Crimes, ILC, 'Report on the Work of its 48th Session', *YILC* (1996), vol. II(2), pp. 49–50, para. 4. This is a different hypothesis from that in which the criminal act targets a single victim but nonetheless can be considered to be part of a systematic policy of targeting the civilian population.

[90] ICTY, *Prosecutor v. Tadić*, TC, Judgment, 7 May 1997, para. 648; ICTY, *Prosecutor v. Blaškić*, TC, Judgment, 3 March 2000, para. 203; ICTY, *Prosecutor v. Kunarac et al.*, TC, Judgment, 22 February 2001, para. 429; ICTR, *Prosecutor v. Akayesu*, TC, Judgment, 2 September 1998, paras. 579–581; ICTR, *Prosecutor v. Kayishema and Ruzindana*, TC, Judgment, 21 May 1999, para. 123. *See* also R. Dixon, supra note 59, p. 126; M. Bettati, supra note 59, p. 299; O. Swaak-Goldman, supra note 59, p. 158; D. Robinson, 'The Context of Crimes against Humanity', supra note 87, p. 63; K. Kittichaisaree, supra note 59, p. 96; Y. Jurovics, supra note 59, pp. 281–288; A. Cassese, supra note 41, p. 65.

[91] ICTY, *Prosecutor v. Vasiljević*, TC, Judgment, 29 November 2002, para. 36. *See* also ICTY, *Prosecutor v. Galić*, TC, Judgment, 5 December 2003, para. 147; ICTY, *Prosecutor v. Simić et al.*, TC, Judgment, 17 October 2003, para. 44; ICTY, *Prosecutor v. Naletilić and Martinović*, TC, Judgment, 31 March 2003, para. 234; ICTY, *Prosecutor v. Kunarac et al.*, TC, Judgment, 12 June 2002, para. 98; ICTY, *Prosecutor v. Krnojelac*, TC, Judgment, 15 March 2002, para. 58; ICTY, *Prosecutor v. Kordić and Čerkez*, TC, Judgment, 26 February 2001, para. 182; ICTY, *Prosecutor v. Kunarac et al.*, TC, Judgment, 22 February 2001, para. 432 (*see*, in particular, note 1109).

Moreover, there is consent among scholars on the assumption that crimes against humanity can be carried out by private groups or organizations.[92] In this case, a connection with aggravated state responsibility is more difficult to establish.

International case law does not require evidence of a state policy to convict individuals for crimes against humanity, and it explicitly rejects any link with aggravated state responsibility. For example, in *Limaj* the ICTY dealt with crimes allegedly perpetrated by the Kosovo Liberation Army, and accepted that crimes against humanity can be committed "by a non-state actor with extremely limited resources, personnel and organization".[93]

However, what may appear at first sight to be a clear difference between individual and state responsibility for international crimes can prove to be a much closer link when one takes into account the way in which the general pre-requisite for crimes against humanity is actually applied in the international case law.

As noted above, the seriousness requirement in relation to aggravated state responsibility is essentially associated with the establishment of a practice of similar wrongful acts carried out by state organs.[94] In other words, it must be found that a sum of events points to the existence of a state policy in carrying out certain breaches of obligations owed to the international community as a whole. On the other hand, in the establishment of individual criminal liability, the international case law has generally adopted a different approach in this respect. What international (and domestic) criminal courts must establish beyond doubt is the criminal conduct of single individuals, that is, a personal participation in the perpetration of international crimes. Thus, their inquiry in principle focuses on the personal

---

[92] Article 18 of the ILC Draft Code of Crimes (ILC, 'Report on the Work of its 48th Session', *YILC* (1996), vol. II(2), p. 49); Article 7 of the ICC Statute (A/CONF.183/9, <www.icc-cpi.int>); ICTY, *Prosecutor v. Kupreškić et al.*, TC, Judgment, 14 January 2000, para. 551; ICTY, *Prosecutor v. Blaškić*, TC, Judgment, 3 March 2000, para. 205 ("Trial Chambers I and II of both this Tribunal and the ICTR have constantly refused to characterize a crime against humanity as an 'act of criminal sovereignty'"); ICTR, *Prosecutor v. Akayesu*, TC, Judgment, 2 September 1998, para. 580; ICTR, *Prosecutor v. Rutaganda*, TC, Judgment, 6 December 1999, para. 69; ICTR, *Prosecutor v. Kayishema and Ruzindana*, TC, Judgment, 21 May 1999, para. 125; Y. Dinstein, supra note 52, p. 906; M.C. Bassiouni, supra note 44, p. 275; O. Swaak-Goldman, supra note 59, pp. 158–159; K. Kittichaisaree, supra note 59, p. 98; A. Cassese, supra note 59, p. 367; Y. Jurovics, supra note 59, pp. 416–417; A. Cassese, supra note 41, p. 83.

[93] ICTY, *Prosecutor v. Limaj*, TC, Judgment, 30 November 2005, para. 191 ("The existence of a 'policy' to conduct an attack against a civilian population is most easily determined or inferred when a State's conduct is in question; but absence of a policy does not mean that a widespread or systematic attack against a civilian population has not occurred. Although not a legal element of Article 5, evidence of a policy or plan is an important indication that the acts in question are not merely the workings of individuals acting pursuant to haphazard or individual design, but instead have a level of organizational coherence and support of a magnitude sufficient to elevate them into the realm of crimes against humanity." Ibid., para. 212).

[94] *See* supra in this Chapter.

conduct of the offender and on the different events in which he or she has taken part.[95] Accordingly, the 'widespread or systematic' criterion must be assessed first of all in the light of the individual behaviour of the alleged perpetrator. In particular, the criminal court will ascertain whether the individual has committed a crime of a particular magnitude[96] or whether he or she has carried out a plurality of crimes according to a similar pattern.[97] For example, in *Vasiljević* the Appeals Chamber concentrated on the conduct of the accused to establish his liability for crimes against humanity:

> The Appeals Chamber does not subscribe to the views of the Appellant that the Trial Chamber erred in finding him guilty of persecution 'solely on the basis of one incident'. First, the Drina River incident consists of the murder of five people and the inhumane acts inflicted on two others. This incident cannot be described as a single act but rather as a series of acts.[98]

---

[95] A particular position is apparently held by M.C. Bassiouni, 'The Normative Framework of International Humanitarian Law: Overlaps, Gaps and Ambiguities', in M.C. Bassiouni (ed.), *International Criminal Law*, vol. I (Ardsley, Transnational Publishers, 1999), p. 625 ("if it is established that a *state* has developed a policy, or carried out a plan, or engaged in acts whose outcomes include the crimes contained in the definition of crimes against humanity, then those persons in the bureaucratic apparatus who brought about, or contributed to, that result could be charged with complicity to commit crimes against humanity").

[96] This is what happened in the *Erdemović* case (ICTY, *Prosecutor v. Erdemović*, TC, Judgment, 29 November 1996), in which the Trial Chamber found that a crime against humanity had been committed. The criminal act was of extreme gravity due, first of all, to the magnitude of the mass execution in which the offender had taken part. Indeed, Erdemović was found to be responsible for "killing between 10 and 100 people", when "during a five-hour period on 16 July 1995" approximately 1,200 unarmed civilians had been killed (para. 85). With respect to the ICTR case law, most of the accused participated in attacks against the Tutsi group, which resulted in thousands of deaths (*see*, for example, ICTR, *Prosecutor v. Rutaganda*, TC, Judgment, 6 December 1999, paras. 299–304; ICTR, *Prosecutor v. Musema*, TC, Judgment, 27 January 2000, para. 756).

[97] The systematic character of crimes against humanity has been assessed by the ICTY and ICTR in a number of cases. For example, in *Kupreškić* (ICTY, *Prosecutor v. Kupreškić et al.*, TC, Judgment, 14 January 2000), the ICTY established the existence of the seriousness requirement of crimes against humanity (persecution, murder and other inhumane acts) with respect to the individual participation of each member of a military group in the attack on the small village of Ahmici in central Bosnia (paras. 749–833). The Trial Chamber focused on the personal conduct of each accused. In particular, it found that the attack against the Muslim civilian population was well planned and well organized (*ibid.*, para. 761). Therefore, the seriousness requirement referred to the personal conduct of the accused individuals and the Chamber did not establish whether such criminal conduct could fit into a more general context of state policy. With respect to the ICTR case law, for example, in the *Musema* case the accused was found guilty of extermination. In particular, the Trial Chamber established the widespread and systematic character of this crime against humanity taking into account not only the number of victims but also the repeated attacks against the Tutsi in which the accused took part (ICTR, *Prosecutor v. Musema*, TC, Judgment, 27 January 2000, paras. 693, 746–751, 754, 796, 945, and 949–951).

[98] ICTY, *Prosecutor v. Vasiljević*, AC, Judgment, 24 February 2004, para. 113.

Thus, when possible, the *ad hoc* tribunals have established the general pre-requisite of crimes against humanity focusing only on the criminal conduct charged in the indictment. They have verified whether the personal conduct of the accused was widespread or systematic, leaving no room for any link with state responsibility.

However, international case law has also accepted that a single act can be regarded as a crime against humanity, if it takes place within the necessary context. For example, a single murder can be part of a pattern that amounts to ethnic cleansing. In *Kupreškić*, the ICTY expressed this concept as follows:

> In general terms, the very nature of the criminal acts over which the International Tribunal has jurisdiction under Article 5, in view of the fact that they must be 'directed against any civilian population,' ensures that what is to be alleged will not be one particular act but, instead, a course of conduct. Nevertheless, *in certain circumstances*, a single act has comprised a crime against humanity when it occurred within the necessary context. For example, the act of denouncing a Jewish neighbour to the Nazi authorities – if committed against a background of widespread persecution – has been regarded as amounting to a crime against humanity.[99]

In such a case, the 'seriousness' criterion for crimes against humanity is established by criminal courts by reference to the broader criminal context, and thus does not strictly depend on the personal conduct of the accused. This is an approach completely different from the first one examined above. It allows criminal courts to establish individual liability for crimes against humanity with respect to conduct not *per se* widespread or systematic but with respect to a criminal context representing the factual framework in which the accused has committed single prohibited acts. To say that criminal courts can deduce individual liability from a general criminal context require only one further step.

All depends on the weight actually given to this general criminal context in establishing individual criminal liability. If international criminal tribunals focus on the personal conduct of the accused and on its widespread or systematic character, then no link with collective criminality will be taken into account, and the widespread or systematic criterion for crimes against humanity will, in a certain sense, be 'individualized'. By contrast, if the emphasis is placed on the pattern of attacks against the civilian population and on the fact that the accused is a member of the group responsible for such widespread or systematic attacks, then

---

[99] ICTY, *Prosecutor v. Kupreškić et al.*, TC, Judgment, 14 January 2000, para. 550 (emphasis added). The ICTY already had the occasion to clarify that: "Crimes against humanity . . . must be widespread or demonstrate a systematic character. However, as long as there is a link with the widespread or systematic attack against a civilian population, a single act could qualify as a crime against humanity. As such, an individual committing a crime against a single victim or a limited number of victims might be recognized as guilty of a crime against humanity if his acts were part of the specific context identified above." (ICTY, *Prosecutor v. Mrkšić*, TC, Review of the indictment pursuant to Rule 61 of the Rules of Procedure and Evidence, 3 April 1996, para. 30).

individual liability for crimes against humanity will be closely connected to and made dependent upon the general criminal context. This second approach widely characterizes the jurisprudence of the *ad hoc* tribunals.

C. *Crimes against Humanity: The Role of the General Criminal Context*

An interesting development has emerged from the ICTY case law. The Tribunal has generalized the approach adopted in previous judgments, holding that the widespread or systematic requirement for crimes against humanity does not concern the conduct of the accused but only the violence carried out against the civilian population, that is, the general criminal context.

In *Kunarac*,[100] the ICTY had to establish the criminal liability of three members of a Bosnian Serb military unit who were charged with war crimes and crimes against humanity committed against the Bosnian Muslim population. With respect to the 'seriousness' criterion of crimes against humanity, the Trial Chamber stated that "*only the attack*, not the individual acts of the accused must be widespread or systematic".[101] In addition, the prohibited conduct of the accused needs only be a part of this attack and, all other conditions being met, a single or relatively limited number of acts on his or her part would qualify as a crime against humanity unless those acts are isolated or random. A single act can be regarded as a crime against humanity if it takes place in the relevant context. This position has been upheld by the Appeals Chamber.[102]

It is not an easy task to evaluate this position of the ICTY concerning the widespread or systematic requirement for crimes against humanity. On the one hand, it must be said that *ad hoc* tribunals have been careful about broadening recourse

[100] ICTY, *Prosecutor v. Kunarac et al.*, TC, Judgment, 22 February 2001.

[101] *Ibid.*, para. 431 (emphasis added).

[102] ICTY, *Prosecutor v. Kunarac et al.*, AC, Judgment, 12 June 2002, para. 96; ICTY, *Prosecutor v. Blaškić*, AC, Judgment, 29 July 2004, para. 101; ICTY, *Prosecutor v. Stakić*, AC, Judgment, 22 March 2006, paras. 245–251. The significant role played by the general criminal context in the establishment of individual liability for crimes against humanity is confirmed by the case law which has dealt with the particular issue of the *actus reus* of persecution. Apart from those listed in the statutes of the *ad hoc* tribunals, 'other' criminal acts can qualify as persecution if they are of the same level of seriousness. This gravity test has been understood as requiring that, in order to amount to persecution, the relevant act must consist of a gross or blatant denial, on discriminatory grounds, of a fundamental right under international customary or treaty law. In particular, the determination of acts amounting to persecution "must be evaluated not in isolation but in context, by looking at their cumulative effect", even though the underlying act may not constitute a violation of international law (*See* ICTY, *Prosecutor v. Kupreškić et al.*, TC, Judgment, 14 January 2000, para. 622, and ICTY, *Prosecutor v. Krnojelac*, TC, Judgment, 15 March 2002, para. 434). Therefore, in order to be regarded as serious, and in order to amount to persecution, certain acts need to be part of a systematic or widespread attack against the civilian population. In other words, they will be established essentially having regard to the general criminal context.

to the general criminal context in finding individuals accountable for crimes against humanity. The existence of a general criminal context – of a widespread or systematic attack against the civilian population – is not enough. To convict the accused it must be proved that there is a link between this general context and his or her personal conduct: the acts of the accused need be a part of the attack.[103] International tribunals have adopted a rigorous approach in considering this link. Most of the accused persons found guilty of crimes against humanity before the ICTY and ICTR committed acts that could have been considered serious. Thus, it has generally been possible for these tribunals to focus on the widespread or systematic nature of the personal conduct of the accused. If we take, for example, the accused persons in *Kunarac*, they were found guilty of torture and rape in a number of cases which could be regarded as widespread or systematic independently of the general context in which they had been carried out. Similarly, in *Blaškić* the Appeals Chamber reviewed the Trial Chamber judgment,[104] and established Blaškić's criminal liability not with respect to the systematic attacks carried out by his troops, but with regard to the conduct of the accused in each attack.[105] Thus, it is possible to say that international case law has generally displayed a rigorous approach in the establishment of the widespread or systematic pre-requisite of crimes against humanity, which is perfectly understandable in the light of the basic principle of personal liability.

Nonetheless, it may reasonably be assumed that the abovementioned interpretation of the widespread or systematic requirement for crimes against humanity has facilitated the task of *ad hoc* tribunals in ascribing individual liability for crimes committed at the collective level. The widespread or systematic nature of the attack is therefore the element of crimes against humanity which allows international tribunals to take the collective dimension of these crimes into account. It represents the link between individual and collective criminality. It is a significant tool at the disposal of criminal tribunals that have to deal mainly with this sort of 'system' criminality. Indeed, the *ad hoc* tribunals have generally addressed large scale atrocities, and the establishment of the 'seriousness' criterion for crimes against humanity

---

[103] *See*, in particular, ICTY, *Prosecutor v. Mrkšić*, TC, Review of the indictment pursuant to Rule 61 of the Rules of Procedure and Evidence, 3 April 1996, para. 30; ICTY, *Prosecutor v. Kunarac et al.*, AC, Judgment, 12 June 2002, para. 96.

[104] The general pre-requisite of crimes against humanity was ascertained with respect to the conduct of the accused as well as that of his subordinate military personnel. In particular, a certain attention was drawn to the pattern of attacks they carried out on various Bosnian villages (ICTY, *Prosecutor v. Blaškić*, TC, Judgment, 3 March 2000, para. 467).

[105] As a consequence of this approach, the Appeals Chamber acquitted him under various counts. ICTY, *Prosecutor v. Blaškić*, AC, Judgment, 29 July 2004.

has not been particularly problematic. Suffice it to recall here some more recent cases of the ICTY dealing with crimes against humanity.[106]

The case law of the ICTY provides ample evidence of the significant role played by the general criminal context in the establishment of individual criminal liability for crimes against humanity.

In *Naletilić*, the ICTY considered serious crimes committed in Mostar and the surrounding region by Bosnian Croats against the Muslim civilian population.[107] The Trial Chamber had no difficulty in finding that, at the time relevant to the indictment, there was a widespread and systematic attack against the Muslim population. Thousands of Muslims were forced to leave their homes. A large number of prisoners of war and civilian prisoners were held at detention centres in the area. The Tribunal was thus satisfied that the acts of the defendants – two military commanders who participated in the fighting – directly contributed to the overall aim of the campaign against the civilian population.

In another important case,[108] the ICTY was called on to hear charges of (*inter alia*) crimes against humanity allegedly carried out by a political leader of the Serbian Democratic Party in Bosnia Herzegovina. The ICTY considered that the relevant events which took place in the municipality of Prijedor constituted a carefully planned attack against the civilian population which culminated in large scale killings of non-Serbs, or at least in their detention. The Tribunal was also satisfied that the conduct of the accused was closely linked to the general criminal context. The accused had participated in a joint criminal enterprise whose purpose was to carry out a discriminatory campaign to ethnically cleanse the municipality of Prijedor by deporting and persecuting Bosnian Muslims and Bosnian Croats. In particular, Stakić

> played a crucial role in the co-ordinated co-operation with the police and army in furtherance of the plan to establish a Serbian municipality in Prijedor. In addition, [he was] one of the main actors in the persecutorial campaign, actively participated in setting up and running [the camps], and took an active role in the organization of the massive displacement of the non-Serb population out of Prijedor municipality.[109]

In *Simić*, three defendants were charged under a theory of joint criminal enterprise for crimes against humanity and war crimes committed in the Bosanski Šamac and Odžak municipalities. Simić was the Bosnian Serb President of the Bosanski Šamac Crisis Staff and of the War Presidency; Tadić was a member of the Crisis

---

[106] All cases dealing with crimes against humanity brought before the ICTR concern conduct which has also entailed charges of genocide, because carried out in a context of notorious widespread and systematic atrocities.

[107] ICTY, *Prosecutor v. Naletilić and Martinović*, TC, Judgment, 31 March 2003, paras. 238–244.

[108] ICTY, *Prosecutor v. Stakić*, TC, Judgment, 31 July 2003, paras. 628–630.

[109] ICTY, *Prosecutor v. Stakić*, AC, Judgment, 22 March 2006, para. 78.

Staff and of the Exchange Commission; and Zarić had served in various positions (Assistant Commander for Intelligence, Reconnaissance, Morale and Information of the 4th Detachment, Chief of National Security Service in Bosanski Šamac, Deputy to the President of the War Council for Security Matters in Odžak, and Assistant Commander of the 2nd Posavina Brigade for Morale and Information) and reported directly to the Crisis Staff. The Tribunal found that the defendants had participated in a joint criminal enterprise and that their acts were part of a widespread and systematic attack against Bosnian Croats and Bosnian Muslims. The attack had been planned and carried out in an organized manner. Hundreds of non-Serbs had unlawfully been detained, a large number of them were subjected to torture or to cruel and inhumane treatment, and hundreds of them had been deported or forcibly transferred.[110]

In *Brđanin*, the ICTY was satisfied that "there was a widespread or systematic attack against the Bosnian Muslim and Bosnian Croat civilian population in the Bosnian Krajina during the period relevant to the Indictment".[111] In several instances, mass killings took place and a policy of ethnic cleansing was systematically implemented by the Bosnian Serbs. Tens of thousands of Bosnian Muslims and Bosnian Croats had forcibly been expelled according to a general pattern of conduct. The acts committed by the accused had been part of this widespread and systematic attack against the civilian population.

Similarly, in *Blagojević*, both defendants were high-ranking officers in brigades which took part in the attack on the Srebrenica enclave. The attack had been directed against the Bosnian Muslim civilian population and was clearly widespread and systematic. It affected approximately 40,000 people. The underlying crimes with which the indictment was concerned were part of the attack.[112]

In some cases it can be more problematic to establish a link between the general criminal context and the conduct of an individual defendant. In particular, when the accused has a leadership position, there may be a physical and structural remoteness between him and the general criminal context. This has not prevented international tribunals from finding a link between the conduct of the accused and the widespread or systematic attack against the civilian population, at the 'cost' of relying on a more flexible form of liability.[113]

---

[110] ICTY, *Prosecutor v. Simić et al.*, TC, Judgment, 17 October 2003, paras. 978–982.

[111] ICTY, *Prosecutor v. Brđanin*, TC, Judgment, 1 September 2004, paras. 159–162.

[112] ICTY, *Prosecutor v. Blagojević and Jokić*, TC, Judgment, 17 January 2005, paras. 550–554.

[113] In *Brđanin*, for example, the Trial Chamber found a link with the criminal context, but considered 'aiding and abetting' to be the most appropriate form of liability (ICTY, *Prosecutor v. Brđanin*, TC, Judgment, 1 September 2004, paras. 354–355: "JCE is not an appropriate mode of liability to describe the individual criminal liability of the Accused, given the extraordinarily broad nature of this case, where the Prosecution seeks to include within a JCE a person as structurally remote

This case law shows that, in a number of cases, the 'seriousness' criterion in relation to crimes against humanity has been applied in a more flexible way which seems indispensable for taking into account of the collective dimension of international crimes such as crimes against humanity. When the personal conduct of the accused is not *per se* widespread and systematic, the *ad hoc* tribunals employ a two-step analysis. They first examine the general criminal context, and then they proceed to a determination of whether the individual conduct of the accused fits into that broader picture. This methodology introduces a precise link between individual liability and collective responsibility. Moreover, international tribunals may establish that certain crimes have been committed at the collective level 'once and for all', so that in subsequent cases the notorious criminal context may be taken as a kind of judicial notice.[114]

This methodology raises the question of whether the establishment of individual responsibility for crimes against humanity necessarily corresponds to a finding of a serious wrongful act, as defined under aggravated state responsibility. Due to the kind of jurisdiction they exercise, international criminal tribunals take into account the general criminal context as a sort of preliminary issue which is necessary to ascribe individual liability. They do not investigate whether the collective criminal phenomenon is the result of a state conduct or of the conduct of group of private individuals, because this is not required under international criminal law. International criminal tribunals focus on collective criminality with the specific purpose of identifying a nexus with the conduct of the accused. While systematic or large scale attacks against the civilian population generally imply an involvement of the state apparatus, the existence of an overlap in the establishment of individual and state responsibility for crimes against humanity can only be decided on a case-by-case basis, and the factual circumstances of each case will be crucial. In some cases the general criminal context taken into account to hold individual offenders accountable for crimes against humanity concerns the conduct of non-state actors.[115] In other cases, international criminal tribunals explicitly refer to a general criminal context taking place at the state level, as in the Darfur case currently before the ICC.[116] What can be stressed is that international criminal tribunals increasingly establish the discussed pre-requisite of crimes against humanity having regard to the general criminal context rather than the personal conduct of the accused, that is, with respect to facts that could be regarded as serious under aggravated state responsibility. As a matter of legal interpretation, the seriousness requirement for

from the commission of the crimes charged in the Indictment as the Accused"). For a discussion of this case and, more generally, of joint criminal enterprise, *see* infra Chapter 6.

114 *See* infra note 127 and accompanying text.

115 *See*, for example, the *Limaj* case, supra note 93 and accompanying text.

116 ICC, *Prosecutor v. Ahmad Harun and Ali Kushayb*, Pre-Trial Chamber, Decision on the Prosecution Application under Article 58(7) of the Statute, 27 April 2007, paras. 65–67.

crimes against humanity relates to the general criminal context, and accordingly it is established in a very similar way with respect to both state and individual responsibility.

D. *Genocide*

According to the well-established definition of genocide, the existence of a specific plan to destroy a protected group does not constitute an element of the crime.[117] Thus, under international criminal law there is no formal seriousness requirement. However, genocide is by nature a collective crime. Its definition requires the (total or partial) physical destruction of the targeted group to be carried out. Thus, it is collective in the sense that the victim is a group. But such a criminal goal would probably be achieved only if the perpetrator is a group as well. Historically, genocide has always been perpetrated by groups, or better by states. The problematic aspect of genocide is that its collective nature from the viewpoint of the perpetrator is not translated into a precise element in the definition of the crime.[118]

As far as state responsibility is concerned, it is not disputed that genocide entails aggravated state responsibility. But no seriousness requirement is explicitly cited with respect to this crime in the Draft Articles on State Responsibility. According to the ILC, genocide is *per se* a serious breach of community obligations. Thus, the question is whether the participation of one state organ in the commission of genocide is sufficient to trigger aggravated state responsibility. While it cannot be excluded that isolated acts of state organs amounting to genocide entail ordinary state responsibility,[119] the answer is arguably negative. One may think of historical precedents or of analogous crimes, such as official torture, which can be carried out by isolated state organs but which entail aggravated state responsibility only if carried out according to a widespread state practice. Moreover, the fact that genocide must be regarded by definition as a serious breach under Article 40 means that its

---

[117] ICTR, *Prosecutor v. Kayishema and Ruzindana*, TC, Judgment, 21 May 1999, para. 94; ICTY, *Prosecutor v. Jelisić*, AC, Judgment, 5 July 2001, para. 48; ICTY, *Prosecutor v. Krstić*, TC, Judgment, 2 August 2001, para. 572. On this particular aspect, *see* J. Verhoeven, 'Le crime de génocide. Originalité et ambiguïté', 24 *RBDI* (1991), p. 25; W.A. Schabas, *Genocide in International Law. The Crime of Crimes* (Cambridge, Cambridge University Press, 2000), pp. 208–209; K. Kittichaisaree, supra note 59, p. 76; A. Cassese, 'Genocide', in A. Cassese *et al.* (eds.), *The Rome Statute of the International Criminal Court. A Commentary*, vol. I (Oxford, Oxford University Press, 2002), p. 350 ("in case of genocide, international rules do not require the existence of a widespread or systematic practice as a legal ingredient of the crime").

[118] *See* G.P. Fletcher and J.D. Ohlin, 'Reclaiming Fundamental Principles of Criminal Law in the Darfur Case', 3 *JICJ* (2005), p. 546; and J.D. Ohlin, 'Three Conceptual Problems with the Doctrine of Joint Criminal Enterprise', 5 *JICJ* (2007), p. 73.

[119] One may think for example of a genocide committed by state A with the contribution of a single state organ of state B. While state A incurs aggravated state responsibility, state B 'only' incurs ordinary state responsibility. On this specific aspect, *see* infra Chapter 8.

collective nature has been taken into account, and that a significant involvement of the state apparatus must be established in order to find aggravated responsibility. If the seriousness requirement is to be regarded as implicit in the definition of genocide, this is because by its very nature this crime requires, in the words of the ILC, "an intentional violation on a large scale".

The approach to the collective nature of genocide under international criminal law is different. As noted above, in order to hold individuals accountable for genocide there is no need to demonstrate a genocidal policy or that the prohibited conduct has been carried out by a group of perpetrators. Abstractly speaking, even a single person can destroy the targeted group:

> Such a case is theoretically possible. The murders committed by the accused are sufficient to establish the material element of the crime of genocide and it is *a priori* possible to conceive that the accused harboured the plan to exterminate an entire group without this intent having been supported by any organization in which other individuals participated. In this respect, the preparatory work of the Convention of 1948 brings out that premeditation was not selected as a legal ingredient of the crime of genocide, after having been mentioned by the *ad hoc* committee at the draft stage, on the grounds that it seemed superfluous given the special intention already required by the text and that such precision would only make the burden of proof even greater. It ensues from this omission that the drafters of the Convention did not deem the existence of an organization or a system serving a genocidal objective as a legal ingredient of the crime. In so doing, they did not discount the possibility of a lone individual seeking to destroy a group as such.[120]

Due to its nature and purpose, international criminal law focuses on the establishment of personal liability. This explains how it is possible to interpret the definition of genocide as to include cases of isolated perpetrators, since no seriousness requirement is provided for under the customary definition of genocide.[121] In principle, the collective nature of genocide needs not be taken into account from the viewpoint of the perpetrator.[122]

The Darfur case clearly epitomizes the abstract possibility of adopting two diverging approaches as far as individual and state responsibility for genocide are concerned. The Commission of Inquiry concludes that genocide has not occurred in Sudan. In particular, it holds that no state genocidal policy existed, and that the crimes (against humanity)[123] committed by the Sudanese Government and the militias under its control were not carried out with the aim to physically destroy

[120] ICTY, *Prosecutor v. Jelisić*, TC, Judgment, 14 December 1999, para. 100.

[121] P.N. Drost, *The Crime of State. Genocide* (Leiden, Sythoff, 1959), p. 85.

[122] Increasingly, scholars criticize this approach and urge the collective nature of genocide to be taken into account. *See* G.P. Fletcher and J.D. Ohlin, supra note 118, pp. 545–550; C. Kress, 'The Darfur Report and Genocidal Intent', 3 *JICJ* (2005), pp. 565–577.

[123] 'Report of the International Commission of Inquiry on Darfur to the United Nations Secretary-General pursuant to Security Council Resolution 1564 of 18 September 2004', supra note 25, para. 519.

the relevant targeted group.[124] As already mentioned, the Commission decided to focus on individual criminal liability, but various passages in the report exclude a direct (aggravated) responsibility of Sudan, even though some of its organs might be implicated in the commission of that crime. Indeed, at the same time the Commission did not rule out "the possibility that in some instances *single individuals*, including Government officials, may entertain a genocidal intent",[125] and it would be for the competent court to establish the criminal liability for genocide of these individuals, in the absence of any involvement of Sudan in the commission of this crime. As will be discussed in the next chapter, in practice it is much more difficult to accept these diverging approaches when looking at the way in which the psychological element is actually established.

In practice, the collective nature of genocide is crucial in ascribing individual accountability for this crime. For obvious reasons, the ICTR has mainly dealt with the crime of genocide. Its case law confirms this rigorous approach, focusing on the personal conduct of the accused regardless of any link with a state genocidal policy. However, the ICTR has tried not only accused persons who have committed flagrant acts of genocide, but also individuals that have carried out acts amounting to genocide because they were part of a broader genocidal context. In particular, the ICTR deemed it necessary, in each trial in which the alleged act of genocide was part of a broader criminal context, for the Prosecution to demonstrate that genocide was carried out in Rwanda and that the accused took part in this genocidal campaign.[126] As already noted with respect to crimes against humanity, this approach allows the Tribunal to ascribe individual liability relying on the general criminal context, and establishes a connection between individual and collective criminality.

But the ICTR has taken one significant step further, and in a recent decision it took judicial notice that genocide occurred in Rwanda, that genocide was a notorious fact.[127] In rejecting the strictly individual approach of the Trial Chamber (according to which the Tribunal should only focus on the personal involvement

[124] *Ibid.*, para. 518.

[125] *Ibid.*, para. 520.

[126] *See*, in particular, ICTR, *Prosecutor v. Akayesu*, TC, Judgment, 2 September 1998, paras. 78–129, and *Prosecutor v. Kayishema and Ruzindana*, TC, Judgment, 21 May 1999, paras. 31–54. The case law of the ICTR concerning genocide will be examined in detail below (*see* infra Chapter 4).

[127] ICTR, *Prosecutor v. Karemera et al.*, AC, Decision on Prosecutor's Interlocutory Appeal of Decision on Judicial Notice, 16 June 2006. By contrast, the ICTY has displayed a more rigorous approach to the matter, admitting only factual findings (and not legal findings) as adjudicated facts of which it can take judicial notice. *See*, for example, ICTY, *Prosecutor v. Krajišnik*, TC, Decision on Prosecution Motions for Judicial Notice of Adjudicated facts and for Admission of Written Statements of Witnesses pursuant to Rule 92*bis*, 28 February 2003.

of the defendant charged with genocide),[128] the Appeals Chamber recognized that the genocide occurred in Rwanda in 1994 was a crime committed at the collective level, and stressed the importance of this general criminal context for understanding the individual's actions and establishing individual criminal liability not only with respect to genocide but also other international crimes, such as crimes against humanity.[129] Indeed, as a consequence of having established once and for all that the Rwandan genocide against the Tutsi group is a 'part of world history', the Prosecution no longer needs to demonstrate the criminal context in which the accused participated with single prohibited acts to convict him for genocide. This approach has the effect not only of taking into account the collective dimension of the crime of genocide but also of establishing a clear relationship between individual and collective criminality. It is the collective criminal phenomenon which is established first, and only then individual liability is ascribed to those who have *participated* in the genocidal campaign. In this case, it is difficult to deny that the judicial notice of the Rwanda genocide – coupled with the fact that the ICTR has convicted high-ranking organs of the state – points to an aggravated responsibility of the state.

Finally, there is an indirect way in which the collective nature of genocide can be taken into account. Genocide as a specific intent crime requires the perpetrator of the prohibited conduct to have acted with the intent to destroy the targeted group. However, it is very difficult to prove the genocidal intent when genocide is not committed in a systematic manner or according to a preconceived plan.[130] Therefore, international and national criminal tribunals have constantly affirmed that the *dolus specialis* can be inferred from a certain number of presumptions of fact, and specifically from the massive and/or systematic nature of the criminal

---

[128] ICTR, *Prosecutor v. Karemera et al.*, AC, Decision on Prosecutor's Interlocutory Appeal of Decision on Judicial Notice, supra note 127, para. 33.

[129] *Ibid.*, paras. 35–36.

[130] A divergent view seems to be expressed in the Elements of Crimes prepared in connection with the ICC Statute. Indeed, the PrepCom has listed among the elements of genocide a further requirement, namely, that "the conduct took place in the context of a manifest pattern of similar conduct directed against that group or was conduct that could itself effect such destruction" (UN Doc. PCNICC/2000/1/Add.2, <untreaty.un.org/cod/icc/index.html>). However, this additional element seems inconsistent with the definition of genocide under both customary law and Article 6 of the ICC Statute (A. Cassese, supra note 117, p. 349). The reason for the introduction of such an additional condition can be found in the drafting history of the Elements of Crimes. Arguably, the requisite context was introduced in order to balance the recognition by the PrepCom that a single act (*e.g.* the 'initial' criminal act) can constitute genocide (V. Oosterveld, 'The Elements of Genocide – The Context of Genocide', in R.S. Lee (ed.), *The International Criminal Court. Elements of Crimes and Rules of Procedure and Evidence* (Ardsley, Transnational Publishers, 2001), pp. 45–47; W.A. Schabas, supra note 117, p. 234). Therefore, it is not possible to say that the Elements of Genocide always make responsibility conditional on the contextual element described above.

acts.[131] Accordingly, the general criminal context can have a certain indirect role in establishing individual criminal liability for genocide, but this particular aspect will be examined in the next chapter.[132]

E. *Aggression*

The crime of aggression is certainly the international crime characterized by the closest connection between state and individual responsibility.[133] The first statements which regarded aggressive war as an international crime addressed a state responsibility issue.[134] Only later, in the *Nuremberg* and *Tokyo* trials, were indi-

---

131 ICTR, *Prosecutor v. Akayesu*, TC, Judgment, 2 September 1998, paras. 477, 523–524, and 728–730; ICTR, *Prosecutor v. Kayishema and Ruzindana*, TC, Judgment, 21 May 1999, para. 93; ICTR, *Prosecutor v. Rutaganda*, TC, Judgment, 6 December 1999, paras. 60–62; ICTR, *Prosecutor v. Musema*, TC, Judgment, 27 January 2000, paras. 166–167; ICTY, *Prosecutor v. Karadžić and Mladić*, TC, Review of the Indictments pursuant to Rule 61 of the Rules of Procedure and Evidence, 11 July 1996, para. 94; ICTY, *Prosecutor v. Jelisić*, TC, Judgment, 14 December 1999, para. 101; ICTY, *Prosecutor v. Krstić*, TC, Judgment, 2 August 2001, para. 572.

132 *See* infra Chapter 4.

133 S. Glueck, *The Nuremberg Trial and Aggressive War* (New York, Knopf, 1946); H. Donnedieu de Vabres, 'Le procès de Nuremberg devant les principes modernes du droit pénal international', 70 *RCADI* (1947), p. 477; G.A. Finch, 'The Nuremberg Trial and International Law', 41 *AJIL* (1947), p. 20; B.V.A. Röling, *The Tokyo Trial and Beyond. Reflections of a Peacemonger* (Cambridge MA, Polity Press, 1993), pp. 65–70; J. Hogan-Doran and B.T. Van Ginkel, 'Aggression as a Crime under International Law and the Prosecution of Individuals by the Proposed International Criminal Court', 43 *NILR* (1996), p. 321; M.C. Bassiouni and B.B. Ferencz, 'The Crime Against Peace', in M.C. Bassiouni (ed.), *International Criminal Law*, vol. I (Ardsley, Transnational Publishers, 1999), p. 313; M. Dumée, 'Le crime d'agression', in H. Ascensio *et al.* (eds.), *Droit international pénal* (Paris, Pedone, 2000), p. 251; B.B. Ferencz, 'The Crime of Aggression', in G. Kirk McDonald and O. Swaak-Goldman (eds.), *Substantive and Procedural Aspects of International Criminal Law*, vol. I (The Hague, Kluwer Law International, 2000), p. 33; S.R. Ratner and J.S. Abrams, supra note 52, pp. 124–128; A. Cassese, supra note 41, pp. 111–116; M. Lippman, 'The History, Development, and Decline of Crimes Against Peace', 36 *The George Washington International Law Review* (2004), p. 957; S. Solera, *Defining the Crime of Aggression* (London, Cameron May, 2007).

134 In 1762, Rousseau already defined war in the following terms: "*La guerre n'est donc point une relation d'homme à homme, mais une relation d'Etat à Etat, dans laquelle les particuliers ne sont ennemis qu'accidentellement, non point comme hommes ni même comme citoyens, mais comme soldats; non point comme membres de la patrie, mais comme ses défenseurs. Enfin chaque Etat ne peut avoir pour ennemis que d'autres Etats et non pas des hommes, attendu qu'entre choses de diverses natures on ne peut fixer aucun vrai rapport*" (J.-J. Rousseau, *Du contrat social* (Paris, Gallimard, 1993), Livre I, Chapitre IV (originally published in 1762)). *See* C. Eagleton, 'Faut-il proscrire seulement les guerres d'agression ou toutes les guerres?', 36 *RGDIP* (1932), p. 498; R.J. Alfaro, 'La question de la définition de l'agression', 29 *RDISDP* (1951), p. 367; I. Brownlie, *International Law and the Use of Force by States* (Oxford, Clarendon Press, 1963); B.V.A. Röling, 'International Law and the Maintenance of Peace', 4 *NYIL* (1973), p. 1; B. Broms, 'The Definition of Aggression', 154 *RCADI* (1977), p. 299; A.M. Rifaat, *International Aggression. A Study of the Legal Concept: Its*

viduals prosecuted for the crime of aggression. Henceforth, the development of international rules relating to such violations had to serve a double purpose: the identification of the conduct giving rise to state responsibility and that giving rise to individual criminal liability. The former, however, remains the characterizing feature of the norms concerning aggression, as this is primarily considered a matter that concerns states. In 2004, the ICJ still conceives of aggression essentially in terms of a relationship between states: self-defence entails an interstate legal relation and it can only be validly invoked in case of an armed aggression "by one State against another State".[135]

The fact that aggression does not entail a legal relation between states and individuals does not exclude the possibility that the international prohibition of (interstate) aggression may also concern individuals. However, it implies that individual liability for aggression presupposes state responsibility, and persons can be convicted for aggression only if a state act of aggression has taken place. This establishes a very close connection between aggravated state responsibility and individual criminal liability for aggression. In order to establish this relationship precisely, three major aspects are relevant, that is, the material element, the seriousness requirement, and the subjective element of the crime in question. While the subjective element will be examined below,[136] the focus here will be on the first two elements, bearing in mind that the seriousness requirement is generally considered to be implicit in the definition of aggression.

The main problem in the identification of such a relationship concerns the exact definition of aggression with respect to both state and individual responsibility. Neither Article 16 of the 1996 Draft Code nor Article 5 of the ICC Statute gives a definition of aggression. The works leading to these texts essentially refer back to the *Nuremberg* judgment and to the 1974 GA Definition of Aggression.[137]

The Nuremberg Charter defines crimes against peace as the planning, preparation, initiation and waging of aggressive war. However, no precise definition of

---

Development and Definition in International Law (Stockholm, Almqvist & Wiksell International, 1979); J. Zourek, 'Enfin une définition de l'agression', 20 *AFDI* (1974), p. 9; Y. Dinstein, *War, Aggression and Self-Defence* (2d edn., Cambridge, Cambridge University Press, 1994); N.A. Nyiri, *The United Nations' Search for a Definition of Aggression* (New York, Peter Lang, 1989).

[135] ICJ, *Legal Consequences of the Construction of a Wall in the Occupied Palestinian Territory*, supra Chapter 1, note 44, para. 139. Consequently, Israel cannot invoke self-defence with respect to acts of terrorism carried out by private individuals. However, it is worth recalling that in recent time the use of force by or against non-state actors has increasingly attracted the attention of international law scholars. For a general discussion of this question with respect to a recent case of international practice, *see* E. Cannizzaro, 'Entités non-étatiques et régime international de l'emploi de la force. Une étude sur le cas de la réaction israélienne au Liban', 111 *RGDIP* (2007), p. 331.

[136] *See* infra Chapter 4.

[137] GA Resolution n. 3314 (XXIX) adopted on 14 December 1974.

'aggressive war' was given in the judgment. The only general definition of aggressive war we can infer from the judgment is that of an illegal use of armed force by state A to attack state B.[138] By contrast, 'aggressive acts' seemed to imply a simple threat to use armed force and under such circumstances individual criminal liability was apparently excluded. Accordingly, the Nuremberg Charter, as interpreted by the IMT, criminalized as crimes against peace acts by individuals leading to an armed attack by state A against state B, and the consequences of maintaining a domination of state B. Indeed, not only were German leaders convicted for the launching of twelve aggressive wars but also for crimes against peace, which included the carrying out of occupation policies. The exclusion of acts of aggression from crimes against peace was challenged in the subsequent Nuremberg proceedings.[139] However, a broad interpretation of the material element of the crime of aggression has arguably been rejected both in the ILC's Draft Code of Crimes and in the GA Definition of Aggression.

Article 16 of the 1996 Draft Code reads as follows: "an individual who, as leader or organizer, actively participates in or orders the planning, preparation, initiation or waging of aggression committed by a State shall be responsible for a crime of aggression." Except for the fact that it simply speaks of aggression and not of war of aggression, this provision completely relies on the *Nuremberg* precedent. The previous provision on the crime of aggression, drafted by the ILC in 1954, embodied a much broader and much more controversial definition. Article 2(1) provided that "any act of aggression" is a crime against the peace and security of mankind, including "activities calculated to foment civil strife" (Article 2(5)), "annexation" (Article 2 (8)) and "coercive measures of an economic or political character" (Article 2(9)). However, this Article was deleted during the second lecture of the Draft Code of Crimes and neither new Article 16 nor its commentary provide for a definition of aggression. The ILC has preferred to refer to the concept of aggression used in the *Nuremberg* judgment and not to codify highly controversial scenarios of aggression.

---

138 'Against another state' because war, in general, is a matter involving states, and aggressive wars, in particular, are considered to be the violation of the distinctive feature of states: their sovereignty. 'Illegal' because the use of armed force is in violation of international law: Germany violated not only specific treaties but also a general customary rule prohibiting the use of war as a means of pursuing national politics. 'Through the use of armed force' because, according to the International Military Tribunal, other situations where armed force was not used – the Austrian *Anschluss*, for example – were considered simply to be *acts* of aggression and not wars of aggression.

139 In the *Ministries* case (US Nuremberg Military Tribunal, *Von Weizsäcker et al.*, 14 April 1949, 16 *ILR* (1949), pp. 344–362), the American Military Tribunal held that the invasions of Austria (1938) and Czechoslovakia (1939) were acts of aggression and accordingly crimes against peace (at 347). These nations surrendered without firing a shot. The charge of aggression therefore concerned an overwhelming military threat, and individual responsibility for crimes against peace was affirmed even in the absence of the use of armed force.

Moreover, a certain vagueness can also serve the purpose of leaving the door open for future developments under customary law.

When compared to international criminal law documents, the GA Definition of Aggression had a much wider scope. It had to identify situations which could give rise to both state and individual responsibility. The definition of aggression is also an important document since – adopted by consensus – it focused only on non-controversial issues which could be agreed upon by the entire international community. The clear outcome of such a process of negotiation was the exclusion from the definition of aggression of interpretations which aimed at broadening the concept of use of force beyond that of armed force, or the definition of crimes against peace beyond aggressive wars.

The definition took armed force as its basic concept. As stated generally in the preamble, aggression is the "most serious and dangerous illegal use of force". In this definition, 'illegal' means action that is not justified by the UN Charter. Thus, in the light of Article 51, which is the only exception to the use of force embodied in the Charter, the definition of aggression concerned the most serious and dangerous uses of force justifying individual or collective self-defence. Opinions in favour of the inclusion of highly controversial issues such as anticipatory self-defence, economic aggression or ideological aggression were rejected because of a lack of unanimity.[140] On the other hand, there was a general agreement in favour of the inclusion of indirect aggression[141] and the consequences of aggression in terms of territorial acquisition or other advantages deemed unlawful.[142]

In the end, the GA agreed upon a definition of armed aggression which does not broaden the notion applied in Nuremberg. Indeed, Article 5 of the definition is clearly inspired by that precedent. Arguably, Article 5 deals with the consequences of aggression with respect to both states and individuals. In particular, it establishes individual criminal liability in the case of wars of aggression, using the same wording as the IMT did. This was done explicitly – at the insistence of the U.K. – in order to avoid the criminalization of further aggressive acts.[143] The result was the exclusion from Article 5 of simple threats to use armed force, in accordance with the general concept of aggression adopted in the definition.

One problematic aspect in Article 5(2) is that it uses two different wordings to address the issues of state and individual responsibility respectively. While 'aggression' gives rise to state responsibility, only 'wars of aggression' give rise to individual liability. Thus, after the adoption of the definition, the debate focused on the

140 B.B. Ferencz, *Defining International Aggression. The Search for World Peace. A Documentary History and Analysis* (Dobbs Ferry N.Y., Oceana Publications, 1975), p. 30.

141 *See* Article 3(g) of the GA Definition of Aggression.

142 *See* Article 5(3) of the GA Definition of Aggression.

143 B.B. Ferencz, supra note 140, p. 43.

puzzling question of the identification of the difference between aggression and war of aggression.[144] Nonetheless, it seems that the easiest solution is to consider that there is one unitary notion – concerning the most serious cases of illegal use of armed force, such as those listed in Article 3 – of aggression giving rise to both aggravated state responsibility and individual criminal liability under international law. This conclusion is confirmed by the general reference to 'aggression' or 'act of aggression' indistinctly in the 1996 Draft Code and in the work of the bodies charged to elaborate a definition of aggression under the ICC Statute.

With respect to the ICC Statute, Article 5 on the subject-matter jurisdiction of the Court gives no definition of aggression. The Final Act of the Rome conference established a Preparatory Commission (PrepCom)[145] and entrusted it with the task of drafting the elements of all crimes falling under the Court's jurisdiction (1999–2002).[146] With the entry into force of the Statute, the Assembly of the States Parties decided to continue and complete the work on the crime of aggression,[147] and established a Special Working Group on the Crime of Aggression (SWGCA).[148] Thus, the PrepCom first and subsequently the SWGCA have been entrusted with the difficult task of preparing a provision on aggression. In their proposals, an act of aggression "means an act referred to in the GA Resolution 33 (XXIX) of 14 December 1974 which is determined to have been committed by the State concerned".[149]

Thus, there is a complete overlap between the act of aggression giving rise to aggravated state responsibility and the crime of aggression giving rise to individual criminal liability. In particular, aggression is limited to the serious breaches listed in Article 3 of the UN GA Resolution, while acts such as economic aggression or

144 *See* the different views expressed by J. Stone, *Conflict through Consensus* (Baltimore, Johns Hopkins University Press, 1977); B.B. Ferencz, supra note 140, pp. 43–44; and Y. Dinstein, supra note 134, p. 126.

145 Resolution F of the Final Act of the Rome Conference, <untreaty.un.org/cod/icc/index.html>.

146 For the final proposal, *see* UN Doc. PCNICC72002/2/Add.2, <untreaty.un.org/cod/icc/index .html>.

147 ICC-ASP/1/Resolution 1, <www.icc-cpi.int>.

148 ICC-ASP/4/32, Annex II, p. 371, <www.icç-cpi.int>.

149 *See* UN Doc. PCNICC/2002/2/Add.2, pp. 3–4, <untreaty.un.org/cod/icc/index.html>, and ICC-ASP/6/SWGCA/INF.1, p. 8, <www.icc-cpi.int>. In the SWGCA, two options have been put forward as concerns the definition of the *actus reus* of the crime of aggression: referring to either a state 'armed attack' or to a state 'act of aggression'. The latter solution was generally agreed upon provided that a seriousness threshold is included in the definition of the act of aggression. Thus, the document just referred to proposes to qualify an act of aggression as an act "which, by its character, gravity and scale, constitutes a manifest violation of the Charter of the United Nations" (*ibid.*, p. 11).

the threat to use armed force are excluded from this definition. Thus, the concrete situations constituting such overlaps are the cases of aggression as defined by the GA in 1974, including the consequences of maintaining an occupation. However, it is not possible to exclude any future broadening of such a definition, due for example to a broad interpretation of Article 5 by the ICC relying on judicial precedents such as the *Ministries* case.[150]

The second aspect to be taken into account when establishing the relationship between state and individual responsibility for aggression is the seriousness requirement. Abstractly, this requirement should establish the dividing line between acts of aggression giving rise to aggravated state responsibility and prohibited uses of force entailing 'only' ordinary state responsibility. It seems however that the seriousness requirement is always fulfilled in the crime of aggression. According to the 1974 Definition, aggression is the most serious use of force. Moreover, the seriousness criterion is generally deemed implicit in the definition of aggression.[151] This is confirmed in other provisions of the definition. In particular, Article 3 (g), which deals with indirect aggression, explicitly requires a certain degree of gravity to be met. Indeed, initially indirect aggression was one of the controversial issues hindering the achievement of an agreement among the members of the ILC. Finally, an agreement on the inclusion of indirect aggression was reached but only on condition that the wrongful act is characterized by a degree of seriousness analogous to that of an armed attack.[152]

With respect to individual criminal liability for aggression, a seriousness requirement must be fulfilled as well. International practice and the studies on aggression point to a complete overlap between the material element of aggression in state and individual responsibility. While perfectly possible in theory, at present international criminal law does not provide for the criminal liability of individuals who have carried out act of aggression not reaching a certain degree of seriousness. Therefore, the seriousness requirement can consequently be considered implicit also in individual criminal liability for aggression. This is confirmed not only by the fact that the 1974 Definition addresses the issue of both state and individual

150 *See* the discussion in the PrepCom, UN Doc. PCNICC/2002WGCA/DP.2, <untreaty.un.org/cod/icc/ index.html>, and the SWGCA, ICC-ASP/6/SWGCA/INF.1, p. 3, <www.icc-cpi.int>.

151 *See* the ILC Commentary on Article 19 (ILC, 'Report on the Work of its 28th Session', *YILC* (1976), vol. II, p. 112) and Article 40 (ILC, 'Report on the Work of its 53rd Session', *YILC* (2001), vol. II(2), p. 112).

152 B.B. Ferencz, supra note 140, p. 39.

responsibility, but also by the ILC works on the Draft Code,[153] and the recent work of the Preparatory Committee for the ICC.[154]

All these factors taken together establish a very close relationship between state and individual responsibility for aggression. In both cases the criminal act is the same, and individual criminal liability arises from the same serious breach entailing aggravated state responsibility. Therefore, it seems impossible to speak of dissociation or complete autonomy of individual criminal liability as far as the crime of aggression is concerned. Rather, individual accountability seems closely connected to aggravated state responsibility arising out of the same conduct.

4. *Concluding Observations*

On closer scrutiny, the seriousness requirement – once limited to human rights breaches and then extended to all breaches giving rise to aggravated state responsibility – can play a dual role. On the one hand, it establishes a dividing line between ordinary and aggravated state responsibility. Once the threshold of seriousness is crossed, individual criminal liability overlaps with aggravated state responsibility. On the other hand, it establishes a connection between these two regimes of international responsibility. In particular, it provides for a criterion according to which typical individual crimes, that is, crimes which can be perpetrated by single individuals in isolation from the state apparatus, can nevertheless trigger aggravated state responsibility. In other words, seriousness fills the gap between a rapidly developing international criminal law, which tends towards an 'atomization' of international accountability, and aggravated state responsibility, which focuses on collective criminal phenomena. These two roles were clearly acknowledged by the ICTY in the *Furundžija* case.[155] Conduct amounting to official torture would normally only lead to individual criminal liability. However, when "carried out as an extensive practice of State officials", individual criminal liability overlaps with aggravated state responsibility.

In principle, the seriousness requirement in aggravated state responsibility is different from the pre-requisites under international criminal law. These pre-requisites are different with respect to each category of international crimes. Sometimes there

[153] Commentary on Article 16 of the 1996 Draft Code of Crimes (ILC, 'Report on the Work of its 48th Session', *YILC* (1996), vol. II(2), para. 5). Moreover, the Draft Code confirms the need for a seriousness requirement in order to hold a state responsible for aggression. In particular, the conduct of the state must be "a sufficiently serious violation of the prohibition contained in Article 2, paragraph 4, of the Charter of the United Nations."

[154] *See* UN Doc. PCNICC/2002/2/Add.2, <untreaty.un.org/cod/icc/ index.html>. *See* also supra note 148.

[155] ICTY, *Prosecutor v. Furundžija*, TC, Judgment, 10 December 1998, para. 142.

is no such requirement to be met. In general, no state involvement is ever required in order to find a person accountable for international crimes. The perspective from which international criminal courts look at widespread and systematic crimes is inevitably different from the perspective one assumes when establishing aggravated state responsibility. This requirement can be 'individualized', and established having regard to the personal conduct of the offender, that is, whether his or her acts evidence a pattern of similar criminal acts or whether they reach a certain threshold of magnitude. On the other hand, an inquiry into the seriousness requirement of aggravated state responsibility implies the establishment of a state practice, that is, a sum of criminal acts committed by state organs.

A clear example of these different approaches is provided by the ICTY investigation on the crimes supposedly committed by NATO in Kosovo. It is well-known that, according to the report of the Prosecutor – which was exceptionally made public – "there was no deliberate targeting of civilians or unlawful military targets by NATO during the campaign".[156] First, the investigation focused on a few selected incidents from the many it was provided with. Second, the analysis was carried out by reference to each single incident, in order to ascertain individual liability. Third, the Committee charged with the investigation did not take into account the general pattern of military conduct. In particular, it explicitly refused to evaluate the cumulative effect of such incidents in establishing whether NATO was responsible for breaches of international law on the conduct of warfare. While referring to the *Kupreškić* decision,[157] which could have justified such an approach, the Committee decided that "the mere *cumulation* of such instances, all of which have been lawful, cannot *ipso facto* be said to amount to a crime", but then the Committee never went through such an inquiry. Thus, it found that no *single* incident was in breach of international law. Arguably, if the Tribunal had adopted an approach similar to that used to assess the seriousness requirement under aggravated state responsibility (that is, evaluating the sum of these 'incidents'), this could have led to a completely different solution.[158]

International criminal tribunals have made plain that they are not competent to establish state responsibility.[159] They are not even entrusted with the establishment

[156] ICTY, Prosecutor's Report on the NATO Bombing Campaign, supra the Introduction, note 4.

[157] ICTY, *Prosecutor v. Kupreškić et al.*, TC, Judgment, 14 January 2000, para. 526.

[158] *See* E. Cannizzaro, 'Le operazioni aeree della NATO contro la Repubblica federale di Iugoslavia e il diritto umanitario', 84 *Riv. Dir. Int.* (2001), pp. 133–135.

[159] ICTY, *Prosecutor v. Delalić et al.*, TC, Judgment, 16 November 1998, para. 230. *See* also Y. Jurovics, supra note 59. This seems to be a well-established rule under international criminal law. Accordingly, with the notable exception of Articles 9 and 10 of the Nuremberg Charter on the crime of membership, the jurisdiction of international criminal tribunals is always limited to natural persons. *See* Article 1 of the ICTY Statute (S.C. Res. 827(1993)), Article 1 of the ICTR Statute (S.C. Res. 955(1994)), Article 1 of the ICC Statute (<www.icc-cpi.int>), Article 1 of

of the historical truth, as stated in *Krstić*.[160] Interestingly, this case is one of the two ICTY cases upon which the ICJ essentially relied in finding that genocide in fact occurred in Srebrenica.[161] This is a good example of the inevitable link between state and individual responsibility for international crimes that can be established through the seriousness requirement. It is true that international criminal courts do not investigate issues of state responsibility and are very rigorous in applying the principle of individual criminal liability. However, when they establish facts pertaining to the general criminal context, and in particular facts in which a state is involved, this can have a deep impact in the parallel establishment of aggravated state responsibility for international crimes.[162]

In practice, the foregoing analysis has revealed that at a closer look the seriousness of the prohibited conduct amounting to an international crime represent a significant point of contact between state and individual responsibility. A case-by-case analysis of the various categories of international crimes shows a general overlap of the prohibited conduct entailing state and individual responsibility.

First, there are international crimes whose definition does not require a 'seriousness' element to be met to entail individual criminal liability. This is the case for example of official torture or certain war crimes. If committed by state organs, such crimes trigger both ordinary state responsibility and individual criminal liability. Only once the seriousness threshold is crossed, individual liability will overlap with aggravated state responsibility. Accordingly, both individual and state responsibility will arise in regard to the same serious conduct.

---

the Statute of the Special Court for Sierra Leone (UN Doc. S/2000/915), Article 1 of the Law establishing extraordinary chambers in the Courts of Cambodia, <www.cambodia.gov.kh/krt>. *See* supra Chapter 3. The same point is made by France in its comments to the Draft Articles on State Responsibility (UN Doc. A/CN.4/488, p. 68).

160 ICTY, *Prosecutor v. Krstić*, TC, Judgment, 2 August 2001, para. 2: "The events of the nine days from July 10–19 1995 in Srebrenica defy description in their horror and their implications for humankind's capacity to revert to acts of brutality under the stresses of conflict. In little over one week, thousands of lives were extinguished, irreparably rent or simply wiped from the pages of history. The Trial Chamber leaves it to historians and social psychologist to plumb the depths of this episode of the Balkan conflict and to probe for deep-seated causes. The task at hand is a more modest one: to find, from the evidence presented during the trial, what happened during that period of about nine days and, ultimately, whether the defendant in this case, General Krstić, was criminally responsible, under the tenets of international law, for his participation in them. The Trial Chamber cannot permit itself the indulgence of expressing how it feels about what happened in Srebrenica, or even how individuals as well as national and international groups not the subject of this case contributed to the tragedy. *This defendant, like all others, deserves individualized consideration and can be convicted only if the evidence presented in court shows, beyond a reasonable doubt, that he is guilty of acts that constitute crimes covered by the Statute of the Tribunal*" (emphasis added).

161 ICJ, *Genocide* case, supra the Introduction, note 1.

162 *See* infra Chapter 7.

Second, there are international crimes which are *per se* serious, and which by definition require the involvement of the state in their perpetration. This is notably the case with aggression, a crime in which individual criminal liability is dependent upon the previous establishment of aggravated state responsibility. Moreover, despite the dearth of international practice concerning such cases, there may be certain war crimes in which the establishment of a substantial involvement of the state military apparatus proves essential to ascribing individual criminal liability.[163] These categories of international crimes entail a clear overlap between aggravated state responsibility and individual criminal liability, since the same conduct trigger both kinds of international responsibility.

Third, there are international crimes characterized by a collective dimension which nonetheless does not necessarily imply an involvement at the state level. While this seriousness element seems differently reflected in the rules governing state and individual responsibility respectively, international practice shows a correspondence in the establishment of the serious conduct entailing both kinds of international responsibility for crimes like genocide or crimes against humanity. In particular, international case law increasingly tends to focus on the collective dimension of these international crimes.

Due to its primary function of establishing personal liability and to the whole set of principles elaborated accordingly, international criminal law might seem at first not prepared to deal efficiently with 'system' criminality.[164] International crimes are generally carried out at the collective level, if not with a substantial involvement of states, and it can be very difficult to ascribe individual liability for similar offences. However, international criminal tribunals have been prepared at least to adopt a particular methodology to establish individual criminal responsibility: individuals who have committed single prohibited acts can be convicted where their conduct fits into a broader criminal context that the tribunal has previously ascertained. Indirectly, this requires the international criminal tribunal to establish first that international crimes have been committed at the collective level. The assessment of the general criminal context largely correspond to a finding of a serious breach which could entail aggravated state responsibility, if carried out by state organs. There are even cases in which the state involvement in the criminal context has been explicitly taken into account. If this particular methodology does not lead to an identity in the establishment of aggravated state responsibility and individual criminal liability (in the sense that it is not required to establish aggravated state

---

163 For a comparative analysis between aggression and war crimes, *see* Y. Dinstein, 'The Distinctions between War Crimes and Crimes against Peace', in Y. Dinstein and M. Tabory (eds.), *War Crimes in International Law* (The Hague, M. Nijhoff, 1996), p. 1 et seq.

164 B.V.A. Röling, 'The Significance of the Laws of War', in A. Cassese (ed.), *Current Problems of International Law* (Milano, Giuffré, 1975), pp. 137–139.

responsibility first, in order to ascribe then individual liability), nonetheless it marks a significant point of contact between the two regimes, since the same criminal context is relevant to establish both kinds of international responsibility.

Chapter 4

The Overlap of the Psychological Element: *Mens Rea* v. Fault

Turning to the psychological element of international crimes, international practice shows that this can represent another important point of contact between aggravated state responsibility and individual criminal liability. This element is normally qualified as *mens rea* under international criminal law, and as fault with respect to state responsibility.

In the former case, the *mens rea* is a fundamental ingredient of individual liability for international crimes, as international criminal law is grounded on the principle of personal culpability. Accordingly, the psychological participation in the offence must always be proved for the accused to be convicted of international crimes. In other words, the *mens rea* is a basic element of individual criminal liability.[1] There are various degrees of *mens rea* under international criminal law,[2] but this fundamental requirement must always be established beyond reasonable doubt. The *mens rea* is a characterizing feature of criminal law in the sense that it is universally recognized that no person can be held criminally liable if no psychological participation can be shown on his part. The same is true with respect to international criminal law.[3]

Under the law of state responsibility the existence of a fault requirement is more controversial. However, there may be international crimes requiring the proof of a psychological element also to establish aggravated state responsibility.

This overlap raises the question of the relationship between state and individual responsibility as far as the psychological element is concerned. Taking, for example, genocide and assuming that a psychological element – a genocidal intent – is required under both international criminal law and aggravated state responsibility, then the question is whether the state genocide intent is identical to the *mens rea* that must be established with respect to individual perpetrators, or whether the collective intent of the state is something different from the *mens rea* of a natural person.

---

[1] *See* supra the Introduction.

[2] *See* A. Cassese, *International Criminal Law* (Oxford, Oxford University Press, 2003), pp. 159–178.

[3] *Ibid.*, p. 137.

In order to address this question, the analysis will briefly concentrate on the more controversial definition of the psychological element under the law of state responsibility, and the way in which the relationship between state and individual responsibility with respect to this element can be abstractly conceived of. Then the relevant international practice will be examined in some detail.

1. *The Psychological Element and State Responsibility*

With respect to state responsibility, the question of fault has always been a very controversial issue. International law scholars are split between supporters of fault as a requirement under state responsibility, and those affirming that no such an element is necessary to establish states' international responsibility.[4]

The ILC codification work does not seem to have put an end to the debate. It is true that Article 2 does not list fault among the elements of state internationally wrongful acts.[5] However, diverging views have been expressed according to which fault still has a certain role to play in the law of state responsibility.

---

[4] *See*, in particular, D. Anzilotti, *Teoria generale della responsabilità dello Stato nel diritto internazionale* (Firenze, Lumachi, 1902); G. Sperduti, 'Sulla colpa in diritto internazionale', 3 *Comun. e Stud.* (1950), pp. 79–104; A. Carlebach, *Le problème de la faute et sa place dans la norme du droit international* (Paris, LGDJ, 1962); I. Brownlie, *International Law and the Use of Force by States* (Oxford, Clarendon Press, 1963), p. 166; R. Luzzatto, 'Responsabilità e colpa in diritto internazionale', 51 *Riv. Dir. Int.* (1968), pp. 53–107; R. Ago, 'La colpa nell'illecito internazionale', in *Scritti giuridici in onore di Santi Romano*, vol. III (Padova, Cedam, 1940), pp. 177–206; C. Lombois, 'La culpabilité en droit international', 24 *Annales de l'Université des sciences sociales de Toulouse* (1976), pp. 137–149; P.-M. Dupuy, 'Le fait générateur de la responsabilité internationale des Etats', 188 *RCADI* (1984), pp. 9–183; P.-M. Dupuy, 'Faute de l'Etat et "fait internationalement illicite"', 5 *Droits* (1987), pp. 51–63; P. De Sena, 'Condotta di singoli organi e condotta dell'apparato statale in tema di colpa nell'illecito internazionale', 71 *Riv. Dir. Int.* (1988), pp. 525–553; G. Arangio-Ruiz, 'Second Report on State Responsibility', *YILC* (1989), vol. II(1), p. 1 et seq.; G. Arangio-Ruiz, 'State Fault and the Forms and Degrees of International Responsibility: Questions of Attribution and Relevance', in *Mélanges Michel Virally. Le droit international au service de la paix de la justice et du développement* (Paris, Pedone, 1991), pp. 25–42; J. Salmon, 'L'intention en matière de responsabilité internationale', in *Mélanges Michel Virally. Le droit international au service de la paix de la justice et du développement* (Paris, Pedone, 1991), pp. 413–422; A Gattini, 'La notion de la faute à la lumière du projet de convention de la Commission du droit international sur la responsabilité internationale', 3 *EJIL* (1992), pp. 253–284; G. Palmisano, 'Colpa dello Stato e colpa dell'organo nella responsabilità internazionale: spunti critici di teoria e di prassi', 19–20 *Comun. e Stud.* (1992), pp. 623–755; G. Palmisano, 'Les causes d'aggravation de la responsabilité des Etats et la distinction entre "crimes" et "délits" internationaux', 98 *RGDIP* (1994), pp. 629–674; A. Gattini, 'Smoking/No Smoking: Some Remarks on the Current Place of Fault in the ILC Draft Articles on State Responsibility', 10 *EJIL* (1999), pp. 397–404.

[5] Article 2 reads: "There is an internationally wrongful act of a State when conduct consisting of an action or omission: (a) Is attributable to the State under international law; and (b) Constitutes a

On the one hand, fault has been regarded as an element of attribution, when the primary norm breached so requires. In other words, attribution of a wrongful act to the state means both attribution of prohibited conduct under international law carried out by a state organ, and attribution of the intent of the state organ.[6] If no intent of the organ can be proved, attribution of the prohibited conduct alone would not be sufficient to entail state responsibility. Thus, state fault corresponds to the *mens rea* of the state organ. This conception is grounded on ancient state practice concerning injuries to aliens. When the ILC started its codification work, international practice on state responsibility substantially concerned cases of injuries to aliens in which state responsibility was invoked for isolated wrongful acts committed by a state to the detriment of another state's nationals. With respect to similar cases, it is arguably possible to equate the conduct of the state with that of the organ committing the international wrongful act. Thus, the old conception according to which there is a perfect identity between the legal person (the state) and the physical person (the monarch) was still regarded as applicable, at least with respect to isolated wrongful acts. In similar cases, it is argued, it is possible to identify state fault with the organs' *mens rea*.[7]

On the other hand, the codification of circumstances precluding wrongfulness is regarded by some authors as requiring that, at least indirectly, no fault of the state ought to be present in order to engage its international responsibility.[8] In other words, it is for the author state to prove the absence of fault on its part, *i.e.*, it can invoke certain circumstances precluding wrongfulness,[9] while the injured state only has to demonstrate the two requirements listed in Article 2. However, this alternative conception does not directly entail a problem of relationship between state fault and individual *mens rea*. Accordingly, it can temporarily be set aside.[10]

Turning to aggravated state responsibility, in principle no element of fault is required under this regime of secondary norms. Aggravated state responsibility is characterized by the seriousness of the state wrongful act,[11] and it seems difficult to require, in addition, proof of a psychological element of the entire state apparatus. Indeed, the ILC codification of state responsibility confirms that, in principle, fault

breach of an international obligation of the State" (ILC, 'Report on the Work of its 53rd Session', *YILC* (2001), vol. II(2), p. 34).

6 *See* R. Ago, supra note 4.

7 P. De Sena, supra note 4.

8 *See* B. Conforti, *Diritto internazionale* (7th edn, Napoli, Editoriale Scientifica, 2006), pp. 333–4; A. Gattini, 'La notion de la faute à la lumière du projet de convention de la Commission du droit international sur la responsabilité internationale', supra note 4, p. 253.

9 These are provided under Articles 20 to 25 of the 2001 ILC Draft Articles on State Responsibility (ILC, 'Report on the Work of its 53rd Session', *YILC* (2001), vol. II(2), pp. 72–80).

10 Circumstances precluding wrongfulness will be examined in detail infra in Chapter 5.

11 *See* supra Chapter 3.

has no role under such a special form of state responsibility. Article 40 does not mention fault[12] and Article 26 excludes the possibility of invoking circumstances precluding wrongfulness in case of serious breaches.[13] Therefore, a general requirement of fault is not taken into account either directly as an element of aggravated state responsibility, or indirectly as a circumstance precluding wrongfulness.

However, to say that fault has no role in aggravated state responsibility may be problematic since there are certain international crimes which by definition can only be carried out with a specific intent. In other words, there may be primary norms prohibiting certain conduct which require an additional element (fault) to be met, for example the norm prohibiting genocide. Thus, one may ask whether aggravated state responsibility for genocide requires the additional proof that the state apparatus has acted with the intent to destroy the targeted group. Arguably, it does. At least this is the answer generally provided by international law scholars,[14] and confirmed by the few elements of international practice on the subject, such as the Commission for Historical Clarification's Report on Guatemala,[15] the position adopted by Serbia-Montenegro in 1999 before the ICJ,[16] the Report of

[12] Article 40 (1) reads: "This Chapter applies to the international responsibility which is entailed by a serious breach by a State of an obligation arising under a peremptory norm of general international law" (ILC, 'Report on the Work of its 53rd Session', *YILC* (2001), vol. II(2), p. 112).

[13] Article 26 reads: "Nothing in this Chapter precludes the wrongfulness of any act of a State which is not in conformity with an obligation arising under a peremptory norm of general international law" (ILC, 'Report on the Work of its 53rd Session', *YILC* (2001), vol. II(2), p. 84).

[14] *See*, in general, A. Cassese, *International Law* (Oxford, Oxford University Press, 2001), p. 271.

[15] The Report was adopted on February 1999, and para. 111 of the Conclusions dealing with the proof of the genocidal intent reads: "Considering the series of criminal acts and human rights violations which occurred in the regions and periods indicated and which were analysed for the purpose of determining whether they constituted the crime of genocide, the CEH concludes that the reiteration of destructive acts, directed systematically against groups of the Mayan population, within which can be mentioned the elimination of leaders and criminal acts against minors who could not possibly have been military targets, demonstrates that the only common denominator for all the victims was the fact that they belonged to a specific ethnic group and makes it evident that these acts were committed 'with intent to destroy, in whole or in part' these groups (Article II, first paragraph of the Convention)", <shr.aaas.org/guatemala/ceh/report/english/toc.html>.

[16] ICJ, *Case Concerning Legality of Use of Force* (Yugoslavia v. Belgium), Request for the Indication of Provisional Measures, Order, 2 June 1999, *ICJ Reports* 1999, para. 35 ("Yugoslavia contends moreover that the sustained and intensive bombing of the whole of its territory, including the most heavily populated areas, constitutes 'a serious violation of Article II of the Genocide Convention'; whereas it argues that 'the pollution of soil, air and water, destroying the economy of the country, contaminating the environment with depleted uranium, inflicts conditions of life on the Yugoslav nation calculated to bring about its physical destruction'; whereas it asserts that it is the Yugoslav nation as a whole and as such that is targeted; and whereas it stresses that the use of certain weapons whose long-term hazards to health and the environment are already known, and the destruction of the largest part of the country's power supply system, with catastrophic consequences of which

the Commission of Inquiry on Darfur,[17] and finally the ICJ itself.[18] This raises the problem of the relationship between aggravated state responsibility and individual criminal liability.

The question is how the fault element is to be determined when specific intent crimes have been committed by a state. In line with what has already been said, there are two options. A first option is to consider that the specific intent of the state corresponds to the *dolus specialis* of the responsible state organs. In other words, state fault is identified with the *mens rea* of the state organ breaching a primary obligation requiring such an additional element to be met. The major problem concerning this option is that aggravated state responsibility normally arises out of the commission of serious breaches of community obligations, of complex wrongful acts carried out by a plurality of state organs, of a general involvement of the state apparatus. Under such circumstances, it is difficult to identify state fault with the psychological attitude of single state organs. Should we take into account the intent of state leaders?[19] Or would that of low-ranking officials be enough? With respect to isolated international crimes, it might be possible to identify state fault and the organs' intent and therefore to consider that not only the material conduct but also the specific intent of the organ are attributed to the state in order to establish its responsibility. However, in general, international crimes require the involvement of the entire state apparatus, and this line of reasoning is much more difficult to accept.[20] In such cases, it is almost impossible to equate the *mens rea* of the state with that of single state organs, since this psychological element is scattered among a plurality of perpetrators.[21]

Therefore, the second option is to conceive of the specific intent of the state as a 'collective fault' which can be inferred from the overall pattern of criminal state acts. In other words, state fault is no longer connected to the psychological attitude of individual state organs, but it is a more 'objective' standard concerning the purpose

---

the Respondent must be aware, 'impl[y] the intent to destroy, in whole or in part, the Yugoslav national group as such'").

[17] *See* supra Chapter 3, note 25. As already noted, while the Commission decided in principle to focus on individual criminal liability only, its report contained various statements concerning state responsibility for the same international crimes.

[18] ICJ, *Genocide* case, supra the Introduction, note 1, paras. 186–189.

[19] For a similar view as far as the crime of genocide is concerned, *see* W.A. Schabas, *Genocide in International Law. The Crime of Crimes* (Cambridge, Cambridge University Press, 2000), p. 441.

[20] P. De Sena, supra note 4, p. 525 et seq.

[21] L. Cavicchioli, 'Sull'elemento soggettivo nei crimini contro la pace e la sicurezza dell'umanità', 76 *Riv. Dir. Int.* (1993), pp. 1047–1097. *See* more generally P.-M. Dupuy, 'International Criminal Responsibility of the Individual and International Responsibility of the State', in A. Cassese *et al.* (eds.), *The Rome Statute of the International Criminal Court. A Commentary*, vol. II (Oxford, Oxford University Press, 2002), p. 1096; A.B. Loewenstein and S.A. Kostas, 'Divergent Approaches to Determining Responsibility for Genocide', 5 *JICJ* (2007), p. 847.

of a legal entity (the state) which can be demonstrated by the existence, for example, of a criminal policy carried out by the state apparatus.[22] With respect to genocide, it is particularly problematic to identify the state collective intent with the *mens rea* of single state organs. Thus, it can be argued that such a collective intent rather corresponds to an additional objective element of the serious wrongful act, which can "be ascertained by induction through a global analysis of the criminal actions taken by the state against the targeted group".[23] This approach has been upheld by the ICJ in its recent judgment concerning the *Genocide* case.[24]

To sum up, from the standpoint of state responsibility, the relationship between state and individual responsibility as far as the *mens rea*/fault requirement is concerned can be problematic with respect to isolated crimes, if one accepts that fault is a necessary ingredient of state responsibility, and even more problematic with respect to collective crimes requiring a specific intent because of the very different nature of the concepts of *mens rea* and fault under international criminal law and state responsibility respectively.

2. *Theoretical Approaches to the Psychological Element*

Generally, even those international law scholars who have explicitly addressed the issue of the relationship between state and individual responsibility for international crimes have paid very little attention to the psychological element. This is probably due to the fact that the psychological element represents one of the most important differences between state and individual responsibility for international crimes, since no such element is generally required under aggravated state responsibility,[25] but this argument is not elaborated further. From a purely theoretical

[22] *See* G. Arangio-Ruiz, 'State fault and the forms and degrees of international responsibility: Questions of attribution and relevance', supra note 4; G. Palmisano, 'Colpa dell'organo e colpa dello Stato nella responsabilità internazionale: spunti critici di teoria e prassi', supra note 4, p. 623; G. Palmisano, 'Les causes d'aggravation de la responsabilité des Etats et la distinction entre 'crimes' et 'délits' internationaux', supra note 4, p. 667.

[23] ICJ, *Application of the Convention on the Prevention and Punishment of the Crime of Genocide* (Bosnia and Herzegovina v. Serbia and Montenegro), Oral pleadings, 20 April 2006, CR/2006/34, para. 33. This is the position advanced by Bosnia and Herzegovina. For the different position of Serbia and Montenegro, *see* infra note 26.

[24] ICJ, *Genocide* case, supra the Introduction, note 1, paras. 242 and 373. Having carefully taken into account the findings of the ICTY relating to genocide, the Court concluded that Bosnia had not established "the existence of that intent on the part of the Respondent, either on the basis of a concerted plan, or on the basis that the events reviewed above reveal a consistent pattern of conduct which could only point to the existence of such intent" (para. 376).

[25] *See*, in particular, A. Nollkaemper, 'Concurrence between Individual Responsibility and State Responsibility in International Law', 52 *ICLQ* (2003), p. 633; A. Viviani, *Crimini internazionali e responsabilità dei* leader *politici e militari* (Milano, Giuffré, 2005), p. 64.

standpoint, it is however possible to describe two diverging theoretical positions to this issue by relying on the basic assumptions of the individual-oriented and the state-oriented approaches.

The basic assumption of the individual-oriented conceptual scheme posits the dissociation between the conduct of the state and that of its organs. Thus, on the one hand, *mens rea* represents one of the fundamental requirements of international criminal law. As noted above, it is indispensable to prove beyond doubt the psychological participation of the accused in order to convict him or her for international crimes. On the other hand, the regime of state responsibility may or may not require a fault element to be met. However, this is completely irrelevant from the viewpoint of international criminal law. Criminal liability is established with respect to natural persons, not the state, and this is done totally independently of the establishment of either ordinary or aggravated state responsibility. Even if the *mens rea* element overlapped with the fault requirement, this would entail *no relationship* between state and individual responsibility for international crimes.

An opposite solution would derive from the state-oriented conceptual scheme. The basic assumption of this scheme posits the identity between the conduct of the state and that of its organs. State organs are held accountable under international criminal law for serious wrongful acts committed by the state. In this perspective, it is the participation in the state crime which is criminalized under international law, and this requires consistency between the elements of international crimes entailing the criminal liability of state organs and the elements of serious wrongful acts entailing aggravated state responsibility. Therefore, if international crimes require a psychological element to be met this must be established in the same way under both state responsibility and individual liability. According to the different theories of state fault examined above, there are two options.

First, one may share the view according to which state fault corresponds to the *mens rea* of the state organ that committed the serious wrongful act.[26] Therefore, establishing state responsibility preliminarily requires an inquiry into the psychological attitude of state organs. As pointed out above, this methodology can be applied to cases of isolated international crimes or to special international crimes entailing only the criminal liability of state leaders, that is, those organs which represent the state and with which the state can be identified.[27] On the other hand, this methodology is hardly applicable to crimes characterized by a general involvement of the state apparatus. In this case, it is difficult to say which state organs have the intent necessary to entail aggravated state responsibility.

---

[26] ICJ, *Application of the Convention on the Prevention and Punishment of the Crime of Genocide* (Bosnia and Herzegovina v. Serbia and Montenegro), Oral pleadings, 15 March 2006, Statements by Serbia and Montenegro, CR/2006/20, paras. 345–347.

[27] *See* infra in this Chapter.

Alternatively, state fault can be conceived of as a collective fault to be established in a more objective way, and in particular it can be inferred from the general context of state criminality. Thus, having ascertained the collective intent of the state – for instance, a state policy aimed at carrying out certain specific intent crimes – the criminal liability of those state organs which have participated in the commission of these crimes should be more easily established, since their *mens rea* can be inferred from this 'collective intent'.[28] For example, if it is found that a state has carried out a genocidal policy, then state organs having murdered members of the targeted group can be said to have had the necessary genocidal intent if they knew about the state policy, with no need to prove that they personally intended to destroy the targeted group. This different methodology requires criminal tribunals to establish the general context of state criminality first, and then to hold state organs accountable for the role they actually played in this broader criminal context.[29] As a result, both state fault and state organs' *mens rea* can be proved in the same, more objective way, which in the end facilitates the establishment of the psychological element required by some specific intent crimes.

Therefore, according to the former view state fault is identified with the *mens rea* of the responsible state organ, while according to the latter the *mens rea* of the responsible state organs is proved through the collective fault of the author state.

3. *The Psychological Element as Applied in the International Case Law*

From the standpoint of the relationship between state and individual responsibility for international crimes, the psychological element is problematic since it is uncertain whether it is a common element of state and individual responsibility

[28] Some international scholars argue that no *dolus specialis* is required and a lower standard of *mens rea* must be accepted with respect to state organs (at least state leaders) when their psychological attitude can be inferred from the broader context of state criminality. This approach is primarily adopted by supporters of the state-oriented approach. *See* L. May, *Crimes Against Humanity: A Normative Account* (Cambridge, Cambridge University Press, 2005), Chapter 8. However, it must be recalled that a similar approach is also shared by those scholars who would like to see the elements of genocide applied according to its collective dimension. Thus, the specific intent should be a collective intent shared by the members of the criminal group and it should be sufficient to convict single perpetrators having knowledge of this collective specific intent. *See* A.K.A. Greenawalt, 'Rethinking Genocidal Intent: The Case for a Knowledge-Based Interpretation', 99 *Colum. L. Rev.* (1999), pp. 2259–2294; J.R.W.D. Jones, 'Whose Intent is it Anyway?', in L.C. Vohrah *et al.* (eds.), *Man's Inhumanity to Man. Essays on International Law in Honour of Antonio Cassese* (The Hague, M. Nijhoff, 2003), p. 467; C. Kress, 'The Darfur Report and Genocidal Intent', 3 *JICJ* (2005), p. 573; H. Van Der Wilt, 'Genocide, Complicity in Genocide and International v. Domestic Jurisdiction', 4 *JICJ* (2006), pp. 241–244.

[29] *See* supra Chapter 3.

or whether two different requirements apply under these regimes. The present section will examine the relevant international practice focusing only on those international crimes that require such an element to be met under both state and individual responsibility. Therefore, it will not include international crimes, such as crimes against humanity, which certainly require a psychological element to be demonstrated under international criminal law, but which do not require an analogous element to be met under state responsibility.

With respect to isolated crimes, the problematic aspect essentially concerns the regime of state responsibility, that is, whether it requires or not a fault element to be met. If no fault element is provided for under state responsibility, then no question of relationship with international criminal law arises. By contrast, assuming that it does, state and individual responsibility can be reconciled through the approach described above that identifies state fault with the *mens rea* of the responsible state organ. In other words, the same psychological requirement would be applicable to establish both ordinary state responsibility and individual criminal liability for isolated crimes, such as torture or certain war crimes.

Finally, there are collective crimes requiring a specific intent to be demonstrated to entail both state and individual responsibility. The analysis of international case law concerning these category of international crimes is particularly interesting. The proof of the psychological element with respect to crimes committed by large organized groups of perpetrators, *i.e.*, crimes committed in collective frameworks, including state apparatuses, is particularly difficult. On closer examination, it seems possible to discern cases in which the separation between state and individual responsibility tends to blur as far as the psychological element is concerned. Indeed, recent international case law shows an interesting development with respect to certain international crimes in which the *mens rea* is established in a more 'objective' way, by taking into account elements of the general criminal context or the conduct of persons other than the accused but taking part in the commission of the offence. On the other hand, there are international crimes, in whose respect there seems to be a perfect overlap between state and individual responsibility also with respect to the *mens rea*/fault requirement.

A. *Genocide*

The crime of genocide can generally be carried out only by organized groups of perpetrators. As already noted, international tribunals have taken into account the collective nature of the crime of genocide in the establishment of material element of this crime.[30] This is also true with respect to the required *mens rea* of the accused, that is, the genocidal intent.

---

[30] *See* supra Chapter 3.

Genocide requires the accused to have the "intent to destroy, in whole or in part, a national, ethnic, racial or religious group, as such". According to a well-established case law, it is certainly possible to demonstrate genocidal intent with circumstantial evidence, but the proof of such a particularly high level of *mens rea* can nonetheless be particularly problematic. Indeed, knowledge is not enough. As the ICTY affirmed in *Jelisić*, "[t]he *Akayesu* Trial Chamber found that an accused could not be found guilty of genocide if he himself did not share the goal of destroying in part or in whole a group even if he knew that he was contributing to or through his acts might be contributing to the partial or total destruction of a group".[31]

In general, an inquiry into genocidal intent is supposed to mainly focus on the personal conduct of the offender such as "words or deeds or a pattern of purposeful action that deliberately, consistently, and systematically targets victims on account of their membership of a particular group while excluding the members of other groups".[32] For example, in the so-called *Media Case*[33] the ICTR found Nahimana, Barayagwiza, and Ngeze guilty of genocide for their leading role in the creation and control of those Rwandan media (RTLM and Kangura) that broadcast a message of ethnic hatred and called for violence against the Tutsi population. Thus, in establishing the specific intent of the accused, the Trial Chamber was able to focus essentially on "their individual statements and acts, as well as the message they conveyed through the media they controlled".[34] Indeed, each of the accused had made statements that evidenced their genocidal intent.[35]

Notwithstanding such cases in which the specific intent of genocide can be established quite easily simply by relying on the personal statements and acts of the accused, it can be "very difficult in practice to provide proof of the genocidal intent of an individual if the crimes committed are not widespread and if the crime charged is not backed by an organization or a system".[36] This explains why a significant role can be recognized to the general context in the establishment of the *dolus specialis* characterizing the crime of genocide. Indeed, it is now well established that the genocidal intent can be inferred not only directly – having regard to the acts and utterances of the accused – but also from the general context. As the ICTR said in *Akayesu*:

> The Chamber considers that it is possible to deduce the genocidal intent inherent in a particular act charged from the general context of the perpetration of other culpable

[31] ICTY, *Prosecutor v. Jelisić*, TC, Judgment, 14 December 1999, para. 86 (referring to ICTR, *Prosecutor v. Akayesu*, TC, Judgment, 2 September 1998, paras. 544–547).

[32] K. Kittichaisaree, *International Criminal Law* (Oxford, Oxford University Press, 2001), p. 74.

[33] ICTR, *Prosecutor v. Nahimana et al.*, TC, Judgment, 3 December 2003.

[34] *Ibid.*, para. 957.

[35] *Ibid.*, paras. 966–969.

[36] ICTY, *Prosecutor v. Jelisić*, TC, Judgment, 14 December 1999, para. 101. *See* also ICTR, *Prosecutor v. Kayishema and Ruzindana*, TC, Judgment, 21 May 1999, para. 94.

> acts systematically directed against that same group, whether these acts were committed by the same offender or by others. Other factors, such as the scale of atrocities committed, their general nature, in a region or a country, or furthermore, the fact of deliberately and systematically targeting victims on account of their membership of a particular group, while excluding the members of other groups, can enable the Chamber to infer the genocidal intent of a particular act.[37]

In other words, the *mens rea* of the accused can be inferred from the collective conduct of persons other than the accused himself, even if such persons are unidentified.[38] In particular, one factor of this collective criminal conduct seems to be of paramount importance in establishing the psychological attitude of the accused, namely, the existence of a plan or policy giving rise to acts covered by the definition of genocide. As already noted, the genocidal policy is not a legal ingredient of the crime of genocide.[39] Nonetheless, "in the context of proving specific intent, the existence of a plan or policy may become an important factor in most cases. The evidence may be consistent with the existence of a plan or policy, or may even show such existence, and the existence of a plan or policy may facilitate proof of the crime."[40]

To a certain extent, modern case law also accepts that the *dolus specialis* of the accused may be deduced from acts not amounting by themselves to genocide, such

---

[37] ICTR, *Prosecutor v. Akayesu*, TC, Judgment, 2 September 1998, para. 523.

[38] ICTY, *Prosecutor v. Krstić*, AC, Judgment, 19 April 2004, para. 34; ICTY, *Prosecutor v. Brđanin*, TC, Judgment, 1 September 2004, para. 707.

[39] This results from the wording of Article 4 of the Genocide Convention ("persons committing genocide or any of the other acts enumerated in Article III shall be punished, whether they are constitutionally responsible rulers, public officials or *private individuals*") as well as the interpretation generally given to it. This was explicitly held by the US Court of Appeals, Second Circuit, *Kadić v. Karadžić*, Decision on subject matter jurisdiction, 13 October 1995, 70 F.3d 232; the ICTY, *Prosecutor v. Jelisić*, TC, Judgment, 14 December 1999, para. 100 ("that the drafters of the Convention did not deem the existence of an organization or a system serving a genocidal objective as a legal ingredient of the crime. In so doing, they did not discount the possibility of a lone individual seeking to destroy a group as such."), and is generally acknowledged by international law scholars. *See*, in particular, J. Verhoeven, 'Le crime de génocide. Originalité et ambiguïté', 24 *RBDI* (1991), p. 12; M.C. Bassiouni, *Crimes against Humanity in International Criminal Law* (The Hague, Kluwer Law International, 1999), pp. 246–247; M. Lippman, 'Genocide', in M.C. Bassiouni (ed.), *International Criminal Law*, vol. I (Ardsley, Transnational Publishers, 1999), p. 609; D.D. Ntanda Nsereko, 'Genocide: A Crime against Mankind', in G. Kirk McDonald and O. Swaak-Goldman (eds.), *Substantive and Procedural Aspects of International Criminal Law*, vol. I (The Hague, Kluwer Law International, 2000), p. 134; K. Kittichaisaree, supra note 32, p. 77. However, this does not prevent a few international law scholars from still considering genocide to be an international crime necessarily committed with the state involvement. *See* J. Verhoeven, 'Le crime de génocide. Originalité et ambiguïté', supra in this note, p. 26; R. Maison, 'Le crime de génocide dans les premiers jugements du Tribunal Pénal international pour le Rwanda', 103 *RGDIP* (1999), pp. 144–145.

[40] ICTY, *Prosecutor v. Jelisić*, AC, Judgment, 5 July 2001, para. 48.

as the deliberate destruction of mosques and houses belonging to the members of the targeted group.[41] Accordingly, the task of international tribunals in establishing genocidal intent may be facilitated by relying on various factors pertaining to the broader criminal context, and giving the general background in which genocide is committed. These are the existence of a genocidal policy, of widespread prohibited acts directed against the targeted group, and even of attacks against that group not amounting to its physical destruction.

Now, when looking at international case law and the way in which the genocidal intent has actually been established, one must admit that international tribunals have been cautious in relying too widely on the general criminal context.

On the one hand, the ICTR held that genocidal intent must be established first having regard to the personal conduct of the accused.[42] And, where possible, the Tribunal has inferred the genocidal intent from 'direct evidence'[43] consisting of the personal conduct of the accused, his statements, and his participation in acts amounting to genocide. In other words, there are cases in which the Tribunal was able to deduce the *mens rea* from a 'pattern of purposeful action' of the accused.[44]

---

41 ICTY, *Prosecutor v. Krstić*, TC, Judgment, 2 August 2001, para. 580 ("The Trial Chamber is aware that it must interpret the Convention with due regard for the principle of *nullum crimen sine lege*. It therefore recognizes that, despite recent developments, customary international law limits the definition of genocide to those acts seeking the physical or biological destruction of all or part of the group. Hence, an enterprise attacking only the cultural or sociological characteristics of a human group in order to annihilate these elements which give to that group its own identity distinct from the rest of the community would not fall under the definition of genocide. The Trial Chamber however points out that where there is physical or biological destruction there are often simultaneous attacks on the cultural and religious property and symbols of the targeted group as well, attacks which may legitimately be considered as evidence of an intent to physically destroy the group. In this case, the Trial Chamber will thus take into account as evidence of intent to destroy the group the deliberate destruction of mosques and houses belonging to members of the group."). *See* also ICTY, *Prosecutor v. Karadžić and Mladić*, TC, Review of the Indictments pursuant to Rule 61 of the Rules of Procedure and Evidence, 11 July 1996, paras. 94–95, ICTR, *Prosecutor v. Akayesu*, TC, Judgment, 2 September 1998, para. 524.

42 ICTR, *Prosecutor v. Baghilishema*, TC, Judgment, 7 June 2001, para. 63 ("evidence of the context of the alleged culpable acts may help the Chamber to determine the intention of the Accused, especially where the intention of a person is not clear from what that person says or does. The Chamber notes, however, that the use of context to determine the intent of an accused must be counterbalanced with the actual conduct of the Accused. The Chamber is of the opinion that the Accused's intent should be determined, above all, from his words and deeds, and should be evident from patterns of purposeful action.").

43 ICTR, *Prosecutor v. Kamuhanda*, AC, Judgment, 19 September 2005, para. 82.

44 ICTR, *Kayishema and Ruzindana*, AC, Judgment, 1 June 2001, paras. 158–159. For similar cases *see* ICTR, *Prosecutor v. Musema*, TC, Judgment, 27 January 2000, para. 927; ICTR, *Prosecutor v. Nahimana et al.* ('Media Trial'), 3 December 2003, paras. 957–969; ICTR, *Prosecutor v. Kajelijeli*, TC, Judgment, 1 December 2003, para. 828; ICTR, *Prosecutor v. Niyitegeka*, TC, Judgment, 16 May 2003, para. 419; ICTR, *Prosecutor v. Elizaphan and Gerard Ntakirutimana*, TC, Judgment,

From the viewpoint of international criminal law, an individualized approach – in which the *mens rea* of the accused is established having regard to his personal conduct – is certainly preferable. This approach is undoubtedly respectful of the fundamental principle of personal guilt.

On the other hand, there are cases in which it was not possible to establish the *mens rea* of the accused in this direct way. Thus, international *ad hoc* tribunals accepted that, alternatively, it is possible to infer the genocidal intent of the accused from the general criminal context. This is first reflected in the methodology generally adopted to prove such a particular requirement. International tribunals generally start by considering the general context in which genocide has been perpetrated and, in particular, whether a genocidal plan or policy existed at the time covered by the Indictment. Only then is the personal conduct of the accused taken into account. If the general context indicates that a genocidal policy has been elaborated and executed, then it is much easier to establish individual criminal liability. On the contrary, to prove that the accused alone wanted to commit genocide is very difficult, if not almost impossible. In this sense the importance of the broader criminal context clearly emerges from a comparative analysis of the overall work of the ICTY and ICTR.

B. *Genocide: The Role of the General Criminal Context*

In Rwanda, the notorious fact that genocide was perpetrated against the Tutsis was a preliminary issue of considerable importance for the allocation of individual criminal liability. Since its first case (*Akayesu*), the ICTR examined the historical events in Rwanda and established that genocide had been committed against the Tutsis. Almost all the accused before the ICTR have been convicted for genocide, and their *dolus specialis* has been established accordingly.

The ICTY took the same methodological approach. For example, in *Blagojević* the Tribunal held: "the Trial Chamber will first determine whether genocide was committed in July 1995 following the fall of the Srebrenica enclave, and if it determines that it was committed, it will consider the legal requirements for complicity in genocide".[45]

When compared to what happened in Rwanda, the general criminal context during the Balkan conflict did not indicate a clear case of genocide. It was very controversial whether the ethnic cleansing campaign in the former Yugoslavia actually amounted to genocide. Thus, even if it could rely on a general criminal context, establishing the specific intent of the alleged perpetrators of genocide in

---

21 February 2003, paras. 789, and 793; ICTR, *Prosecutor v. Muhimana*, TC, Judgment, 28 April 2005, paras. 513–518. *See* also ICTY, *Prosecutor v. Jelisić*, TC, Judgment, 14 December 1999, paras. 102–108).

[45] ICTY, *Prosecutor v. Blagojević and Jokić*, TC, Judgment, 17 January 2005, para. 638.

the Balkan conflict has been a challenging task for the ICTY. Indeed, only in a few cases has the Prosecutor charged persons with genocide, and the Tribunal has never found that the accused possessed the requisite genocidal intent.[46] These cases are particularly interesting since the *mens rea* of the accused charged with genocide was either absent or impossible to establish merely taking into account his personal conduct, and the Tribunal had to turn to the general criminal context.

The case law of the *ad hoc* tribunals can be classified in three groups as far as the genocidal intent is concerned. First, there are cases in which no genocidal context was established, and the accused possessed no genocidal intent. In most cases dealing with genocide, the ICTY was not able to establish either the existence of a genocidal plan or the genocidal intent of the accused persons, who nonetheless all had a discriminatory intent.[47] In particular, in *Stakić* and *Brđanin* the ICTY affirmed that the political agenda of Bosnian Serb leaders was aimed at the removal and not at the physical destruction of the victim group,[48] and *accordingly* the accused showed a discriminatory not a genocidal intent. In *Krajišnik*, the ICTY proceeded with a two-stage inquiry into genocidal intent, both at the level of the material perpetrators of the relevant crimes and at the level of the leadership of the Srpska Republic, which included the accused. The Tribunal found that the required intent had not been demonstrated by the Prosecution at any level.[49]

Second, there are cases in which the genocidal context was actually established, but the accused possessed no genocidal intent. In *Krstić* and *Blagojević*, the ICTY has in fact found that genocide occurred in Bosnia.[50] However, it was not able to find beyond any reasonable doubt that either Krstić or Blagojević had a genocidal intent. Thus, in *Blagojević* the Tribunal convicted the accused for complicity in

---

46 ICTY, *Prosecutor v. Jelisić*, TC, Judgment, 14 December 1999, para. 107; ICTY, *Prosecutor v. Stakić*, TC, Judgment, 31 July 2003, para. 554; ICTY, *Prosecutor v. Brđanin*, TC, Judgment, 1 September 2004, para. 989; ICTY, *Prosecutor v. Krstić*, AC, Judgment, 19 April 2004, para. 134; ICTY, *Prosecutor v. Blagojević and Jokić*, TC, Judgment, 17 January 2005, para. 786; and ICTY, *Prosecutor v. Krajišnik*, TC, Judgment, 27 September 2006, paras. 867–869.

47 ICTY, *Prosecutor v. Jelisić*, TC, Judgment, 14 December 1999, para. 75; ICTY, *Prosecutor v. Stakić*, TC, Judgment, 31 July 2003, para. 826; ICTY, *Prosecutor v. Brđanin*, TC, Judgment, 1 September 2004, para. 1053, and 1070; and ICTY, *Prosecutor v. Krajišnik*, TC, Judgment, 27 September 2006, para. 1118.

48 ICTY, *Prosecutor v. Stakić*, TC, Judgment, 31 July 2003, para. 553; ICTY, *Prosecutor v. Brđanin*, TC, Judgment, 1 September 2004, para. 981.

49 ICTY, *Prosecutor v. Krajišnik*, TC, Judgment, 27 September 2006, paras. 867–869, and 1091–1094. Interestingly, the Tribunal affirmed that the "peculiarity of the present case, which involves multiple levels of actors, is that a crime committed by a person of low political or military rank without genocidal intent may nevertheless be characterized as an act of genocide if it was procured by a person of higher authority acting with that intent" (ICTY, *Prosecutor v. Krajišnik*, TC, Judgment, 27 September 2006, para. 857).

50 ICTY, *Prosecutor v. Krstić*, TC, Judgment, 2 August 2001, para. 599; and ICTY, *Prosecutor v. Blagojević and Jokić*, TC, Judgment, 17 January 2005, para. 677.

genocide.[51] An aider or abettor only needs to *know* that the principal perpetrators harboured the genocidal intent. The *Krstić* case is more complex. In the trial judgment the ICTY found that genocide had been committed by Bosnian Serb forces, and that Krstić *shared* the genocidal intent with other participants in a joint criminal enterprise aimed at the destruction of the Bosnian Muslim population of Srebrenica.[52] However, the Appeals Chamber reversed the trial judgment. According to the Appeals Chamber, the evidence showed that the accused *knew* of the existence of a genocidal plan, but this was not sufficient to infer that he also shared this specific intent with the principal perpetrators of the said joint criminal enterprise.[53] Since the accused did not have genocidal intent, the appropriate form of his responsibility was aiding and abetting.[54]

Third, there are cases in which genocidal context was established, and the accused had the requisite genocidal intent. These are cases in which the impossibility of inferring genocidal intent from the personal conduct of the accused is 'counterbalanced' this time with a wide reliance on the broader criminal context. As noted above, the ICTR has proved the genocidal intent having mainly regard to the personal conduct of the accused. The ICTR has generally viewed that the acts of genocide entailing the individual criminal liability of the accused as part of the broader criminal context in Rwanda. However, it had the occasion to specify that the genocidal intent was established taking into account the personal conduct of the accused and not merely inferred from the overall genocidal campaign.[55] More interesting are those cases in which the general context played a substantial role before the ICTR. Thus, in *Kayishema*, notwithstanding the contrary view of the

---

[51] ICTY, *Prosecutor v. Blagojević and Jokić*, TC, Judgment, 17 January 2005, paras. 785–786.

[52] ICTY, *Prosecutor v. Krstić*, TC, Judgment, 2 August 2001, para. 633.

[53] ICTY, *Prosecutor v. Krstić*, AC, Judgment, 19 April 2004, paras. 100–134.

[54] Aiding and abetting as a form of complicity does not require specific intent to be demonstrated but only requires the accused to be aware, to know that the principal perpetrator has the requisite *dolus specialis*.

[55] The Appeals Chamber in *Rutaganda* explicitly held that "the Appellant was not convicted of the crime of genocide on the basis of any particular theory of guilt by association. Paragraph 399 of the Trial Judgment clearly shows that the Trial Chamber found that the Appellant was possessed of the specific intent based on his specific acts, namely his direct participation in the widespread massacres committed against the members of the Tutsi group, and his ordering and abetting the commission of crimes against the Tutsi. The Trial Chamber also noted that the victims were systematically selected on account of their membership of the Tutsi group. Viewed in its context, the additional reference to the Appellant's position of authority underscores the impact of his presence at the scene of the crimes and his exceptional ability to aid and abet the commission of the said crimes against members of the Tutsi group, due to the position of influence he held in the community. Furthermore, it emerges from the Trial Judgment that the Trial Chamber considered the impact of the general context of the acts aimed at destroying the Tutsi group after having noted, based on the Appellant's acts, that he had indeed the specific intent." (ICTR, *Prosecutor v. Rutaganda*, AC, Judgment, 26 May 2003, paras. 529–530).

Appeals Chamber,[56] the Trial Chamber seems to rely essentially on the existence of a genocidal plan implemented at prefecture levels (Kayishema was the Prefect of Kibuye), on the number of victims, on the methodical character of the planned and programmed massacres, on the superior position of the accused, and on the utterances by the accused and *other* individuals.[57] Similarly, in *Ndindabahizi* the ICTR strongly relies on the general context, the superior position of the accused (Minister of Government), and on the fact that he "was well aware that his remarks and actions were part of a wider context of ethnic violence, killing and massacres in Rwanda during this period."[58] Finally, in *Simba* genocidal intent was established as follows: "Given the scale of the killings and their context, the only reasonable conclusion is that the assailants who physically perpetrated the killings possessed the intent to destroy in whole or in part a substantial part of the Tutsi group. This genocidal intent was shared by all participants in the joint criminal enterprise, including Simba."[59]

In the description of the Tribunal, the conduct of the accused appears to be essentially characterized as aiding and abetting and his *mens rea* corresponds to knowledge. However, the Trial Chamber convicted him for participation in a joint criminal enterprise, and strongly relied on the general criminal context to infer that all the participants thereto must have shared the genocidal intent.[60] In comparison, a more rigorous approach has been adopted by the ICTY in the just mentioned *Krstić* case. As already noted, the Trial Chamber finding on the genocidal intent of the accused[61] was reversed by the Appeals Chamber because all that could be reasonably inferred from the facts pleaded at trial was that the accused had knowledge of the genocidal intent of the other perpetrators, but did not share it.

This case law shows above all that there are no cases in which the accused was found to have the requisite genocidal intent, in the absence of a broader genocidal context. That is, the genocidal intent has always been established in connection to the existence of a genocidal campaign. Accordingly, the general criminal context has played a pivotal role in establishing the genocidal intent of the accused. In fact the *dolus specialis* of the defendant charged with genocide can be substantially

---

[56] ICTR, *Prosecutor v. Kayishema and Ruzindana*, AC, Judgment, 1 June 2001, para. 148.

[57] ICTR, *Prosecutor v. Kayishema and Ruzindana*, TC, Judgment, 21 May 1999, paras. 527–540.

[58] ICTR, *Prosecutor v. Ndindabahizi*, TC, Judgment, 15 July 2004, para. 463.

[59] ICTR, *Prosecutor v. Simba*, TC, Judgment, 13 December 2005, para. 416.

[60] The conviction of Simba has been confirmed on appeal: ICTR, *Prosecutor v. Simba*, AC, Judgment, 27 November 2007, para. 269.

[61] ICTY, *Prosecutor v. Krstić*, TC, Judgment, 2 August 2001, para. 572. ("the killings were planned: the number and nature of the forces involved, the standardised coded language used by the units in communicating information about the killings, the scale of the executions, the invariability of the killing methods applied, indicate that a decision was made to kill all the Bosnian Muslim military aged men."). *See* also paras. 606–645.

inferred the general criminal context when it is shown that he or she took part in the genocidal campaign.

The *ad hoc* tribunals have adopted a methodology according to which the general context is investigated first, and only subsequently is the *mens rea* of the accused established in connection to that general context. Thus, there are cases in which the genocidal intent is substantially inferred from the general criminal context, and therefore established in a more 'objective' manner, and even independently from the intent of the material perpetrators.[62] This methodology has been both criticized and strongly supported.[63] In any case, a more 'objective' *mens rea* can be essential in dealing with collective crimes like genocide, which are characterized by a collective intent. Otherwise, this particular psychological element would be almost impossible to prove in most cases. Even though the genocidal context does not correspond to a state policy, this dramatically reduces the distance between individual criminal liability and aggravated state responsibility. Both the specific intent of the accused and state fault are established, with respect to genocide, having regard to the same general criminal context.[64]

Finally, there is another way of facilitating the establishment of individual criminal liability for genocide which characterizes certain cases brought before the *ad hoc* tribunals. They have relied on modes of liability requiring a lower psychological element to be met. Genocidal intent is particularly difficult to demonstrate because of the collective dimension of the crime of genocide. Therefore, relying on particular modes of liability specifically elaborated to deal with collective crimes, whose elements are shared by a multiplicity of perpetrators, can make it easier to establish this specific intent. For example, an accused can be charged with 'aiding and abetting' in the commission of genocide, a form of liability which only requires *knowledge* of the genocidal campaign. The same is arguably true with respect to 'joint criminal enterprise'.[65] Of course, the accused charged under joint criminal enterprise needs to have had genocidal intent, but the psychological element is

---

[62] *See* supra note 49 and accompanying text.

[63] Strong criticism has been expressed by G.P. Fletcher and J.D. Ohlin, 'Reclaiming Fundamental Principles of Criminal Law in the Darfur Case', 3 *JICJ* (2005), pp. 545–548. *See* also R. Maison, supra note 39, p. 139; W.A. Schabas, supra note 19, pp. 222–224; S.R. Ratner and J.S. Abrams, *Accountability for Human Rights Atrocities in International Law* (Oxford, Oxford University Press, 2001), p. 37; Y. Jurovics, *Réflexions sur la spécificité du crime contre l'humanité* (Paris, LGDJ, 2002), pp. 320–321; A. Cassese, 'Genocide', in A. Cassese *et al.* (eds.), *The Rome Statute of the International Criminal Court. A Commentary*, vol. I (Oxford, Oxford University Press, 2002), p. 344. For the opposite view, *see* supra note 28.

[64] In this respect, it is interesting to compare the *Genocide* case decided by the ICJ (*see* supra the Introduction, note 1) and the ICTY judgment in *Krajišnik* (supra note 49). More generally, the relation between the establishment of state and individual responsibility for the same international crimes is examined below (*see* infra Chapter 7).

[65] *See* infra Chapter 6.

shared by the members of this enterprise. Thus, it is much easier to demonstrate that the accused *shared* the specific intent with other perpetrators than to prove he alone intended to destroy the targeted group by his actions.

Similarly, one may share the view that command responsibility does not require proof of genocidal intent on the part of the commander, who must only have knowledge that his subordinates have committed genocide.[66] The issue is still controversial since international tribunals at first took diverging positions. The ICTR has generally convicted those responsible for genocide under both Article 6(1) and Article 6(3) of its Statute. Therefore, in these cases genocidal intent was already demonstrated. On one occasion, it had convicted an accused for genocide under the doctrine of command responsibility, without showing its genocidal intent.[67] The ICTY, on the other hand, at first excluded the possibility of relying on command responsibility where the commander or his subordinates do not have genocidal intent.[68] However, in two more recent judgments the Tribunal seems to have reviewed its position, holding that command responsibility does not require a showing that the accused has genocidal intent.[69]

Thus, under certain modes of liability which specifically aim at collective forms of perpetration of international crimes, individuals can be convicted for genocide without showing that they individually possessed a genocidal intent. Their *mens rea* is essentially established having regard to the general criminal context, that is, the same facts that could be investigated to establish state fault. This confirms the fundamental role played by the general criminal context in the ascertainment of individual criminal responsibility, and points out a significant similarity in the establishment of state and individual responsibility for genocide.

---

66 Command responsibility takes into account the case of crimes carried out by members of an *organized group* – be it a military group or otherwise. Under such circumstances, a lower threshold of *mens rea* with respect to genocide can be justified in the light of the 'institutional' role of superiors and of the broader and more complex framework in which such collective crimes are generally carried out. *See* A. Cassese, supra note 2, p. 211, and W.A. Schabas, supra note 19, pp. 226–229. For a more critical approach, *see* K. Ambos, 'Superior Responsibility', in A. Cassese *et al.* (eds.), *The Rome Statute of the International Criminal Court. A Commentary*, vol. I (Oxford, Oxford University Press, 2002), p. 871.

67 ICTR, *Prosecutor v. Ntagerura et al.*, TC, Judgment, 25 February 2004, para. 654. The conviction of Imanishimwe for genocide under Article 6(3) of the ICTR St. was set aside by the Appeals Chamber because the relevant charges had not been properly pleaded in the indictment (ICTR, *Prosecutor v. Ntagerura et al.*, AC, Judgment, 7 July 2006, paras. 164–165).

68 ICTY, *Prosecutor v. Stakić*, TC, Judgment, 31 July 2003, para. 559.

69 ICTY, *Prosecutor v. Brđanin*, TC, Judgment, 1 September 2004, para. 718; ICTY, *Prosecutor v. Blagojević and Jokić*, TC, Judgment, 17 January 2005, para. 686.

C. *War Crimes*

Generally, war crimes are not specific-intent crimes. However, there are some primary norms prohibiting conduct amounting to war crimes and requiring such a *dolus specialis*. A recent case before the ICTY has in fact dealt with a specific intent war crime. This case merits a closer examination because the Tribunal has widely relied on the general criminal context to infer the *mens rea* of the accused.

In *Galić*, an international tribunal for the first time convicted an individual for the 'crime of terror against the civilian population'. Indeed the Tribunal found that such a crime has legal basis under a rule of customary international law.[70] General Galić has been held responsible for having ordered a "protracted campaign of shelling and sniping upon civilian areas of Sarajevo and upon the civilian population thereby inflicting terror and mental suffering upon its civilian population".

The Trial Chamber of the ICTY did not list seriousness among the elements of this particular violation of the laws and customs of war.[71] However, the Prosecutor insisted on demonstrating that this crime was carried out in a widespread and systematic manner. Although unnecessary, this additional element was finally essential to proving the *mens rea* of the accused. Indeed, the crime of terror against the civilian population was treated by the Trial Chamber as a specific-intent crime, thus requiring a *dolus specialis* to be demonstrated. In this case, it had to be established that the accused had the specific intent of terrorizing the civilian population.

As with the cases dealing with genocide examined above, the general context and the proof of a widespread pattern of criminal conduct has substantially helped the Prosecutor in proving such a particular *mens rea*.[72] In *Galić*, the Trial Chamber first established that the accused knew that his subordinates had committed the crimes proved at trial having due regard to their 'seriousness'.[73] This allowed the Tribunal to find Galić's command responsibility.[74] Then, the Tribunal turned to

---

[70] ICTY, *Prosecutor v. Galić*, Trail Chamber, TC, Judgment, 5 December 2003.

[71] *Ibid.*, para. 133.

[72] *Ibid.*, paras. 703–706, and 741–747. The same reasoning was accepted and applied by the IACHR in *Velásquez* (supra Chapter 3, note 20 and accompanying text) where it had to establish state responsibility for serious breaches of human rights.

[73] *See* supra Chapter 3.

[74] ICTY, *Prosecutor v. Galić*, TC, Judgment, 5 December 2003, paras. 703–705: "it would be inconceivable that given the importance of artillery assets for a Corps commander, especially one with an infantry disadvantage, the Accused was not fully appraised of the use of SRK artillery. At a minimum, and as mentioned by witnesses, the daily ammunition expenditure had to be recorded and be known. *The Trial Chamber has already made findings in relation to the widespread character of unlawful activities. These criminal activities had to be carried out by using a vast amount of ammunition. The rate of use of ammunition which would have been in excess of what was required for regular military operations, is among the reasons which allow the Trial Chamber to infer that the Accused knew of criminal activities by his troops.* The Trial Chamber is convinced that the Accused, as a Corps commander, was in full control of SRK artillery assets and knew of the rate of use of

his direct responsibility for having ordered the unlawful campaign of sniping and shelling civilians in Sarajevo. And the specific intent of the accused was essentially inferred from the general context:

> According to the Majority, there is an irresistible inference to be drawn from the evidence on the Trial Record that what the Trial Chamber has found to be widespread and notorious attacks against the civilian population of Sarajevo could not have occurred without it being the will of the commander of those forces which perpetrated it and that the lack of measures to prevent illegal sniping and shelling activities was deliberate.[75]

The crime of terror against the civilian population is a particular crime requiring a certain organization and various persons for its execution. The specific intent is necessarily scattered among the perpetrators, and this element may be difficult to prove unless the general context is duly taken into account.[76] As noted above, this approach may be very useful in ascribing individual liability for collective crimes. From a more general perspective, this results in establishing a closer connection between state and individual responsibility. At a minimum, even with respect to certain collective war crimes, this case shows the need to establish some form of co-ordination between these two regimes of international responsibility, which cannot be achieved by relying too rigorously on the principle of individual criminal liability alone.

D. *Aggression*

The crime of aggression merits particular attention. As already noted, aggression is characterized by a complete overlap between aggravated state responsibility and individual criminal liability as far as the material element is concerned. The same is true with respect to the subjective element.

Indeed, only political and military leaders can be held accountable for this crime under international criminal law. It must be stressed that, in theory, nothing prevents the international legal order from regarding aggression as an international crime which can also be committed by private individuals.[77] However, international

---

ammunition. Third, *in view of the circumstances which prevailed during the conflict, the notoriety of certain of the incidents scheduled in the Indictment and the systematic character of these criminal acts which extended over a prolonged period of time, in conjunction with the media coverage of which the SRK Corps command was aware, renders the Accused's professed ignorance untenable.* The Trial Chamber finds that General Galić, beyond reasonable doubt, was fully appraised of the unlawful sniping and shelling at civilians taking place in the city of Sarajevo and its surroundings." (emphasis added).

[75] *Ibid.*, para. 742. *See* also paras. 745–746.

[76] For a similar case, *see* ICTY, *Prosecutor v. Milošević*, TC, Judgment, 12 December 2007.

[77] In this sense, *see* L. Condorelli, 'Conclusions Générales', in M. Politi and G. Nesi (eds.), *The International Criminal Court and the Crime of Aggression* (Aldershot, Ashgate, 2004), pp. 156–157.

practice reveals a completely different conception of aggression, which is strictly defined in terms of state action.

The *Nuremberg* judgment held that possible perpetrators of crimes against peace were members of a government, persons having high-level posts in the military, diplomats, politicians and industrialists.[78] While the IMT tried those individuals who were in control and who had established the German policy resulting in crimes against peace, the subsequent trials had to deal with the same offences but the defendants were either low-ranking officers or private individuals. In particular, the question of who could be held accountable for aggression was examined in the *Farben* case.[79] The issue was addressed in practical terms: the Tribunal held that it was not possible to depart from the concept that only 'major war criminals' may be held liable for waging wars of aggression; otherwise, the result would be the possibility of collective guilt and mass punishments.[80] "The participation [of the defendants] was that of the followers and not leaders. If we lower the standard of participation to include them, it is difficult to find a logical place to draw the line between the guilty and the innocent among the great mass of German people."[81]

Thus, the Tribunal decided not to depart from the mark already set by the IMT, according to which only 'high public officials' and 'high military officers' can be responsible for the crime of aggression.

International criminal law has not departed from this principle, and today aggression is commonly regarded as a 'leadership crime'.[82] This has the practical

---

78 IMT Judgment, supra Chapter 1, note 90, p. 223.

79 US Nuremberg Military Tribunal, *Krauch and Others* (*Farben* case), 29 July 1948, 15 *ILR* (1948), p. 678 et seq.

80 *Ibid.*, p. 669 ("Under such circumstances there would be no practical limitation on criminal responsibility that would not include, on principle, the private soldier on the battlefield, the farmer who increased his production of foodstuffs to sustain the armed forces, or the housewife who conserved fats for the making of munitions. Under such a construction the entire manpower of Germany could, at the uncontrolled discretion of the indicting authorities, be held to answer for waging wars of aggression").

81 *Ibid.*, p. 670.

82 Domestic criminal courts have underscored this specific feature of the crime of aggression (*see*, for example, Audiencia Nacional, *Scilingo* case, *Sentencia por crimenes contra la humanidad en el caso Adolfo Scilingo*, 19 April 2005, <www.derechos.org>). On the other hand, this nature of the crime of aggression has been codified by the ILC in Article 16 of the Draft Code of Crimes against the Peace and Security of Mankind. According to the ILC commentary, "the perpetrators of an act of aggression are to be found only in the categories of individuals who have the necessary authority or power to be in a position potentially to play a decisive role in committing aggression" (ILC, 'Report on the Work of its 48th Session', *YILC* (1996), vol. II(2), p. 45, para. 2; *see* also M. Dumée, 'Le crime d'agression', in H. Ascensio *et al.* (eds.), *Droit international pénal* (Paris, Pedone, 2000), p. 251). This clearly shows a complete adherence to the approach of the *Nuremberg* judgment and subsequent trials. Moreover, the fact that aggression is a leadership crime was one of the few uncontroversial starting points of the PrepCom working on Article 5 of the ICC

effect of excluding the criminal responsibility of subordinates. In other words, the crime of aggression exceptionally provides for a complete defence of superior orders which can be invoked by all state organs unless it is demonstrated that they had the necessary authority or power to potentially play a decisive role in committing aggression. Only decision-makers can be held accountable; all other participants are excused. The individuals who can be held accountable are those who represent the state. State leaders are responsible for deciding state policy, and they can entirely posses the required *mens rea*. Therefore, they are the only ones who can properly bear the responsibility on behalf of the state, even if they have not committed any atrocity with their own hands. By contrast, it is *a priori* excluded that executioners in the broad sense possess the requisite *mens rea* and the defence of obedience to superior orders is consequently available to all of them. It is the fact that aggression can only be committed by the state apparatus which justifies such a different conclusion.

This brings us to the psychological element of the crime of aggression. While there is a complete overlap between state and individual responsibility with respect to both the material and the subjective elements of this crime, it is still possible to wonder whether these regimes differ as far as the psychological element is concerned.

International criminal law requires the *mens rea* of the accused to be established, even in case of aggression. Indeed, the planning, preparation, initiation or waging of aggression must be intentional. However, the problem with the psychological element of aggression (*animus aggressionis*) is that this requirement can be interpreted in two different ways, that is, as requiring on the part of the accused either a specific intent to commit aggression or simple knowledge that his conduct is contributing to the perpetration of aggression. If we rely on the only precedents to date, the *Nuremberg* and *Tokyo* judgments, no specific intent is necessary to hold the perpetrator criminally accountable for aggression.[83] To convict the accused

Statute, *see* UN Doc. PCNICC/2002/2/Add.2, p. 4, para. II, <untreaty.un.org/cod/icc/index.html> ("the perpetrator was in a position effectively to exercise control over or to direct the political and military action of the State which committed an act of aggression"). The PrepCom lists only two principles governing individual liability for aggression which are well-established, and the first one is the "principle under which the crime of aggression is committed by political or military leaders of a State" (UN Doc. PCNICC/2001/L.1/Rev.1, 9 March 2001, p. 20, <untreaty.un.org/cod/icc/index.html>). The same view has been confirmed in the work of the SWGCA, *see* ICC-ASP/6/SWGCA/INF.1, p. 3, <www.icc-cpi.int>. The debate in SWGCA concerns the better placement of the leadership clause. While most members agree that it should be included in the definition of the crime of aggression, other members stress the importance to replicate the leadership clause in Article 25 dealing with principle of individual criminal responsibility and the modes of liability for international crimes. Indeed, the leadership nature of the crime of aggression implies that some modes of liability would hardly be applicable to this crime.

83 This is the view generally shared by international law scholars. *See* J. Hogan-Doran and B.T. Van Ginkel, 'Aggression as a Crime under International Law and the Prosecution of Individuals by the

persons for aggression, the IMT relied on the fact that they had *knowledge* of Hitler's aggressive plans.[84]

In principle, the same controversial issue concerns aggravated state responsibility for aggression since it is possible to think either that no state fault must be demonstrated or that the state activity must evidence a specific aggressive purpose. However, it is generally held that no specific intent needs to be demonstrated to establish aggravated state responsibility for aggression.[85] The same result emerges from international practice. In particular, the relevant case law of the International Court of Justice shows that no specific intent is required on the part of a state to show that it has committed aggression.[86]

Accordingly, the psychological element remains a distinguishing feature of individual criminal liability, when compared to aggravated state responsibility, also with respect to the crime of aggression. While state responsibility for aggression can be proved in an objective manner, to hold a state military or political leader accountable for this crime requires the proof of his or her *mens rea*. On the other hand, in order to establish this psychological element an international criminal tribunal will probably rely on the general criminal context. In the end, even if the psychological element is a distinguishing feature of international criminal law, it is possible to assume that the surrounding context (state aggression) will be crucial to demonstrate the knowledge of state leaders that their behaviour is contributing to the commission of an act of aggression. This is not to say that state and individual responsibility for aggression will automatically coincide. For example, the accused can invoke defences excluding that he or she participated in the commission of the crime with the requisite *mens rea*.[87] However, this does not eliminate the fact

---

Proposed International Criminal Court', 43 *NILR* (1996), p. 336; Y. Dinstein, *War, Aggression and Self-Defence* (2d edn., Cambridge, Cambridge University Press, 1994), pp. 139–140; A. Cassese, supra note 2, p. 115; G. Werle, *Principles of International Criminal Law* (The Hague, TMC Asser Press, 2005), p. 399.

[84] *See* IMT Judgment, supra Chapter 1, note 90, in particular with respect to the defendants Schact, Bormann, and Streicher. According to T. Taylor, *The Anatomy of the Nuremberg Trials* (New York, Knopf, 1992), Chapter 8, the IMT required a specific intent only for the crime of conspiracy to commit aggression.

[85] R.J. Alfaro, 'La question de la définition de l'agression', 29 *RDISDP* (1951), p. 380; J. Stone, *Aggression and World Order* (London, Stevens & Sons Limited, 1958), p. 141; J. Zourek, 'Enfin une définition de l'agression', 20 *AFDI* (1974), p. 26; B.B. Ferencz, *Defining International Aggression. The Search for World Peace. A Documentary History and Analysis* (Dobbs Ferry N.Y., Oceana Publications, 1975), p. 31; B. Broms, 'The Definition of Aggression', 154 *RCADI* (1977), p. 345; J. Hogan-Doran and B.T. Van Ginkel, supra note 83, p. 336; Y. Dinstein, supra note 83, p. 131; M. Lippman, 'The History, Development, and Decline of Crimes Against Peace', 36 *The George Washington International Law Review* (2004), p. 1036.

[86] *See* the jurisprudence of the ICJ cited supra Chapter 1, note 44.

[87] *See* infra Chapter 5.

that the psychological element of the accused charged with aggression can widely be inferred from the general criminal context, as noted with respect to other international crimes. And individual and state responsibility for aggression will largely overlap also with respect to this element. It is not to be forgotten that, according to the preparatory works, the ICC will try state leaders for aggression only after the establishment of state responsibility for aggression.[88] Therefore, it would in principle be able to rely on this previous assessment in finding both the material and the psychological element of individual criminal liability for the same crime.

On the other hand, the view has been expressed that aggression should be regarded as a *specific intent* crime.[89] Thus, in order to hold political and military leaders accountable for aggression it must be shown that they intended, for example, to achieve territorial gains or to obtain economic advantages. This also implies that the state act of aggression needs to be carried out with an analogous specific intent. The purpose of the present analysis is not to criticize this peculiar approach, but to see what impact it can have in terms of the relationship between state and individual responsibility for aggression.

Arguably, this approach reveals an even closer relationship between state and individual responsibility, because state fault would in the end correspond to the *dolus specialis* of the state organs whose conduct is attributed to the state. Aggression is a particular international crime because criminal liability is limited to a few state leaders, that is, those decision-makers who represent the state. Accordingly, the *mens rea* of the accused can more easily be identified with state fault.[90] If there is a substantial equivalence between the conduct of the state and that of a limited number of its organs, state fault may be equated with that of a few isolated state organs.[91] The crime of aggression is rooted on the basic assumption of identity between the conduct of the state and its political and military leaders, that is, those organs who can be held responsible on its behalf. Not only is the *actus reus* necessarily a state serious breach of obligations owed to the entire international community, but the only persons who can be held criminally liable are those highest ranking organs representing the state as a whole and deciding the state general

[88] *See* infra Chapter 7.

[89] S. Glaser, 'Culpabilité en droit international pénal', 99 *RCADI* (1960), pp. 504–505. It should be added that the work of the PrepCom for the ICC is not always clear as to whether a specific intent is required in the definition of the crime of aggression. One of the options of this definition (option 1, variation 2) requires the armed attack amounting to aggression to be carried out "with the object or result of establishing a military occupation of, or annexing, the territory of" the victim state (UN Doc. PCNICC/2001/L.1/Rev.1, 9 March 2001, p. 17, <untreaty.un.org/cod/icc/index.html>).

[90] *See* supra in this Chapter.

[91] On this point, *see* J. Stone, supra note 85, p. 141.

policies. Thus, assuming that aggravated state responsibility for aggression requires a specific intent to be demonstrated, according to this line of reasoning state fault will correspond to the *dolus specialis* of state leaders. And the establishment of state and individual responsibility for aggression would almost coincide.

This approach is interesting because it essentially relies on a unitary notion of aggression under both state and individual responsibility. Then, the question of the specific intent nature of this crime must be solved consistently under both regimes of responsibility. In this regard, an alternative view has been proposed, according to which the *dolus specialis* of aggression could only be required under international criminal law, and not under the law of state responsibility.[92] This approach is interesting because it splits the unitary notion of aggression into two separate concepts,[93] one applicable to state conduct and the other applicable to individual conduct. Accordingly, it would be possible to keep a certain separation between state and individual responsibility also with respect to the crime of aggression.

To sum up, the crime of aggression is particularly interesting because it reflects a very close relationship – or even an equivalence – between state and individual responsibility with respect to both the subjective and the psychological element. In particular, the latter element is certainly a distinguishing feature of individual criminal liability, but the foregoing analysis shows how difficult it is to conceive of individual liability for aggression in a way completely separated from state responsibility for the same wrongful act. A first option is to consider that there is not a necessary legal link between state and individual responsibility for aggression because the psychological element is not required under the former. Then, the relationship between these regimes will largely depend on the way in which the *mens rea* of state leaders is proved to establish their criminal liability. Arguably, the general criminal context (state aggression) can have a crucial role in showing the psychological element of aggression, as happens with respect to other international crimes. The second option is to consider that state and individual responsibility for aggression do share a common psychological element (*dolus specialis*). In this case, a very close relationship between these regimes is due to the fact that state fault can be identified with the psychological attitude of those few state leaders that can be held accountable for aggression.[94]

---

92 A. Cassese, supra note 2, p. 116.

93 A. Cassese, *International Criminal Law* (2nd edn., Oxford, Oxford University Press, 2008), pp. 152–161.

94 However, it is difficult to justify this second option on the basis of past and more recent international practice. The SWGCA for example seems opposed to the inclusion of a clause which would limit the definition of aggression to acts having "the object or result of establishing a military occupation of, or annexing, the territory of another State or part thereof" (*see* ICC-ASP/6/SWGCA/INF.1, pp. 12, and 21, <www.icc-cpi.int>).

4. *Concluding Observations*

The analysis of the psychological element of international crimes confirms that in principle, the *mens rea* marks a difference between aggravated state responsibility and individual criminal liability. Indeed, the assessment of aggravated state responsibility is generally independent of the establishment of individual criminal liability which requires an additional element (*mens rea*) to be demonstrated. And international criminal tribunals generally apply the principle of personal guilt in a very rigorous manner.

However, recent international case law shows interesting cases in which the two regimes tend to be more closely connected, and the *mens rea*/fault element can represent a point of contact between them.

On the one hand, certain international crimes require a specific intent to be met and the analysis of international practice has shown that this element can be established in a more 'objective' way. This happens in particular with respect to collective crimes because the proof of the *dolus specialis* is particularly difficult. Thus, in order to demonstrate this requirement, international tribunals have been willing to rely on elements of the general criminal context, such as the conduct of persons other than the accused or even acts not amounting to the crime entailing individual criminal liability. In particular, this has led international criminal tribunals to adopt a two-step inquiry into the specific intent of the accused: they first take the general criminal context into account, and then they evaluate the personal conduct of the accused in the light of this surrounding context to see whether it shows the necessary specific intent. This inevitably leads to a shift in the emphasis (in the tribunals' approach) from the psychological attitude of the accused to the broader criminal context. Taking into account the general context in the establishment of individual liability is an important tool for allocating individual criminal liability with respect to crimes of a collective nature.

In practice, this approach brings the ascertainment of individual criminal liability closer to the ascertainment of aggravated state responsibility. The psychological element is established in very similar ways under both regimes. This does not mean that it is the same requirement. State fault, if required, is ascertained through an examination of the general conduct of the state, and patterns of behaviour that characterize such conduct. Under international criminal law, the focus is on the personal conduct of the accused, even though the general criminal conduct is crucial to infer his or her specific intent. However, the emphasis put on the existence of a systematic pattern of criminal behaviour or a criminal policy dramatically reduces the distance that in principle characterizes the establishment of state fault, on the one hand, and the *mens rea* of a state organ, on the other. This inquiry into the general criminal context do not correspond to an establishment of aggravated state responsibility, and such an establishment is not a preliminary requirement to hold state organs accountable for international crimes. The relevant criminal context (useful to infer the *dolus specialis* of the accused) can consist of the behaviour of non-state actors, for example. In other words, the collective criminal context does not necessarily take place at the state level. However, when state and individual responsibility are to be investigated with respect to the same crimes, this collective dimension can establish a direct link between the two regimes of responsibility for international crimes, in particular, as regards the way in which the psychological element is ascertained. At least with respect to the relevant conduct, both the *mens rea* of the accused and state fault for the same crimes will be proved in a similar way, that is, focusing on the same collective criminal context.

On the other hand, with respect to isolated international crimes, state fault can correspond to the *mens rea* of the responsible state organ. This case is not particularly relevant because isolated crimes do not give rise to an overlap between aggravated state responsibility and individual criminal liability. However, international crimes committed by isolated state organs may trigger ordinary state responsibility.[95] Therefore, this case shows an analogous overlap of the psychological element even though it concerns the relationship between individual liability and ordinary state responsibility.

An exception is represented by the crime of aggression. Under international criminal law, only a few state leaders can be held accountable for this crime. From the standpoint of the material element, aggression can hardly be viewed as an isolated crime. However, from the standpoint of the subjective element, individual criminal liability for aggression can only be imposed on a few decision-makers whose intent is essential to establish state fault. Therefore, the psychological element of this crime is likely to be established in the same way under both regimes.

If no fault element is required to establish aggravated state responsibility for aggression, the *mens rea* of the accused can largely be inferred from the general criminal context (state aggression). Even in the absence of a common legal ingredient, the psychological element required under international criminal law can be established in a more 'objective' way relying on the facts that would constitute the seriousness requirement under aggravated state responsibility.

Alternatively, if we consider that state and individual responsibility for aggression do share the same psychological element, then the relationship between these regimes is even closer. The *mens rea* of state leaders charged with aggression is likely to be used as the main proof of the existence of state fault. Therefore, two apparently separated requirements can be regarded as analogous and be established almost in the same way.

---

[95] This particular relationship between ordinary state responsibility and individual criminal liability is examined below. *See* infra Chapter 8.

Chapter 5

Defences and Circumstances Precluding Wrongfulness

The previous chapters have dealt with the basic elements of state and individual responsibility for international crimes and with the problems stemming from their relationship as far as these basic elements are concerned. It is now opportune, for the sake of completeness, to take into account other elements of state and individual responsibility such as defences and circumstances precluding wrongfulness. Indeed, both these regimes provide for particular circumstances under which either wrongfulness or liability are precluded. For example, a state can claim that it has used force in self-defence and avoid a determination that its conduct amounted to an act of aggression. Similarly, an individual can in principle invoke duress and avoid punishment.

The present analysis is limited to the relationship between defences in international criminal law and circumstances precluding wrongfulness in state responsibility. It will not address the particular issue of the distinction between justifications and excuses under international criminal law,[1] and between circumstances precluding wrongfulness and circumstances precluding responsibility in state responsibility.[2] From the comparative viewpoint of this analysis, it is not necessary to deal with these specific distinctions. More general aspects will be taken into account here: whether there is an overlap between certain defences and the corresponding circumstances precluding wrongfulness, whether the same notions are actually applied under both state and individual responsibility, and whether they can be regarded as an additional point of contact between these two regimes of international responsibility.

---

1 *See* in general G.P. Fletcher, *Basic Concepts of Criminal Law* (New York-Oxford, Oxford University Press, 1998).

2 Here the expression 'circumstances precluding wrongfulness' will be used simply because it is the one adopted by the ILC in its codification work on State Responsibility. This does not mean that certain circumstances listed in Articles 20 to 25 are arguably better understood as circumstances precluding responsibility. For a comprehensive analysis of circumstances precluding wrongfulness under state responsibility, *see* R. Ago, 'Eighth Report on State Responsibility', *YILC* (1979), vol. II(1), p. 3 et seq., and *YILC* (1980), vol. II(1), p. 13 et seq.

1. *Theoretical Approaches to the Relationship Between Defences and Circumstances Precluding Wrongfulness*

From the viewpoint of the relationship between aggravated state responsibility and individual criminal liability, defences and circumstances precluding wrongfulness raise two main questions. First, assuming that the same circumstance amounts to a defence under international criminal law and to a circumstance precluding wrongfulness under state responsibility, one may wonder whether this circumstance must necessarily be interpreted and applied in the same way. Second, one may ask whether circumstances precluding wrongfulness can play a role under international criminal law, and, in addition to defences, prevent individuals from being punished for international crimes, even if these circumstances belong to a different field of international law.

The first question is whether a consistent application of state and individual responsibility must be guaranteed as far as defences and circumstances precluding wrongfulness are concerned. For example, if duress[3] is invoked by a state organ accused of having committed an international crime and distress,[4] the corresponding circumstance precluding wrongfulness under state responsibility, is invoked by the state, should duress and distress be interpreted and applied in the same way? If so, the unlawful conduct will either simultaneously entail state and individual responsibility (since it does not meet the common requirements of duress and distress) or be excused and engage neither state nor individual responsibility. In this way, a co-ordination between state and individual responsibility is established.

---

[3] On the notion of duress, *see* in general A. Cassese, *International Criminal Law* (Oxford, Oxford University Press, 2003), p. 242 et seq. The ICTY mentions as essential conditions for duress to be accepted: "1) the act charged was done to avoid an immediate danger both serious and irreparable; 2) there was no adequate means of escape; 3) the remedy was not disproportionate to the evil" (ICTY, *Prosecutor v. Erdemović*, TC, Judgment, 29 November 1996, para. 17). The ICC Statute refers to duress in the following terms: "The conduct which is alleged to constitute a crime within the jurisdiction of the Court has been caused by duress resulting from a threat of imminent death or of continuing or imminent serious bodily harm against that person or another person, and the person acts necessarily and reasonably to avoid this threat, provided that the person does not intend to cause a greater harm than the one sought to be avoided. Such a threat may either be: i) Made by other persons; or ii) Constituted by other circumstances beyond that person's control" (Article 31, 1, d, <www.icc-cpi.int>).

[4] The notion of distress is defined in the ILC Draft Articles on State Responsibility. Article 24 reads: "1) The wrongfulness of an act of a State not in conformity with an international obligation of that State is precluded if the author of the act in question has no other reasonable way, in a situation of distress, of saving the author's life or the lives of other persons entrusted to the author's care. 2) Paragraph 1 does not apply if: a) The situation of distress is due, either alone or in combination with other factors, to the conduct of the State invoking it; or b) The act in question is likely to create a comparable or greater peril" (ILC, 'Report on the Work of its 53rd Session', *YILC* (2001), vol. II(2), p. 78).

By contrast, if duress and distress are interpreted and applied differently, the same conduct could entail either state or individual responsibility without necessarily entailing the other.

The second question essentially concerns the possibility for individuals to avoid international criminal liability, not by invoking the defences provided for under international criminal law, but by claiming that their conduct is not unlawful under the regime of state responsibility, that is, by invoking a circumstance precluding wrongfulness. The classical example would be the crime of aggression. If state A launches an armed attack against state B and this attack can be regarded as a lawful reaction in self-defence, then state A is not responsible for aggression. Arguably, in the absence of an act of aggression on the part of state A, political and military leaders of that state cannot be held individually accountable for the crime of aggression. Thus, the question revolves around the possibility to conceive of cases in which individuals might invoke a circumstance precluding the wrongfulness of the state conduct to avoid their personal punishment, as in the case of aggression. For example, can individuals charged with international crimes claim that their conduct amounted, for example, to a lawful reprisal?

From a theoretical point of view, these issues are differently addressed by the individual-oriented and state-oriented conceptual schemes.

According to the state-oriented conceptual scheme and its assumptions, individual criminal liability is in fact a measure indirectly aimed at sanctioning the wrongful state. State organs cannot be punished for conduct not amounting to state serious wrongful acts, that is, for acts not entailing aggravated state responsibility under international law. Accordingly, the responses to the two questions raised above should logically be consistent. Defences and the corresponding circumstances precluding wrongfulness should be interpreted and applied in the same way; otherwise individual liability might apply independently of state responsibility. By the same token, circumstances precluding wrongfulness should have a role in international criminal law and should preclude individual liability alongside traditional defences.

On the other hand, according to the individual-oriented conceptual scheme, individual criminal liability under international law may well exist even if no corresponding state responsibility can be established. Thus, defences can certainly be conceived of and applied in a manner which is different from that used under state responsibility with respect to the corresponding circumstances precluding wrongfulness.[5] For example, the personal conduct of the accused may be excused by duress,

---

[5] *See*, in particular with respect to self-defence, G.-J. Knoops, *Defenses in Contemporary International Law* (Ardsley, Transnational Publishers, 2001), p. 211 ("The fact... that a State may legitimately use force in self-defense does not automatically imply that its military personnel, agents or other nationals are endowed with the private right to use force in self-defense and are therefore allowed

while state responsibility can nonetheless be affirmed since it is entailed by a wider criminal conduct carried out by the state which does not meet the requirements of distress. On the other hand, individual criminal liability can arguably be precluded only by those defences expressly provided under international criminal law. Since state and individual responsibility are regarded as totally separated, circumstances precluding the wrongfulness of state conduct can hardly have an impact on the different issue of individual accountability, unless there is a corresponding defence under international criminal law. Of course, from this point of view, the critical question is to identify with precision such defences under customary international law.

Undeniably, these approaches address the problem of the relationship between defences and circumstances precluding wrongfulness according to diverging criteria and lead to conflicting results. In the end, they both deny any relationship between state and individual responsibility for international crimes. However, the analysis of international practice reveals a different scenario. Defences and circumstances precluding wrongfulness are governed by different sets of secondary rules, but at the same time they represent a point of contact between state and individual responsibility for international crimes.

2. *Overlapping Defences and Circumstances Precluding Wrongfulness*

International case law, and in particular modern case law, has rarely dealt with defences. Before international *ad hoc* tribunals, the accused persons have generally pleaded not guilty for not having committed the crime, and at most they have claimed to have an alibi. Of course, the rigorous approach of these tribunals has not encouraged a wide reliance on defences on the part of the accused. However, a few cases can be relevant to the present analysis.

The *Erdemović* case[6] is probably the most interesting one. Erdemović was a soldier responsible for having killed dozens of Muslims during the conflict in the former Yugoslavia. Before the ICTY, he invoked duress as an excuse for his conduct, since he maintained that he was threatened to do so.

In 1997, the Appeals Chamber of the *ad hoc* tribunals found that duress does not afford a complete defence for crimes involving the killing of innocent human beings.[7] This narrow interpretation of duress can raise concern when taking into account the relationship between state and individual responsibility for international

to commit, under this shield, international crimes. The concept of individual criminal and command responsibility must be assessed independently from the use of force by a State").

6 ICTY, *Prosecutor v. Erdemović*, TC, Judgment, 29 November 1996.

7 ICTY, *Prosecutor v. Erdemović*, AC, Judgment, 7 October 1997, para. 19.

crimes. Indeed, if distress is not interpreted in the same way as duress, then the same conduct will entail the personal liability of the state organ under international criminal law, but will not also give rise to state responsibility due to the broader scope of distress under the latter regime.

One commentator has been very critical regarding such a possible consequence.[8] Gaeta strongly affirms the need "to co-ordinate the relevance of duress in both fields of international law, namely State responsibility and international criminal liability", and to give equal weight to duress in both of these fields.[9] Unfortunately, *Erdemović*-like situations are not so clear-cut and merit a closer examination from two different perspectives.

One may first look at the definition of duress and distress from the viewpoint of the relationship between *ordinary* state responsibility and individual criminal liability. When state responsibility arises out of isolated breaches of state organs, it seems correct to support the need for a co-ordination between state and individual responsibility. The conduct of the state overlaps with the conduct of one of its organs, and therefore the two wrongful acts are identifical. Gaeta gives an interesting example: the case of a killing of a prisoner of war by a state official (soldier) forced to do so by a civilian, who threatens that otherwise he will kill both the soldier and the prisoner of war.[10] The soldier will be charged with a typical 'individual' war crime committed independently of any broader involvement of the state apparatus.[11] And in these circumstances he will probably invoke duress. On the other hand, if the soldier has been forced by a civilian, it seems perfectly correct to consider that the state has nothing to do with the crime and that distress can be invoked to preclude the wrongfulness of the state conduct. Thus, the co-ordination between state and individual responsibility will depend on the interpretation given to duress and distress respectively. In similar cases, it is arguably correct to maintain that distress should be interpreted in the same way as duress, since the same conduct gives rise to both ordinary state responsibility and individual criminal liability. In particular, independently of the fact that one may or may not share the approach of the ICTY in *Erdemović*, in this case a defence is invoked to exclude the *mens*

[8] P. Gaeta, 'War Crimes Trials Before Italian Criminal Courts: New Trends', in H. Fischer *et al.* (eds.), *International and National Prosecution of Crimes under International Law: Current Developments* (Berlin, Spitz, 2001), p. 751 et seq.

[9] *Ibid.*, pp. 763–764.

[10] *Ibid.*

[11] *See* B.V.A. Röling, 'Aspects of the Criminal Responsibility for Violations of the Laws of War', in A. Cassese (ed.), *The New Humanitarian Law of Armed Conflict* (Napoli, Editoriale Scientifica, 1980), p. 203; P.-M. Dupuy, 'International Criminal Responsibility of the Individual and International Responsibility of the State', in A. Cassese *et al.* (eds.), *The Rome Statute of the International Criminal Court. A Commentary*, vol. II (Oxford, Oxford University Press, 2002), p. 1093. The classification of international is discussed below in Chapter 9.

rea of the state organ whose conduct is attributable to the state. Therefore, it is difficult to see how, when turning to *ordinary* state responsibility, distress can be interpreted in a different way from the same circumstance which can exclude the liability of the state organ.

From the viewpoint of the relationship between *aggravated* state responsibility and individual criminal liability, things are arguably different. If we take the facts in the *Erdemović* case, it dealt with a completely different crime. In 1995, the Srebrenica safe area[12] fell to the Bosnian Serb forces and thousands of Muslim civilians tried to flee the area. But the Bosnian Serb forces were able to separate an undetermined number of Muslim men from the women and children and transport them by bus out of the enclave to various locations where they were to be executed.[13] While Erdemović was found guilty since duress was not regarded as a complete defence with respect to such a grave crime, on the other hand, it seems impossible for the state to invoke distress with respect to a wrongful act such as that in which Erdemović took part. Due to the magnitude of the crime and the broad involvement of the Serb forces, Erdemović was clearly not implicated in a typical isolated individual crime. From the standpoint of state responsibility, the relevant conduct is not limited to Erdemović's action, but it corresponds to a much broader criminal context, which includes the preparation and organization of the crime, the participation of various state organs, the order of the superior, the execution by various subordinates, and the number of victims. When considered in its entirety, this conduct is arguably sufficient to fulfil the requirements of aggravated state responsibility.

However, while the ICTY in *Erdemović* apparently guarantees a certain coordination between state and individual responsibility – because both the state and the state organ are accountable – this merely derives from the nature of the crime and not from an identical interpretation of duress and distress. It is perfectly possible to share the criticism of the Erdemović solution with regard to duress, to support the possibility for individuals to rely on duress even in such circumstances,[14] and to hold that *aggravated* state responsibility does not necessarily cumulate with individual criminal liability. Duress and distress can be interpreted in different ways because they are defined with respect to two completely different conducts: duress refers to the personal conduct of the accused, whereas distress (allegedly) refers to the overall activity of the state, and not to the conduct of an isolated state organ as far as serious breaches are concerned. Thus, with respect to collective crimes it

---

12 *See* SC Res. 819(1993), <www.un.org/Docs/sc>.

13 ICTY, *Prosecutor v. Erdemović*, TC, Judgment, 29 November 1996, paras. 77, 78 and 80.

14 *See* the Separate and Dissenting Opinion of Judge Cassese appended to the 1997 *Erdemović* judgment, <www.un.org/icty>.

is abstractly possible for a state organ to successfully invoke duress, while the state cannot claim to have acted in distress.

A. *The Scope of the Overlap Between Defences and Circumstances Precluding Wrongfulness*

More generally, with respect to serious breaches of community obligations entailing aggravated state responsibility, it seems almost impossible for the state to invoke those circumstances precluding wrongfulness which are typical of isolated wrongful acts, such as distress, necessity or *force majeure*. For example, it is difficult to justify genocide or crimes against humanity because of "the occurrence of an irresistible force or of an unforeseen event, beyond the control of the State, making it materially impossible in the circumstances to perform the obligation". Indeed, aggravated state responsibility is defined in terms of collective involvement of the state in the carrying out of the wrongful act, and it is mainly due to the seriousness requirement that most of the time circumstances precluding wrongfulness cannot operate with respect to serious breaches.

Thus, a connection between state and individual responsibility, as far as defences and circumstances precluding wrongfulness are concerned, is very unlikely to arise. In practice the overlap between defences and circumstances precluding wrongfulness is very limited. This is essentially due to the fact that most circumstances precluding wrongfulness cannot be applied with respect to serious breaches entailing aggravated state responsibility. According to the ILC, such serious breaches have a peremptory character and in no case can their wrongfulness be precluded by those circumstances applying to ordinary state responsibility.[15] Even leaving aside the peremptory character of certain primary obligations, it is clear that the factual preconditions of certain circumstances precluding wrongfulness are such as to be applied only with respect to isolated wrongful acts, and not with respect to *serious* breaches entailing aggravated state responsibility. For example, this is the case of distress, necessity or *force majeure*. Moreover, the application of certain other circumstances can be excluded simply by taking into account the non-reciprocal nature of obligations owed to the entire international community. Thus, the wrongfulness of serious breaches cannot be precluded, for example, by consent of the injured state,[16] because this circumstance only operates at the bilateral level. As far as

[15] *See* Article 26 which reads: "Nothing in this chapter precludes the wrongfulness of any act of a State which is not in conformity with an obligation arising under a peremptory norm of general international law" (ILC, 'Report on the Work of its 53rd Session', *YILC* (2001), vol. II(2), p. 84).

[16] The same reasoning can be applied to countermeasures. Article 50 of the Draft Articles on State Responsibility excludes the lawfulness of countermeasures prohibited under international humanitarian law (ILC, 'Report on the Work of its 53rd Session', *YILC* (2001), vol. II(2), p. 131).

non-reciprocal obligations are concerned, the consent of one state (or more generally a bilateral circumstance precluding wrongfulness) does not exclude the wrongfulness of the serious breach with respect to all other states.

Consequently, as far as defences and circumstances precluding wrongfulness are concerned, the overlap between state and individual responsibility is essentially limited to self-defence. Indeed, both customary law and the UN Charter provide for the inherent right of states to act in (individual and collective) self-defence in case of aggression. One may see self-defence as part of the primary norm defining (that is, limiting the definition of) state aggression rather than a circumstance precluding wrongfulness. In both cases, the rationale for self-defence is the same: the legal order exceptionally admits a derogation to the norm protecting a collective interest (international peace) allowing an individual interest perceived as fundamental (the survival of the state) to prevail over the former.[17]

On the other hand, self-defence can also be regarded as a specific defence under international criminal law, a defence having the same rationale as self-defence under the law of state responsibility. In *Kordić*, the ICTY explicitly dealt with the definition of self-defence and affirmed that it is provided for under customary international law:

> The notion of self-defence may be broadly defined as providing a defence to a person who acts to defend or protect himself or his property (or another person or person's property) against attack, provided that the acts constitute a reasonable, necessary and proportionate reaction to the attack. The Trial Chamber notes that the Statute of the International Tribunal does not provide for self-defence as a ground for excluding criminal responsibility. 'Defences' however form part of the general principles of criminal law which the International Tribunal must take into account in deciding the cases before it.[18]

Similarly, both the *ad hoc* tribunals have rejected the *tu quoque* argument with respect to international humanitarian norms embodying absolute, non-reciprocal obligations. *See* ICTY, *Prosecutor v. Kupreškić et al.*, TC, Judgment, 14 January 2000, paras. 515–520, and ICTR, *Prosecutor v. Gacumbtsi*, TC, Judgment, 17 June 2004, para. 165. This issue is discussed in more detail infra in this Chapter.

[17] G.P. Fletcher, supra note 1. This explains why, under such exceptional circumstances, particular requirements, like proportionality, are essential to strike a balance between the private and the collective interests involved.

[18] ICTY, *Prosecutor v. Kordić and Čerkez*, TC, Judgment, 26 February 2001, para. 449. Then in paras. 450–451 the Trial Chamber explained that "Paragraph (1)(c) of Article 31 of the Statute of the ICC, entitled 'Grounds for excluding criminal responsibility', which provides for the exclusion of criminal liability in situations where a person acts reasonably to defend himself or another person, or certain types of property, reads: '1. In addition to other grounds for excluding criminal responsibility provided for in this Statute, a person shall not be criminally responsible if, at the time of that person's conduct: … (c) The person acts reasonably to defend himself or herself or another person or, in the case of war crimes, property which is essential for the survival of the person or another person or property which is essential for accomplishing a military mission against an imminent

Thus, the possibility for individuals charged with international crimes to invoke self-defence under international criminal law is confirmed in the most recent international case law, in the ICC Statute, and in the ILC codification of Crimes against the Peace and Security of Mankind.[19]

From a comparative point of view, self-defence is very interesting because it has two different meanings under state and individual responsibility, but at the same time it can be regarded as a point of contact between these two regimes.

On the one hand, self-defence under international criminal law is arguably different from self-defence under state responsibility. According to the ILC:

> It is important to distinguish between the notion of self-defence in the context of criminal law and the notion of self-defence in the context of Article 51 of the Charter of the United Nations. The notion of self-defence in the criminal law context relieves an individual of responsibility for a violent act committed against another human being that would otherwise constitute a crime such as murder. In contrast, the notion of self- defence in the context of the Charter of the United Nations refers to the lawful use of force by a State in the exercise of the inherent right of individual or collective self-defence, and which would therefore not constitute aggression by that State.[20]

---

and unlawful use of force in a manner proportionate to the degree of danger to the person or the other person or property protected. The fact that the person was involved in a defensive operation conducted by forces shall not in itself constitute a ground for excluding criminal responsibility under this subparagraph'. The principle of self-defence enshrined in this provision reflects provisions found in most national criminal codes and may be regarded as constituting a rule of customary international law. Article 31(1)(c) of the ICC Statute sets forth two conditions which must be met in order for self-defence to be accepted as a ground for excluding criminal liability: (a) the act must be in response to 'an imminent and unlawful use of force' against an attack on a 'protected' person or property; (b) the act of defence must be 'proportionate to the degree of danger'. In relation to the specific circumstances of war crimes, the provision takes into account the principle of military necessity." This position was then upheld by the Appeals Chamber in its judgment of 17 December 2004, paras. 835–838.

[19] *See* Article 14 and, in particular, para. 8 of its commentary: "Self-defence was recognized as a possible defence in some of the war crime trials conducted after the Second World War. The United Nations War Crimes Commission concluded that 'A plea of self-defence may be successfully put forward, in suitable circumstances, in war crime trials as in trials held under municipal law'. The plea of self-defence may be raised by an accused who is charged with a crime of violence committed against another human being resulting in death or serious bodily injury. The notion of self-defence could relieve an accused of criminal responsibility for the use of force against another human being resulting in death or serious injury if this use of force was necessary to avoid an immediate threat of his own death or serious injury caused by that other human being. The right of an individual to act in self-defence is implicitly recognized in the saving clause contained in the Convention on the Safety of United Nations and Associated Personnel (article 21)" (ILC, 'Report on the Work of its 48th Session', *YILC* (1996), vol. II(2), p. 40).

[20] *Ibid.*

The same distinction was taken into account by the ICTY in *Kordić*.[21] As mentioned above, the Trial Chamber relied on a notion of *individual* self-defence and excluded the possibility that "military operations in self-defence" could provide a justification for serious violations of international humanitarian law. Thus, in principle two different and separate notions of self-defences apply under international criminal law and state responsibility.[22]

B. *The Particular Case of the Crime of Aggression*

On the other hand, self-defence plays a very peculiar role as regards the crime of aggression. Indeed, with respect to aggression both state and individual responsibility arise out the same serious breach: a state act of aggression. Accordingly, the circumstance that is capable of justifying both state and individual conduct is arguably the same. To be more precise, it is the customary notion of *state* self-defence which excludes an armed attack from being qualified as aggression under international law. Therefore, if the conduct cannot be regarded as an unlawful act of aggression, neither aggravated state responsibility nor individual criminal liability can arise at the international level.[23]

With respect to the crime of aggression, there is arguably only one notion of self-defence which applies to both state and individual responsibility. This is due to the particular nature of this crime. The sole act which can be qualified as aggression is the state wrongful act. Individuals are not held criminally accountable for 'personal' acts of aggression, but for acts of "aggression committed by a State".[24] Individual criminal liability of political and military leaders derives from the fact that they represent the state and they are the ultimate decision-makers to whom responsibility for aggression can be ascribed. Those particular individuals, and only those, are responsible for the state aggressive policy. This reveals a clear

---

21 ICTY, *Prosecutor v. Kordić and Čerkez*, TC, Judgment, 26 February 2001, para. 452.

22 A similar approach is adopted by L. Condorelli, 'Responsabilité Etatique et Responsabilité Individuelle pour Violations Graves du Droit International Humanitaire', in L.C. Vohrah *et al.* (eds.), *Man's Inhumanity to Man. Essays on International Law in Honour of Antonio Cassese* (The Hague, M. Nijhoff, 2003), p. 218.

23 The ILC in its commentary on Article 16 of the Draft Code of Crimes affirms that, "[i]ndividual responsibility for such a crime is intrinsically and inextricably linked to the commission of aggression by a State. The rule of international law which prohibits aggression applies to the conduct of a State in relation to another State. Therefore, only a State is capable of committing aggression by violating this rule of international law which prohibits such conduct" (ILC, 'Report on the Work of its 48th Session', *YILC* (1996), vol. II(2), p. 43).

24 Article 16 of the Draft Code of Crimes (ILC, 'Report on the Work of its 48th Session', *YILC* (1996), vol. II(2), p. 42). For a particular interpretation of the international law rule on self-defence which goes back to domestic criminal law concepts, see G.P. Fletcher and J.D. Ohlin, *Defending Humanity. When Force is Justified and Why* (Oxford, New York, Oxford University Press, 2008).

point of contact between state and individual responsibility for aggression. This particular crime is defined in terms of state action, and when (state) self-defence applies, no wrongful act can be said to exist under international law. Accordingly, no individual can be held criminally accountable for a legitimate use of force under international law.

C. *Concluding Remarks*

The foregoing analysis prompts three general remarks with respect to the relationship between state and individual responsibility for international crimes as far as the definition of defences and circumstances precluding wrongfulness is concerned. First, there is a very limited overlap between aggravated state responsibility and individual criminal liability, which essentially concerns self-defence and, as will be discussed below, countermeasures. It is true that a broader overlap characterizes the relationship between ordinary state responsibility and individual criminal liability, and there may be a need to apply defences and circumstances precluding wrongfulness in a consistent way. But this need for co-ordination derives from factual circumstances. When international crimes are the result of isolated acts of state organs, it seems reasonable to interpret these norms consistently and qualify the same relevant conduct consistently in order to have either both state and individual responsibility engaged or none of them. On the other hand, the seriousness of international crimes and the non-reciprocal nature of obligations owed to the entire international community explain the very limited overlap between aggravated state responsibility and individual criminal liability as far as defences and circumstances precluding wrongfulness are concerned.

Second, it is possible to interpret defences and circumstances precluding wrongfulness differently, because they refer to two different kinds of conduct: the former apply to a serious wrongful state act, whereas the latter have to do with individual conduct amounting an international crime. Even self-defence can be seen as a general principle embodying two different notions, one applicable to states and the other one to individuals. Thus, state and individual responsibility for international crimes can in principle be regarded as separate regimes also with respect to defences and circumstances precluding wrongfulness. However, a first point of contact between these regimes concerns the notion of self-defence as applicable to the crime of aggression.

Third, the particular nature of the crime of aggression derives from its definition under customary international law. The primary norm defining aggression excludes the wrongfulness of armed attacks carried out in self-defence. Accordingly, no state serious wrongful act can be said to have been carried out where the use of armed force is a reaction to a previous act of aggression. The conduct of the state is perfectly lawful under international law. This primary norm (concerning state conduct) is also the basis for establishing individual liability for the crime of aggression. Therefore, it seems correct to maintain that, in the absence of a state act of aggression, no state leader can be held criminally liable for aggression. This means that the very same notion of (state) self-defence is applicable to both state and individual responsibility under international law.

3. *Circumstances Precluding Wrongfulness and International Criminal Law*

The crime of aggression is an example of a crime allowing individuals to invoke a defence not expressly provided under international criminal law, a circumstance (self-defence) pertaining to the definition of the lawfulness of state action, a circumstance which has nothing to do with their private conduct. This brings us to the second problematic aspect of the relationship between aggravated state responsibility and individual criminal liability as far as circumstances precluding wrongfulness are concerned, namely, whether circumstances precluding wrongfulness can actually play a role under international criminal law.

The question an international criminal tribunal may have to deal with is whether, in establishing the criminal liability of an accused who has participated in the commission of a crime carried out at the state level, it can take into account the fact that the corresponding state conduct is not unlawful under international law due to a circumstance precluding its wrongfulness, and therefore whether it must acquit the accused. In other words, there may be cases in which certain conduct in principle gives rise to both state and individual responsibility, but whose wrongfulness may be precluded under state responsibility. In this case, the question is whether the (state) circumstance precluding wrongfulness can be relied upon to exclude individual criminal liability as well.

According to the overlap identified above, it does not seem to be controversial for (state) self-defence to be applicable with respect to the crime of aggression. A more problematic situation concerns countermeasures and, in particular, so-called belligerent reprisals. In general, it must be recalled that under the law of state responsibility there are certain "obligations which by reason of their character must not be the subject of countermeasures at all".[25] In particular, the ILC Draft Articles on State Responsibility separately lists obligations for the protection of fundamental human rights (Article 50 (1) (b)), and obligations of a humanitarian character prohibiting reprisals (Article 50 (1) (c)). It is generally accepted and recognized that the former include genocide, crimes against humanity, and

---

[25] Commentary on Art. 50 (ILC, 'Report on the Work of its 53rd Session', *YILC* (2001), vol. II(2), p. 131, para. 2).

torture.[26] For example, genocide cannot justify counter-genocide.[27] Thus, with respect to certain obligations owed to the entire international community there is a general and absolute prohibition of reprisals under international law. The breach of these non-reciprocal obligations always entails state responsibility, even if the serious breach is committed in response to the breach of the same obligations by another state. Consequently, with respect to genocide, crimes against humanity and torture, there is no room left for invoking the countermeasure argument under international criminal law.

Apparently, this conclusion does not extend to war crimes. However, it is not entirely clear to what extent individuals charged with war crimes are entitled to rely on the belligerent reprisal defence to avoid punishment. To answer this question, it is first necessary to ascertain whether and to what extent belligerent reprisals can preclude state responsibility.

Going back to the ILC codification of state responsibility, it emerges that international humanitarian law is treated separately from fundamental human rights law. More interestingly, while Article 50 (1) (b) sets out a general prohibition of countermeasures, Article 50 (1) (c) has a narrower scope and refers only to those humanitarian law obligations *already prohibiting reprisals*. As the ILC explains in its commentary, "the paragraph reflects the basic prohibition of reprisals *against individuals*, which exists in international humanitarian law."[28]

Thus, to establish whether and to what extent states can take countermeasures in this particular field of international law, we must look at its specific provisions. This is a very controversial question.[29] The 1949 Geneva Conventions and Additional Protocol I of 1977 clearly set out a prohibition of reprisals against protected persons and objects in situations of international armed conflicts. But reprisals have not been formally prohibited in certain areas, namely, methods and means of warfare and internal armed conflicts. Moreover, the absolute prohibition of reprisals against the civilian population has continued to be a matter of considerable controversy. In

---

[26] Commentary on Art. 26 (ILC, 'Report on the Work of its 53rd Session', *YILC* (2001), vol. II(2), p. 85, para. 5).

[27] As the ICJ noted, "in no case could one breach of the Convention serve as an excuse for another" (*Case Concerning Application of the Convention on the Prevention and Punishment of the Crime of Genocide* (Bosnia and Herzegovina v. Yugoslavia), *Counter-Claims*, Order, 17 December 1997, *ICJ Reports* 1997, p. 258, para. 35).

[28] Commentary on Article 50 (ILC, 'Report on the Work of its 53rd Session', *YILC* (2001), vol. II(2), p. 132, para. 8, emphasis added).

[29] *See* F. Kalshoven, *Belligerent Reprisals* (Leiden, M. Nijhoff, 1971); R. Bierzanek, 'Reprisals as a Means of Enforcing the Laws of Warfare: The Old and the New Law', in A. Cassese (ed.), *The New Humanitarian Law of Armed Conflict* (Napoli, Editoriale Scientifica, 1980), pp. 232–257; C. Greenwood, 'The Twilight of the Law of Belligerent Reprisals', 20 *NYIL* (1989), pp. 35–69; F. Kalshoven, 'Belligerent Reprisals Revisited', 21 *NYIL* (1990), pp. 43–80.

particular, certain reservations to the Geneva Conventions and Protocols apparently assume the lawfulness of reprisals in kind taken in extreme circumstances.[30]

Recent international case law has cast some light on the long-debated question of belligerent reprisals. The ICTY has taken the view that there is a general and absolute prohibition of reprisals against the civilian population under customary international law, notwithstanding the international or internal character of the armed conflict. A first statement in that sense can be found in the *Martić* decision.[31] But it is in *Kupreškić* that the Tribunal dealt in more detail with this question. In particular, it carefully examined the *opinio juris* before concluding that a rule has emerged under customary law providing for the absolute prohibition of reprisals against civilians in all armed conflicts.[32] This conclusion is perfectly consistent with

---

[30] *See*, for example, the UK reservation to the 1977 Additional Protocol: "If any adverse party makes serious and deliberate attacks against the civilian population or civilians or civilian objects, the United Kingdom will regard itself as entitled to take measures otherwise prohibited to the extent that it considers such measures necessary for the sole purpose of compelling the adverse party to cease committing violations, but only after formal warning to the adverse party requiring cessation of the violations has been disregarded and then only after a decision taken at the highest level of government."

[31] ICTY, *Prosecutor v. Martić*, TC, Review of the Indictment pursuant to Rule 61, 8 March 1996, para. 17 ("the rule which states that reprisals against the civilian population as such, or individual civilians, are prohibited in all circumstances, even when confronted by wrongful behaviour of the other party, is an integral part of customary international law and must be respected in all armed conflicts").

[32] ICTY, *Prosecutor v. Kupreškić et al.*, TC, Judgment, 14 January 2000, paras. 531–534 ("First, even before the adoption of the First Additional Protocol of 1977, a number of States had declared or laid down in their military manuals that reprisals in modern warfare are only allowed to the extent that they consist of the use, against enemy armed forces, of otherwise prohibited weapons – thus *a contrario* admitting that reprisals against civilians are not allowed. In this respect one can mention the United States military manual for the Army (The Law of Land Warfare), of 1956, as well as the Dutch 'Soldiers Handbook' (Handboek voor de Soldaat) of 1974. True, other military manuals of the same period took a different position, admitting reprisals against civilians not in the hands of the enemy belligerent. In addition, senior officials of the United States Government seem to have taken a less clear stand in 1978, by expressing doubts about the workability of the prohibition of reprisals against civilians. The fact remains, however, that elements of a widespread *opinio necessitatis* are discernible in international dealings. This is confirmed, first of all, by the adoption, by a vast majority, of a Resolution of the U.N. General Assembly in 1970 which stated that 'civilian populations, or individual members thereof, should not be the object of reprisals'. A further confirmation may be found in the fact that a high number of States have ratified the First Protocol, thereby showing that they take the view that reprisals against civilians must always be prohibited. It is also notable that this view was substantially upheld by the ICRC in its Memorandum of 7 May 1983 to the States parties to the 1949 Geneva Conventions on the Iran-Iraq war and by Trial Chamber I of the ICTY in Martić. Secondly, the States that have participated in the numerous international or internal armed conflicts which have taken place in the last fifty years have normally refrained from claiming that they had a right to visit reprisals upon enemy civilians in the combat area. It would seem that such claim has been only advanced by Iraq in the Iran-Iraq

and confirmed by the ICTY case law on the definition of the war crime 'attack on civilian population'. Notwithstanding early uncertainties,[33] the ICTY case law now regards the prohibition against attacking civilians and civilian objects as an absolute prohibition that may not be derogated from because of military necessity.[34]

This general prohibition refers to reprisals against civilian population and objects and also extends to internal armed conflict.[35] According to the ICTY, reprisals against civilians are always prohibited and cannot be regarded as a circumstance

war of 1980–1988 as well as – but only in abstracto and hypothetically, by a few States, such as France in 1974 and the United Kingdom in 1998. The aforementioned elements seem to support the contention that the demands of humanity and the dictates of public conscience, as manifested in *opinio necessitatis*, have by now brought about the formation of a customary rule also binding upon those few States that at some stage did not intend to exclude the abstract legal possibility of resorting to the reprisals under discussion. The existence of this rule was authoritatively confirmed, albeit indirectly, by the International Law Commission. In commenting on sub-paragraph d of Article 14 (now Article 50) of the Draft Articles on State Responsibility, which excludes from the regime of lawful countermeasures any conduct derogating from basic human rights, the Commission noted that Article 3 common to the four 1949 Geneva Conventions 'prohibits any reprisals in non-international armed conflicts with respect to the expressly prohibited acts as well as any other reprisal incompatible with the absolute requirement of humane treatment'. It follows that, in the opinion of the Commission, reprisals against civilians in the combat zone are also prohibited. This view, according to the Trial Chamber, is correct. However, it must be supplemented by two propositions. First, Common Article 3 has by now become customary international law. Secondly, as the International Court of Justice rightly held in Nicaragua, it encapsulates fundamental legal standards of overarching value applicable both in international and internal armed conflicts. Indeed, it would be absurd to hold that while reprisals against civilians entailing a threat to life and physical safety are prohibited in civil wars, they are allowed in international armed conflicts as long as the civilians are in the combat zone."). It must be recalled that the Trial Chamber held that international humanitarian law "is however an area where *opinio iuris sive necessitatis* may play a much greater role than *usus*" (*ibid.*, para. 527).

33 *See* ICTY, *Prosecutor v. Blaškić*, TC, Judgment, 3 March 2000, para. 180, and ICTY, *Prosecutor v. Kordić and Čerkez*, TC, Judgment, 14 February 2001, para. 328. In these cases the ICTY implicitly held that attack on the civilian population could have been justified by military necessity.

34 *See* ICTY, *Prosecutor v. Galić*, TC, Judgment, 5 December 2003, paras. 41–62; ICTY, *Prosecutor v. Blaškić*, AC, Judgment, 29 July 2004, para. 109; ICTY, *Prosecutor v. Kordić and Čerkez*, AC, Judgment, 17 December 2004, para. 54 (NB: *see* corrdigendum of 26 January 2005); ICTY, *Prosecutor v. Strugar*, TC, Judgment, 31 January 2005, para. 280; ICTY, *Prosecutor v. Martić*, TC, Judgment, 12 June 2007, paras. 66–72. On the other hand, in the Draft Code of Crimes the ILC apparently excludes the possibility that military necessity could be considered a defence under international criminal law (Commentary on Article 14, ILC, 'Report on the Work of its 48th Session', *YILC* (1996), vol. II(2), p. 41, para. 11).

35 For a very critical position towards the ICTY case law concerning belligerent reprisals, *see* F. Kalshoven, 'Reprisals and the Protection of Civilians: Two Recent Decisions of the Yugoslavia Tribunal', in L.C. Vohrah *et al.* (eds.), *Man's Inhumanity to Man. Essays on International Law in Honour of Antonio Cassese* (The Hague, M. Nijhoff, 2003), pp. 481–510.

precluding wrongfulness under state responsibility.[36] This consequently excludes the possibility that reprisals against civilians could have an indirect impact on international criminal law, that in other words individuals charged with war crimes could invoke such circumstances as a defence.

Yet the ICTY has not completely ruled out the lawfulness of other kinds of belligerent reprisals. Indeed, in *Kupreškić* it felt the need to spell out those fundamental requirements that should be met to regard belligerent reprisals as lawful:

> It should also be pointed out that at any rate, even when considered lawful, reprisals are restricted by; (a) the principle whereby they must be a last resort in attempts to impose compliance by the adversary with legal standards (which entails, amongst other things, that they may be exercised only after a prior warning has been given which has failed to bring about the discontinuance of the adversary's crimes); (b) the obligation to take special precautions before implementing them (they may be taken only after a decision to this effect has been made at the highest political or military level; in other words they may not be decided by local commanders); (c) the principle of proportionality (which entails not only that the reprisals must not be excessive compared to the precedent unlawful act of warfare, but also that they must stop as soon as that unlawful act has been discontinued) and; (d) 'elementary considerations of humanity' (as mentioned above).[37]

The main question thus concerns the precise identification of the types of belligerent reprisals which are not prohibited under international humanitarian law. Taking into account the general prohibitions set out in the above-mentioned case law, belligerent reprisals are arguably lawful and can be envisaged "in the choice of weapons and in the methods of combat used against military objectives".[38] This means, for example, that a state can validly claim to have used prohibited weapons as a reprisal against the enemy state which had previously breached international humanitarian law obligations.

From the standpoint of the relationship between state and individual responsibility, this leaves open the question of the possibility for an individual charged with certain war crimes to claim that his conduct amounted to a lawful belligerent reprisal. Can a state organ be convicted for a war crime with respect to a conduct that would be regarded as a lawful reprisal of the state under international humanitarian law? In other words, is the international norm on belligerent reprisal directed only at states, or it also applies to individuals? In the absence of international case law explicitly dealing with this subject, the question can only be addressed abstractly,

---

36 It must be stressed that in *Kordić and Čerkez* (AC, Judgment, 17 December 2004, para. 54) the ICTY quotes the ICJ's *Nuclear Weapons* case (supra Chapter 1, note 44) to conclude that this 'intransgressible' principle of customary international law consistently applies to all states and individuals (para. 78).

37 ICTY, *Prosecutor v. Kupreškić et al.*, TC, Judgment, 14 January 2000, para. 535.

38 ICRC Commentary to Article 51 of Additional Protocol I, para. 1985, <www.icrc.org>.

according to the general approach one adopts with respect to the relationship between state and individual responsibility.

The first option is to try to include lawful belligerent reprisals among the justifications of international criminal law.[39] However, such an approach might be problematic because, if one adopts a rigorous individual-oriented approach, the defendants would be permitted to invoke only those defences expressly provided for under international criminal law. To hold that belligerent reprisals amount to a defence under international criminal law, it must be demonstrated that a customary rule with such a content exists at present. This is however a very hard task. International practice on the subject is very poor: the ILC in its commentary to the Draft Code of Crimes does not mention the problem; the statutes of international criminal tribunals and courts are silent on the subject; the few post-WWII trials which have dealt with reprisals have largely lost their relevance;[40] and among recent judgments only *Kupreškić* implicitly admits the existence of lawful belligerent reprisals under international law without giving any indication as to their precise content and definition under international criminal law.

Furthermore, reprisals are a typical form of state conduct and can hardly be conceived of in terms of strict individual conduct. Defences under international criminal law are exceptional circumstances justifying or excusing the personal conduct of the accused, while reprisals render lawful the entire state conduct. An individual claiming that his conduct is part of a lawful reprisal admits that his personal behaviour is unlawful under international criminal law but claims that the state conduct as a whole is lawful under the law of state responsibility.

The second option is to consider that, once a circumstance precluding wrongfulness applies, the relevant conduct is definitely lawful under international law, no matter whether state or individual responsibility is at stake. It may seem reasonable to apply consistently the rules of international humanitarian law on belligerent reprisals to both state and individual responsibility for war crimes. The difference with the previous option is that there is no attempt to bring the (state) reprisal mechanism into the defences available under international criminal law. In other words, there is no need to operate at the level of secondary norms. This is due to the fact that the rule on (the lawfulness of) belligerent reprisals can be understood as a corollary of the primary norms of international humanitarian law prohibiting certain means and methods of warfare. Accordingly, there is one relevant conduct to establish the lawfulness of a belligerent reprisal, and this is the global conduct of the state, not the personal behaviour of the accused. Therefore, state and individual responsibility for war crimes can be ascertained consistently, because they originate

---

[39] A. Cassese, supra note 3, p. 221.

[40] For a detailed analysis of this case law, *see* F. Kalshoven, *Belligerent Reprisals*, supra note 29, pp. 216–263.

from the same conduct, which cannot be lawful and at the same time unlawful under international humanitarian law.

If we accept the *Kupreškić* requirements, as some states apparently do,[41] reprisals "may be taken only after a decision to this effect has been made at the highest political or military level". Reprisals concerning the means of warfare are a typical instance of state conduct not only because they are decided at the highest state levels, but also because they generally require the involvement of the state military organization in order to be carried out. This is the typical situation in which an international crime is carried out by a group of persons, and its perpetration is possible only because of the existence of a state apparatus in which the crime is planned, decided, organized, and finally executed. These crimes are regarded as heinous because they have at their disposal the entire state apparatus. It is the 'system' that in a sense legalizes the commission of the international crime. A rigorous individual-oriented conceptual scheme focusing only on the personal conduct of the accused is clearly ill-equipped to deal with such situations. A different approach, allowing international tribunals to take into account the general context in which international crimes are carried out, proves more effective in securing the punishment of the persons charged with international crimes.[42] In particular, the lawfulness of a belligerent reprisal can only be established at the state level, that is, taking into account the general conduct of the state.

Thus, this is a particular case in which individual criminal liability can be established only once the relevant conduct (the state reprisal) is found to be lawful or not. As the ICTY did in *Kupreškić*,[43] the relevant provisions of international humanitarian law are investigated and interpreted first as regards state responsibility and the question of individual liability is then solved accordingly. With respect to international humanitarian law rules addressing state conduct but having an impact on individual liability, international criminal tribunals cannot but try to guarantee a consistency between state and individual responsibility. They should be able to take into account the fact that, for example, a military operation is lawful under international law, and that the accused cannot be held accountable for a legitimate conduct, or that a military action is an unlawful belligerent reprisal, and that this can be an aggravating factor for the commander who has abused his leadership position. This necessarily entails a very close connection between state and individual responsibility for war crimes, because the rules on belligerent reprisals must be consistently applied under both regimes of international responsibility.

---

[41] *See* the UK reservation to the Additional Protocol supra note 30. For the drafting history of the Additional Protocol I and the willingness of some states to accept that recourse to reprisals should be decided by the Government, *see* R. Bierzanek, supra note 29.

[42] *See* supra Charters 3 and 4.

[43] *ICTY, Prosecutor v. Kupreškić et al.*, TC, Judgment, 14 January 2000.

4. *Concluding Observations*

This chapter has examined the question of whether defences and circumstances precluding wrongfulness can be regarded as a point of contact between state and individual responsibility for international crimes. International case law on the subject is not abundant. A few cases show how problematic the co-ordination between these regimes can be.

In principle, it is possible to say that international case law confirms a rigorous approach in the application of the principle of personal liability. It appears that even similar defences and circumstances precluding wrongfulness can be interpreted in different ways under state and individual responsibility, when they apply to different conduct. In particular, circumstances precluding wrongfulness are hardly applicable under aggravated state responsibility, and the corresponding defences can receive an autonomous application under international criminal law. For example, the same wrongful act does not necessarily entail both state and individual responsibility since in most cases the state organ would be able to invoke a defence that is not available to the state. Self-defence is the major exception to this conclusion, which undoubtedly applies under both state and individual responsibility. However, a distinction has been made also with respect to self-defence, which in principle has two different meanings under state and individual responsibility. Thus, to a certain extent aggravated state responsibility and individual criminal liability can be regarded as separate regimes when taking into account defences and circumstances precluding wrongfulness.

In practice, no generalization seems to be possible and there are at least two significant exceptions essentially due to the fact that both state and individual responsibility for certain international crimes are to be established with respect to the same conduct. First, self-defence marks a clear link between state and individual responsibility as far as the crime of aggression is concerned. The same notion of (state) self-defence is applicable under both state and individual responsibility. The crime of aggression rests on the assumption that the state conduct is the basis for holding political and military leaders accountable under international law. Therefore, if the state conduct is a lawful reaction in self-defence then no individual is accountable under international criminal law. This close link between the two regimes is due to the fact that the same international rule determines both state and individual responsibility.

Second, the lawfulness of certain belligerent reprisals under international humanitarian law can arguably have a deep impact on the establishment of individual liability for war crimes. While it is difficult to include a typical circumstance precluding the wrongfulness of state conduct among the defences available under international criminal law, it seems nonetheless necessary to keep a certain consistency in the application of the rules on belligerent reprisals under both state and individual responsibility. Indeed, when a (state) conduct is to be regarded as lawful under international humanitarian law, it can hardly be used to affirm the criminal liability of individuals. Where the same conduct is at stake, it seems reasonable to maintain that it should receive the same qualification in terms of both aggravated state responsibility and individual criminal liability. According to the same rationale, when an isolated conduct entail both ordinary state responsibility and individual criminal liability, it seems correct to apply defences and the corresponding circumstances precluding wrongfulness in a consistent manner.

As a final remark, it can be said that the analysis of defences and circumstances precluding wrongfulness shows, in line with previous chapters, the difficulty of relying on a pure either state-oriented or individual-oriented conceptual scheme to solve the problems raised by the relationship between state and individual responsibility for international crimes. While a certain separation characterizes in principle these regimes, there are also close links due to the definition of certain crimes under international law, and to factual circumstances which are relevant to establish both aggravated state responsibility and individual criminal liability.

Chapter 6

Ascribing Responsibility for Collective Crimes: Modes of Liability

The previous chapters have discussed the elements of international crimes. In the following pages, the analysis continues to focus on the conduct capable of entailing a dual responsibility under international law, but from a different perspective. The relationship between state and individual responsibility for international crimes is examined from the standpoint of international criminal law. Because international criminal tribunals generally focus on large-scale crimes, they have not only interpreted the elements of international crimes in a way which takes their collective dimension into account, they have also developed specific modes of liability by which to ascribe individual criminal liability to the participants in collective criminality. This confirms the fact that the collective dimension of international crimes plays a crucial role in ascribing individual criminal liability.

Indeed, the analysis of international case law reveals a gradual shift from purely individual to collective responsibility. International criminal tribunals increasingly rely on specific modes of liability allowing them to deal with vast scale crimes more efficiently. This is because individual liability is attached to individual members of a criminal group according to their participation in a wider criminal enterprise. Therefore, the emphasis shifts from the personal behaviour of the suspect to collective criminality, or even state criminality. While it is not technically possible to speak of an overlap between state and individual responsibility as far as modes of liability are concerned, these particular modes represent an additional element pointing to a substantial overlap of the way in which conduct entailing a dual responsibility is ascertained at the international level.

The analysis of these typical elements of international criminal law will start by considering the various ways in which individual criminal liability can in principle be linked to collective responsibility. It will then trace the evolution of international criminal law as far as modes of collective liability are concerned. Finally, it will discuss the connections that are entailed by this recent development in terms of the relationship between individual and state responsibility for international crimes.

1. *Linking Individual Liability to Collective Criminal Conduct*

When international crimes are committed at the collective or state level, the main challenge is to secure prosecution in an effective way. From the viewpoint of international law – a body of law traditionally concentrating on state responsibility only, it might seem natural to focus first and foremost on collective responsibility and then try to derive individual responsibility from the prior establishment of the commission of a collective crime.

Abstractly speaking, there are at least three ways in which to link the establishment of criminal liability of individual perpetrators to a previous finding of collective responsibility. One of the easiest ways is to consider that, if a certain group is responsible for an international crime, then *all* the members of the group must be held criminally liable. In other words, mere membership in the criminal group is enough to automatically entail the criminal liability of each member of the group for the crimes committed by the group.[1] This mechanism is undoubtedly unacceptable from the perspective of individual liability, because it totally disregards the basic principles of international criminal law, according to which the material and psychological participation of each member of the group must be demonstrated. But it is also problematic from the viewpoint of state responsibility. If the group is a state, then a finding of aggravated state responsibility would necessarily entail the criminal responsibility of all the members belonging to the state community. No similar consequence can be justified under international law.

Second, it is possible to limit the effect of a previous finding on group responsibility, and to say that it should only entail the criminal liability of a restricted number of members of the group, namely, only the leaders of the group. Since it can be regarded as not materially possible or not fair to punish *all* the members of group, one could focus only on those persons who have planned, decided, and organized the commission of the relevant collective crimes. In other words, only a few decision-makers can be held criminally liable on behalf of the entire group. Thus, it is the group as a whole to be indirectly sanctioned through the punishment of its 'major responsible' members. Again, if the group is a state, this second option could be consistent with a state-oriented conceptual scheme, but finds no support in international practice. Except for aggression, international crimes do not include in their definition any such limitation with respect to the offenders that can be put on trial. And this option is clearly at odds with the basic principle

[1] This was arguably the aim of the American proposal which led to the inclusion of the crime of membership in the IMT Statute annexed to the London Charter. *See* S. Darcy, *Collective Responsibility and Accountability under International Law* (Leiden, Koninklijke Brill NV, 2007), pp. 257–262. As will be discussed below, however, the IMT had been very careful in triggering such a mechanism (*see* infra in this Chapter).

of individual guilt and the fundamental purpose of international criminal law, which is to fight against impunity and bring to justice all those who have committed international crimes.

Third, the collective responsibility of the entire group can be said to entail only the criminal liability of those members who have actually participated in the collective criminal conduct. In other words, a more limited connection between the collective nature of the crime and those who can bear criminal liability for it can be taken into account. According to this third option, if the entire group is declared criminal, the prosecution of individual members of the group can only rely on partial presumptions. Thus, while the *actus reus* can be presumed – or better yet, while membership in the criminal group should be regarded as the *actus reus* of the crime in question – the criminal court will nonetheless have to establish beyond doubt the *mens rea* of the member who participated in the collective criminal context. This third option may be acceptable from the standpoint of international criminal law, since the previous finding on collective responsibility does not automatically give rise to individual liability, but it has the legal effect of allowing criminal courts to establish individual liability more easily.

International practice shows no such case of a direct link between the establishment of aggravated state responsibility and individual liability for international crimes. The only precedent can be traced back to the IMT Statute, where individual liability is linked to a previous establishment of collective responsibility for international crimes. Accordingly, two questions arise. First, whether such a link (or a similar link) between collective and individual responsibility for international crimes can still be relied upon today. Second, how the collective dimension of international crimes can be a point of contact between state and individual responsibility.

2. *The Crime of Membership in a Criminal Organization*

After WWII, the prosecution of those responsible for the widespread crimes committed during the war was faced with a major problem, namely that of bringing to justice an amazingly high number of perpetrators. Therefore, it was necessary to find prompt ways to put the suspects on trial. The special mechanism elaborated in order to deal with collective international crimes was the crime of membership. According to Article 9 (1) of the IMT Statute:

> At the trial of any individual member of any group or organization the Tribunal may declare (in connection with any act of which the individual may be convicted) that the group or organization of which the individual was a member was a criminal organization.

Then, Article 10 added that:

> In cases were a group or organization is declared criminal by the Tribunal, the competent national authority of a Signatory shall have the right to bring individuals to trial for membership therein before national, military, or occupation courts. In any such case the criminal nature of the group or organization is considered proved and shall not be questioned.

Thus, the IMT was competent to assign criminal status to German organizations that were responsible for the most serious international crimes committed during WWII. Then every member of such organizations would be subject to trial and punishment before the competent national courts. In particular, members of criminal organizations would be found guilty for mere participation in those organizations, not for having committed specific international crimes. In other words, mere membership was regarded as criminal. Accordingly, Control Council Law No. 10 provided that acts recognized as crimes included "membership in categories of a criminal group or organization declared criminal by the International Military Tribunal".[2]

The crime of membership was elaborated by the US according to the common law notion of corporate liability, and with the aim to concentrate international efforts (that is, the IMT jurisdiction) on the prosecution of crimes committed by state leaders and criminal organizations, while leaving subordinates to domestic courts.[3] Thus, the crime of membership was conceived of to facilitate the attribution of liability for collective crimes to the various members of the criminal groups. Since it was impossible for the IMT to prosecute all those responsible for crimes committed during WWII, this mechanism allowed national courts to deal with intermediate and minor players, and more generally with all the members of the organizations which would have been declared criminal by the IMT.

However, the crime of membership was problematic from the viewpoint of the principle of individual criminal liability. If applied literally, the mechanism provided under Articles 9 and 10 of the IMT Statute would have meant disregarding the basic principle according to which "no one may be held answerable for acts or omissions of organizations to which he belongs, unless he bears personal responsibility for a particular act, conduct or omission".[4] Indeed, the main problem with the crime of membership was that it indirectly provided for a mechanism of collective punishment. The risk of guilt by association was acknowledged by the IMT, and it explicitly rejected the possibility of mass punishments (as did domestic courts in subsequent trials).[5]

---

[2] *See* Article II (1)(d) of Control Council Law N. 10.

[3] *See*, in general, H. Meyrowitz, *La répression des crimes contre l'humanité par les tribunaux allemands en application de la loi n.10 du Conseil de Contrôle Allié* (Paris, LGDJ, 1960).

[4] A. Cassese, *International Criminal Law* (Oxford, Oxford University Press, 2003), p. 137.

[5] IMT Judgment, supra Chapter 1, note 90, p. 251 ("criminal guilt is personal, and mass punishment must be avoided"). The same position was clearly shared by domestic courts pronounc-

In its judgment, the IMT was very careful in applying Article 9. First, it declared criminal only a few German organizations, namely, the Leadership Corps of the Nazi Party, the Gestapo, the SD, and the SS. These organizations were established and used for purposes which were criminal under international law; membership in these organizations was voluntary; and their members were involved in the commission of the most serious crimes perpetrated by the Nazi regime during WWII. Second, the IMT made a careful evaluation of the legal consequences of such declarations as far as the individual criminal liability of their members was concerned. In particular, it held that:

> A criminal organization is analogous to a criminal conspiracy in that the essence of both is co-operation for criminal purposes. There must be a group bound together and organized for a common purpose. The group must be formed or used in connection with the commission of crimes denounced by the Charter. Since the declaration with respect to the organizations and groups will, as has been pointed out, fix the criminality of its members, that definition should exclude persons who had no *knowledge* of the criminal purposes or acts of the organization and those who were drafted by the State for membership, unless they were personally implicated in the commission of acts declared criminal by Article 6 of the Charter as members of the organization. Membership *alone* is not enough to come within the scope of these declarations.[6]

In other words, the IMT tried to bring back this crime to the traditional concepts of criminal law.

> A member of an organization which the Tribunal has declared to be criminal may be subsequently convicted of the crime of membership and be punished for that crime by death. This is not to assume that international or military courts which will try these individuals will not exercise appropriate standards of justice.[7]

To be sure, the main legal consequence of the declaration was to fix the criminality of its members, that is, to regard membership as the *actus reus* of the crime in question. However, the IMT required domestic courts to establish, in addition, that membership was voluntary and that the accused had knowledge that the group or organization was used for the commission of international crimes. In that way, the IMT required the *mens rea* of the member to be established. Of course, where members of the organization were found to have personally committed international crimes, this would be enough to entail their criminal liability independently of the fact that their membership in the criminal organization was voluntary.

---

ing in subsequent trials. *See* the *Flick* case, US Nuremberg Military Tribunal, *Flick and Others*, 22 December 1947, 14 *ILR* (1947), p. 266 et seq., the *Krupp* case, US Nuremberg Military Tribunal, *Krupp and Others*, 30 June 1948, 15 *ILR* (1948), p. 627 et seq., and the *Farben* case, supra Chapter 4, note 79.

6 IMT Judgment, supra Chapter 1, note 90, p. 251 (emphasis added).

7 *Ibid.*, p. 250.

As a result, the crime of membership was not considered to be a mechanism which automatically ascribed liability for the crimes committed by the group or organization to all its members, including those who had not participated in their execution. The IMT considered the crime of membership to be a separate international offence in which the *actus reus* is membership in a criminal organization or group, and the *mens rea* is knowledge of the criminal purpose of that organization or group.

On the one hand, it was mere membership that was to be criminalized (independently of the commission of international crimes), since it was considered that criminal groups or organizations had been the main instruments of the German state for the planning and execution of international crimes. On the other hand, this separate offence did not call into question the principle of individual criminal liability, since the IMT defined it according to the principle of personal guilt.[8]

Thus, the crime of membership could be seen as a useful tool in the prosecution of international crimes committed by the state apparatus. In particular, it established a direct legal link between those state structures declared criminal by the IMT and the individual criminal responsibility of the members of such organizations.

3. *Modes of Collective Liability under International Criminal Law*

Yet modern international criminal law seems to have abandoned such a mechanism. The crime of membership was exceptionally included in the London Charter, and no similar tool has been inserted since that time in the statutes of international criminal tribunals. Moreover, such tribunals have no jurisdiction over collective entities, but only over natural persons. While various domestic legal systems provide for the criminalization of membership in groups or organizations established for the purpose of committing crimes, it seems impossible to assert the existence of a similar offence under modern international criminal law[9] in the absence of any explicit provision or of any relevant practice in that regard, apart from the Nuremberg precedent. However, international criminal tribunals have elaborated other tools to deal with crimes committed in a collective context. In particular, they increasingly rely on specific modes of liability which can facilitate the appraisal of collective criminal phenomena and the establishment of the individual liability of the members of criminal groups.

---

8 Subsequent trials which applied the crime of membership respected the definition and recommendations made by the IMT. *See*, in particular, the *Ministries* case (supra Chapter 3, note 139), and the *Einsatzgruppen* case (US Nuremberg Military Tribunal, *Ohlendorf et al.*, 10 April 1948, 15 *ILR* (1948), pp. 656–668).

9 *See* S. Bouiffror and C. Derycke, 'Les organisations criminelles', in H. Ascensio *et al.* (eds.), *Droit international pénal* (Paris, Pedone, 2000), pp. 167–179.

Command responsibility, for example, was elaborated with the precise aim of facilitating the attribution of collective crimes committed in hierarchically organized contexts to those allegedly most responsible, *i.e.*, commanders. Since the *Yamashita* case, command responsibility has significantly broadened its scope and today not only military commanders but also civilian superiors can be held accountable for not having prevented or punished the crimes committed by their subordinates. However, despite its very broad scope, command responsibility has been applied by international tribunals in a very rigorous manner and only in a very few cases has the Prosecutor successfully charged persons under this form of liability. Since direct responsibility is always to be preferred, in the end command responsibility has been confined to a few cases of military-like situations, and has been successfully applied to low-ranking military commanders.[10]

Another form of liability has proved more successful in the prosecution of collective crimes, and is increasingly relied upon by *ad hoc* tribunals: this is 'aiding and abetting'. Indeed, this form of liability presupposes that the crime has been carried out by a group of persons, and, since it distinguishes between perpetrators and accomplices, it allows international tribunals to ascribe individual liability to those persons who have not directly committed international crimes, but who (knowingly) have substantially contributed to the commission of these crimes.

Thus, aiding and abetting is a form of liability which can be very useful to deal with collective crimes, which are characterized by the fact of being carried out by large amounts of organized perpetrators. Under such circumstances the offence is generally so complex that it can only be perpetrated with the contribution of various offenders, each of them performing a very specialized task which has nonetheless a substantial effect on the achievement of the criminal purpose. Thus, it can be very difficult to appraise all the criminal acts which, taken together, result in

---

[10] For a general overview of the *ad hoc* tribunals' case law concerning command responsibility *see* B.I. Bonafè, 'Finding a Proper Role for Command Responsibility', 5 *JICJ* (2007), p. 599 et seq. For two recent cases, *see* ICTY, *Prosecutor v. Orić*, TC, Judgment, 30 June 2006, and ICTY, *Prosecutor v. Strugar*, TC, Judgment, 31 January 2005. In the former case, the accused was found guilty under the doctrine of command responsibility and sentenced to two years' imprisonment, but the AC reversed his conviction under Article 7(3) of the ICTY Statute (ICTY, *Prosecutor v. Orić*, AC, Judgment, 3 July 2008). In the latter case, the AC upheld the accused's conviction under Article 7(3) of the ICTY Statute (ICTY, *Prosecutor v. Strugar*, AC, Judgment, 17 July 2008). For a particular conception of superior responsibility, *see* N.L. Reid, 'Bridging the Conceptual Chasm: Superior Responsibility as the Missing Link between State and Individual Responsibility under International Law', 18 *Leiden Journal of International Law* (2005), p. 827. The author maintains that superior responsibility is a mode of liability capable of reconciling state and individual responsibility for international crimes. Since both kinds of responsibility originate from the breach of the same duty to prevent or punish the commission of international crimes, the establishment of superior responsibility would lead to the parallel establishment of state responsibility. For further reflections on this issue, *see* infra Chapter 7, notes 47–48 and accompanying text.

the commission of international crimes. Aiding and abetting is a form of liability which can help in identifying those offenders who are structurally remote from the commission of international crimes but who have otherwise played a substantial role in their perpetration, *i.e.*, accomplices.

Aiding and abetting is now a well-established form of liability. Since its first case, the ICTY had the occasion to illustrate the two basic requirements that must be fulfilled to hold the accomplice criminally liable.[11] The actions of the accused must have a substantial and direct effect on the commission of the international crime, and the accused must have the knowledge of the likely effect of his or her actions.[12] Subsequent case law has further clarified that notion, and identified specific situations in which it can be said that the accomplice knowingly gave "practical assistance, encouragement, or moral support" having a substantial effect on the perpetration of collective crimes.[13]

---

[11] ICTY, *Prosecutor v. Tadić*, TC, Judgment, 7 May 1997, paras. 663–692.

[12] According to recent case law, "The *actus reus* of aiding and abetting is that the support, encouragement or assistance of the aider and abettor has a substantial effect upon the perpetration of the crime. There is no requirement of a causal relationship between the conduct of the aider or abettor and the commission of the crime, or proof that such conduct was a condition precedent to the commission of the crime. An omission may, in the particular circumstances of the case, constitute the *actus reus* of aiding and abetting. Further, the assistance may occur before, during or after the principal crime has been perpetrated. While each case turns on its own facts, mere presence at the scene of a crime will not usually constitute aiding or abetting. However, where the presence bestows legitimacy on, or provides encouragement to, the actual perpetrator, that may be sufficient. In a particular case encouragement may be established by an evident sympathetic or approving attitude to the commission of the relevant act. For example, the presence of a superior may operate as an encouragement or support, in the relevant sense. The *mens rea* required is knowledge that, by his or her conduct, the aider and abettor is assisting or facilitating the commission of the offence. This awareness need not have been explicitly expressed. It may, of course, be inferred from all relevant circumstances. The aider and abettor need not share the *mens rea* of the perpetrator, but he or she must be aware of the essential elements of the crime ultimately committed by the perpetrator, and must be aware of the perpetrators' state of mind. This is not to say that the aider and abettor must be aware of the specific crime that will be committed by the perpetrator. If the aider and abettor is aware that one of a number of crimes will probably be committed by the perpetrator, and one of those crimes is in fact committed, than he has intended to assist or facilitate the commission of that crime, and is guilty as an aider and abettor." (ICTY, *Prosecutor v. Limaj et al.*, TC, Judgment, 30 November 2005, paras. 517–518).

[13] ICTY, *Prosecutor v. Furundžija*, TC, Judgment, 10 December 1998, paras. 190–257. For the relevant case law, *see* ICTY, *Prosecutor v Delalić et al.*, TC, Judgment, 16 November 1998, paras. 327–329; ICTY, *Prosecutor v. Aleksovski*, TC, Judgment, 25 June 1999, paras. 62–65; ICTY, *Prosecutor v. Kunarac et al.*, TC, Judgment, 22 February 2001, paras. 391–393; ICTY, *Prosecutor v. Kvočka et al.*, TC, Judgment, 2 November 2001, paras. 253–263; ICTY, *Prosecutor v. Krnojelac*, TC, Judgment, 15 March 2002, paras. 88–90; ICTY, *Prosecutor v. Vasiljević*, TC, Judgment, 29 November 2002, paras. 70–71; ICTY, *Prosecutor v. Naletilić and Martinović*, TC, Judgment, 31 March 2003, para. 63; ICTY, *Prosecutor v. Krnojelac*, AC, Judgment, 17 September 2003, para. 33; ICTY, *Prosecutor v. Simić et al.*, TC, Judgment, 17 October 2003, paras. 161–165; ICTY, *Prosecutor v. Vasiljević*,

Interestingly, due to the nature of collective crimes, aiding and abetting is increasingly relied on to deal with crimes committed by superiors or leaders. Indeed, superiors and leaders generally do not physically participate in the commission of international crimes. These are normally carried out by 'executioners', whose direct criminal responsibility can be established quite easily. It is much more difficult to prove a direct involvement on the part of leaders. One can assume that leaders generally play a major role in conceiving and planning the commission of collective crimes. But this is very difficult to demonstrate. Charges for having planned, ordered or instigated the commission of international crimes are rarely successful. Thus, aiding and abetting can be a form of liability which at least allows the tribunal to convict leaders for the role they played in facilitating the commission of collective crimes. For example, the ICTY relied on aiding and abetting to convict two commanders of the Bosnian Serb Army. General Krstić, Commander of the Drina Corps, and Colonel Blagojević, Commander of the Bratunac Brigade, were both convicted for aiding and abetting genocide.[14] Similarly, aiding and abetting was the form of liability which allowed the ICTR to convict as accomplices in the Rwandan genocide leading political figures, such as the Minister of Finance of the Interim Government.[15] Although aiding and abetting can facilitate the prosecution of international crimes, paradoxically it has the effect of turning state leaders into simple accomplices.[16]

From the standpoint of the present analysis, the most interesting form of liability is undoubtedly joint criminal enterprise. The possibility of relying on joint criminal

AC, Judgment, 25 February 2004, para. 102; ICTY, *Prosecutor v. Krstić*, AC, Judgment, 19 April 2004, paras. 135–144; ICTY, *Prosecutor v. Blaškić*, AC, Judgment, 29 July 2004, paras. 43–52; ICTY, *Prosecutor v. Brđanin*, TC, Judgment, 1 September 2004, paras. 271–274; ICTY, *Prosecutor v. Blagojević and Jokić*, TC, Judgment, 17 January 2005, paras. 726–728; ICTY, *Prosecutor v. Strugar*, TC, Judgment, 31 January 2005, paras. 349–350. The ICTR has also relied on this form of liability. However, it has generally convicted persons who could be regarded, at the same time, as direct perpetrators and as accomplices. *See* ICTR, *Prosecutor v. Akayesu*, TC, Judgment, 2 September 1998, paras. 484, and 693; ICTR, *Prosecutor v. Kayishema and Ruzindana*, TC, Judgment, 21 May 1999, paras. 199–201, and 500; ICTR, *Prosecutor v. Musema*, TC, Judgment, 27 January 2000, paras. 125–126, and 944; ICTR, *Prosecutor v. Kajelijeli*, TC, Judgment, 1 Decemebr 2003, paras. 757, and 765–769; ICTR, *Prosecutor v. Kamuhanda*, TC, Judgment, 22 January 2004, paras. 588, and 596–600; *Prosecutor v. Ntagerura et al.*, TC, Judgment, 25 February 2004, paras. 763, and 802.

14 ICTY, *Prosecutor v. Krstić*, AC, Judgment, 19 April 2004, paras. 135–144; ICTY, *Prosecutor v. Blagojević and Jokić*, TC, Judgment, 17 January 2005, paras. 723–728, and 770–787.

15 *See* ICTR, *Prosecutor v. Semanza*, TC, Judgment, 15 May 2003, paras. 433–436. But *see* also ICTR, *Prosecutor v. Elizaphan and Gerard Ntakirutimana*, TC, Judgment, 21 February 2003, paras. 787–790, and ICTR, *Prosecutor v. Ndindabahizi*, TC, Judgment, 15 July 2004, paras. 455–457, 464, and 485.

16 K. Gustafson, 'The Requirement of an "Express Agreement" for Joint Criminal Enterprise', 5 *JICJ* (2007), p. 152.

enterprise was affirmed for the first time by the ICTY in the *Tadić* case,[17] and now this form of liability is routinely applied in the jurisprudence of both the ICTY and the ICTR. The ICC Statute also includes joint criminal enterprise among the forms of liability provided under Article 25.[18]

The reasons for the success of this form of liability are quite obvious. International crimes are generally carried out by groups of perpetrators, and joint criminal enterprise allows international tribunals to take this collective dimension into account.[19] This was explicitly recognized by the ICTY in *Tadić*. The Appeals Chamber acknowledged that, according to the Statute, all those who have committed international crimes, "whatever the manner in which they may have perpetrated, or participated in the perpetration of those violations, must be brought to justice", and put the emphasis on the collective nature of international crimes in order to conclude that the Statute also embraces modes of collective liability, as joint criminal enterprise.[20]

---

[17] ICTY, *Prosecutor v. Tadić*, AC, Judgment, 15 July 1999, paras. 185–229.

[18] "In accordance with this Statute, a person shall be criminally responsible and liable for punishment for a crime within the jurisdiction of the Court if that person: . . . (d) In any other way contributes to the commission or attempted commission of such a crime by a group of persons acting with a common purpose. Such contribution shall be intentional and shall either: (i) Be made with the aim of furthering the criminal activity or purpose of the group, where such activity or purpose involves the commission of a crime within the jurisdiction of the Court; or (ii) Be made in the knowledge of the intention of the group to commit the crime" (Article 25(3)(d) of the Rome Statute). There are diverging opinions on the actual scope of this provision. For an interpretation consistent with the case law of the *ad hoc* tribunals concerning joint criminal enterprise, *see* A. Cassese, 'The Proper Limits of Individual Responsibility under the Doctrine of Joint Criminal Enterprise', 5 *JICJ* (2007), p. 132. For a narrower interpretation, *see* K. Ambos, 'Joint Criminal Enterprise and Command Responsibility', 5 *JICJ* (2007), p. 159.

[19] *See* N. Piacente, 'Importance of the Joint Criminal Enterprise Doctrine for the ICTY Prosecutorial Policy', 2 *JICJ* (2004), pp. 446–454.

[20] "[The Statute] does not exclude those modes of participating in the commission of crimes which occur where *several persons* having a common purpose embark on criminal activity that is then carried out either jointly or by some members of this plurality of persons. Whoever contributes to the commission of crimes by the group of persons or some members of the group, in execution of a common criminal purpose, may be held to be criminally liable, subject to certain conditions, which are specified below. The above interpretation is not only dictated by the object and purpose of the Statute but is also warranted by the *very nature of many international crimes* which are committed most commonly in wartime situations. *Most of the time these crimes do not result from the criminal propensity of single individuals but constitute manifestations of collective criminality*: the crimes are often carried out by groups of individuals acting in pursuance of a common criminal design. Although only some members of the group may physically perpetrate the criminal act (murder, extermination, wanton destruction of cities, towns or villages, etc.), the participation and contribution of the other members of the group is often vital in facilitating the commission of the offence in question. It follows that the moral gravity of such participation is often no less – or indeed no different – from that of those actually carrying out the acts in question. Under these

Thus, joint criminal enterprise is aimed at making possible the conviction of the members of a criminal group. But this is not a way to ascribe criminal liability for mere membership in a criminal organization. This point has been made quite clear. Joint criminal enterprise does not resuscitate the Nuremberg crime of membership. Joint criminal enterprise is simply a form of liability, not a new offence criminalizing participation in a criminal group or organization. To be convicted, the accused must have personally carried out international crimes, even if he or she has done so together with other perpetrators.[21]

The fact that joint criminal enterprise requires the offence to have actually been carried out is useful to distinguish this notion from that of conspiracy. The latter was included in the IMT Statute, even though it only applied to crimes against peace. Indeed, in the case of conspiracy, mere agreement is sufficient to convict an accused who has not materially carried out the relevant crime, whereas "the liability of a member of a joint criminal enterprise will depend on the commission of criminal acts in furtherance of that enterprise".[22]

---

circumstances, *to hold criminally liable as a perpetrator only the person who materially performs the criminal act would disregard the role as co-perpetrators of all those who in some way made it possible for the perpetrator physically to carry out that criminal act.* At the same time, depending upon the circumstances, to hold the latter liable only as aiders and abettors might understate the degree of their criminal responsibility. This interpretation, based on the Statute and the inherent characteristics of many crimes perpetrated in wartime, warrants the conclusion that international criminal responsibility embraces actions perpetrated by a *collectivity of persons* in furtherance of a common criminal design" (ICTY, *Prosecutor v. Tadić*, AC, Judgment, 15 July 1999, paras. 190–193, emphasis added). For a different view, advocating a more literal interpretation of the ICTY Statute, *see* J.D. Ohlin, 'Three Conceptual Problems with the Doctrine of Joint Criminal Enterprise', 5 *JICJ* (2007), p. 69.

21 The ICTY had the occasion to clarify that: "[j]oint criminal enterprise is different from membership of a criminal enterprise which was criminalized as a separate criminal offence in Nuremberg and in subsequent trials held under Control Council Law No 10. As pointed out by the *United Nations War Crimes Commission*, what was to be punished in relation to the latter was 'no mere conspiracy to commit crimes but a knowing and voluntary membership of organizations which did in fact commit crimes, and those on a wide scale'. No such offence was included in the Tribunal's Statute. The Secretary-General made it clear that only natural persons (as opposed to juridical entities) were liable under the Tribunal's Statute, and that mere membership in a given criminal organization would not be sufficient to establish individual criminal responsibility... Criminal liability pursuant to a joint criminal enterprise is not a liability for mere membership of for conspiring to commit crimes, but a form of liability concerned with the participation in the commission of a crime as part of a joint criminal enterprise, a different matter. The Prosecution in the present case made that point clear when it said that Ojdanić was being charged not for his membership in a joint criminal enterprise but for his part in carrying it out. The indictment talks of his 'having significantly contributed' to the execution of the joint criminal enterprise by 'using the *de jure* and *de facto* powers available to him'." (ICTY, *Prosecutor v. Milutinović et al.*, AC, Decision on Ojdanić's Motion challenging Jurisdiction – Joint Criminal Enterprise, 21 May 2003, paras. 25–26).

22 *Ibid.*, para. 23.

According to a now well-established case law, joint criminal enterprise is a form of liability requiring the members of the group to actually participate in the commission of the crime. The objective elements (*actus reus*) of joint criminal enterprise are: 1) a plurality of persons; 2) the existence of a common plan, design or purpose which amounts to or involves the commission of an international crime; and 3) participation of the accused in the common design involving the perpetration of an international crime.[23] The ICTY identified three different types of joint criminal enterprise, and accordingly three different *mens rea* requirements.[24]

The 'basic' form of joint criminal enterprise includes cases where all co-perpetrators, acting pursuant to a common purpose, possess the same criminal intention. This first category requires the intent to perpetrate a certain crime to be shared by all co-perpetrators. The 'systemic' form of joint criminal enterprise is a variant of the basic form characterized by the existence of an organized system of ill-treatment, and concerns the so-called concentration camp cases. It requires the accused to have personal knowledge of the system of ill-treatment as well as the intent to further this common concerted system. The 'expanded' form of joint criminal enterprise concerns cases involving a common purpose to commit an international crime where one of the perpetrators commits an act which, while outside the common purpose, is nevertheless a natural and foreseeable consequence of the carrying out of that common purpose. This third category requires the accused to have the intention to participate in the criminal purpose and to contribute to the joint criminal enterprise. In addition, the accused is liable for a crime not agreed upon in the common plan if the commission of this crime was foreseeable, and he or she willingly took that risk.

As noted above, international tribunals now routinely rely on this form of liability. Despite some clarification, they apply the definition of joint criminal enterprise as set out in early case law. From the viewpoint of the present analysis, two sets of consequences deriving from reliance on joint criminal enterprise must be pointed out. First, the major legal consequence in terms of criminal responsibility is that all of the participants in a joint criminal enterprise "are equally guilty of the crime regardless of the part played by each in its commission".[25] Therefore, it is at the sentencing stage that the specific contribution of the accused will be evaluated.[26] Second, joint criminal enterprise is a form of liability specifically aimed at address-

---

[23] ICTY, *Prosecutor v. Tadić*, AC, Judgment, 15 July 1999, para. 227.

[24] *Ibid.*, para. 228, and ICTY, *Prosecutor v. Vasiljević*, AC, Judgment, 22 February 2004, paras. 97–99.

[25] ICTY, *Prosecutor v. Vasiljević*, TC, Judgment, 29 November 2002, para. 67. *See* also ICTY, *Prosecutor v. Brđanin and Talić*, TC, Decision on Form of Further Amended Indictment and Prosecution Application to Amend, 26 June 2001, para. 26; ICTY, *Prosecutor v. Krnojelac*, TC, Judgment, 15 March 2002, para. 82.

[26] ICTY, *Prosecutor v. Vasiljević*, AC, Judgment, 25 February 2004, para. 110.

ing international crimes committed at the collective level. This has the effect of changing the perspective of the tribunal which has to establish individual liability for collective crimes.

As far as *mens rea* is concerned, relying on a form of liability like joint criminal enterprise necessarily implies a different approach in proving this element. Indeed, the tribunal has to investigate the intent *shared* by the co-perpetrators, and not that of an isolated offender. This may considerably facilitate its task. Of course, joint criminal enterprise requires the psychological element to be demonstrated, and the fact of relying on this particular form of liability cannot alter the *mens rea* required by international crimes. Thus, for example, a participant in a joint criminal enterprise aimed at persecuting the civilian population must posses the requisite discriminatory intent.[27]

With respect to the establishment of the *shared mens rea*, there are also cases in which the organization among the members of the criminal enterprise is *per se* an *indicium* of the psychological attitude of the accused. For example, the 'systemic' form of joint criminal enterprise seems to render less difficult the establishment of a shared *mens rea*. In *Krnojelac*, the Appeals Chamber of the ICTY held that:

> with regard to Krnojelac's duties, the time over which he exercised those duties, his knowledge of the system in place, the crimes committed as part of that system and their discriminatory nature, a trier of fact should reasonably have inferred from the above findings that *he was part of the system and thereby intended to further it*. The same conclusion must be reached when determining whether the findings should have led a trier of fact reasonably to conclude that *Krnojelac shared the discriminatory intent* of the perpetrators of the crimes of imprisonment and inhumane acts.[28]

While proof of the shared intent is certainly easier than proof of the intent of an individual perpetrator, it must be admitted that this element is always difficult to demonstrate. In particular, the shared intent is not easily demonstrated with respect to specific intent crimes. One can think of the *Krstić* and the *Blagojević* cases examined above.[29] In similar cases, the Tribunal turned to another mode of liability typical of collective crimes which requires a lower *mens rea*, and has convicted the accused as aiders and abettors.

As far as *actus reus* is concerned, reliance on joint criminal enterprise means that the tribunal will not evaluate the personal conduct of one single offender, but that

---

[27] ICTY, *Prosecutor v. Stakić*, TC, Judgment, 31 July 2003, para. 826. This aspect has raised considerable controversy, because the third category of joint criminal enterprise requires a lower standard of *mens rea* and hardly seems applicable to specific intent crimes. For an attempt to reconcile this apparent inconsistency, *see* E. Van Sliedregt, 'Joint Criminal Enterprise as a Pathway to Convicting Individuals for Genocide', 5 *JICJ* (2007), p. 184.

[28] ICTY, *Prosecutor v. Krnojelac*, AC, Judgment, 17 September 2003, para. 111 (emphasis added).

[29] These cases have been examined supra in Chapter 4. *See* also ICTY, *Prosecutor v. Vasiljević*, AC, Judgment, 24 February 2004, paras. 115–132.

of a plurality of perpetrators. In this respect, the *ad hoc* tribunals have adopted a more liberal approach. In particular, they will focus on the final result of the collective conduct of a group of offenders in achieving their common purpose, for example in persecuting the civilian population. Concretely, this means that the tribunal focuses on a collective criminal context. The personal conduct of the accused must 'only' evidence some form of participation in the commission of the relevant international crime.

The fact that international criminal tribunals do not seem to be willing to excessively broaden the scope of joint criminal enterprise with respect to the personal contribution of the accused does not exclude reliance on the doctrine of joint criminal enterprise in cases in which the accused played only a secondary role in the furtherance of the common criminal purpose. The ICTY required that participation and contribution of individual members be "significant".[30] This does not mean, however, that the member of the joint criminal enterprise must have physically committed any part of the *actus reus* of the relevant crime, nor that his contribution must have had a substantial effect on the commission of the crime, as in aiding and abetting.[31] The level of participation in a joint criminal enterprise is "less than the level of participation necessary to graduate an aider or abettor to a co-perpetrator of that enterprise."[32] Arguably, the reason for this lower involvement is twofold. Joint criminal enterprise is characterized by the common criminal purpose, and additionally requires the accused to share the intent with other participants, while an aider and abettor only needs to have knowledge of the principal's intent.[33] Thus, whether the participation of an individual accused person in a joint criminal enterprise can be regarded as significant is established on a case-by-case basis, according to the particular characteristics of the collective criminal phenomenon at issue.[34]

---

30 ICTY, *Prosecutor v. Brđanin*, AC, Judgment, 3 April 2007, para. 430.

31 ICTY, *Prosecutor v. Vasiljević*, AC, Judgment, 24 February 2004, para. 102.

32 ICTY, *Prosecutor v. Kvočka et al.*, TC, Judgment, 2 November 2001, para. 287.

33 *Ibid.*, para. 288.

34 Nonetheless, the Tribunal has indicated some factors which can be relevant in establishing the necessary level of participation in a joint criminal enterprise. *Ibid.*, para. 311: "The level of participation attributed to the accused and whether that participation is deemed significant will depend on a variety of factors, including the size of the criminal enterprise, the functions performed, the position of the accused, the amount of time spent participating after acquiring knowledge of the criminality of the system, efforts made to prevent criminal activity or to impede the efficient functioning of the system, the seriousness and scope of the crimes committed and the efficiency, zealousness or gratuitous cruelty exhibited in performing the actor's function".

4. *Joint Criminal Enterprise and Mass Atrocities*

One of the most controversial aspects concerning joint criminal enterprise is whether this doctrine can apply to very broad cases in which the Prosecution includes among the members of a criminal enterprise a large amount of persons, in particular, political or military leaders who have not physically committed any relevant crime, and who are structurally remote from those having materially perpetrated these crimes.

It need hardly be recalled that joint criminal enterprise requires a common purpose among the participants, and that they participated in the commission of international crimes in furtherance of the common purpose. Excessively broadening its scope, it is maintained, creates a risk that joint criminal enterprise will be transformed into what is essentially guilt by association.[35] In practice, however, international crimes are most of the time committed by large groups of perpetrators and the criminal design is often elaborated at the level of political and military leaders. Joint criminal enterprise could be a very useful tool to ascribe liability to those offenders that have not materially committed any international crime, and more generally to deal with collective criminality.[36]

In *Brđanin*, the Trial Chamber of the ICTY considered that joint criminal enterprise was not the appropriate mode of liability to describe the individual criminal liability of the accused.[37] The Prosecutor alleged that many individuals participated in a joint criminal enterprise with the purpose of forcibly removing the Bosnian Muslim and Bosnia Croat population from the territory of the planned Serbian state. These included Momir Talić, other members of the ARK Crisis Staff, the leadership of the SerBiH and the SDS, including Radovan Karadžić, Momcilo Krajišnik and Biljana Plavšić, members of the Assembly of the Autonomous Region of Krajina and the Assembly's Executive Committee, the Serb Crisis Staffs of the ARK municipalities, the army of the Republika Srpska, Bosnian Serb paramilitary forces and others. Since the accused did not physically commit any of the crimes charged in the indictment, the Prosecutor had to establish whether there had been an agreement (to commit the relevant crime) between the accused and the other persons listed above. However, the Tribunal did not examine the existence of a joint

[35] *See* S. Darcy, supra note 1, pp. 245–253, who expresses criticism over both joint criminal enterprise and command responsibility as modes of liability "tend to raise the spectre of collective responsibility", (p. 366); J.D. Ohlin, supra note 20, p. 88; H. Van Der Wilt, 'Joint Criminal Enterprise: Possibilities and Limitations', 5 *JICJ* (2007), p. 69; E. Van Sliedregt, supra note 27, p. 184.

[36] A. Cassese, supra note 18, p. 109; K. Gustafson, supra note 16, p. 134; A.M. Danner and J.S. Martinez, 'Guilty Associations: Joint Criminal Enterprise, Command Responsibility, and the Development of International Criminal Law', 93 *Calif. L. Rev.* (2005), pp. 75–169.

[37] ICTY, *Prosecutor v. Brđanin*, TC, Judgment, 1 September 2004, paras. 343–355.

criminal enterprise between the accused and Momir Talić, other members of the ARK Crisis Staff, the leadership of the SerBiH and the SDS (including Radovan Karadžić, Momcilo Krajišnik and Biljana Plavšić), members of the ARK Assembly and the Assembly's Executive Committee and the Serb Crisis Staffs of the ARK municipalities, since the latter did not physically commit any of the relevant crimes. As far as the remaining alleged participants in the joint criminal enterprise, that is, the accused and "members of the army and Serb paramilitary forces ('Relevant Physical Perpetrators')", the Tribunal found that no agreement between them had been established. In particular,

> given the physical and structural remoteness between the Accused and the Relevant Physical Perpetrators and the fact that the Relevant Physical Perpetrators in most cases have not even been personally identified, the Trial Chamber is not satisfied that the only reasonable conclusion that may be drawn from the Accused's and the Relevant Physical Perpetrators' respective actions aimed towards the implementation of the Common Plan is that the Accused entered into an agreement with the Relevant Physical Perpetrators to commit a crime.[38]

Thus, since reliance on joint criminal enterprise requires proof of an agreement between the accused and the "relevant physical perpetrators",[39] the Trial Chamber held that this form of liability is not appropriate for cases of an "extraordinarily broad nature";[40] it is rather applicable to smaller criminal enterprises in which a closer connection between the accused and the perpetrators can be established.[41]

The Prosecution appealed this part of the judgment, and the Appeals Chamber granted the appeal.[42] The Appeals Chamber clarified that an accused can be liable for his or her participation in a common criminal purpose where the *actus reus* is perpetrated by persons who do *not* share the common purpose, that is, persons *outside* the joint criminal enterprise.[43] There may be joint criminal enterprises including only political or military leaders when they use persons outside the joint criminal enterprise to carry out the *actus reus* of an international crime.[44]

---

[38] *Ibid.*, para. 354.

[39] *Ibid.*, para. 353.

[40] *Ibid.*, para. 355.

[41] *Ibid.*, note 890 reads: "ICTY cases have applied JCE to enterprises of a smaller scale, limited to a specific military operation and only to members of the armed forces (*Krstić* Trial Judgment, para. 610); a restricted geographical area (*Simić* Trial Judgment, paras 984–985); a small group of armed men acting jointly to commit a certain crime (*Tadić* Appeal Judgment, paras. 232 *et seq.; Vasiljević* Trial Judgment, para. 208); or, for the second category of JCE, to one detention camp (*Krnojelac* Trial Judgment, para. 84)".

[42] ICTY, *Prosecutor v. Brđanin*, AC, Judgment, 3 April 2007, paras. 357–450.

[43] *Ibid.*, paras. 349, 404, and 414.

[44] *Ibid.*, paras. 410–413.

In addition, the Appeals Chamber held that joint criminal enterprise does not require proof of an explicit agreement between the accused and the physical perpetrators to commit a particular crime.[45] This form of liability requires the existence of a common purpose amounting to or involving the commission of an international crime.[46] Thus, the Appeals Chamber found that joint criminal enterprise can be applied to large-scale cases.[47] Once the elements of joint criminal enterprise are properly defined and are supported by the evidence, there is no risk that this doctrine might lapse into guilt by mere association.[48]

This means that, in principle, joint criminal enterprise is capable of addressing large collective criminal phenomena, including international crimes committed by the entire state apparatus, in particular crimes elaborated at the highest level of the state hierarchy. In practice, the possibility to ascribe liability to state leaders under the doctrine of joint criminal enterprise will largely be a matter of evidence. As recognized by the Appeals Chamber, it would not be correct to invoke those practical difficulties to preclude the application of this doctrine to large-scale cases.[49] Therefore, the crucial aspect concerns the exact definition of the elements of joint criminal enterprise when applied to state leaders. If narrowly construed, the broad scope that this doctrine might have in theory can disappear in practice, as happens with command responsibility.

In *Brđanin*, the Appeals Chamber was very careful in putting forward the elements of joint criminal enterprise when applied to large-scale cases, in particular when the physical perpetrators do not belong to the joint criminal enterprise. The Tribunal must be satisfied beyond reasonable doubt that there is a plurality of persons belonging to the criminal enterprise; that the common criminal purpose is sufficiently specified and is common to all the members of the joint criminal enterprise; that the accused made a significant contribution to the furtherance of the common purpose; that the accused has the intent to commit an international crime; and that the crime can be imputed to the accused because he or she used the physical perpetrators in accordance with the common plan.[50] The Appeals Chamber concluded that, when all these requirements are met, the accused can

---

[45] *Ibid.*, para. 419.

[46] *Ibid.*, para. 418.

[47] For some precedent decisions of the *ad hoc* tribunals reaching the same conclusion, *see* ICTR, *Prosecutor v. Rwamakuba*, AC, Decision on interlocutory appeal regarding application of joint criminal enterprise to the crime of genocide, 22 October 2004, para. 25; ICTR, *Prosecutor v. Karemera and others*, AC, Decision on jurisdictional appeals: Joint criminal enterprise, 12 April 2006, para. 16; ICTY, *Prosecutor v. Stakić*, AC, Judgment, 22 March 2006, paras. 68–70; ICTY, *Prosecutor v. Krajišnik*, TC, Judgment, 27 September 2006, para. 876.

[48] ICTY, *Prosecutor v. Brđanin*, AC, Judgment, 3 April 2007, paras. 424–425.

[49] *Ibid.*, para. 424.

[50] *Ibid.*, paras. 430–431.

appropriately be held liable under both the first and the third category of joint criminal enterprise.[51]

The content of this judgment is likely to raise some criticism, as the trial court's judgment already did. However, from the standpoint of the present analysis, it is interesting to note which elements of large-scale joint criminal enterprise among those listed above can bring individual criminal liability closer to state responsibility.

First, the common criminal purpose plays a crucial role. When the physical perpetrators are outside the joint criminal enterprise, "the key issue remains that of ascertaining whether the crime in question forms part of the common criminal purpose".[52] The common purpose is certainly the distinctive feature of this doctrine, and with respect to somewhat smaller enterprises the proof of the common criminal purpose may not be too problematic. For example, the 'systemic' form of joint criminal enterprise does not require proof of an agreement among the co-perpetrators.[53] Arguably, this is due to the particular circumstances of this form of joint criminal enterprise. The so-called 'concentration camp cases' refer to structured, organized, even hierarchical forms of co-perpetration in which the agreement is expressed by the very system which has made the commission of the relevant collective crimes possible.[54] However, with respect to large-scale cases, it can be very difficult in practice to show that there is such a common purpose among state leaders, and that it is shared by all the members of the joint criminal enterprise. In addition, it is uncertain whether the ICTY would accept to rely on joint criminal enterprise in cases other than those in which common goals can only be achieved by collective action.

In *Simić*, the Tribunal dealt in particular with the basic form of joint criminal enterprise and it stressed that:

> The common goal to commit these acts of persecution [arrest, detention, cruel and inhumane treatment, deportation, forcible transfer] could not have been achieved without the joint actions of the police, paramilitaries, the Tactical Group of the JNA and Crisis Staff. No participant could have achieved the common goals on their own.[55]

This case was not particularly problematic because the accused (Simić) "was at the apex of the joint criminal enterprise at the municipal level".[56] However, it is unclear whether the Tribunal was simply discussing the specific circumstances of

---

51 *Ibid.*, para. 431.

52 *Ibid.*, para. 418.

53 *See* ICTY, *Prosecutor v. Krnojelac*, AC, Judgment, 17 September 2003, para. 97; ICTY, *Prosecutor v. Kvočka et al.*, AC, Judgment, 28 February 2005, para. 118.

54 A. Cassese, supra note 18, p. 112.

55 ICTY, *Prosecutor v. Simić et al.*, TC, Judgment, 17 October 2003, para. 991.

56 *Ibid.*, para. 992.

the case before it, or whether it was setting out a general requirement that could also be regarded as applicable to other cases. In other words, it remains to be seen whether in future cases joint criminal enterprise would be limited to common criminal goals which can *only* be achieved through collective action.

What is certain is that the Tribunal focuses on the collective dimension of the criminal enterprise, not on each single contribution provided by the members of the joint criminal enterprise. When it had to deal with the claim of an accused who contended that his role was insignificant because the joint criminal enterprise would have been successful even without his contribution, the ICTY simply rejected this "piecemeal approach".[57] When otherwise dealing with political leaders, the Tribunal has accorded a fundamental role to the general criminal context. In *Krajišnik*, more than 50 pages are dedicated to the description of the administration of Bosnian-Serb Republic, and about 100 pages deal with the connection between the state machinery and the accused in order to establish his personal responsibility under the doctrine of joint criminal enterprise.[58]

Thus, as in the establishment of aggravated state responsibility, the focus is on collective action. When applied to state leaders, the common criminal purpose or plan can correspond to the state policy elaborated at the highest levels of the state hierarchy, and the facts which can lead to the establishment of the common criminal purpose are the same as those that can be relied upon to ascertain the seriousness of the wrongful state act, that is, aggravated state responsibility. Therefore, the broad notion of joint criminal enterprise upheld in *Brđanin* shows that the greater the emphasis put on the common criminal purpose, the closer joint criminal enterprise comes to collective responsibility. As long as joint criminal enterprise is detached from the material commission of international crimes, a greater co-ordination with state responsibility is needed.

Second, large-scale joint criminal enterprises including only political or military leaders can be problematic because a link must be established between the accused and the physical perpetrators to say that the former participated in the common criminal purpose. The Appeals Chamber in *Brđanin* held that the crimes committed by the physical perpetrators can be imputed to the accused when he or she has used these persons to act in accordance with the common plan.[59] Unfortunately, the judgment does not further clarify what "to use the principal perpetrators" means, nor does it elaborate on the criteria according to which the criminal conduct of the physical perpetrators is "imputable" to the accused. The Appeals Chamber simply stated that the link must be assessed on a case-by-case basis.[60]

---

[57] ICTY, *Prosecutor v. Kvočka et al.*, AC, Judgment, 28 February 2005, paras. 419–420.

[58] ICTY, *Prosecutor v. Krajišnik*, TJ, Judgment, 27 September 2006, pp. 54–109, and 306–406.

[59] ICTY, *Prosecutor v. Brđanin*, AC, Judgment, 3 April 2007, paras. 413 and 430.

[60] *Ibid.*, para. 414.

Similarly, the judgment in *Krajišnik* was not entirely satisfactory in setting out the legal requirements necessary to prove the link between the members of the joint criminal enterprise and the physical perpetrators. However, this case is interesting because it shows that crimes committed by mid or low-level perpetrators can be 'attributed' to the leadership having the power and authority over political and military organs so that it can be said that they are responsible for, among other things, the "creation", "support", "direction", and "control" of the state machinery which has conceived of and carried out a criminal policy.[61]

Thus, the question is how the link between the joint criminal enterprise of political and military leaders and the physical perpetrator can be established. The mere reference to "imputation" or to criteria such as "direction" and "control" immediately recalls the rules of state responsibility on the attribution of wrongful acts. Is it possible that the Tribunal implicitly referred to criteria such as those codified by the ILC in 2001? What seems indisputable is that attribution of the (large scale) criminal conduct of the physical perpetrators to a joint criminal enterprise composed of state leaders only comes very close to attribution of state organs' conduct to the state. In both cases, there is a collective entity which acts through physical perpetrators and whose responsibility can only be established by 'imputing' certain conduct to this collective entity. It is possible that the Tribunal will develop criteria of 'attribution' similar to those existing under the law of state responsibility. At any rate, while the criteria of such an imputation can be a matter of controversy, the underlying idea is very similar. When both state and state leaders responsibility is assessed with respect to the same international crimes, it would be very difficult to maintain a rigorous separation between these two regimes. A certain degree of consistency must inevitably be guaranteed in the parallel establishment of state and individual responsibility for the same conduct. In the end, this particular form of joint criminal enterprise dramatically reduces the distance between aggravated state responsibility and individual criminal liability of state leaders for international crimes.

5. *Modes of Collective Liability and State Responsibility*

Aggravated state responsibility arises out of serious international crimes. It is established with respect to large scale atrocities and general criminal practices carried out by the state apparatus. If necessary, collective fault must be demonstrated to hold a state responsible for certain international crimes, like genocide. In sum, aggravated state responsibility deals with collective responsibility.

---

[61] ICTY, *Prosecutor v. Krajišnik*, TJ, Judgment, 27 September 2006, paras. 1120–1121.

By contrast, international criminal law focuses on individual accountability. It attaches responsibility to individual perpetrators, even though international crimes are normally carried out by large and organized groups of perpetrators, if not by the state itself. Because it is very difficult to conceive of international crimes in pure individual terms, international criminal law faces two main challenges: holding political and military leaders accountable, and properly taking the collective dimension of international crimes into account.[62] The foregoing analysis shows that the constant concern of international criminal law has been the elaboration of particular tools allowing international criminal tribunals to address collective criminal phenomena. If international criminal tribunals cannot rely on a direct link between collective and individual responsibility, other tools, and in particular specific modes of liability, can help to ascribe individual liability for international crimes.

It must be recalled that criminal responsibility is in no way ascribed to groups as such. Today, international criminal law does not provide for any specific offence criminalizing mere participation in a criminal organization. Joint criminal enterprise is not the crime of membership. It does not establish a direct legal connection between collective responsibility and individual liability, as the crime of membership did.[63] International criminal tribunals have been rigorous in convicting the perpetrators of collective crimes in a manner which is respectful of the basic principle of personal liability.[64]

Therefore, one of the major problems with international crimes is that these are prohibited under international rules directed at either states or individuals, when in practice international crimes are most often committed by groups of perpetrators. International law does not address these crimes in terms of collective responsibility of criminal groups,[65] but in terms of either state or individual responsibility. According to one commentator, international crimes committed by groups "are unlikely to be prevented nor will compliance with the relevant provisions of international law be significantly improved through punishment of one single individual".[66] This can

[62] H. Van Der Wilt, supra note 35, pp. 91–92; K. Gustafson, supra note 16, pp. 135–136; E. Van Sliedregt, supra note 27, pp. 185–187.

[63] However, there are international law scholars which would welcome the criminalization of mere participation in an organization whose purpose is to commit international crimes. *See* A. Viviani, *Crimini internazionali e responsabilità dei* leader *politici e militari* (Milano, Giuffré, 2005), pp. 194 and 202.

[64] A. Cassese, supra note 18, p. 109.

[65] *See* L. Zegveld, *The Accountability of Armed Opposition Groups in International Law* (Cambridge, Cambridge University Press, 2002), pp. 55–58, and 223. According to this author, there is a major obstacle in holding armed opposition groups accountable for international humanitarian law violations. This is regarded as "incompatible with the fundamental right of the state to preserve its existence and to remain the only authority" (*ibid.*, p. 163).

[66] *Ibid.*, p. 133.

help to explain the increasing focus on the collective dimension of international crimes, and the need for international criminal law to provide for specific mechanisms allowing international (and domestic) criminal tribunals to deal with such crimes. In other words, international case law tries to find acceptable ways to bridge the gap between the individual and the state by taking into account intermediate social structures which have no clear status under international law but which are most often responsible for the commission of international crimes. From this standpoint, this approach can lead to the establishment of a certain relationship between state and individual responsibility.

It results from the present analysis that the increasing attention given to group criminality has been possible thanks to two main elements. First, the definition of certain international crimes requires these crimes to be carried out at the collective level. As noted above, international tribunals have accepted that a single prohibited type of conduct can amount to, for example, a crime against humanity if it is part of the general criminal context, or that the genocidal intent can be inferred from the general criminal context. Accordingly, the elements of certain international crimes have been interpreted in a way that has allowed international tribunals to establish the collective criminal context first, and then to evaluate whether the individual conduct was part of it. If so, it is possible to hold the accused (or rather the member of the criminal group) accountable for participating in the relevant collective crimes.

Second, international criminal law has increasingly focused on modes of liability making it possible to address collective crimes more efficiently. This seems to be one of the most important developments that international criminal law has recently undergone. Reliance on modes of liability such as command responsibility and joint criminal enterprise is essential to ascribe liability for international crimes which otherwise would have been difficult to conceive of as the mere sum of isolated instances of criminal conduct. In particular, joint criminal enterprise radically changes the way in which individual liability for collective crimes is established: the *actus reus* is the global criminal conduct carried out by the participants in the furtherance of a common criminal design, and the *mens rea* is the shared intent of the members of the criminal group.[67] This arguably brings individual liability closer to aggravated state responsibility. Indeed, the collective dimension of international crimes assumes a primary role in the establishment of individual criminal responsibility.

[67] E. Van Sliedregt, *The Criminal Responsibility of Individuals for Violations of International Humanitarian Law* (The Hague, TMC Asser Press, 2003), p. 353, refers to joint criminal enterprise as the 'modern version' of the Nuremberg crime of membership.

While certain modes of liability, like command responsibility,[68] are only capable of addressing smaller groups criminality,[69] and of ascribing liability to low-ranking officials, other modes of liability are capable, at least in principle, of addressing larger groups or state criminality. In particular, joint criminal enterprise can be used to ascribe criminal liability to political or military state leaders for international crimes. It is not possible to say whether this form of liability will be successfully applied to future large-scale cases. For example, the elements of this particular joint criminal enterprise could be construed very narrowly. In any way, this is a very significant development of international criminal law, which would have at its disposal not only tools to take the collective dimension of international crimes into account, but also a specific mode of liability to deal with crimes orchestrated by political and military leaders.[70]

The developments examined above witness a clear shift in focus from strictly personal to collective criminal conduct. In particular, the modes of collective liability lead to a certain relationship between state and individual responsibility for international crimes. They do not entail a direct legal connection between these regimes, but they show the growing need to develop tools capable of taking into account the collective dimension of international crimes, and overcome the limits of a rigorous individually-focused methodology. In particular, reliance on modes of collective liability (such as joint criminal enterprise) has the effect of establishing individual criminal liability in a way which is increasingly similar to the assessment of aggravated state responsibility for the same internationally prohibited conduct.

---

[68] B.I. Bonafè, supra note 10, p. 599.

[69] According to G.P. Fletcher and J.D. Ohlin, 'Reclaiming Fundamental Principles of Criminal Law in the Darfur Case', 3 *JICJ* (2005), p. 547, "International criminal law has oriented itself toward these discrete smaller groups precisely because the larger groups – nations and states – cannot be the appropriate object of *criminal* responsibility".

[70] As this book was going to press, the Prosecutor of the ICC requested an arrest warrant against the president of Sudan, Omar Hassan Al Bashir, on the ground that he committed genocide, crimes against humanity, and war crimes. The interest of this case lies in the fact that the Prosecutor relies on a particular mode of liability (perpetration by means) and alleges that Al Bashir committed crimes 'through' members of the state apparatus, the army and the Militia/Janjaweed. The criteria according to which the crimes can be attributed to Al Bashir are described by the Prosecutor as follows: "Al Bashir *controls* and *directs* the perpetrators. The commission of those crimes on such a scale, and for such a long period of time, the targeting of civilians and in particular the Fur, Masalit and Zaghawa, the impunity enjoyed by the perpetrators, and the systematic cover-up of the crimes through public official statements, are evidence of a plan based on the mobilization of the state apparatus, including the armed forces, the intelligence services, the diplomatic and public information bureaucracies, and the justice system." (ICC Office of the Prosecutor, 'Summary of the case: Prosecutor's Application for Warrant of Arrest under Article 58 Against Omar Hassan Ahmad Al Bashir', 14 July 2008, p. 7, emphasis added, <www.icc-cpi.int/library/organs/otp/ICC-OTP-Summary-20081704–ENG .pdf>). What is worth stressing here is the striking similarity of such criteria with those provided for under the law of state responsibility as far as state agency determination is concerned.

When coupled with the possibility of taking judicial notice that certain international crimes have been perpetrated at the collective level and are part of 'world history',[71] then individual criminal liability turns into an establishment of mere *participation* in a collective international crime whose commission has been assessed once and for all. As a consequence, this particular methodology in the judicial establishment of individual criminal liability inevitably resembles that used to ascertain aggravated state responsibility. The same context of collective criminality is at the basis of both kinds of international accountability because it is crucial in the proof of the various elements of international crimes and of the modes of liability. The assessment of the collective commission of international crimes becomes the unavoidable factual finding to establish both state and individual responsibility. Once this basic assessment of the prohibited material conduct is carried out, what these regimes additionally require is the application of specific rules on attribution to an individual or to a state.

6. *Concluding Observations*

This chapter has examined the way in which specific modes of liability could entail a relationship between state and individual responsibility for international crimes. International case law shows interesting developments on this subject. While a direct legal connection between collective and individual responsibility had exceptionally been provided for under the IMT Statute, today no similar tool exists. International criminal tribunals have therefore relied on the modes of liability at their disposal to appraise the collective nature of international crimes.

As for command responsibility, reliance on joint criminal enterprise has been both strongly criticized and enthusiastically welcomed.[72] The reaction could hardly have been different. These modes of collective liability represent a challenge, from the standpoint of international criminal law. They try to apply to collective phenomena a set of legal standards conceived and developed for individual conduct. However, it is generally recognized that, when applied in a very careful manner, these modes of liability represent an indispensable tool for international criminal tribunals to address collective criminality. In a sense, they try to bridge the gap between individual and state responsibility.

The relationship between state and individual responsibility entailed by these modes of liability is partially different from the other points of contact illustrated in previous chapters. Modes of collective liability bring the establishment of indi-

---

[71] *See* supra Chapter 3, note 127, and accompanying text.

[72] *See* in particular the contributions to the symposia on command responsibility and joint criminal enterprise published in 5 *JICJ* (2007).

vidual criminal liability closer to the establishment of aggravated state responsibility. More generally, these modes of liability are another sign of the radical change of perspective that characterizes the recent evolution of international criminal law. International criminal tribunals no longer focus on individual behaviour, but they establish that international crimes have been committed at the collective level and that the required psychological attitude was shared by all the participants to the joint criminal enterprise. This results in an establishment of individual responsibility which is much closer to that of state responsibility for international crimes.

Accordingly, the way in which the commission of collective and state crimes is carried out becomes very similar. In particular, joint criminal enterprise can be applied to hold state leaders accountable for international crimes. It is uncertain whether this particular form of joint criminal enterprise would share some standards with state responsibility, but it shows an additional point of contact between state and individual responsibility for international crimes. As these two kinds of international responsibility become closer, because they focus on the same conduct, there is an increasing need to guarantee a certain consistency in the way each evolves.

Chapter 7

Establishing State and Individual Responsibility for International Crimes

In principle, one of the clearest signs of the separation between state and individual responsibility for international crimes is that there are different and independent bodies charged with enforcing obligations of states and obligations of individuals under international law. Individual liability is established by international (and domestic) criminal tribunals. State responsibility is dealt with by competent political bodies, internationals courts, or is simply left to the more traditional means of peaceful settlement of international disputes.

For example, with respect to the genocide that took place in the former Yugoslavia, it seems natural to say that international law ascribes responsibility in different ways with respect to individuals, on the one hand, and states on the other. Thus, the task of the ICTY is to establish whether certain individuals have actually committed genocide, whereas the task of the ICJ is to ascertain issues of state responsibility.

In *Krstić*, the ICTY judgment started making clear that, while dealing with notorious crimes committed during the conflict in the former Yugoslavia, it would not address the question of collective responsibility, because its task was to establish individual criminal liability only.[1] On the other hand, the ICJ has been asked to settle the dispute between Bosnia and Herzegovina and Serbia and to ascertain whether the latter was responsible for the genocide that occurred in the former Yugoslavia.[2] And Bosnia has from the very beginning made it clear that it was looking for neither revenge nor collective guilt.[3]

---

[1] ICTY, *Prosecutor v. Krstić*, TC, Judgment, 2 August 2001, para. 2. *See* also ICTY, *Prosecutor v. Delalić et al.*, TC, Judgment, 16 November 1998, para. 230, in which the Tribunal explicitly says that it "is a criminal judicial body, established to prosecute and punish individuals for violations of international humanitarian law, and not to determine State responsibility for acts of aggression and unlawful intervention."

[2] ICJ, *Genocide* case, supra the Introduction, note 1.

[3] "*Cette affaire ne blâme pas tous les Serbes pour les actes de génocide. Nous ne visons pas les citoyens de Sérbie-Monténégro ou les citoyens de la République des Serbes de Bosnie, qui ont été induits en erreur par leurs chefs. Nous cherchons à établir la responsabilité d'un Etat*" (S. Maupas, 'Ouverture du procès pour 'génocide' de la Bosnie contre la Serbie', Le Monde, 28 February 2006).

Yet one may have doubts about such an absolute separation between state and individual responsibility for international crimes as far as enforcement mechanisms are concerned. Indeed, there are cases in which the establishment of state and individual responsibility is somehow connected. In particular, the present chapter will investigate two of them. First, in establishing individual liability for certain international crimes, international criminal tribunals might have to apply rules belonging to the law of state responsibility. Second, there might be instances in which state and individual responsibility for international crimes are not established in perfect isolation from each other because either the same body deals with situations entailing both kinds of international responsibility or certain international crimes require a parallel determination of state and individual responsibility. These are cases that can unveil a closer relationship between state and individual responsibility than one might have expected.

1. *Issues of State Responsibility before International Criminal Tribunals*

The best example of the first class of issues is the criterion respectively used in international criminal law and in the law of state responsibility to attribute the conduct of *de facto* state organs to the state.[4] The starting point of this analysis is a consideration of the diverging decisions of the ICJ in *Nicaragua* and of the ICTY in *Tadić*. These cases have been the object of considerable debate among international law scholars.[5] They have also been viewed as an element of increasing fragmentation of the international legal order, attracting the attention and concern of the ILC.[6] However, from the standpoint of the present analysis, this kind of case merits close examination for a different reason: it shows a clear point of contact in the establishment of state and individual responsibility for international crimes.

In *Tadić*, the ICTY was confronted with the question of whether certain war crimes had been committed in international or internal armed conflicts by organ-

[4] The precise identification of the customary rules on state agency is a very complicated question, which the codification of State responsibility seems to leave at least partially unsettled. *See*, in general, P. Palchetti, *L'organo di fatto dello Stato nell'illecito internazionale* (Milano, Giuffré, 2007).

[5] *See*, in particular, C. Kress, 'L'organe *de facto* en droit international public. Réflexions sur l'imputation à l'Etat de l'acte d'un particulier à la lumière des développements récents', 105 *RGDIP* (2001), pp. 93–144; F. Dopagne, 'La responsabilité de l'Etat du fait des particuliers: les causes d'imputation revisitées par les Articles sur la responsabilité de l'Etat pour fait internationalement illicite', 34 *RBDI* (2001), pp. 492–525. For a critical view on the 1997 Trial Chamber decision, *see* M.P. Scharf, 'Trial and Error: An Assessment of the First Judgment of the Yugoslavia War Crimes Tribunal', 30 *NYU J. Int'l L. Pol.* (1998), pp. 167–200.

[6] The work of the ILC on the topic is summarized in its last 'Report of the Study Group on Fragmentation of International Law, finalized by M. Koskenniemi', UN Doc. A/CN.4/L.682, of 13 April 2006, <untreaty.un.org/ilc/guide/gfra.htm>.

ized military groups.[7] The Tribunal had to establish individual criminal liability, but to do so it considered that it was necessary to apply the relevant rules of the law of state responsibility.

As is well known, the conflict took place in the Republic of Bosnia and Herzegovina between the Bosnian governmental armed forces and the Bosnian Serb forces.[8] The Bosnian Serb forces were supported by the JNA (the armed forces of the Federal Republic of Yugoslavia). The alleged crimes were perpetrated by the accused as a member of the Bosnian Serb armed forces. Thus, according to the Trial Chamber, it had to decide whether the Bosnian Serb forces were *de facto* agents of the Federal Republic of Yugoslavia or not,[9] so as to determine whether to apply the rules concerning international armed conflicts or rather the rules concerning internal armed conflicts. In the former case, the accused could be found liable for the violation of the more advanced and precise international rules referred to in Article 2 of the ICTY Statute; otherwise, the accused could be found guilty under Article 3 of the more limited and generic prohibitions relating to internal armed conflicts.[10]

The Tribunal found that, prior to 19 May 1992, the JNA had control over a substantial portion of Bosnia and Herzegovina,[11] and that it had played a significant role in training and equipping the Bosnian Serb paramilitary forces.[12] Before that date, Bosnian Serb forces co-operated with and acted under the command of and within the framework of the JNA. Thus, crimes perpetrated before May 1992 could be considered acts of *de facto* agents of the Federal Republic of Yugoslavia, that is, as crimes committed in an international armed conflict.

But on 15 May 1992, the SC demanded that all interference from outside Bosnia and Herzegovina by units of the JNA cease immediately.[13] It further demanded that those units either be withdrawn, or be placed under the authority of the Government of the Republic of Bosnia and Herzegovina, or be disbanded and disarmed.[14] Consequently, the VRS (Bosnian Serb forces of the *Republika Srpska*) was created

---

7 ICTY, *Prosecutor v. Tadić*, TC, Judgment, 7 May 1997, and AC, Judgment, 15 July 1999.

8 The Bosnian Serb forces controlled territory under the banner of the *Republika Srpska* and revolted against the *de jure* Government of the Republic of Bosnia and Herzegovina.

9 ICTY, *Prosecutor v. Tadić*, TC, Judgment, 7 May 1997, para. 584: "acts of the armed forces of the *Republika Srpska*, although nationals of the Republic of Bosnia and Herzegovina, after 19 May 1992 in relation to opstina Prijedor may be imputed to the Federal Republic of Yugoslavia (Serbia and Montenegro) if those forces were acting as de facto organs or agents of that State".

10 *See* Articles 2 and 3 of the ICTY Statute (SC Res, 827(1993)), and the explanations given by the Appeals Chamber of the ICTY in *Prosecutor v. Tadić*, 2 October 1995, paras. 79–95, as regards their different application.

11 ICTY, *Prosecutor v. Tadić*, TC, Judgment, 7 May 1997, para. 113.

12 *Ibid.*, para. 593.

13 SC Resolution 752(1992), <www.un.org/Docs/sc>.

14 ICTY, *Prosecutor v. Tadić*, TC, Judgment, 7 May 1997, para. 582.

in May 1992, and the Federal Republic of Yugoslavia transferred units, materials, and soldiers to the VRS force.

Even though there remained the same weapons, the same equipment, the same officers, the same commanders, largely the same troops, the same logistics centres, the same suppliers, the same infrastructure, the same source of payments, the same goals and mission, the same tactics, and the same operations,[15] the Trial Chamber found that "after 19 May 1992 the armed forces of the *Republika Srpska* could not be considered as *de facto* organs or agents of the Government of the Federal Republic of Yugoslavia".[16] Therefore, the Trial Chamber concluded that the armed forces of the *Republika Srpska* were nothing more than mere allies, "albeit highly dependent allies, of the Government of the Federal Republic of Yugoslavia (Serbia and Montenegro) in its plan to achieve a Greater Serbia from out of the remains of the former Yugoslavia."[17]

Indeed, the Court chose to apply the 'effective control' test established by the ICJ in the *Nicaragua* case,[18] according to which a general relationship of dependence and control is not enough to entail state responsibility. Confronted with this very high threshold, the Prosecution failed to show that Serbia and Montenegro exercised the required control over the VRS.[19] Consequently, the Court decided that, after 19 May 1992, the VRS could not be regarded as *de facto* organs or agents of Serbia and Montenegro.[20] Since the theory of an 'international conflict' was not

---

[15] *Ibid.*, Judge McDonald Dissenting Opinion, para. 7.

[16] ICTY, *Prosecutor v. Tadić*, TC, Judgment, 7 May 1997, para. 607.

[17] *Ibid.*, para. 606. *See* also para. 605: "there is no evidence on which this Trial Chamber can conclude that the Federal Republic of Yugoslavia (Serbia and Montenegro) and the VJ ever direct or, for that matter, ever felt the need to attempt to direct, the actual military operations of the VRS, or to influence those operations beyond that which would have flowed naturally from the coordination of military objectives and activities by the VRS and VJ at the highest levels."

[18] ICJ, *Case Concerning Military and Paramilitary Activities in and against Nicaragua* (Nicaragua v. USA), supra Chapter 1, note 44, para. 115: "United States participation, even if preponderant or decisive, in the financing, organizing, training, supplying and equipping of the *contras*, the selection of its military or paramilitary targets, and the planning of the whole of its operation, is still insufficient in itself, on the basis of the evidence in the possession of the Court, for the purpose of attributing to the United States the acts committed by the *contras* in the course of their military or paramilitary operations in Nicaragua. All the forms of United States participation mentioned above, and even the general control by the respondent State over a force with a high degree of dependency on it, would not in themselves mean, without further evidence, that the United States directed or enforced the perpetration of the acts contrary to human rights and humanitarian law alleged by the applicant State. Such acts could well be committed by members of the *contras* without the control of the United States. *For this conduct to give rise to legal responsibility of the United States, it would in principle have to be proved that that State had effective control of the military or paramilitary operations in the course of which the alleged violations were committed*" (emphasis added).

[19] ICTY, *Prosecutor v. Tadić*, TC, Judgment, 7 May 1997, para. 588.

[20] *Ibid.*, para. 587.

accepted by the majority of the Trial Chamber (with Judge McDonald dissenting), the accused was found responsible for war crimes perpetrated in the context of an internal armed conflict under Article 3 of the Statute.

In her dissenting opinion, Judge McDonald essentially maintained that the 'effective control' test is not the appropriate standard for agency determination in the *Tadić* case.[21] On the one hand, she advanced a particular interpretation of the *Nicaragua* judgment[22] which the ICJ seems to have subsequently upheld.[23] More interestingly from the viewpoint of the present analysis, Judge McDonald focused on the differences between state responsibility and individual liability.[24] First of all, while state responsibility fundamentally entails the right of the injured state to monetary damages, in cases of individual criminal liability, reparations are not at issue.[25] Second, the general context of the *Tadić* case is completely different from the situation which gave rise to the Nicaragua-USA dispute.[26] Finally, her dissenting opinion emphasizes the differences between the general principles underlying international humanitarian law and those underlying state responsibility.[27] In short, her argument seems to imply that reliance on a different criterion of attribution of *de facto* organs' conduct to the state was justified in *Tadić* because of the different nature of individual criminal liability.[28]

---

[21] The first alternative argument, however, was that "if effective control is the degree of proof required to establish agency under *Nicaragua*, I conclude that this standard has been met" (ICTY, *Prosecutor v. Tadić*, 7 May 1997, Judge McDonald Dissenting Opinion, para. 15).

[22] Indeed, she stated that, according to the *Nicaragua* judgment, "it appears that there are two bases on which the acts of the VRS could be attributed to the Federal Republic of Yugoslavia (Serbia and Montenegro): where the VRS acted as an agent of the Federal Republic of Yugoslavia (Serbia and Montenegro), which could be established by a finding of dependency on the one side and control on the other; or where the VRS was specifically charged by the Federal Republic of Yugoslavia (Serbia and Montenegro) to carry out a particular act on behalf of the Federal Republic of Yugoslavia (Serbia and Montenegro) thereby making the act itself attributable to the Federal Republic of Yugoslavia (Serbia and Montenegro). In *Nicaragua*, the Court required a showing of effective control for this latter determination" (*ibid.*, para. 25).

[23] ICJ, *Genocide* case, supra the Introduction, note 1, paras. 385–412, where the Court applies two different standards to establish either 1) whether the VRS can be equated with Serbian state organs or 2) whether the VRS could have acted under the direction or control of Serbia.

[24] ICTY, *Prosecutor v. Tadić*, 7 May 1997, Judge McDonald Dissenting Opinion, para. 27: "This is recognized even by the majority, which notes that *Nicaragua* was concerned ultimately with the responsibility of a State for a breach, *inter alia*, of rules of international humanitarian law, while the instant case is concerned ultimately with the responsibility of an individual for the breach of such rules".

[25] *Ibid.*, para. 28.

[26] *Ibid.*, para. 29.

[27] *Ibid.*, para. 33.

[28] *See* T. Meron, 'Classification of Armed Conflict in the Former Yugoslavia: *Nicaragua's* Fallout', 92 *AJIL* (1998), pp. 236–242.

The Trial Chamber's judgment was appealed, and the Tribunal discussed both the question of the relationship between state and individual responsibility, and the problem of the right test to apply. As to the first issue, the Appeals Chamber stated that the question did not concern the distinction between state and individual responsibility. Rather, the point was merely the application of the rules concerning attribution provided for under the law of state responsibility.[29] More generally, the Chamber held that: "international humanitarian law does not include legal criteria regarding imputability specific to this body of law. Reliance must therefore be had upon the criteria established by general rules on State responsibility."[30] As to the right test to apply in state agency determination, the Tribunal held that, in the *Tadić* case, the *Nicaragua* test of the 'effective control' was not applicable.

The Appeals Chamber started by analysing the rationale of international rules on state agency,[31] and accordingly distinguished various situations with different degrees of control required. First, in cases of private individuals acting on behalf of the state, it would be necessary to demonstrate that the state issued *specific instructions* concerning the commission of the illegal act.[32] Second, in cases where individuals make up an "organized and hierarchically structured group," agency determination requires that the group as a whole be under the *overall control* of the state in order to attribute the conduct of the group to the state.[33] The rationale behind such a finding is that otherwise "States might easily shelter behind, or use

---

[29] ICTY, *Prosecutor v. Tadić*, AC, Judgment, 15 July 1999, para. 104: "what is at issue is not the distinction between the two classes of responsibility. What is at issue is a preliminary question: that of the conditions on which under international law an individual may be held to act as a de facto organ of a State. Logically these conditions must be the same both in the case: (i) where the court's task is to ascertain whether an act performed by an individual may be attributed to a State, thereby generating the international responsibility of that State; and (ii) where the court must instead determine whether individuals are acting as de facto State officials, thereby rendering the conflict international and thus setting the necessary precondition for the 'grave breaches' regime to apply. In both cases, what is at issue is not the distinction between State responsibility and individual criminal responsibility. Rather, the question is that of establishing the criteria for the legal imputability to a State of acts performed by individuals not having the status of State officials."

[30] *Ibid.*, para. 105.

[31] "[T]he requirement of international law for the attribution to State of acts performed by private individuals is that the State exercises control over the individuals. The degree of control may, however, vary according to the factual circumstances of each case" (*ibid.*, para. 117). Indeed, the Court explained that "the rationale behind this rule [article 8 of the Draft on State Responsibility] is to prevent States from escaping international responsibility by having private individuals carry out tasks that may not or should not be performed by State officials, or by claiming that individuals actually participating in governmental authority are not classified as State organs under national legislation and therefore do not engage State responsibility."

[32] *Ibid.*, paras. 118–119.

[33] *Ibid.*, paras. 120 and 131.

as a pretext, their internal legal system or the lack of any specific instructions in order to disclaim international responsibility."[34] It is important to note that the Appeals Chamber justified the distinction between different degrees of control – *i.e.*, specific instructions, and overall control – according to the nature of the perpetrator of international crimes, namely, isolated individuals or organized groups.[35] International law also embraces a third test: "the *assimilation* of individuals to State organs on account of their actual behaviour within the structure of the State".[36] Finally, the Appeals Chamber reported many cases confirming that judicial and state practice adhere to such rules on agency determination.

Thus, the right test to apply under the circumstances of the *Tadić* case – that is, with respect to organized and hierarchically structured groups – was the 'overall control' test.[37] Accordingly, the accused was to be held responsible for war crimes committed in the context of an international armed conflict under article 2 of the Statute. Subsequent case law shows that, today, the 'overall control' test is well established and normally applied by the ICTY.[38]

From the viewpoint of the present analysis, it is irrelevant whether the overall control test is the right test or not. Abstractly speaking, the ICTY could have relied on other international law rules to determine whether the armed conflict was international or internal. What must be stressed here is that, once the Tribunal decided to apply the rules on state attribution, it had to do so in a consistent way with the interpretation they receive under the law of state responsibility. From this perspective, the *Tadić* case is remarkable because it shows a clear willingness to rely on the rules provided under the law of state responsibility, even when these rules must be applied in a different context, that is, when they must be applied to a preliminary question in a criminal proceeding. Indeed, the Appeals Chamber

---

[34] *Ibid.*, para. 123.

[35] *Ibid.*, para. 120 ("Plainly, an organized group differs from an individual in that the former normally has a structure, a chain of command and a set of rules as well as the outward symbols of authority. Normally a member of the group does not act on his own but conforms to the standards prevailing in the group and is subject to the authority of the head of the group.").

[36] *Ibid.*, para. 141. Later the Court explained that "private individuals acting within the framework of, or in connection with, armed forces, or in collusion with State authorities may be regarded as de facto State organs. In these cases it follows that the acts of such individuals are attributed to the State, as far as State responsibility is concerned, and may also generate individual criminal responsibility" (para. 144).

[37] *Ibid.*, paras. 146–162.

[38] *See* ICTY, *Prosecutor v. Blaškić*, TC, Judgment, 3 March 2000, paras. 95–123; ICTY, *Prosecutor v. Aleksovski*, AC, Judgment, 24 March 2000, paras. 137–146; *ICTY, Prosecutor v. Kordić and Čerkez*, TC, Judgment, 26 February 2001, para. 111; ICTY, *Prosecutor v. Naletilić and Martinović*, TC, Judgment, 31 March 2003, paras. 181–8 and 197–202; ICTY, *Prosecutor v. Brđanin*, TC, Judgment, 1 September 2004, para. 148.

made it clear that it was applying the same general criterion of control that applies in cases of state responsibility.

Therefore, the *Tadić* case shows a particular point of contact between state and individual responsibility for international crimes. In establishing individual liability for war crimes, international tribunals first have to determine the nature of the armed conflict. If recourse is had to the customary rules on state attribution, then these rules must be consistently applied in both fields of international law. This case reveals a precise legal connection between state and individual responsibility concerning the establishment of a general pre-requisite of war crimes, *i.e.*, the nature of the armed conflict, on the one hand, and one of the basic requirements in the establishment of state responsibility on the other. In this sense, *Tadić* guarantees a co-ordination between aggravated state responsibility and individual criminal liability.

The reply of the ICJ to the *Tadić* jurisprudence came in 2007, when the Court had to pronounce on the same facts, this time from the point of view of state responsibility.[39] The ICJ did not uphold the overall control test set out in *Tadić*.[40] The Court referred back to *Nicaragua* and applied the effective control test, arguably in a slightly narrower way than in the famous precedent.[41]

It seems that the criticism of the Court over *Tadić* mainly concerned the decision of the ICTY to apply the rules on state attribution to a preliminary question, that is, the nature of the conflict. On the one hand, it is possible to agree with the Court that the ICTY could have relied upon other international law rules to decide this specific issue.[42] On the other hand, it has been proposed to use the unity of substantive law as a remedy for jurisdictional fragmentation and to

---

[39] ICJ, *Genocide* case, supra the Introduction, note 1. The judgment has been the object of detailed analysis by international law scholars. *See* the various comments published in 18 *EJIL* (2007), 5 *JICJ* (2007), and 111 *RGDIP* (2007).

[40] ICJ, *Genocide* case, supra the Introduction, note 1, paras. 399–412. On this specific issue, *see* in general A. Cassese, 'The *Nicaragua* and *Tadić* Tests Revisited in Light of the ICJ Judgment on Genocide in Bosnia', 18 *EJIL* (2007), pp. 649–668.

[41] *See* H. Ascensio, 'La responsabilité selon la Cour internationale de Justice dans l'affaire du génocide bosniaque', 111 *RGDIP* (2007), p. 290.

[42] For example, the nature of the conflict could have been decided having recourse to the rules on international legal personality. *See* the approach adopted by the Trial Chamber in *Delalić*, ICTY, *Prosecutor v. Delalić et al.*, TC, Judgment, 11 November 1998, para. 231. From April 1992 the conduct of VRS forces could have been seen by the Tribunal as autonomous actions of an 'independent entity', in order to qualify the conflict between Bosnia and that entity as international. This seems to be the only way to characterize that conflict as international, and at the same time to deny attribution of the VRS conduct to Serbia. However, this line of reasoning implies the very difficult matter of proving that that 'independent entity' could have been regarded as a *de facto* government – a possibility that the ICJ seems to exclude in its judgment in the *Genocide* case, supra the Introduction, note 1, para. 420.

reconcile the decision of the Court with the jurisprudence of the ICTY.[43] From the present standpoint, the attitude of the Court is mainly problematic because it suggests that the same rule can, "without logical inconsistency", have two different meanings according to the context in which it is applied.[44] In other words, this case raises concern because it epitomizes the danger of inconsistency underlying a conception that tries to maintain, at any cost, a strict separation between state and individual responsibility for international crimes.[45] When dozens of individuals can be convicted for grave breaches because their conduct is attributable to a state, it is difficult to maintain that at the same time that state would not be responsible under international humanitarian law because the conduct of such individuals is not attributable to the state. Therefore, it would have seemed more 'logical' to conclude that either two different international rules apply to two different legal questions, or that the same international rule should be consistently interpreted and applied to the same legal question.

Another aspect of the *Tadić* case which must be pointed out here is that it shows a certain willingness of the ICTY to mark a distinction between individual criminal liability and state responsibility. State agency determination in case of crimes committed by organized military groups is a situation somewhat similar to the establishment of command responsibility. However, the ICTY relies on an 'overall control' test to attribute the conduct of military groups to the state, whereas it applies an 'effective control' test to establish the existence of a superior-subordinate relationship under the doctrine of command responsibility.[46] Thus, with respect to crimes committed in the framework of military or paramilitary groups, this results in the application of two different criteria in relation to the establishment of state responsibility and of the criminal liability of commanders respectively. This dual approach has been explained by the different nature of state responsibility

---

[43] *See* E. Cannizzaro, 'Interconnecting International Jurisdictions: A Contribution from the Genocide Decision of the ICJ', 1 *European Journal of Legal Studies* (2007), <www.ejls.eu>. In particular, it is the substantive unity of the issue brought before two different international jurisdictions which "would plead for the unity of the legal assessment of the same conduct under the same rule of law" (p. 6).

[44] ICJ, *Genocide* case, supra the Introduction, note 1, paras. 404–405. The issue of applying two different tests to the qualification of the armed conflict and to state agency determination is discussed in detail by M. Spinedi, 'On the Non-Attribution of the Bosnian Serbs' Conduct to Serbia', 5 *JICJ* (2007), pp. 829–838. The author concludes that it is not "very easy" "to prove that the criteria of attribution of conduct to states for determining participation in a conflict are different than those applicable for the attribution of wrongful acts" (p. 837).

[45] Arguably, the Court could have relied on the fact that the ICTY was dealing with a preliminary question, and accordingly it could have treated it differently from the other facts that the ICTY must establish beyond doubt in order to convict an accused for international crimes. On the relevance of the *ad hoc* tribunals judgments for the ICJ, *see* infra Chapter 9.

[46] *See* supra Chapter 6.

and individual criminal liability.[47] Indeed, it might be argued that holding commanders criminally responsible for the crimes committed by their subordinates should require more rigorous conditions than those necessary to attribute the same conduct to the state (and give rise to its responsibility under international law). However, the interesting aspect of this approach from the viewpoint of the relationship between state and individual responsibility for international crimes is that it reveals a tendency to conceive of state and individual responsibility for international crimes as two different regimes. Thus, while under certain circumstances the *ad hoc* tribunals may have to apply rules of state responsibility, these very rules are kept separate from rules concerning similar notions that are specific to individual criminal liability.[48]

2. *Connections in the Establishment of State and of Individual Responsibility*

Another aspect which may undermine the strict separation between state and individual responsibility for international crimes concerns a certain blurring of the distinction between international bodies charged with establishing aggravated state responsibility and those responsible for establishing individual criminal liability.

It is generally true that international criminal tribunals only focus on individual criminal liability under international law. However, the foregoing analysis has shown that there are cases in which aggravated state responsibility needs at least to be taken into account. On the other hand, a different point of contact between state and individual responsibility derives from the fact that there may be international bodies – charged, at least in principle, with state responsibility issues only – that in practice also deal with individual criminal liability. The most blatant example is provided by the practice of the UN SC.

A very controversial issue at the end of the twentieth century was the establishment of the ICTY by the SC. International law scholars were essentially divided on the question of whether or not the SC had the power to establish such juris-

47 A. Viviani, *Crimini internazionali e responsabilità dei* leader *politici e militari* (Milano, Giuffré, 2005), p. 65, note 132. The different nature and purposes of state and individual responsibility for international crimes will be examined below in Chapter 8.

48 It must be noted however that it is not always easy to keep these notions separate. For example, the Report of the Commission of Inquiry for Darfur shows a certain blurring between the notions of overall control referred to state conduct and that of effective control required under the doctrine of command responsibility. *See*, 'Report of the International Commission of Inquiry on Darfur to the United Nations Secretary-General pursuant to Security Council Resolution 1564 of 18 September 2004', supra Chapter 3, note 25, para. 123.

dictional bodies under the law of the UN Charter.[49] From the viewpoint of the present analysis, the precise identification of legal foundations of the SC's power to establish international criminal tribunals is not so important. What matters is the fact that the SC's power to address issues of individual liability challenges the strict separation between the establishment of state responsibility, on the one hand, and individual criminal liability, on the other. Indeed, if one assumes that the regimes of state and individual responsibility are mutually autonomous, it is striking to realize that the power to take measures against both states and individuals responsible for international crimes could be concentrated in the hands of one organ traditionally entrusted to deal only with the maintenance of international peace and security.[50] By contrast, if one adopts the opposite approach, according to which individual liability is nothing but a particular way of indirectly sanctioning the author state, then the power of the SC to establish *ad hoc* tribunals is perfectly logical because these tribunals are essentially aimed at sanctioning wrongful state acts.[51] This difference in approach is arguably one of the reasons why the establishment of the ICTY by the SC has been so controversial, as was the establishment of the Iraqi Compensation Commission.[52]

An important question that arises is how this twofold role of the SC is possible. What seems worth noting here is that the establishment of the ICTY, and of the ICTR a year later, are not isolated acts in the practice of the SC. Indeed, the practice of the SC shows an ever-increasing number of resolutions dealing with the conduct of individuals, resolutions explicitly directed at individuals, and resolutions in which measures are taken against individuals under Chapter VII.[53] Both the ICTY and the ICTR have upheld the SC's power to establish international criminal tribunals.[54] International practice shows that today a broad interpretation of the SC's powers under Chapter VII of the Charter prevails, in particular with

---

49 *See* supra Chapter 2, note 68 and accompanying text.

50 *See* A.C. Carpenter, 'The International Criminal Court and the Crime of Aggression', 64 *Nord. J. Int'l L.* (1995), p. 233; G.P. Fletcher and J.D. Ohlin, 'Reclaiming Fundamental Principles of Criminal Law in the Darfur Case', 3 *JICJ* (2005), p. 542.

51 *See* E. Sciso, 'I rapporti fra Consiglio di sicurezza e Corte penale internazionale', in S.I.D.I., *Cooperazione fra Stati e giustizia penale internazionale. III Convegno. Siena 12 e 13 giugno 1998* (Napoli, Editoriale Scientifica, 1999), p. 246.

52 For different opinions on the SC power to establish the Compensation Commission, *see* G. Arangio-Ruiz, 'On the Security Council's 'Law-Making'', 83 *Riv. Dir. Int.* (2000), pp. 717–719; D. Caron, 'The Legitimacy of the Collective Authority of the Security Council', 87 *AJIL* (1993), p. 552; B. Graefrath, 'Iraqi Reparations and the Security Council', 55 *ZaöRV* (1995), pp. 1–68.

53 *See* I. Cameron, 'UN Targeted Sanctions, Legal Safeguards and the European Convention on Human Rights', 72 *Nord. J. Int'l L.* (2003), pp. 159–214.

54 ICTY, *Prosecutor v. Tadić*, AC, Decision on the Defence Motion for Interlocutory Appeal on Jurisdiction, 2 October 1995; ICTR, *Prosecutor v. Kanyabashi*, TC, Decision on the Defence Motion on Jurisdiction, 18 June 1997.

respect to the possibility for this body to take measures not only against states but also against individuals, *as far as such measures serve the function of maintaining international peace and security*. Thus, while the drafters of the UN Charter arguably intended to confine the SC's powers to state action, today the power of the SC to address issues of individual liability no longer seems to be an open question under international law.[55]

It is against this background that the establishment of the ICTY and ICTR must be evaluated. Acting under Chapter VII was certainly the most expeditious way to bring those responsible to justice, and no other *ad hoc* tribunal has been established since.[56] But the power of the SC to set up such tribunals is only one element of the broader international practice pointing to the recognition of the SC's power to address individual conduct.

The ICC Statute can be cited as a confirmation of the significant role that the SC can have in the enforcement mechanisms of international criminal law. Indeed, under the Rome Statute, the SC has the power not only to refer situations to the Court (Article 13) but also to defer investigation or prosecution (Article 16).[57] On

---

[55] L. Condorelli, 'Legalità, legittimità, sfera di competenza dei Tribunali penali *ad hoc* creati dal Consiglio di sicurezza delle Nazioni Unite', in F. Lattanti and E. Sciso (eds.), *Dai Tribunali penali internazionali ad hoc a una Corte permanente* (Napoli, Editoriale Scientifica, 1996), pp. 47–63. Condorelli maintains that, according to Article 31 of the Vienna Convention, subsequent practice can have such an effect on the interpretation of the UN Charter.

[56] The lack of political will to set up new *ad hoc* tribunals seems mainly due to the fact that such tribunals are very expensive and rather slow in the prosecution and punishment of the indicted persons, and due also to the fact that the permanent ICC has now come into being. *See* 'Report of the International Commission of Inquiry on Darfur to the United Nations Secretary-General pursuant to Security Council Resolution 1564 of 18 September 2004', supra Chapter 3, note 25, para. 574.

[57] On the relationship between the ICC and the SC, *see* S. Yee, 'A Proposal to Reformulate Article 23 of the ILC Draft Statute for an International Criminal Court', 19 *Hastings Int'l & Comp. L. Rev.* (1995–6), pp. 529–538; C.L. Blakesley, 'Jurisdiction, Definition of Crimes, and Triggering Mechanisms', 25 *Den. J. Int'l L. & Pol'y* (1996–7), pp. 233–280; H.P. Kaul, 'Towards a Permanent International Criminal Court. Some Observations of a Negotiator', 18 *HRLJ* (1997), p. 172; G. Arangio-Ruiz, 'Fine prematura del ruolo preminente di studiosi italiani nel progetto di codificazione della responsabilità degli Stati: specie a proposito di crimini internazionali e dei poteri del Consiglio di sicurezza', 81 *Riv. Dir. Int.* (1998), pp. 110–129; V. Gowlland-Debbas, 'The Relationship between the Security Council and the Projected International Criminal Court', 3 *JACL* (1998), pp. 97–119; A. Zimmermann, 'The Creation of a Permanent International Criminal Court', 2 *Max Planck Y. UN L.* (1998), pp. 169–237; P. Gargiulo, 'The Controversial Relationship between the International Criminal Court and the Security Council', in F. Lattanzi and W.A. Schabas (eds.), *Essays on the Rome Statute of the International Criminal Court* (Ripa di Fagnano Alto, Il Sirente, 1999), pp. 67–103; S.R. Ratner, 'The Relationship between the International Criminal Court and the Security Council: An Appraisal of the United States Position', in S.I.D.I., *Cooperazione fra Stati e giustizia penale internazionale. III Convegno. Siena 12 e 13 giugno 1998* (Napoli, Editoriale Scientifica, 1999), pp. 237–243; E. Sciso, supra note 51, p. 245; L. Yee, 'The

the one hand, the existence of a permanent ICC guarantees a certain separation between state and individual responsibility under international law. On the other hand, in Rome a clear majority of states nonetheless supported the SC's power of so-called 'judicial intervention'.

The power of the SC to refer cases to the Court was already present in the 1993 Working Group proposal, and it was maintained both by the ILC (in its 1994 Report) and by the PrepCom (in the 1998 Draft). Except for a few isolated positions,[58] during the Rome conference this power was not called into question, and it was finally embodied in Article 13.[59]

The SC power to block the Court was more controversial. A number of states opposed what was perceived as a serious threat to the independence of the future criminal court, and this led to a significant modification of the original proposal on this issue. Indeed, according to the ILC proposal the Court could not exercise its jurisdiction as long as the situation was being dealt with by the SC under Chapter VII (Article 23).[60] This provision was inserted in order to co-ordinate the activity of the SC with that of the future ICC, and was inspired by Article 12 of the UN Charter with the purpose of co-ordinating the activity of the GA and the SC. However, one may doubt that Article 12 is the most appropriate source of inspiration: unlike the GA, the ICC is not an organ of the UN, and arguably

International Criminal Court and the Security Council: Articles 13(b) and 16', in R.S. Lee (ed.), *The International Criminal Court. The Making of the Rome Statute. Issues, Negotiations, Results* (The Hague, Kluwer, 1999), pp. 143–152; M.H. Arsanjani, 'Reflections on the Jurisdiction and Trigger Mechanism of the International Criminal Court', in A.M. Von Hebel *et al.* (eds.), *Reflections on the International Criminal Court. Essays in Honour of Adrian Bos* (The Hague, TMS Asser Press, 1999), pp. 57–76; L. Arbour and M. Bergsmo, 'Conspicuous Absence of Jurisdictional Overreach', in A.M. Von Hebel *et al.* (eds.), *Reflections on the International Criminal Court. Essays in Honour of Adrian Bos* (The Hague, TMS Asser Press, 1999), pp. 129–140; F. Berman, 'The Relationship between the International Criminal Court and the Security Council', in A.M. Von Hebel *et al.* (eds.), *Reflections on the International Criminal Court. Essays in Honour of Adrian Bos* (The Hague, TMS Asser Press, 1999), pp. 173–180; G.H. Oosthuizen, 'Some Preliminary Remarks on the Relationship between the Envisaged International Criminal Court and the UN Security Council', 46 *NILR* (1999), pp. 313–342; M. Bergsmo, 'Occasional Remarks on Certain State Concerns about the Jurisdictional Reach of the International Criminal Court, and Their Possible Implications for the Relationship between the Court and the Security Council', 69 *Nord. J. Int'l L.* (2000), pp. 87–113; J.F. Escudero Espinosa, *La Corte penal internacional y el Consejo de seguridad* (Madrid, Dilex, 2004).

58 *See* the press releases by India and Pakistan of 16 June 1998 (L/ROM/8, L/ROM/9) and 17 July 1998 (L/ROM/22), <www.un.org/icc/index.htm>.

59 Article 13 reads: "The Court may exercise its jurisdiction with respect to a crime referred to in article 5 in accordance with the provisions of this Statute if: . . . (b) A situation in which one or more of such crimes appears to have been committed is referred to the Prosecutor by the Security Council acting under Chapter VII of the Charter of the United Nations", <www.icc-cpi.int>.

60 ILC, 'Report on the Work of its 46th Session', *YILC* (1994), vol. II(2), p. 43. For a comment on Article 23, *see* S. Yee, supra note 57, p. 529.

Article 12 has lost most of its original authority.[61] Thus, one can rather turn to the relationship between the SC and the ICJ.[62] Despite the absence of specific provisions on the subject, the Court has maintained that there is nothing "irregular in the simultaneous exercise of their respective functions";[63] the SC has its political functions whereas the Court has its judicial functions.[64] Thus, as a matter of principle, it is perfectly conceivable that the SC and the ICC exercise their respective and different functions with respect to the same situation.

A compromise was found during the Rome conference thanks to the so-called 'Singapore proposal', according to which a formal decision of the SC under Chapter VII was necessary to block an investigation or prosecution before the ICC. In this way, it was possible to co-ordinate the action of the SC under Chapter VII and the jurisdiction of the ICC, and at the same time to guarantee the independence of the ICC. Thus, an explicit decision under Chapter VII is necessary to block the activity of the Court, while the sole fact that a situation is put on the SC agenda is not sufficient to do so.[65]

From the viewpoint of the present analysis, the most significant aspect is the role the SC has gradually assumed with respect to individuals committing serious breaches of community obligations. The drafting history of the ICC Statute and the final outcome of the Rome conference confirm that the SC has the power to address the conduct of individuals who breach of the most fundamental rules of the international community. Indeed, the Rome Statute is not capable of conferring new powers on the SC. Articles 13 and 16 are necessarily grounded on the powers entrusted to the SC by the UN Charter.[66]

Thus, the existence of a political body which centralizes the adoption of measures with respect to both states and individuals represents a significant point of contact between state and individual responsibility for international crimes. And

---

[61] ICJ, *Legal Consequences of the Construction of a Wall in the Occupied Palestinian Territory*, supra Chapter 1, note 44, para. 28. *See* S.R. Ratner, supra note 57, p. 241.

[62] *See* R. Higgins, 'The Relationship between the International Criminal Court and the International Court of Justice', in A.M. Von Hebel *et al.* (eds.), *Reflections on the International Criminal Court. Essays in Honour of Adrian Bos* (The Hague, TMS Asser Press, 1999), pp. 163–172.

[63] ICJ, *Case Concerning United States Diplomatic and Consular Staff in Teheran* (United States of America v. Iran), Judgment, 24 May 1980, *ICJ Reports* 1980, para. 40.

[64] ICJ, *Case Concerning Military and Paramilitary Activities in and against Nicaragua* (Nicaragua v. United States of America), Jurisdiction of the Court and Admissibility of the Application, Judgment, 26 November 1984, *ICJ Reports* 1984, para. 95.

[65] Article 16 now reads: "No investigation or prosecution may be commenced or proceeded with under this Statute for a period of 12 months after the Security Council, in a resolution adopted under Chapter VII of the Charter of the United Nations, has requested the Court to that effect; that request may be renewed by the Council under the same conditions", <www.icc-cpi.int>.

[66] *See* A. Zimmermann, supra note 57, p. 216; F. Berman, supra note 57, p. 176; M. Bergsmo, supra note 57, p. 94; J.F. Escudero Espinosa, supra note 57, p. 153.

this is not only an abstract point of contact due to the fact that one body has the power to deal with both state and individual conduct with respect to the same situation. This broad power of the SC may establish a concrete link between the establishments of state and individual responsibility. Indeed, this situation can lead to such a close link that a separation between state and individual responsibility is difficult to maintain in practice.

First, the SC has played a role in the enforcement of international criminal law (by establishing *ad hoc* tribunals or by referring a case to the ICC) in situations where international crimes had arguably been committed in the framework of a state policy or with the involvement of the state apparatus. In other words, international prosecution of international crimes has been put in place by the SC once it has been found that a certain situation not only was a threat to international peace and security under Article 39 of the UN Charter but also entailed some degree of state involvement. In practice, it seems possible to maintain that the prosecution of core crimes at the international level has generally focused on cases which implied a dual responsibility of the state and its organs. A certain degree of state responsibility seems undeniable, for instance with respect to the crimes committed in Former Yugoslavia, Rwanda, and Darfur. In a sense, the SC has exercised its powers with respect to individuals in cases of international crimes generally perpetrated at the state level.

Second, an unlimited power of the SC to address individual conduct can have a detrimental effect on international criminal law, which creates a risk that it may be used to attain different goals from its own. The SC power to bar an ICC proceeding "would effectively extend the privileged position of certain states to the Court and call into question the principle of equality before the law".[67] The intrusion of a political organ in the judicial function of the ICC can result in selective justice, as shown by the SC decision to grant immunity from the Court's jurisdiction to peacekeeping personnel from states not party to the Rome Statute. In 2002, the SC adopted Res. 1422 which, according to Article 16 of the Rome Statute, requested the ICC not to commence or proceed with investigation or prosecution of cases involving current or former personnel from those states for a twelve month period. The same request was renewed in 2003.[68] It is true that immunity was granted to such persons 'only' temporarily. However, the SC has subsequently decided in two specific situations that current or former peacekeeping personnel from states not party to the Rome Statute "shall be subject to the exclusive jurisdiction of that contributing State for all alleged acts and omissions arising out of or related to" the forces operating in Liberia and Sudan.[69] This results in two *ad hoc* cases of

[67] V. Gowlland-Debbas, supra note 57, p. 109.

[68] *See* SC Resolution 1487(2003), <www.un.org/Docs/sc>.

[69] *See* SC Resolutions 1497(2003), para.7, and 1593(2005), para. 6, <www.un.org/Docs/sc>.

permanent immunity from the ICC jurisdiction, and seriously calls into question the principle of equality before the law.[70]

Furthermore, the increasing focus of the SC on individual conduct may lead, to a certain extent, to a substitution of individual accountability for international crimes for state responsibility, thus establishing an even closer link between state and individual responsibility. Instead of discharging its traditional functions under the UN Charter and adopting measures towards states endangering international peace and security, the SC may be induced to concentrate on the role of individuals in similar situations of international crisis. The ultimate function of international criminal law, *i.e.*, "to combat impunity and render justice to the victims of war crimes and crimes against humanity",[71] is arguably different from the primary responsibility of the SC under Chapter VII, *i.e.*, the maintenance of international peace and security.[72] And measures adopted against individuals can hardly have the same effect of measures adopted against states in order to fulfil the very function of maintaining international peace and security.[73] Nonetheless, the practice of the SC clearly reveals a growing importance of individual accountability, to the detriment of state responsibility.[74]

What has happened with respect to the situation in Darfur is a very good example of this trend. International crimes – war crimes and crimes against humanity – have been committed in a widespread and systematic manner. These crimes are substantially attributable to Sudan.[75] The SC determined that "the situation in Sudan constitutes a threat to international peace and security and to stability in the region".[76] The SC has dealt with the situation in Darfur essentially by adopting measures against individuals and non-governmental entities.[77] A few months later, having acknowledged that Sudan was not complying with its obligations under international law, the SC declared that it

[70] *See* G. Gaja, 'Immunità squilibrate dalla giurisdizione penale in relazione all'intervento armato in Liberia', 86 *Riv. Dir. Int.* (2003), p. 763.

[71] This is the way in which the ICTY interprets its mandate by the SC (*see* the ICTY Completion Strategy, UN Doc. S/2002/678).

[72] For a comparative analysis of the nature and functions of state and individual responsibility, *see* infra Chapter 8.

[73] Less doubtful is the situation in which measures taken by the SC against individuals are only part of a broader set of measures taken against states endangering international peace and security.

[74] *See* infra note 85.

[75] *See* supra Chapter 3, note 27.

[76] SC Resolution 1556(2004), <www.un.org/Docs/sc>.

[77] As the SC has stated: "all states shall take the necessary measures to prevent the sale or supply, to all *non-governmental entities and individuals*, ... of arms and related materiel of all types" (*ibid.*, para. 7, emphasis added).

> shall consider taking additional measures as contemplated in Article 41 of the Charter of the United Nations, such as actions to affect Sudan's petroleum sector and the Government of Sudan or individual members of the Government of Sudan, in order to obtain such full compliance or full cooperation.[78]

No such measures towards Sudan have ever been taken. The SC has extended the measures adopted in Res. 1556 to all parties to the internal conflict, including therefore also the Government of Sudan.[79] However, the Government of Sudan can request the SC for an exemption from the prohibition of the movement of military equipment and supplies into the Darfur region.[80] In the end, this measure will concern only the above-mentioned non-governmental entities.

By contrast, the SC has adopted new measures against those individuals responsible for the international crimes in Sudan.[81] Following the proposal of the Commission of Inquiry previously established to investigate the violations committed in Darfur,[82] the SC has for the first time referred a situation to the ICC according to Article 13 of the Rome Statute.[83] This decision is certainly to be welcomed. However, no parallel action against Sudan was decided. Thus, on the one hand, one may wonder whether future proceedings before the ICC in which high-ranking Sudanese organs will be charged with the international crimes committed in Darfur[84] are an adequate response to a situation endangering international peace. On the other hand, the situation in Darfur is now growing worse, the involvement of other states in the crisis is not unlikely, and one may doubt whether measures addressing only individual conduct are appropriate to fulfil the primary function of the SC, that is, maintaining international peace and security.[85]

---

[78] SC Resolution 1564(2004), para. 14, <www.un.org/Docs/sc>.

[79] SC Resolution 1591(2005), <www.un.org/Docs/sc>.

[80] *Ibid.*, para. 3 (a)(v), and para. 7.

[81] Additional measures against individuals have been adopted under Res. 1591(2004), and a list of such individuals has subsequently been included in Resolution 1672(2006), <www.un.org/Docs/sc>.

[82] The Commission of Inquiry focused only on the identification of individual perpetrators (supra Chapter 3, note 25). However, nothing in the letter of SC Resolution 1564(2004) prevented the Commission from interpreting its mandate in broader terms and including issues of state responsibility.

[83] SC Resolution 1593(2005), <www.un.org/Docs/sc>.

[84] *See* supra Chapter 6, note 70.

[85] According to Rao, "by emphasizing the individual criminal responsibility and merely punishing individuals, we will not be able in the long run to stamp out the situations that provide the environment for lawless behavior" (P.S. Rao, 'International Crimes and State Responsibility', in M. Ragazzi (ed.), *International Responsibility Today: Essays in Memory of Oscar Schachter* (Leiden, Boston, M. Nijhoff, 2005), p. 80). *See* also V.D. Degan, 'Responsibility of States and Individuals for International Crimes', in S. Yee and W. Tieya (eds.), *International Law in the Post-Cold War World: Essay in Memory of Li Haopei* (London, New York, Routledge, 2001), pp. 209, and 211, pointing out the risk that, in practice, state responsibility has no real consequences.

3. *Establishing State and Individual Responsibility for Aggression*

The crime of aggression was, and still is, one of the most controversial aspects of the ICC Statute. According to Article 5, the ICC will have jurisdiction over the crime of aggression, but only once the Assembly of States Parties agrees on a definition of this crime and on the conditions under which the Court is to exercise its jurisdiction. In addition, Article 5 specifies that the future provision on the crime of aggression "shall be consistent with the relevant provisions of the Charter of the United Nations". In other words, the judicial action of the ICC with respect to aggression must not impinge on, and must be co-ordinated with, the SC's primary role under Chapter VII, and in particular its power under Article 39 to determine when a state act of aggression has been carried out.

Abstractly speaking, the relationship between the ICC and the SC as far as aggression is concerned can be considered from two different perspectives: that of the relationship between the Rome Statute and the UN Charter, and that of the relationship between state and individual responsibility. From the standpoint of the law of treaties, the ICC Statute contains a provision requiring respect for the primary responsibility of the SC under Chapter VII. However, there is no need to establish a procedure that automatically subordinates the exercise of the ICC jurisdiction over individuals charged with the crime of aggression to a prior determination that state aggression has actually occurred. The ICC must simply 'respect' the determinations of the SC concerning state conduct. If there is a determination under Chapter VII, the ICC should respect it as far as state aggression is concerned, but at least in principle it would be free to deviate from that determination as far as *individual* liability is concerned.[86] Absent a determination under Article 39, the ICC will be free to exercise its jurisdiction over the alleged perpetrators of the crime of aggression.

From the standpoint of the relationship between state and individual responsibility, things are arguably different. If the crime of aggression is strictly defined in terms of state action, liability cannot be ascribed to individuals lacking an assessment of the relevant state conduct. If a state has not committed aggression, its political and military leaders cannot be charged with aggression. However, the ICC cannot pronounce on issues of state responsibility, since its jurisdiction is strictly limited to natural persons.[87] Thus, the action by the Court would necessarily be

[86] *See* Fourth Session of the Assembly of the States Parties to the ICC Statute, ICC-ASP/4/32, Annex II, para. 64, <www.icc-cpi.int>. For example, if the offender lacks the requisite *mens rea* it cannot be convicted.

[87] For opinions in favour of the ICC power to proceed even if state aggravated responsibility has not been previously established, *see* V. Gowlland-Debbas, supra note 57, p. 106; G. Gaja, 'The Respective Roles of the ICC and the Security Council in Determining the Existence of an Aggression', in M. Politi and G. Nesi (eds.), *The International Criminal Court and the Crime of Aggres-*

subordinated to the previous assessment concerning state aggression by a different international body having the power to address state conduct. Naturally, the SC is the first on the list, but it is not the only one. The GA may pronounce on similar issues. So too can the ICJ. This raises the problem of the choice of the competent body, which is not an easy task. But there is an even more problematic aspect: in principle, if the international body charged with determining state aggression is unable to pronounce on a particular situation, then action by the ICC would be completely precluded.

If it were possible to regard the crime of aggression as a crime which could also be committed by private individuals, no prior assessment of the state conduct would be necessary.[88] The ICC would thus be totally free to exercise its jurisdiction independently of the position adopted, for instance, by the SC with respect to the different question of state aggression. However, at present international law seems clearly oriented towards a definition of aggression rigorously framed in terms of state conduct. The analysis carried out in previous chapters has pointed out the particular features of the crime of aggression with respect to the material element, the perpetrators, the seriousness requirement, and defences. On the other hand, the case law of the ICJ has undoubtedly confined aggression to state conduct.[89]

With respect to the amendment process of Article 5 of the ICC Statute, the outcome is highly uncertain. The crime of aggression raises various questions, and some of them are very controversial. However, the works of the PrepCom and of the SWGCA have also highlighted the existence of essentially three relatively well-established aspects concerning aggression. First, the crime of aggression is a 'leadership' crime. Aggression can only be committed by political and military leaders, *i.e.*, in the words of the PrepCom and the SWGCA, by persons "being in a position effectively to exercise control over or to direct the political and military action of a State."[90] Second, aggression is strictly defined in terms of state conduct. Therefore, an act of aggression "means an act referred to in GA Resolution 3314 (XXIX) of 14 December 1974, which is determined to have been committed by

sion (Aldershot, Ashgate, 2004), p. 123; S.M. Yengejeh, 'Reflections on the Role of the Security Council in Determining an Act of Aggression', in M. Politi and G. Nesi (eds.), *The International Criminal Court and the Crime of Aggression* (Aldershot, Ashgate, 2004), pp. 130–131; M. Lehto, 'The ICC and the Security Council: About the Argument of Politicization', in M. Politi and G. Nesi (eds.), *The International Criminal Court and the Crime of Aggression* (Aldershot, Ashgate, 2004), p. 148.

[88] *See* supra Chapter 4, note 77 and accompanying text.

[89] ICJ, *Legal Consequences of the Construction of a Wall in the Occupied Palestinian Territory*, supra Chapter 1, note 44; ICJ, *Case Concerning Armed Activities on the Territory of the Congo* (Democratic Republic of the Congo v. Uganda), supra Chapter 1, note 44, para. 165.

[90] ICC-ASP/2/10, p. 234, <www.icc-cpi.int>, previously issued as PCNICC/2002/2/Add.2, <untreaty.un.org/cod/icc/index.html>. *See* supra Chapter 4.

the State concerned".[91] Third, the ICC could not proceed against individuals unless there is a prior determination of the state act of aggression. This is due to the fact that "it is necessary to determine that a state act of aggression has occurred before it can be determined that an individual crime of aggression is at hand".[92]

The fact that there is an agreement on such basic assumptions does not lead to an analogous convergence of opinions on the definition of aggression,[93] and the conditions for the exercise of the ICC jurisdiction. As to the latter, the proposal of the PrepCom and the SWGCA reads as follows:

> Where the Prosecutor intends to proceed with an investigation in respect of a crime of aggression, the Court shall first ascertain whether the Security Council has made a determination of an act of aggression committed by the State concerned. If no Security Council determination exists, the Court shall notify the Security Council of the situation before the Court.[94]

This provision tries to co-ordinate the jurisdiction of the ICC with the SC's power under Chapter VII, so that the Rome Statute is consistent with the UN Charter. If the SC makes a determination with respect to state aggression, then the ICC must take it into account. However, this does not solve the problem where the SC takes no action.[95]

There are considerable differences of opinion on this point. Two approaches have emerged: one in favour of the exclusive competence of the SC, and the other supporting such competence for other bodies as well, such as the UN GA or the ICJ.[96] In the end, two alternatives have been included in the PrepCom and SWGCA proposals: 1) the ICC jurisdiction would be precluded if there is no prior determination of aggression made by a competent organ outside the Court; or 2)

---

[91] *Ibid.*. *See* supra Chapter 3.

[92] *Ibid.*, p. 385.

[93] While aggression is a leadership crime and subordinates cannot be charged with it, the question of whether command responsibility would be applicable under such circumstances is controversial. More generally, the debate revolves around the forms of liability which are applicable to the crime of aggression (*see* ICC-ASP/4/32, Annex II, para. 18–31, <www.icc-cpi.int>). A similar problem concerns the possibility to hold individuals accountable for the attempt to commit aggression (*see* ICC-ASP/4/32, Annex II, para. 33–43, <www.icc-cpi.int>). The question is even more difficult when state aggression has not fully materialised, since 1) the definitions of state aggression and of the individual crime of aggression may be different in this respect, and 2) this situation puts in question the role of an outside body that might be called upon to determine whether state aggression has occurred.

[94] *See* PCNICC/2002/2/Add.2, <untreaty.un.org/cod/icc/index.html>, and ICC-ASP/5/SWGCA/2, p. 4, <www.icc-cpi.int>.

[95] The SC has determined the existence of a state aggression only on very few occasions. *See* supra Chapter 1, note 43. Moreover, the inactivity of the SC is generally due to the veto power of the permanent member states. These states would thus be able to leave the ICC in a state of paralysis.

[96] ICC-ASP/4/32, Annex II, paras. 63–74, <www.icc-cpi.int>.

the ICC would be able to proceed with the case.[97] In the end, this proposal leaves open the door to different solutions, but it shows the two major problems concerning the exercise of the ICC jurisdiction over the crime of aggression. First, there is uncertainty over the legal effects of the prior determination of state aggression (by the SC or another international body) with respect to the establishment of individual liability by the ICC.[98] Second, the proposal seeks, at all costs, to keep the determination of state aggression and the establishment of individual criminal liability for aggression separate, in order to preserve the autonomy of the ICC and to respect the basic principles of international criminal law.

These uncertainties concerning the crime of aggression can only be explained by the fact that the dilemma faced by the drafters of these proposals is that of trying to look at the crime of aggression from the perspective of *individual* criminal liability (that is, with the aim of defining the elements of an individual crime and of keeping a strict separation between the activity of the ICC and issues of state responsibility), but having assumed that the crime of aggression has a particular nature, that is, it is a *state* crime. Thus, the paradox of the crime of aggression is that, due to its nature, a close link with state responsibility is unavoidable, but at the same time the specific features of the individual crime of aggression must be identified.[99] To be sure, it is a very difficult task. At a certain point the SWGCA recognized that its ultimate task is "*to delineate clearly the point of intersection between individual responsibility on the one hand and State responsibility on the other.*"[100] Thus, with respect to aggression, there are clear connections between state and individual responsibility and they raise particular problems that cannot be solved if there is no clarity concerning the theoretical underpinnings concerning this crime.

On the one hand, the establishment of personal criminal liability for the crime of aggression necessarily requires the corresponding act of state aggression to be established. This implies the assessment of both material conduct (amounting to aggression) and the fact that this conduct is attributable to a state. Where there is such a prior determination of state aggression, the question concerns the legal effects of this determination for the ICC.[101] The prior finding of fact relating to the material conduct amounting to aggression can be seen as a preliminary question necessary to establish individual criminal liability. Although it can be maintained,

[97] ICC-ASP/2/10, p. 234, <www.icc-cpi.int>, previously issued as PCNICC/2002/2/Add.2, para. 5, <untreaty.un.org/cod/icc/index.html>, and ICC-ASP/5/SWGCA/2, p. 4, <www.icc-cpi.int>.

[98] ICC-ASP/4/32, Annex II, paras. 60–62, <www.icc-cpi.int>.

[99] The SWGCA explicitly states that it has to distinguish between the collective act of and individual participation in aggression (ICC-ASP/4/32, pp. 362–364, <www.icc-cpi.int>).

[100] *Ibid.*, para. 62 (emphasis added).

[101] *See* G.H. Oosthuizen, supra note 57, who examines both the review power of the ICC and the binding effect of SC resolutions from an institutional viewpoint. As to the former aspect, *see* also J.F. Escudero Espinosa, supra note 57, p. 162.

abstractly speaking, that the ICC has the power to review this finding according to elements not previously taken into account, such as self-defence,[102] in practice it is difficult to accept two different qualifications of the same act of aggression. A certain consistency must be guaranteed when the same international rule defines aggression under both state and individual responsibility. On the other hand, this does not prevent the ICC from considering elements specific to international criminal law which can exclude individual criminal responsibility notwithstanding a determination that a state act of aggression has taken place, such as certain defences typical of individual conduct. Turning to the legal finding on state attribution, arguably the ICC cannot depart from it. While this particular aspect has no direct impact on the subsequent trial of state leaders for aggression, it can play an indirect role before the ICC. Once it is established that a state has committed an act of aggression, the *actus reus* has already been determined, and the *mens rea* of political and military leaders can be easily inferred from the general criminal context.[103] How is it possible for state leaders to deny "intention or knowledge"[104] of the relevant act of aggression? In the end, it seems very difficult to keep the establishment of state and individual responsibility for aggression separate. Prior determination is likely to have a very profound impact on the ICC.[105]

On the other hand, there is a clear need to maintain the separation between the determination of state aggression and the establishment of individual accountability for aggression. The efforts of the PrepCom and the SWGCA have been aimed at elaborating proposals which could guarantee a certain autonomy for the ICC. If the jurisdiction of the ICC is made dependent on a prior determination of state aggression, the major risk is that of a paralysis of the Court if the competent body cannot reach a decision on that issue. From this perspective, the option concerning

---

102 A. Zimmermann, supra note 57, considers the binding effect of SC resolutions to be limited to the extent that it reaches a determination on the merits of the act of aggression. "Thus, the ICC itself would eventually have to consider and determine all those elements of the crime which are not already contained in the determination made by the Security Council under Article 39 of the Charter" (p. 203). *See* also ICC- ASP/4/32, Annex II, para. 61, <www.icc-cpi.int>. However, this possibility can be problematic because the SC generally limit itself to very concise determinations under Article 39. If the SC simply states that aggression has occurred, does this mean that the ICC can review this decision according to the elements of state responsibility for aggression not taken into account?

103 *See* supra Chapter 4.

104 *See* ICC-ASP/2/10, p. 234, <www.icc-cpi.int>, previously issued as PCNICC/2002/2/Add.2, para. 1, <untreaty.un.org/cod/icc/index.html>.

105 According to one commentator, if the prior determination of the SC were binding upon the ICC, it would leave the Court "only the remaining task of determining the role of individuals involved in the act of aggression, much in the same style of a compensation commission administering individual claims after a country such as Iraq has been determined to be liable for all amounts" (S. Yee, supra note 57, pp. 532–533).

the competence, for example, of the ICJ is less problematic, even though it raises concerns as to the introduction of a hierarchy between these two institutions.[106] A solution could be to admit that the ICC "can proceed" even in the absence of a prior determination of state aggression.[107] However, it is not clear what exactly this second option means. Assuming that the Court can establish the material conduct amounting to aggression but that it cannot attribute such conduct to a state, would this imply that the Court is supposed to focus on individual liability only? This might be inconsistent with the definition of the crime of aggression. By contrast, does this mean that the Court has given the power to ascertain that a state act of aggression has taken place? However, such a possibility might imply that the Court would apply the relevant rules of state responsibility.

In both cases, whether the ICC has a review power or "may proceed", the main problem would be to guarantee a consistent application of international primary rules called into question under both state and individual responsibility. As recognized by the SWGCA, the ICC and the SC have "autonomous, but complementary roles, which could best be advanced if both institutions [have] broadly compatible rules regarding the determination of an act of aggression".[108]

To sum up, the debate over the crime of aggression is particularly interesting because it highlights the contradictions necessarily connected to the lack of a clear theoretical approach over this crime. On the one hand, it is taken for granted that there must be a separation between the enforcement mechanisms of state and individual responsibility. While the SC is called on to establish the existence of a *state* wrongful act, the ICC jurisdiction is limited to the prosecution of *individuals* for aggression. And this scheme is never called into question in the recent proposal concerning the exercise of the ICC jurisdiction over the crime of aggression. On the other hand, the nature of this crime is not disputed either. Aggression is a crime which can be committed only by states. There is a general overlap between the elements of state responsibility for aggression and the elements of the crime of aggression entailing individual liability. Thus, the criminal liability of political and military leaders would be almost inextricably connected to the prior determination of a state act of aggression.[109] And if the Court "may proceed" without such a prior determination, state responsibility would be implicit in the conviction of military or political state leaders.

---

106 ICC-ASP/5/35, p. 14, <www.icc-cpi.int>.

107 *See* ICC-ASP/6/SWGCA/INF.1, Annex III ("Non-paper submitted by the Chairman on the exercise of jurisdiction"), pp. 18–20, <www.icc-cpi.int>. This document seems to admit that, in any case, the Court can proceed. It is unclear whether the option according to which – absent a prior determination – the ICC may not proceed has been set aside.

108 *Ibid.*, p. 11. *See* also E. Sciso, supra note 51, p. 258.

109 *See* T.L.H. McCormack and G.J. Simpson, 'A New International Criminal Law Regime?', 42 *NILR* (1995), p. 196; V. Gowlland-Debbas, supra note 57, p. 107.

4. *Concluding Observations*

When taking into account the establishment of international responsibility for the most serious crimes of concern to the international community as a whole, there is a consistently reaffirmed division of tasks between international bodies entrusted with the establishment of state responsibility, and international bodies having to exercise criminal jurisdiction over individuals responsible for international crimes.

The ICJ has recently affirmed its discretion in interpreting issues of general international law with respect to previous decisions of international criminal tribunals.[110] At the same time, the Court based its judgment on previous findings of fact of the ICTY. In other words, this seems to confirm the view according to which there is a certain division of competences between international bodies dealing with either state or individual responsibility to be respected. However, this strict division of compenteces may prove problematic in the establishment of international responsibility for international crimes.

The present chapter has examined various situations in which such a 'natural' assumption is called into question. First, there are cases in which notions of state responsibility must be consistently applied before international criminal tribunals. The *Tadić* case has been examined in detail. The crime of aggression raises a similar question. Once it is accepted that the material element of this crime corresponds to a rule governing state responsibility, a certain co-ordination between state and individual responsibility for aggression needs to be guaranteed. Absent a determination on the state conduct, and assuming that the ICC can proceed, it can only do so by relying on the relevant rules of general international law governing state aggression. These examples show that, if a separation between the establishment of state and individual responsibility for international crimes is to be maintained, it must be counterbalanced by an effective co-ordination of these regimes.

Second, there are cases in which this division of competences disappears, or more precisely, where it becomes unidirectional. The analysis has focused on the powers of the SC and its practice addressing both state and individual conduct. When no separation exists between the body charged to deal with state responsibility and that exercising criminal jurisdiction over the individuals responsible for international crimes, there is the risk that the basic principles of international criminal law may be frustrated or that the intervention of a political body in such matters may result in selective justice. In addition, individual criminal liability would be closely connected to state responsibility, and would essentially be established with respect to crimes entailing a dual responsibility under international law. Taking into account the crime of aggression, the prior determination of state aggression is capable of having a considerable impact on the establishment of state leaders'

---

110 ICJ, *Genocide* case, supra the Introduction, note 1, para. 403.

criminal liability. Furthermore, this increases the possibility for individual criminal liability to be used as an alternative or substitute for state responsibility. In other words, the risk is to use individual criminal liability for different purposes from those that naturally characterize this field of international law. The separate but connected establishment of state and individual responsibility shows all the difficulties of finding a fair balance between the need to combat impunity for international crimes and the need to guarantee state compliance with international rules in an effective way.

Part III

The Relationship Between State and Individual Responsibility for International Crimes

Chapter 8

Complementarity Between State and Individual Responsibility for International Crimes

The analysis of international practice carried out in Part II has concentrated on both the differences and the points of contact between state and individual responsibility for international crimes. The main result is that the relationship between these regimes entails an increasing number of problematic issues concerning their co-ordination. Thus, it no longer seems possible to simply disregard this relationship or assume that these issues can be efficiently addressed on a case-by-case basis. The purpose of the following two chapters is to discuss the general outcomes of the foregoing analysis of international practice and shape a theoretical framework capable of explaining the relationship between state and individual responsibility accordingly.

1. *The Relationship Between State and Individual Responsibility for International Crimes according to International Practice*

International practice prompts two general remarks on the relationship between state and individual responsibility. Aggravated state responsibility and international criminal law are in principle regarded as separate regimes under international law. However, in practice there are various points of contact between these regimes. A special plea must finally be reserved to the crime of aggression which is generally considered to be a crime of an exceptional nature with respect to which no complete separation between state and individual responsibility seems possible.

Undoubtedly, international practice shows a certain tendency to keep state responsibility separate from individual liability. These regimes may well share a common origin, *i.e.*, the breach of obligations owed to the entire international community. Nonetheless, they remain two different legal regimes of international responsibility aiming at governing the consequences of distinct types of conduct.

In particular, international criminal law only concerns individual conduct, not state conduct. The principle of individual criminal liability applies to all individuals, both state organs and private individuals. International case law has made it plain that no state policy need be demonstrated as a condition for holding state organs accountable when they commit international crimes which by definition must be carried out in a widespread or systematic way. To be convicted, every defendant must have had a certain *mens rea*, and this element can never be presumed, not even with respect to high ranking state organs. Defences under international criminal law do not necessarily have the same meaning of circumstances precluding wrongfulness under the law of state responsibility. The modes of liability that can be relied upon to ascribe liability for crimes committed at the collective level do not require a previous establishment of state responsibility.

All in all, international practice points to a separation between state and individual responsibility for international crimes. With respect to crimes entailing a dual responsibility under international law, this separation arguably derives from the dissociation between the conduct of the state and that of its organs. This dissociation also explains why state organs can be prosecuted even if they have committed the relevant international crimes in the exercise of governmental authority. At the same time, this dissociation does not prevent state organs' conduct from being attributed to the state, and accordingly it does not relieve the state of responsibility for the same crimes.[1]

On the other hand, the analysis of international practice also reveals that, notwithstanding the separation between state and individual responsibility for international crimes, and independently of the particular case of the crime of aggression, there are various points of contact between these two regimes which can hardly be eliminated. The way in which the material element of international crimes is established by international criminal tribunals is very similar to the way in which the wrongful state act amounting to a crime is demonstrated. The general criminal context plays a fundamental role in proving the material element of international crimes. The same importance of the general criminal context characterizes the

---

[1] The issue of state organs' immunity has not been examined in detail here. I had the occasion to discuss the relation between international crimes and immunity from jurisdiction elsewhere. *See* B.I. Bonafè, 'Imputazione all'individuo di crimini internazionali e immunità dell'organo', 87 *Riv. Dir. Int.* (2004), pp. 393–426. The dissociation between state conduct and that of its organs justifies both the separation between state and individual responsibility for international crimes, and a certain point of contact between them. While state organs cannot invoke immunity *ratione materiae* to escape punishment for international crimes, their conduct is still attributable to the state. Accordingly, the state is immune from jurisdiction even though it is accused of having committed international crimes, and certain state organs can validly invoke immunity *ratione personae* (before domestic courts) because the protection afforded to states in order to guarantee a peaceful development of international relations prevails over the general interest to fight against impunity and prosecute all those responsible for international crimes. *See* also P.-M. Dupuy, 'Crimes et immunités, ou dans quelle mesure la nature des premiers empêche l'exercice des secondes', 103 *RGDIP* (1999), pp. 289–295; A. Cassese, 'When May Senior State Officials Be Tried for International Crimes? Some Comments on the *Congo v. Belgium* Case', 13 *EJIL* (2002), pp. 853–875; and M. Frulli, *Immunità e crimini internazionali* (Torino, Giappichelli, 2007).

establishment of the *mens rea* for specific intent crimes. For example, there is no case of an offender possessing the genocidal intent in which the general criminal context was not also established. Furthermore, particular modes of liability have been elaborated to address the collective dimension of international crimes more efficiently. The more international criminal law focuses on and develops tools to deal with collective criminality, the more the assessment of individuals' crimes reveals traits of overlap with the assessment of states' crimes. At a minimum, it deals with the same facts that are capable of entailing aggravated state responsibility.

Other aspects can lead to an even more direct link between state and individual responsibility for international crimes. A number of international law rules need to be applied under both state responsibility and international criminal law. This is, for instance, the case of the rules of international humanitarian law governing belligerent reprisals. Another example could be provided by the rules on state attribution, if these are confirmed to be the right standard to determine the nature of an armed conflict.

Furthermore, the strict separation between state and individual responsibility is put into question by the fact that at the international level there are organs having the power to deal with both state and individual conduct amounting to international crimes. In particular, the SC has increasingly addressed issues of individual liability and even has a significant role in the enforcement mechanisms of international criminal law. For all the reasons pointed out above, the existence of some form of relationship between state and individual responsibility for international crimes at the international level seems to be undeniable.

Against this background, the specific features of the crime of aggression seem to differentiate this crime from other international crimes. The crime of aggression is defined in terms of state conduct. The material element of aggression entailing individual liability corresponds to the definition of the state acts of aggression entailing aggravated state responsibility, that is, to those uses of armed force considered to be *per se* among the most serious breaches of obligations owed to the entire international community. Aggression is a leadership crime, and only political or military state leaders can be convicted for aggression. Even with respect to the *mens rea*, this crime shows a certain overlap between state and individual responsibility. The same notion of self-defence seems to be applicable to both state and individual responsibility for aggression. Therefore, this crime is at first sight characterized by an almost inextricable link between state and individual responsibility under international law.[2] However, recent developments and in particular the insertion

[2] The particular nature of this crime also explains why jurisdiction over aggression can only be exercised by either an international criminal court or the domestic courts of the state of nationality of the defendants (*see* Article 8 of the ILC Draft Code of Crimes against the Peace and Security of Mankind). This marks a considerable difference with respect to other crimes that can be prosecuted

of aggression in the ICC Statute has involved a certain change in perspective. As discussed above, considerable efforts are being made in order to keep the establishment of state and individual responsibility for aggression separate.

2. *A Functional Analysis of State and Individual Responsibility for International Crimes*

Leaving aside for the moment the crime of aggression, the analysis of the functions of state and individual responsibility respectively confirms the two main results illustrated above, that is, the substantial difference of these regimes, and at the same time the existence of inevitable points of contact between them.

On the one hand, it is generally acknowledged that one of the major differences between state and individual responsibility for international crimes concerns their respective functions.[3] An analogous difference has been pointed out by international courts.[4] It is maintained that international crimes committed by individuals give rise

according to the principle of universal jurisdiction (*see* supra Chapter 1, notes 16–18). According to the ILC, "This principle of exclusive jurisdiction is the result of the unique character of the crime of aggression in the sense that the responsibility of an individual for participation in this crime is established by his participation in a sufficiently serious violation of the prohibition of certain conduct by States contained in Article 2, paragraph 4, of the Charter of the United Nations. The aggression attributed to a State is a *sine qua non* for the responsibility of an individual for his participation in the crime of aggression. An individual cannot incur responsibility for this crime in the absence of aggression committed by a State. Thus, a court cannot determine the question of individual criminal responsibility for this crime without considering as a preliminary matter the question of aggression by a State. The determination by a national court of one State of the question of whether another State had committed aggression would be contrary to the fundamental principle of international law *par in parem imperium non habet*" (ILC, 'Report on the Work of its 48th Session', *YILC* (1996), vol. II(2), p. 30). For a recent case raising the issue of domestic jurisdiction over the crime of aggression, *see* C. Kress, 'The Iraqi Special Tribunal and the Crime of Aggression', 2 *JICJ* (2004), pp. 347–352.

3 According to Cassese, "The primary goal of [individual] responsibility is to punish the culprit.... The primary goal of [state] responsibility is to bring about cessation of the breach or reparation of the damage, not the punishment of the delinquent State; a reparative rather than punitive outlook is taken" (A. Cassese, *International Law* (Oxford, Oxford University Press, 2001), p. 271). *See* also P.-M. Dupuy, 'International Criminal Responsibility of the Individual and International Responsibility of the State', in A. Cassese *et al.* (eds.), *The Rome Statute of the International Criminal Court. A Commentary*, vol. II (Oxford, Oxford University Press, 2002), p. 1097; M. Kamto, 'Responsabilité de l'Etat et responsabilité de l'individu pour crime de génocide. Quels mécanismes de mise en œuvre?', in K. Boustany and D. Dormoy (eds.), *Génocide(s)* (Bruxelles, Bruylant, 1999), pp. 500 and 509; G. Werle, *Principles of International Criminal Law* (The Hague, TMC Asser Press, 2005), pp. 35–36.

4 *See* ICTY, *Prosecutor v. Kunarac et al.*, TC, Judgment, 22 February 2001, para. 470; and IACHR, *Velásquez Rodriguez case*, supra the Introduction, note 7, para. 134.

to a set of secondary rules which aim at completely different purposes from those characterizing the law of state responsibility. As to the major goals of individual criminal liability, reference is generally made to social functions such as punishment and deterrence,[5] or more generally to forms of social control.[6]

On the other hand, some authors have supported the existence of a regime of state criminal responsibility consisting of the punishment of state organs, and other authors have tried to bring individual criminal liability back to the framework of more traditional consequences belonging to the law of state responsibility.[7] However, there is general agreement that the punishment of state organs does not preclude the application of the traditional consequences of state responsibility. Therefore, it is generally affirmed that individual criminal liability cannot be regarded as a substitute for state responsibility.[8] The criminal liability of state organs is provided under customary international law alongside the traditional consequences of state responsibility.

Therefore, the question is whether state and individual responsibility for international crimes are in fact completely different sets of secondary rules or whether, at least under certain circumstances, there is an overlap between these regimes as far as their general objectives are concerned. The analysis will begin by focusing on the functions of international criminal law in order to see whether the consequences of state responsibility include measures serving the functions of international criminal law. Subsequently, the opposite perspective will be adopted, and international criminal law will be examined in the light of the traditional functions of state responsibility, with a view to determining whether the punishment of state organs responsible for international crimes could be framed among the consequences of the law of state responsibility. Only then will it be possible

---

5 ICTY, *Prosecutor v. Erdemović*, TC, Judgment, 29 November 1996, paras. 58–65; ICTY, *Prosecutor v. Furundžija*, TC, Judgment,10 December 1998, paras. 288–289, and 291; ICTY, *Prosecutor v. Blaškić*, TC, Judgment, 3 March 2000, paras. 763–764; ICTY, *Prosecutor v. Aleksovski*, AC, Judgment, 24 March 2000, para. 185; ICTY, *Prosecutor v. Delalić et al.*, AC, Judgment, 20 February 2001, para. 806; ICTY, *Prosecutor v. Todorović*, TC, Judgment, 31 July 2001, para. 28.

6 M. Foucault, *Surveiller et punir. Naissance de la prison* (Paris, Gallimard, 1975).

7 *See* supra Chapter 2.

8 *See*, in particular, C.T. Eustathiades, 'Les sujets du droit international et la responsabilité internationale. Nouvelles tendances', 84 *RCADI* (1953), p. 603; S.C. McCaffrey, 'Article 5: Responsibility of States', in M.C. Bassiouni (ed.), *Commentaries on the International Law Commission's 1991 Draft Code of Crimes against the Peace and Security of Mankind* (Erès, Paris, 1993), pp. 129–130; A. Pellet, 'La responsabilité pénale individuelle, alternative aux sanctions collectives?', in V. Gowlland-Debbas (ed.), *United Nations Sanctions and International Law* (The Hague, Kluwer Law International, 2001), p. 105; A.A. Cançado Trinidade, 'Complementarity between State Responsibility and Individual Responsibility for Grave Violations of Human Rights: The Crime of State Revisited', in M. Ragazzi (ed.), *International Responsibility Today: Essays in Memory of Oscar Schachter* (Leiden, Boston, M. Nijhoff, 2005), pp. 261, and 267.

to illustrate the complementarity between state and individual responsibility for international crimes.

A. *The Functions of International Criminal Law and State Responsibility*

First of all, it is difficult to maintain that state responsibility and international criminal law each share a punitive function. The regime of state responsibility has undergone a long and difficult process of codification, but in the end states have certainly been reluctant to support the establishment of their criminal responsibility for the breach of community obligations.[9]

The Draft Articles adopted by the ILC in 1976 contained a provision, Article 19, defining 'crimes of States'. However, even Article 19 did not intend to establish a criminal responsibility of states. The Commentary on Article 19 is very explicit on that point:

> in adopting the designation 'international crime', the Commission intends only to refer to 'crimes' of the State, to acts attributable to the State as such. Once again it wishes to sound a warning against any confusion between the expression 'international crime' as used in this article and similar expressions, such as 'crime under international law', 'war crime', 'crime against peace', 'crime against humanity', etc., which are used in a number of conventions and international instruments to designate certain heinous individual crimes.[10]

Since then, any possible reference to criminal responsibility of states has been deleted from the Draft Articles on State Responsibility. Moreover, the ILC has eliminated the few other elements which could have been related to a regime of criminal state

[9] *See* G. Abi-Saab, 'The Uses of Article 19', 10 *EJIL* (1999), p. 351; C. Dominicé, 'La question de la double responsabilité de l'Etat et de son agent', in E. Yakpo and T. Boumedra (eds.), *Liber Amicorum Judge Mohammed Bedjaoui* (The Hague, Kluwer Law International, 1999), p. 157, and more generally supra Chapter 1.

[10] Commentary to Article 19 (ILC, 'Report on the Work of its 28th Session', *YILC* (1976), vol. II (2), para. 59). As Spinedi points out: "the Commission had no intention to link the wrongful acts that it called international crimes with consequences of a type unknown to international law currently in force. The Commission wished to indicate in Draft Article 19 that there are wrongful acts regarded by the international community as more serious than all others because they affect essential interests of the Community. As a consequence, these wrongful acts entail a regime of responsibility different from that attaching to other wrongful acts. According to the Commission the differences relate to the forms of responsibility and to the subjects that may implement it. This does not mean, however, that the Commission had the intention to attach to these acts forms of responsibility similar to those provided in the penal law of modern domestic legal systems" (M. Spinedi, 'International Crimes of State. The Legislative History', in J.H.H. Weiler *et al.* (eds.), *International Crimes of State. A Critical Analysis of the ILC's Draft Article 19 on State Responsibility* (Berlin, De Gruyter, 1989), p. 52). With respect to the recent 'decriminalization' of state responsibility, *see* also L.-A. Sicilianos, 'The Classification of Obligations and the Multilateral Dimension of the Relations of International Responsibility', 13 *EJIL* (2002), p. 1128.

responsibility. These are the recognition of punitive damages, specific consequences of state crimes, and disciplinary or penal action as a form of satisfaction.

With respect to punitive damages,[11] the text adopted on the first reading contained Article 45 (2), providing that satisfaction may take the form of "damages reflecting the gravity of the infringement".[12] When he first took this provision into account, Special Rapporteur Crawford acknowledged that the ILC had rejected the concept of punitive damages for the purposes of Article 45. Moreover, due to states' concern about punitive damages, he proposed that punitive damages should be confined to Article 19, that is, in the limited framework of the consequences of international crimes.[13] Accordingly, the Drafting Committee eliminated all references to particular damages in the general provision dealing with satisfaction,[14] and discussed the possibility of introducing punitive damages in relation to aggravated state responsibility only. This is why, in 2000, provisional Article 42 ("Consequences of serious breaches of obligations to the international community as a whole") left open the question by simply stating that a serious breach "may involve, for the responsible State, damages reflecting the gravity of the breach."[15] A clear position on the issue was finally taken by Special Rapporteur Crawford in his Fourth Report. First, "damages reflecting the gravity of the breach" are not punitive damages. Second, punitive damages are not permitted under international law. Accordingly, Article 42 should be retained but reviewed in the light of Governments' criticism of punitive damages.[16] What happened in the end is well

[11] H.W. Briggs (ed.), *The Law of Nations: Cases, Documents and Notes* (New York, Appleton-Century-Crofts, 1952), p. 754; I. Brownlie, *International Law and the Use of Force by States* (Oxford, Clarendon Press, 1963), p. 148; G. Carella, 'I *punitive damages* e la riparazione del danno morale in diritto internazionale', 67 *Riv. Dir. Int.* (1984), p. 751; C.D. Gray, *Judicial Remedies in International Law* (Oxford, Clarendon Press, 1987), p. 26; I. Brownlie, *Principles of Public International Law* (6th edn, Oxford, Oxford University Press, 2003), p. 464; A. De Hoogh, *Obligations* Erga Omnes *and International Crimes. A Theoretical Inquiry into the Implementation and Enforcement of the International Responsibility of States* (The Hague, Kluwer, 1996), pp. 166–7; N.H.B. Jørgensen, 'A Reappraisal of Punitive Damages in International Law', 68 *BYIL* (1997), p. 247; N.H.B. Jørgensen, *The Responsibility of States for International Crimes* (Oxford, Oxford University Press, 2000), p. 187.

[12] ILC, 'Report on the Work of its 48th Session', *YILC* (1996), vol. II(2), p. 67. The provision was elaborated by G. Arangio-Ruiz in his 'Fifth Report on State Responsibility', *YILC* (1993), vol. II(1), p. 32.

[13] J. Crawford, 'Third Report on State Responsibility', UN Doc. A/CN.4/507/Add.1, paras. 174 and 190.

[14] *See* Article 38 of the text provisionally adopted in 2000 (UN Doc. A/CN.4/L.600).

[15] The position of the Drafting Committee is illustrated in the Statement of the Chairman of the Drafting Committee Mr. G. Gaja at the 2662nd meeting of the ILC, 17 August 2000, pp. 22 and 27, <www.lcil.cam.ac.uk/projects/state_responsibility_document_collection.php>.

[16] J. Crawford, 'Fourth Report on State Responsibility', UN Doc. A/CN.4/517, para. 45. *See* also IACHR, *Velásquez Rodriguez case*, Compensatory damages, Judgment, 21 July 1989, *Annual Report*

known. All references to particular damages disappeared from Article 41 of the text finally adopted in 2001.

Article 52 of the 1996 Draft Articles established two specific consequences to be attached to the commission of international crimes by states.[17] First, the injured state was entitled to obtain restitution in kind even if the burden of providing restitution was out of all proportion to the benefit gained by the injured state instead of compensation, and even if restitution could seriously jeopardise the political independence or economic stability of the responsible state.[18] Second, the injured state was entitled to obtain satisfaction even with demands which could impair the dignity of the responsible state.[19] These specific consequences have been taken into account by Special Rapporteur Crawford, who nonetheless considered them to be problematic.[20] In particular, with respect to satisfaction, he held that its main element "is now proportionality, and there is no need to 'humiliate' even a State which has committed a gross breach of a community obligation".[21] Accordingly, the Special Rapporteur proposed to delete those specific consequences. Due to the importance of the values underlying international crimes, he proposed other specific consequences such as punitive damages, additional obligations for third states, and a general clause leaving the door open to future developments under customary international law.

As noted above, the Drafting Committee rejected Crawford's proposal on 'penal' consequences, and Article 52 was replaced with a 'without prejudice' clause on further consequences arising under international law.[22] Thus, Article 41 of the text adopted in 2001 makes no reference to consequences with a punitive or humiliating character, but simply lists a few additional obligations for third states[23] and the without prejudice clause just mentioned.

---

of the Inter-American Court of Human Rights, Ser. C, No. 7 (1990), paras. 37–38, and IACtHR, *Godinez case*, Compensatory damages, Judgment, 21 July 1989, *Annual Report of the Inter-American Court of Human Rights*, Ser. C, No. 8 (1990), paras. 35–36.

17 ILC, 'Report on the Work of its 48th Session', *YILC* (1996), vol. II(2), p. 76.

18 To be precise, Article 52 established that the restitution was not subject to the limitations set out in subparagraphs c) and d) of Article 43 (*ibid.*).

19 Similarly, Article 52 established that the satisfaction was not subject to the restriction set out in paragraph 3 of Article 45 (*ibid.*).

20 J. Crawford, 'Third Report on State Responsibility', UN Doc. A/CN.4/507/Add.4, para. 408. *See* also P.-M. Dupuy, 'L'unité de l'ordre juridique international', 297 *RCADI* (2002), p. 367.

21 *Ibid.*, This is an important aspect because it shows that even satisfaction is conceived of in compensatory terms rather than punitive.

22 The position of the Drafting Committee is illustrated in the Report of its Chairman, G. Gaja (*see* supra note 15). *See* Article 42, para. 3 of the Draft Articles provisionally adopted in 2000, UN Doc. A/CN.4/L.600.

23 These are the duty of co-operation (*see* supra Chapter 1), the obligation not to recognize as lawful a situation created by a serious breach, and the obligation not to render aid or assistance in maintaining that situation.

A third consequence to be taken into account is disciplinary or penal action against the responsible individuals. This was an undisputed form of satisfaction supported by international practice (mostly cases of state responsibility concerning the treatment of aliens). Accordingly, the Draft Articles adopted in 1996 established that: "in cases where the internationally wrongful act arose from the serious misconduct of officials or from the criminal conduct of officials or private parties, [satisfaction may take the form of] disciplinary action against, or punishment of, those responsible".[24]

This general provision on satisfaction was not intended to codify a special consequence of crimes of states. However, it soon raised the question of the relationship between state and individual responsibility for international crimes. In particular, this provision could have been interpreted as including in general terms individual criminal liability among the consequences of wrongful state acts.

The approach of Special Rapporteur Crawford was sceptical with respect to this particular consequence. He took into account that states' opinions were rather divided on that issue.[25] He also affirmed that it was not clear "whether prosecution of criminal conduct was sought by way of satisfaction or as an aspect of performance of some primary obligation".[26] In other words, prosecution of nationals for international crimes may simply derive from an international obligation to prosecute or extradite the perpetrators of such offences, which has nothing to do with the legal relation between the injured state and the responsible state deriving from the commission of a wrongful act and governed by secondary rules. The problem was then addressed and, in some way solved, by the Drafting Committee: disciplinary or penal action, one of the typical consequences of state responsibility, was simply omitted from the final text of the Draft Articles.[27]

The same question was brought up again with respect to the consequences of crimes of state. Indeed, during the plenary debate it was suggested that the ILC took into account the 'transparency' of states in case of serious breaches of obligations towards the international community as a whole.[28] In other words, it was proposed to consider the criminal liability of state organs for international crimes

---

[24] Article 45, para. 2 (d), ILC, 'Report on the Work of its 48th Session', *YILC* (1996), vol. II(2), p. 67.

[25] J. Crawford, 'Third Report on State Responsibility', UN Doc. A/CN.4/507/Add.1, para. 175.

[26] *Ibid.*, para. 192.

[27] "There was some discussion in the Plenary and then in the Drafting Committee on the question of whether Article 38 [45] should refer, among the modalities of satisfaction, to disciplinary or penal action relating to the individuals whose conduct caused the internationally wrongful act. Given the divergent views on this issue and also the fact that paragraph 2 does not intend to provide an exhaustive list, the Committee decided not to mention disciplinary or penal action in the text", Statement of the Chairman of the Drafting Committee Mr. G. Gaja at the 2662nd meeting of the International Law Commission, 17 August 2000, p. 22 (*see* supra note 15).

[28] *Ibid.*, p. 53.

as a special consequence of state 'serious breaches' since aggravated state responsibility was viewed as a pre-condition to bring state organs to trial.[29] However, the Drafting Committee was "unable to accept this proposal",[30] because

> the articles do not address the question of the individual responsibility under international law of any person acting in the capacity of an organ or an agent of a State. While this could already be inferred from the fact that the articles only address the issues related to the responsibility of States, the Committee felt that a specific provision added clarity. As a result you have article 58 entitled 'Individual responsibility'. Again this article amounts to a 'without prejudice clause'.[31]

Thus, neither the provisional draft of 2000 nor the final text addresses the problem of the relationship between the punishment of state organs for international crimes and punishment for aggravated state responsibility.[32] The 'without prejudice' clause embodied in Article 58 does not exclude the existence of a separate body of international law governing the responsibility of individuals for international crimes,

---

[29] The theory in question has been strongly supported by A. Pellet, 'La responsabilité des dirigeants pour crime international de l'Etat. Quelques remarques sommaires au point de vue du droit international', in G. Doucet (ed.), Terrorisme, victimes et responsabilité pénale internationale (Paris, Calmann-Lévy, 2003): "*lorsque l'individu en question est un gouvernant,... l'Etat qu'il dirige devien[t] 'transparent' et... les immunités traditionnelles, source d'impunité, disparaissent*" (p. 198); "*l'engagement de la responsabilité personnelle des gouvernants est une manière de sanctionner, concrètement, les comportements étatiques contraires au droit des gens*" (p. 200). *See* also A. Pellet, supra note 8, pp. 105–116. Pellet rejects the possibility of considering individual criminal liability as an alternative to collective sanctions against states responsible for serious breaches of obligations owed to the international community as a whole. However, he puts the emphasis on the close link between state and individual responsibility. In particular, he points out the fact that, when the exercise of jurisdiction over state organs allegedly responsible for international crimes – who are entitled to immunity – is possible, "*c'est parce que [l'Etat] a, par eux, commis un crime que le voile étatique peut être percé. L'une des conséquences du concept de crime, totalement oubliée par le projet d'articles de la CDI, est, en effet, la 'transparence' de l'Etat grâce à laquelle la responsabilité des individus par l'intermédiaire desquels il a agi (ou qui ont agi par son intermédiaire?) peut être recherchée sans qu'ils puissent se retrancher derrière leurs fonctions officielles*" (p. 108). *See* also A. Pellet, 'Vive le crime! Remarques sur les degrés de l'illicite en droit international', in *Le droit international à l'aube du XXIème siècle – Réflexions de codificateurs* (New York, United Nations, 1997), pp. 287–315, and A. Pellet, 'Can a State Commit a Crime? Definitely, Yes!', 10 *EJIL* (1999), pp. 425–434.

[30] Similarly, the ILC rejected the 'transparency' theory and decided not to deal with individual criminal liability in the Draft Articles on State Responsibility (*see* ILC, 'Report on the Work of its 52nd Session', *YILC* (2000), vol. II(2), paras. 383 and 388).

[31] G. Gaja, Statement of the Chairman of the Drafting Committee at the 2662nd meeting of the International Law Commission, 17 August 2000, p. 53, supra note 15.

[32] The commentary on Article 58 "makes clear that the Articles as a whole do not address any question of the individual responsibility under international law of any person acting on behalf of a State. It clarifies a matter which could be inferred in any case from the fact that the Articles only address issues relating to the responsibility of States" (ILC, 'Report on the Work of its 53rd Session', *YILC* (2001), vol. II(2), p. 142).

nor does it exclude that there may be a relationship between state and individual responsibility for international crimes. The Commission is silent on this relationship, but it seems to start at least from the assumption that these regimes are separate and that individual liability cannot exhaust aggravated state responsibility.

> Where crimes against international law are committed by State officials, it will often be the case that the State itself is responsible for the acts in question or for failure to prevent or punish them. In certain cases, in particular aggression, the State will by definition be involved. Even so, the question of individual responsibility is *in principle distinct* from the question of State responsibility. The State is *not exempted* from its own responsibility for internationally wrongful conduct by the prosecution and punishment of the State officials who carried it out. Nor may those officials hide behind the State in respect of their own responsibility for conduct of theirs which is contrary to rules of international law which are applicable to them.[33]

To sum up, there is no doubt that the long work of codification of state responsibility has highlighted a general agreement on the absence of any punitive purpose of aggravated state responsibility.[34] This confirms the substantive difference with

[33] *Ibid.*, para. 3. An analogous position was explicitly held by the ILC in 1976. The commentary on Article 19 reads: "it must be added at once that it would be wrong to identify the right-duty of certain States to punish individuals who have committed such crimes with the 'special form' of international responsibility applicable to the State in cases of this kind. The obligation to punish personally individuals who are organs of the State and are guilty of crimes against the peace, against humanity, and so on does not, in the Commission's view, constitute a form of international responsibility of the State, and such punishment certainly does not exhaust the prosecution of the international responsibility incumbent upon the State for internationally wrongful acts which are attributed to it in such cases by reason of the conduct of its organs. Punishment of those in charge of the State machinery who have started a war of aggression or organized an act of genocide does not *per se* release the State itself from its own international responsibility for such acts. Conversely, as far as the State is concerned, it is not necessarily true that any 'crime under international law' committed by one of its organs for which the perpetrator is held personally liable to punishment, despite his capacity as a State organ, must automatically be considered not only as an internationally wrongful act of the State concerned, but also as an act entailing a 'special form' of responsibility for that State" (ILC, 'Report on the Work of its 28th Session', *YILC* (1976) vol. II(2), pp. 103–104). The point is further made clear that: "the attribution to the State of an internationally wrongful act characterized as an 'international crime' is quite different from the incrimination of certain individuals-organs for actions connected with the omission of an 'international crime' of the State, and that the obligation to punish such individual actions does not constitute the form of international responsibility specially applicable to a State committing an 'international crime' or, in any case, the sole form of this responsibility" (*ibid.*, p. 119). *See* also M. Spinedi, 'La responsabilité de l'État pour 'crime': une responsabilité pénale?', in H. Ascensio *et al.* (eds.), *Droit international pénal* (Paris, Pedone, 2000), pp. 93–114.

[34] Interestingly, the existence of a criminal regime of state responsibility was excluded by the ICTY in *Prosecutor v. Blaškić*, AC, Judgment on the Request of the Republic of Croatia for Review of the Decision of Trial Chamber II of 18 July 1997, 29 October 1997, para. 25. *See* C. Tomuschat, 'International Law: Ensuring the Survival of Mankind on the Eve of a New Century', 281 *RCADI*

respect to individual liability for international crimes, which has as its essential purpose the punishment of the wrongdoer.

Deterrence is generally regarded as the other fundamental purpose of individual criminal liability. Thus, the punishment of individuals responsible for international crimes is also conceived of as a future-oriented measure which is able to prevent the commission of similar offences. From this perspective, can individual convictions be regarded as a special consequence of aggravated state responsibility? In other words, is there a purpose of deterrence in aggravated state responsibility?

Taking into account the codification of aggravated state responsibility, Article 41 does not mention such a purpose. The only notion which can be considered close to deterrence is that of 'assurances and guarantees of non-repetition'[35] embodied in Article 30. This is a general provision of the regime of ordinary state responsibility, and as such it is also applicable in case of serious breaches.[36]

However, individual criminal liability has never been considered to be a guarantee of non-repetition by the ILC. Assurances and guarantees of non-repetition are not a special consequence of the regime of aggravated state responsibility. One can even doubt that assurances and guarantees of non-repetition are an autonomous secondary rule under customary international law. According to the Special Rapporteur's view, they appear rather as a particular form of cessation. Indeed, they are essentially associated with the continuation of the breach and, therefore, are irrelevant when the breach has ceased.[37] In its commentaries, the ILC refers to

(1999), p. 290; A. Bos, 'Crimes of State: In Need of Legal Rules?', in G. Kreijen (ed.), *State, Sovereignty, and International Governance* (Oxford, Oxford University Press, 2002), p. 235. The ICJ has recently come to the same conclusion (*Genocide* case, supra the Introduction, note 1, paras. 170, and 178).

[35] The Commentary on Article 30, para. 9, holds that: "they share the characteristics of being future-looking and concerned with other potential breaches. They focus on prevention rather than reparation" (ILC, 'Report on the Work of its 53rd Session', *YILC* (2001), vol. II(2), p. 90). *See* also P.-M. Dupuy, supra note 20, p. 371.

[36] Article 30 is certainly applicable to serious breaches according to the without prejudice clause of Article 41, para. 3. Moreover, the special consequences of Article 41 focus on cessation of the serious breach. In particular, para. 1 codifies the duty of co-operation with respect to cessation of serious breaches (ILC, 'Report on the Work of its 53rd Session', *YILC* (2001), vol. II(2), p. 113).

[37] J. Crawford, 'Third Report on State Responsibility', UN Doc. A/CN.4/507, paras. 53 and 59. To be more precise, he concludes that "they are cognate to cessation" (*ibid.*, para. 57). *See* also J. Crawford *et al.*, 'The ILC's Articles on Responsibility of States for Internationally Wrongful Acts: Completion of the Second Reading', 12 *EJIL* (2001), p. 988 ("assurances and guarantees of non-repetition are *not necessary part* of the legal consequences of an international wrongful act. Much will depend on the circumstances of the case, including the *nature* of the obligation and of the breach", emphasis added).

the ICJ's *LaGrand* case.[38] However, in the conception of the ILC assurances and guarantees of non-repetition "are better treated as an aspect of the continuation and repair of the legal relationship affected by the breach".[39]

Therefore, it is difficult to identify a specific purpose of deterrence in aggravated state responsibility or particular secondary rules aiming towards that end. This marks a major difference with respect to individual criminal liability. From this point of view, aggravated state responsibility can hardly be regarded as a measure serving a typical function of individual criminal liability.

B. *The Functions of State Responsibility and International Criminal Law*

The relationship between state and individual responsibility for international crimes can be examined from a different point of view. Taking into account the contents of aggravated state responsibility, it is possible to see whether the punishment of state organs can be assimilated to some of the consequences attached to state serious breaches under international law. In other words, one may wonder whether individual criminal liability can serve the typical functions of state responsibility.

With respect to countermeasures, the question of their function and purpose has traditionally been very controversial.[40] As noted above, there have been attempts to regard the punishment of state organs for international crimes as a specific reprisal under the law of state responsibility.[41] However, when looking more generally at the codification work of state responsibility, it seems that the ILC has constantly taken a different approach on the matter.[42] Indeed, countermeasures are considered as exceptional measures which have the aim of inducing the responsible state to comply with its obligations. In other words, the general purpose of countermeasures is never punitive.[43] According to this prevailing approach, it is difficult to identify a

---

[38] ICJ, *LaGrand Case* (Germany v. United States of America), *Merits*, Judgment, 27 June 2001, *ICJ Reports* 2001, p. 466. *See* also ICJ, *Case Concerning Avena and other Mexican Nationals* (Mexico v. USA), Judgment, 31 March 2004, *ICJ Reports* 2004, p. 12, in particular, paras. 148–149.

[39] Commentary on Article 37, ILC, 'Report on the work of its 53rd Session', *YILC* (2001), vol. II(2), para. 11. For a different opinion, *see* G. Palmisano, 'Les garanties de non-répétition entre codification et réalisation juridictionnelle du droit: à propos de l'affaire LaGrand', 106 *RGDIP* (2002), p. 753.

[40] *See* in general C. Focarelli, *Le contromisure nel diritto internazionale* (Milano Giuffré, 1994).

[41] *See* supra Chapter 2.

[42] Special Rapporteur Arangio-Ruiz in his overview of the literature on the subjects concludes that "a broad consensus also exists on the function of the countermeasures taken by the injured State. Indeed, while no one questions that they might be adopted to bring about cessation of 'criminal' conduct or, by way of an *extrema ratio*, to guarantee reparation *lato sensu*, nearly all rule out the possibility of their being used for purely punitive purposes" (G. Arangio-Ruiz, 'Fifth Report on State Responsibility', *YILC* (1993), vol. II(1), para. 152).

[43] J. Crawford, 'Third Report on State Responsibility', UN Doc. A/CN.4/507/Add.3, paras. 294 and 296; Statement of the Chairman of the Drafting Committee, G. Gaja, supra note 15, p. 40; A. De

connection between state and individual responsibility. With respect to the general purpose of countermeasures, it hardly seems possible to consider individual criminal liability to be a measure with no punitive purpose which is aimed at guaranteeing compliance with states' primary obligations.

Similarly, individual criminal liability can hardly be regarded as a form of cessation of the wrongful state act. The punishment of state organs that have committed international crimes normally takes place after the relevant state serious breaches have ceased. The same conclusion must be reached, albeit for different reasons, with respect to restitution and compensation. It is difficult to regard the punishment of state organs as a way "to re-establish the situation which existed before the wrongful act was committed"[44] or a way to compensate any financially assessable damage caused by the internationally wrongful act.[45] Thus, these typical consequences of the regime of state responsibility do not establish a connection between state and individual responsibility for international crimes.

However, a certain link may exist between individual criminal liability and state responsibility as far as satisfaction is concerned. Satisfaction can take various forms, as recognized by the ILC.[46] But there is one particular form of satisfaction, which is capable of playing a significant role with respect to state responsibility for international crimes, namely, the punishment of the responsible state organs, in particular, if it can amount to a 'declaratory judgment'.[47] The question may arise as to whether the judgment of criminal courts prosecuting state organs for international crimes can also be conceived of as a form of satisfaction for the injured state. In particular, the question concerns judgments pronounced by international

Hoogh, supra note 11, p. 269. The Commentaries on the final text make clear that countermeasures are exceptional in character, that they can only be taken "in order to induce the responsible state to comply with its obligation", that they are "intended as instrumental, in other words, since they are taken with a view to procuring cessation of and reparation for the internationally wrongful act and not by way of punishment, they are temporary in character and must be as far as possible reversible in their effects in terms of future legal relations between the two States" (Commentary on Chapter 2, ILC, 'Report on the Work of its 53rd Session', *YILC* (2001), vol. II(2), p. 128, paras. 2, 3, and 6), and, finally, that they "are not intended as a form of punishment for the wrongful conduct" of states (Commentary on Article 49, *ibid.*, p. 129, para. 1).

44 Article 35 of the ILC Draft Articles on State Responsibility (*ibid.*, p. 96).

45 Article 36 of the ILC Draft Articles on State Responsibility (*ibid.*, p. 98).

46 Under Article 37, para. 2, satisfaction "may consist in an acknowledgement of the breach, an expression of regret, a formal apology or another appropriate remedy" (*ibid.*, p. 105). Moreover, according to the ILC, satisfaction "is the remedy for those injuries, not financially assessable, which amount to an affront to the State. These injuries are frequently of a symbolic character, arising from the very fact of the breach of the obligation, irrespective of its material consequences for the State concerned" (commentary on Article 37, *ibid.*, p. 106, para. 3).

47 "One of the most common modalities of satisfaction provided in the case of moral or non-material injury to the State is a declaration of the wrongfulness of the act by a competent court or tribunal", Commentary on Article 37, *ibid.*, p. 106, para. 6).

criminal tribunals. Indeed, when established with the support of the entire international community, these have been regarded by some authors as 'measures' taken against the responsible state. The crucial issue is thus whether these judgments – theoretically limited to individual criminal liability – can also be seen as a general recognition of aggravated state responsibility. A positive answer to this question has been advanced in the literature. According to Rosenne, "adequate punishment of an accused whose acts are attributable to a State may be adequate satisfaction *if the responsibility of that State is established*".[48]

Two main remarks can be made with respect to the possibility of regarding individual criminal liability as a form of satisfaction under aggravated state responsibility. The first one concerns the fact that international criminal tribunals cannot ascertain state responsibility. They do not apply the secondary norms governing state responsibility. Their jurisdiction is limited to natural persons. They focus on individual – not state – conduct prohibited under international law. The principle of individual criminal liability is applied in a rigorous manner. However, there may be cases in which there is not such a strict separation between the establishment of state responsibility and the establishment of individual liability. In particular, there are cases in which the material breach amounting to an international crime is established in a very similar way and irrespective of the fact that it entails state or individual responsibility. The foregoing analysis has revealed that there are certain international crimes which are defined in terms of state action, and which require international tribunals – if not to establish aggravated state responsibility – at least to take into account that the relevant individual conduct has taken place in the context of a state serious breach before ascribing personal criminal liability. International criminal tribunals have increasingly focused their attention on crimes committed at the collective level, and have refined the tools at their disposal to address the collective dimension of international crimes. Thus, it is not possible to exclude that the punishment of certain state organs for certain international crimes can require, at least indirectly, a previous assessment of the same facts giving rise to aggravated state responsibility.

The second remark concerns the different nature of ordinary and aggravated state responsibility. From a purely bilateral point of view, it is arguably possible to regard the punishment of state organs responsible for *isolated* crimes as a form of satisfaction for the injured state in the framework of *ordinary* state responsibility. In this case, both kinds of responsibility originate from the very same conduct. This hypothesis is more common than one may at first sight imagine. A comprehensive study on reparation has pointed out that injured states seldom ask for reparation.

[48] S. Rosenne, 'State Responsibility and International Crimes: Further Reflections on Article 19 of the Draft Articles on State Responsibility', 30 *NYU J. Int'l L. Pol.* (1997–1998), p. 164 (emphasis added).

They normally try to obtain the cessation of the wrongful act or the punishment of the wrongdoer, and only as a last resort do they adopt countermeasures.[49] It has been pointed out that satisfaction is characterized by the fact of being a 'self-inflicted' measure,[50] which "settles the matter completely and definitively".[51] In a sense, the state acknowledges that a wrongful act has been committed by one of its organs, but at the same time the punishment of the culprit can be seen as a proof of the lack of any involvement of the state apparatus considered in its entirety. In other words, rather than a secondary obligation properly speaking, satisfaction may be better understood as a possibility offered to the author state to dissociate itself from the responsible organ and avoid other consequences provided for under the law of ordinary state responsibility. In this sense, the punishment of state organs for isolated crimes by the author state can have a twofold effect under international criminal law and under ordinary state responsibility, and be regarded as a significant point of contact between these two regimes because individual liability can exhaust ordinary state responsibility.

By contrast, *aggravated* state responsibility originates from *serious*, that is, widespread or systematic, breaches. When there is a general involvement of the state apparatus, it is difficult to conclude that the punishment of a few state organs is capable of settling the matter completely as far as state responsibility is concerned. The conviction of a state organ by an international criminal tribunal cannot be understood as the settlement of a bilateral dispute between the author state and the injured state; it is adopted in a multilateral framework. As discussed in previous chapters, it does not correspond to a judicial assessment of aggravated state responsibility, even though it may take into account the same facts that entail state responsibility. Therefore, when there is a general involvement of the state in the commission of international crimes, the punishment of isolated state organs can hardly be conceived of as a measure that exhausts aggravated state responsibility. In a very broad sense, the conviction of state organs for international crimes committed by the state can be seen as a reaffirmation of the fundamental principles breached, but in no way can it operate as a circumstance precluding aggravated state responsibility. Although the punishment of state organs could be included in a special notion of satisfaction, it seems appropriate to conclude that this *sui generis* form of satisfaction for the immaterial injury suffered by the international community as a whole does not eliminate the need for the author state to comply

[49] M. Iovane, *La riparazione nella teoria e nella prassi dell'illecito internazionale* (Milano, Giuffré, 1990).

[50] G. Arangio-Ruiz, 'Second Report on State Responsibility', *YILC* (1989), vol. II(1), p. 42; G. Morelli, *Nozioni di diritto internazionale*, (edn, Padova, Cedam, 1967), p. 358.

[51] *See* B. Conforti, *International Law and the Role of Domestic Legal Systems* (Dordrecht, M. Nijhoff, 1993), p. 200, and M. Iovane, supra note 49, pp. 200–205.

with its secondary obligations under the law of state responsibility.[52] The conviction of isolated state organs would not exhaust aggravated state responsibility and would not preclude that the commission of the relevant international crimes by the state entails the typical consequences of this regime, in particular, the duty to repair the injury caused to another state or to the beneficiaries of the obligation breached. The same position has been expressed by the ILC in its commentary on former Article 19 on State Responsibility,[53] and it has been confirmed by the ICJ in its recent judgment in the *Genocide* case.[54]

3. *The Complementarity Between State and Individual Responsibility for International Crimes*

The functional analysis of state and individual responsibility confirms the results emerging from the study of international practice. In principle, these can be regarded as separate and independent regimes. State and individual responsibility are different because they deal with different subjects, apply different legal standards, and serve different functions under international law.

However, individual criminal liability and aggravated state responsibility can be seen as complementary and, to a certain extent, overlapping regimes.[55] As noted

---

[52] Indeed, with respect to breaches entailing aggravated state responsibility the re-affirmation of the primary obligation breached can 'satisfy' the general interest of the international community, but it is arguably not enough to 'satisfy' the injured state or the beneficiaries of the obligation breached. In the bilateral framework of ordinary state responsibility, the punishment of state organs can be seen as a declaratory judgment sufficient to settle an interstate dispute. The ICJ in the *Genocide* case seems to apply this same reasoning (supra the Introduction, note 1, paras. 462–465). However, Serbia's ordinary responsibility arose out of the breach of a due diligence duty (for not having prevented or punished the commission of genocide). Therefore, it is disputable whether a duty of reparation was still owed in that case (*see* C. Tomuschat, 'Reparation in Cases of Genocide', 5 *JICJ* (2007), pp. 907–911). What can be inferred, *a contrario*, from the reading of the ICJ's judgment (para. 462) is that, had Serbia been found responsible for having directly committed genocide – that is, in the framework of aggravated state responsibility – a declaratory judgment would not have been enough, and it would not have exhausted other secondary rules, such as compensation.

[53] "Punishment of those in charge of the State machinery who have started a war of aggression or organized an act of genocide does not *per se* release the State itself from its own international responsibility for such acts" (ILC, 'Report on the Work of its 28th Session', *YILC* (1976), vol. II(2), p. 104).

[54] ICJ, *Genocide* case, supra the Introduction, note 1, paras. 173–174.

[55] For a similar view, *see* H. Gros Espiell, 'International Responsibility of the State and Individual Criminal Responsibility in the International Protection of Human Rights', in M. Ragazzi (ed.), *International Responsibility Today: Essays in Memory of Oscar Schachter* (Leiden, Boston, M. Nijhoff, 2005), p. 160, and A.A. Cançado Trinidade, 'Complementarity between State Responsibility and

above, state and individual responsibility for international crimes share the same origin, that is, the breach of the most important obligations owed to the international community as a whole. The types of conduct to which those obligations correspond entail a dual responsibility because the international legal order considers it to be necessary to attach two complementary – different but overlapping – sets of consequences, neither of which can exhaust the other.

Nonetheless, a generic statement on the complementarity between state and individual responsibility for international crimes does not say much about the precise relationship between these regimes. As summarized above, the study of international practice has indicated the existence of a considerable number of points of contact between individual criminal liability and aggravated state responsibility. The functional analysis of state and individual responsibility for international crimes confirms that these regimes are separate and at the same time that there are links between them. Indeed, at least with respect to isolated international crimes, individual criminal liability of state organs can be seen as a particular form of satisfaction under the law of ordinary state responsibility. With respect to crimes entailing a dual responsibility under international law, there is always a certain kind of relationship between these regimes, or more precisely between individual criminal liability and ordinary state responsibility. What remains to be established is the general framework capable of explaining the complementarity between state and individual responsibility for international crimes.

Individual Responsibility for Grave Violations of Human Rights: The Crime of State Revisited', in M. Ragazzi (ed.), *International Responsibility Today: Essays in Memory of Oscar Schachter* (Leiden, Boston, M. Nijhoff, 2005), pp. 258, 260, and 268. According to the latter author, state and individual responsibility must be regarded as complementary to each other and ineluctably intertwined, "despite the insufficient development of the matter, reflected in the persistent compartmentalized approach to the international responsibility of the State and the international criminal responsibility of individuals".

Chapter 9

Towards a Dual Responsibility Paradigm?

Coming now to the determination of a general framework capable of explaining the relationship between state and individual responsibility for international crimes, we can take, as a starting point, an observation which has already been put forward. When international crimes entail a dual responsibility, international practice shows that the elements of individual criminal liability can only be established by duly taking into account the general criminal context; that there are defences that must be applied in a consistent manner under both regimes; and that there are modes of liability specifically aimed at addressing the collective nature of international crimes. In particular, when political and military leaders are charged with large-scale crimes, individual criminal liability tends to be established in a way which is very similar to that used to prove aggravated state responsibility. All in all, with respect to certain crimes there are direct links between the establishment of state responsibility and the establishment of individual responsibility.

Thus, having found that a certain relationship between these regimes of international responsibility for international crimes emerges from empirical analysis, the final question to be examined here concerns the identification of a general framework that can explain the different elements of this relationship which result from international practice. To answer this question it is necessary to go back to the conceptual schemes described in Part I, and to evaluate whether and to what extent these general approaches are a useful guide in describing the complementarity between state and individual responsibility.

1. *Theoretical Approaches and the Complementarity Between State and Individual Responsibility for International Crimes*

International practice shows that neither the individual-oriented conceptual scheme nor the state-oriented conceptual scheme is, in its entirety, capable of explaining the variety of the relationship between state and individual responsibility for all international crimes.

According to a pure individual-oriented conceptual scheme as described in Part I, aggravated state responsibility and individual criminal liability are not only governed by different sets of secondary norms but they also originate from different primary norms. However, the analysis of international practice carried out in Part II reveals that such a complete separation, in particular with respect to primary norms, is not justified. Among other crimes, war crimes are a clear example of international crimes prohibited under primary norms aiming at both state and individual conduct. For example, the violation of the same 'intransgressible' principles of international humanitarian law entails both state and individual responsibility.[1] But it is also possible to recall other articulations of primary norms intended to narrow, under specific circumstances, the scope of certain prohibited conduct, and directed at both states and individuals, such as self-defence with respect to the prohibition of aggression or belligerent reprisals with respect to certain war crimes. In such cases, the relevant conduct cannot be regarded as a breach of a primary norm and therefore it is perfectly lawful under international law independently of the fact that it has been carried out by states or individuals. Accordingly, if a certain use of force amounts to a legitimate action taken in self-defence or if a certain type of conduct represents a lawful belligerent reprisal, it cannot entail either aggravated state responsibility or individual criminal liability. In addition, international crimes are commonly collective criminal acts whose material element is established in very similar, if not identical, ways from the standpoint of both state and individual responsibility.

According to a pure state-oriented conceptual scheme as described in Part I, state and individual responsibility are not only governed by the same primary norms, they also belong to the same set of secondary norms governing the special consequences to be attached to the commission of international crimes by states. However, the analysis of international practice reveals that such a complete overlap, in particular, of secondary norms, is not justified. One may recall the fact that the consequences especially provided for under international criminal law also apply to international crimes committed by private individuals and the punishment of such individuals has nothing to do with state responsibility. More generally, the functional analysis of the regimes of state and individual responsibility has shown how difficult it is to include a traditional criminal sanction, such as the punishment of those state organs who are responsible for international crimes, among the secondary rules governing aggravated state responsibility. In particular, these two regimes differ as to some of their basic requirements, such as the *mens rea* which is a characterizing feature of international criminal law. As discussed above, even if the punishment of state organs for the commission of isolated international crimes could be regarded as a measure that, under certain circumstances, can preclude ordinary state responsibility from arising, this would not be true with respect to aggravated state responsibility, that is, the consequences to be attached to the serious breaches of obligations owed to the international community as a whole.

---

[1] *See* supra Chapter 5, note 36.

More generally, the individual-oriented scheme is problematic because it tends to reduce international crimes to private facts, when they are normally carried out as large scale or systematic offences which require the involvement of a plurality of organized perpetrators, if not the state itself. In so doing, it removes the connection with state responsibility. The state-oriented scheme has the advantage of taking into account the relationship between state and individual responsibility for international crimes. However, in order to be regarded as a special consequence under the law of state responsibility, individual criminal liability is so closely connected to state responsibility that, in the end, the relationship between these regimes fades out and, ultimately, disappears.

The second option is to consider that the state-oriented and the individual-oriented conceptual schemes have no general application, but they can both be useful in explaining the relationship between state and individual responsibility with respect to different categories of international crimes. In fact, one may be tempted to say that these two theoretical schemes should not be set aside; that a separation can be re-introduced in the evaluation of the results emerging from the analysis of international practice; and that the state-oriented scheme and the individual-oriented scheme have two different, albeit limited, scopes of validity.

This is an interesting option because it can help to solve, for example, the problem of the particular nature of the crime of aggression.[2] There would be two different kinds of relationship between state and individual responsibility governed by the state-oriented scheme and the individual-oriented scheme respectively. One would be used for crimes rigorously defined in terms of state action and whose punishment can be regarded as a special sanction towards the author state, and the other for crimes defined in terms of individual conduct and whose punishment has nothing to do with state responsibility. Therefore, the relationship between state and individual responsibility would not necessarily be explained according to the same abstract scheme for all international crimes, and for example the crime of aggression could be treated differently from crimes against humanity.

However, this option necessarily posits the possibility to classify international crimes in two separate groups according to their nature, and requires the relationship between state and individual responsibility for each category of international crimes to vary in correspondence to one of the general schemes described above. This assumption can hardly be verified both from a practical and a theoretical point of view.

---

[2] *See* B.V.A. Röling, *The Tokyo Trial and Beyond. Reflections of a Peacemonger* (Cambridge MA, Polity Press, 1993), pp. 65–70 and 98–100. This author seems to implicitly adopt a similar view. Putting the emphasis on the peculiarity of the crime of aggression, he suggests that while this crime is characterized by a very close relationship between state and individual responsibility, a different solution could be adopted with respect to other international crimes.

On the one hand, this option presupposes the existence of a category of individual crimes based on a complete dissociation between the conduct of the state and that of natural persons, and entailing no relationship between state and individual responsibility. In particular, the punishment of those responsible for such crimes depends on the application of primary and secondary norms that are totally separate from those governing aggravated state responsibility. It is true that international practice shows a tendency to keep state and individual responsibility separate, and to apply the principle of individual criminal liability in a very rigorous manner. It is also true that certain international crimes can be carried out by isolated individuals on their own initiative, and not as a consequence of a state or group criminal policy.[3] However, the foregoing analysis has revealed that even though these are isolated crimes, the same prohibition applies to states and that, if committed by state organs, they entail at least ordinary state responsibility. This is, for example, what happens with war crimes that can be perpetrated in perfect isolation by single soldiers or the autonomous crime of torture. The breach of these primary norms always entails a dual responsibility under international law, because individual criminal liability for such crimes overlaps with state responsibility.

On the other hand, this option presupposes the existence of a separate category of international crimes based on the identity between the conduct of the state and that of its organs, and in respect of which the punishment of the responsible state organs can be seen as a sanction against the author state. In the works of international law scholars it is possible to find various references to "system crimes",[4] "state-sponsored crimes",[5] and crimes committed by the "state as a whole".[6] However, these scholars do not appear to agree on a precise definition of this category of

---

[3] *See* the definition of individual crimes advanced by B.V.A. Röling, 'Aspects of the Criminal Responsibility for Violations of the Laws of War', in A. Cassese (ed.), *The New Humanitarian Law of Armed Conflict* (Napoli, Editoriale Scientifica, 1980), p. 203, and P.-M. Dupuy, 'International Criminal Responsibility of the Individual and International Responsibility of the State', in A. Cassese *et al.* (eds.), *The Rome Statute of the International Criminal Court. A Commentary*, vol. II (Oxford, Oxford University Press, 2002), p. 1088.

[4] B.V.A. Röling, 'The Significance of the Laws of War', in A. Cassese (ed.), *Current Problems of International Law* (Milano, Giuffré, 1975), pp. 137–139; A. Bos, 'Crimes of State: In Need of Legal Rules?', in G. Kreijen (ed.), *State, Sovereignty, and International Governance* (Oxford, Oxford University Press, 2002), *passim*.

[5] B.M. Yarnold, 'The Doctrinal Basis for the International Criminalization Process', in M.C. Bassiouni (ed.), *International Criminal Law*, vol. I (Ardsley, Transnational Publishers, 1999), p. 148.

[6] A. Nollkaemper, 'Concurrence between Individual Responsibility and State Responsibility in International Law', 52 *ICLQ* (2003), p. 623. Similarly, some Italian authors refer to crimes "*riconducibili alla complessiva organizzazione dello Stato*". *See* M. Iovane, *La tutela dei valori fondamentali nel diritto internazionale* (Napoli, Editoriale scientifica, 2000), pp. 516, and 560–561; P. De Sena, *Diritto internazionale e immunità funzionale degli organi statali* (Milano, Giuffré, 1996), pp. 167, 176, 182, and 185–187; F. Lattanzi, 'Riflessioni sulla competenza di una Corte penale internazionale', 76 *Riv. Dir. Int.* (1993), p. 674.

international crimes, which must necessarily be committed by states. The analysis of international practice has revealed that only the crime of aggression requires an explicit link between the establishment of the state act of aggression and the crime of aggression entailing individual criminal liability, and that the same could probably be said of certain war crimes which require a larger involvement of the state military apparatus to be carried out.

However, this overlap of primary norms whose breach entails both state and individual responsibility does not automatically imply a corresponding unity at the level of secondary norms. If we take aggression, for instance, the study of international practice shows that the regime of individual criminal liability remains separated from the regime of aggravated state responsibility. Not only there is a tendency to maintain a separation in the establishment of state and individual responsibility for aggression, but a finding of (aggravated) state responsibility for aggression does not automatically entail the individual criminal liability of state leaders for the same serious breach. Individuals can always be found not guilty because they lacked the required *mens rea*, or they could rely on specific defences.[7]

Thus, one is led to assume that the fact that state and individual responsibility originate from the same material act of aggression does not necessarily imply that they are governed by the same secondary rules. As discussed above, the seriousness of the breach and the nature of the primary norm breached are the reasons why the conviction of a state leader for aggression cannot substitute the traditional consequences entailed under the law of state responsibility with respect to the author state.

Accordingly, this second option must also be set aside, since it can hardly be reconciled with the results emerging from the analysis of international practice. If it is particularly difficult to identify two separate categories of pure individual and state crimes, it is even more difficult to accept this option from a theoretical viewpoint. In fact, it would result in the parallel application of two conceptual schemes which in the end deny any relationship between state and individual responsibility for international crimes. This second option has the merit of reflecting the different features of certain international crimes, but from a theoretical viewpoint it seems no more than an *escamotage* to set aside again the legal relationship between these regimes. Although many clues point to the existence of such a relationship, this approach seems incapable of capturing its precise content.

---

[7] *See* A. Gattini, *Le riparazioni di guerra nel diritto internazionale* (Padova, Cedam, 2003), p. 689.

2. The Theoretical Framework Explaining the Complementarity Between State and Individual Responsibility for International Crimes

The elaboration of a general framework capable of explaining the relationship between state and individual responsibility for international crimes can only be based on the outcomes of the analysis of international practice.

International practice undoubtedly shows a certain complementarity between these regimes. Complementarity, however, remains a vague concept. To explain in its entirety the relationship between state and individual responsibility for international crimes, two apparently diverging aspects must be taken into account. First, the theoretical framework should be capable of explaining the separation of these regimes. Second, it must at the same time explain the various points of contact between these regimes which emerged from the foregoing analysis. In other words, one is inevitably brought to the conclusion that the sole general framework capable of explaining international practice in its entirety is a conceptual scheme according to which state and individual responsibility originate from the same primary rules but are governed by different sets of secondary rules.[8]

From a very general standpoint, this particular conception of the relationship between state and individual responsibility for international crimes can help to illustrate the fact that diverging views have been expressed by international law scholars in this regard. Indeed, it can explain why some authors have focused on the close links between these regimes, while others have rather pointed out the differences.[9] Similarly, the position adopted by the ILC and in particular the 'without prejudice' clauses inserted in the Draft Articles on State Responsibility and the Draft Code of Crimes respectively become clearer if one takes into account the need to keep the codification of these two sets of secondary norms separate, without excluding a certain overlap, and therefore a certain relationship between them.[10] Indeed, the challenging aspect of dealing with this relationship is to insert these regimes in a unitary legal framework without losing sight of their differences. The proposed conceptual scheme – according to which state and individual responsibility for

[8] For a historical explanation of the overlap of primary norms prohibiting core international crimes with respect to both states and individuals, *see* P. Fois, 'Sul rapporto tra i crimini internazionali dello Stato e i crimini internazionali dell'individuo', 87 *Riv. Dir. Int.* (2004), pp. 929–954. *See* also N.L. Reid, 'Bridging the Conceptual Chasm: Superior Responsibility as the Missing Link between State and Individual Responsibility under International Law', 18 *Leiden Journal of International Law* (2005), p. 797, who starts from the premise that state and individual responsibility "share origins depending on the primary obligations concerned, but they diverge when it comes to their practical content". However, Reid does not venture to demonstrate the validity of that basic assumption.

[9] *See* supra Chapter 2.

[10] *See* supra Chapter 1.

international crimes share a common origin but are governed by different sets of secondary norms – is an attempt to explain both sides of the complementarity between state and individual responsibility.

More specifically, this conceptual scheme seems capable of providing a general framework for the solution of the various problems entailed by the relationship and examined in Part II. The foregoing analysis of international practice shows that these problems substantially concern the need for a certain co-ordination between state and individual responsibility for international crimes. The mere need for co-ordination points to the existence of a legal relationship between these regimes, a co-ordination which otherwise would make no sense between two completely separate fields of international law. Therefore, the proposed conceptual scheme is shaped in a way which makes it possible to justify the co-ordination and the consistent application of two different sets of secondary rules both aiming at the protection of the most important obligations owed to the international community as a whole.

First, positing the unity of state and individual responsibility for international crimes at the level of primary norms is essential to determine the actual content of the relationship between these two regimes, as revealed by the analysis of international practice.

A crucial element of this relationship is the correspondence of the conduct amounting to an international crime and giving rise to both state and individual responsibility. Therefore, conduct triggering a dual responsibility under international law cannot be qualified differently (*i.e.*, as lawful or unlawful) according to whether that conduct is assessed from the perspective of state versus individual responsibility. There is little doubt that the same prohibition of aggression is provided for under a primary norm directed at both states and individuals. Thus, the same conduct (a state act of aggression) simultaneously leads to aggravated state responsibility and individual criminal liability under international law. The foregoing analysis shows that the same is true with respect to war crimes and torture, whose definition is: provided for under specific international conventions; corresponds to customary international law; and applies to both individual crimes and state wrongful acts.[11] Similarly, the prohibition of genocide provided for under customary international law and codified in the 1948 Convention is aimed at both state and individual conduct.[12] Finally, as discussed above, crimes against humanity do share a common

[11] The ILC, in its Commentary on Article 40 of the Draft Articles on State Responsibility (ILC, 'Report on the Work of its 53rd Session', *YILC* (2001), vol. II(2), p. 84), recognizes aggravated state responsibility for breaches of international humanitarian law, and for torture as defined in Article 1 of the 1984 Convention (para. 5).

[12] ICJ, *Genocide* case, supra the Introduction, note 1.

definition under both state and individual responsibility because they essentially include widespread and systematic violations of fundamental human rights.

Understood from this perspective, the unity of primary norms can satisfactorily explain the relationship between state and individual responsibility with respect to the elements of international responsibility examined above. As discussed in previous chapters, this relationship is not always clear because a certain conceptual confusion may concern the precise qualification of these elements as primary or secondary norms.

A good example comes from the consideration of the seriousness requirement. Although the issue may be controversial, the foregoing analysis leads to the conclusion that it is a requirement under the secondary rules of aggravated state responsibility. The seriousness element has no corresponding general requirement under international criminal law. As such, seriousness is a specific feature of aggravated state responsibility that needs not be co-ordinated with, and is independent from, the requirements of international criminal law. In practice, the existence of such a threshold in aggravated state responsibility does not exclude that the same conduct amounting to international crimes but not reaching the required degree of seriousness entail both individual criminal liability and ordinary state responsibility, as may happen for instance with respect to isolated war crimes. However, with respect to certain international crimes, the seriousness requirement is directly provided for under the relevant primary norms whose breach triggers a dual responsibility under international law. This is, for instance, the case of aggression or crimes against humanity. In such cases, the seriousness of the prohibited conduct represents an element common to both state and individual responsibility. To see whether both regimes are implicated by the same 'serious' conduct one needs only look at the way in which the relevant breaches are established. The analysis of international practice has shown that the same methodology is used to ascertain the carrying out of those collective crimes that are capable of triggering a dual responsibility under international law.[13] The material element of collective crimes is normally established having regard first to the general criminal context and then to the participation of the accused in this general context. This is confirmed by the increasing reliance on modes of collective liability (such as joint criminal enterprise) and the way in which these specific features of international criminal law have actually been interpreted and applied in international case law.[14] Therefore, when seriousness is a common element of state and individual responsibility (because it is directly provided for under the relevant primary norms), it is possible to conclude that it is essentially assessed in an analogous way under both aggravated state responsibility and individual criminal liability.

---

[13] *See* supra Chapter 3.

[14] *See* supra Chapter 6.

Similar reasoning can be applied to the *mens rea*/fault element. The *mens rea* is a specific requirement under international criminal law. While it has no formal correspondence under state responsibility, the latter body of international law does not exclude that the fault of the state may be taken into account if required by the relevant primary norms. The classical example is the crime of genocide. At first sight, this element might also be seen as potentially problematic, because it is unclear whether and to what extent it can entail a relationship between these regimes. However, from the standpoint of the proposed conceptual scheme, the relationship between state and individual responsibility is limited to those primary norms requiring a *mens rea*/fault element to trigger both kinds of responsibility. The foregoing analysis has revealed that what might have appeared to be a diverging element has proved to be a much closer link between state and individual responsibility.[15] While an overlap of the notions of *mens rea* and fault can be justified with respect to isolated crimes, as far as collective crimes are concerned these elements are established in a very similar way under both state and individual responsibility.

The unity of primary norms is also useful to explain another element of the relationship between state and individual responsibility for international crimes. The need to proceed with a consistent application of certain international norms (such as self-defence or belligerent reprisals) under both state and individual responsibility has just been recalled above. These rules can be conceived of as articulations of primary norms intended to narrow the scope of certain unlawful conduct. Thus, self-defence limits the scope of the crime of aggression and belligerent reprisals limit the scope of certain war crimes. Accordingly, the material conduct (of states or individuals) which can be justified as self-defence or belligerent reprisals cannot be unlawful under international law. A consistent application of these primary norms implies a clear link between state and individual responsibility for international crimes, or rather that neither state nor individual responsibility can be triggered with respect to conduct that is regarded as lawful under international law.[16]

The main consequence of the described unity at the level of primary norms is that the material conduct amounting to an international crime is the same under both regimes of international responsibility.[17] Once established for the purpose of, for example, state responsibility, the same conduct is relevant for (consistently) ascertaining individual criminal liability. In other words, there is a correspondence in the assessment of the structural elements of international crimes under both regimes of international responsibility. This link between the establishment of state

[15] *See* supra Chapter 4.

[16] *See* supra Chapter 5.

[17] For an analogous view as regards the crime of genocide, *see* E. Cannizzaro, 'Interconnecting International Jurisdictions: A Contribution from the Genocide Decision of the ICJ', 1 *European Journal of Legal Studies* (2007), <www.ejls.eu>.

responsibility and the establishment of individual responsibility for international crimes has recently been confirmed by the ICJ in the *Genocide* case. The Court noted that the fact-finding process of the ICTY falls within the evidence that merits special attention in the determination of state responsibility,[18] and it concluded that the relevant findings of fact made by the Tribunal at trial "should in principle be accepted as highly persuasive".[19] Another example concerns the situation in Darfur. The UN Commission of Inquiry had the task of establishing whether international crimes had occurred in that region, and the ICC actually relies on this previous establishment of the relevant facts when it has to pronounce on questions relating to the individual criminal liability of single defendants.[20] This does not mean that both state and individual responsibility are simultaneously and automatically ascertained. This requires a further step consisting of the application of the different rules governing aggravated state responsibility and individual criminal liability respectively. In other words, the (common) primary international norm concerns a certain prohibited material conduct. But it does not define its scope *ratione personae*. Thus, the determination of the applicable responsibility regime and, accordingly, the consequences of the commission of the crime depend on specific international rules on attribution and the relevant secondary rules governing either state or individual responsibility.

Second, the proposed conceptual scheme posits the separation of the sets of secondary norms governing aggravated state responsibility and individual criminal liability respectively. The foregoing analysis of international practice presents a collection of cases in which the separation and differences between the regime of state responsibility and that of individual criminal liability have been consistently reaffirmed. In particular, the establishment of state responsibility is independent from the establishment of state organs' criminal responsibility, and state responsibility for international crimes can be ascertained even though no state organ has previously been convicted for the same breaches allegedly committed at the state level.

---

[18] ICJ, *Genocide* case, supra the Introduction, note 1, para. 214. On the concurrent jurisdiction of the ICJ and the ICC, *see* M. Boot, *Genocide, Crimes against Humanity, War Crimes: Nullum Crimen Sine Lege and the Subject Matter Jurisdiction of the International Criminal Court* (Antwerpen, Oxford, New York, Intersentia, 2002), pp. 62–65. The jurisdiction of international criminal tribunals is only marginally taken into account by Y. Shany, *The Competing Jurisdictions of International Courts and Tribunals* (Oxford, Oxford University Press, 2003), pp. 39–40.

[19] *Ibid.*, para. 223. In fact, the Court saw no reason to depart from the similar findings of the ICTY, and concluded that the acts committed at Srebrenica were to be qualified as acts of genocide under international law (paras. 296–297). *See* also S. Rosenne, 'War Crimes and State Responsibility', in Y. Dinstein and M. Tabory (eds.), *War Crimes in International Law* (The Hague, M. Nijhoff, 1996), p. 104.

[20] *See*, for example, ICC, *Prosecutor v. Ahmad Harun and Ali Kushayb*, Pre-Trial Chamber, Decision on the Prosecution Application under Article 58(7) of the Statute, 27 April 2007, paras. 59 and 75, <www.icc-cpi.int>.

More generally, the foregoing analysis has revealed the separation between state and individual responsibility for international crimes lies at the level of the secondary rules. In particular, this separation concerns the different requirements and functions characterizing the two regimes of responsibility for international crimes.

For example, the seriousness requirement differentiates aggravated state responsibility from individual criminal liability when this element is not present as a general requirement of the relevant crime under international criminal law. As in the case of the autonomous crime of torture, the same conduct amounting to official torture and entailing individual criminal liability cannot also lead to aggravated state responsibility if it is not carried out in a widespread or systematic way.[21]

To give another example, the *mens rea* requirement remains a general feature of international criminal law, even though fault can play a role under state responsibility with respect to certain international crimes. Accordingly, the same conduct amounting to an international crime and entailing aggravated state responsibility cannot also lead to individual criminal liability where the *mens rea* is not proved beyond any reasonable doubt.

The functional analysis of state and individual responsibility confirms that these regimes pursue different objectives and are substantively different. Indeed, this separation easily explains the fact that state and individual responsibility for international crimes are generally ascertained by different bodies at the international level. While the unity at the level of primary norms can justify the existence of international bodies competent to adopt measures against both states and individuals responsible for the commission of international crimes, this situation can be problematic because one single organ would be called to adopt measures serving different functions at the international level.[22]

As already noted, even with respect to the crime of aggression a separation in the establishment of state and of individual responsibility is maintained. The reason for this separation lies in the completely different nature of state and individual responsibility. A distinction in the application of the rules pertaining to international criminal law and aggravated state responsibility respectively is maintained even though the relevant crime is defined in terms of state action and a previous determination of state responsibility is necessary to proceed against the defendants. This is not to deny that there are particularly close ties between state and individual responsibility for aggression, but these links do not justify a different solution as far as the independence of secondary norms of state and individual responsibility are concerned.

This general framework proves useful to explain two final aspects concerning the relationship between state and individual responsibility for international crimes.

---

[21] ICTY, *Prosecutor v. Furundžija*, TC, Judgment, 10 December 1998, para. 142.

[22] *See* supra Chapter 7.

As illustrated above, one of the major consequences of the described separation at the level of secondary norms is that state organs' criminal liability cannot substitute aggravated state responsibility for the same serious breach. However, the foregoing analysis has pointed out that under particular circumstances the punishment of state organs responsible for isolated international crimes can exhaust ordinary state responsibility for the same conduct. The reason for this apparently problematic solution is that individual responsibility in this case is better understood as a measure capable of preventing the relevant conduct from being regarded as unlawful. By contrast, with respect to serious crimes committed with a general involvement of the state apparatus it is not possible to regard the punishment of a few state organs as a measure exhausting aggravated state responsibility.[23]

On the other hand, the proposed conceptual scheme in no way intends to disregard another aspect emerging from the study of international practice, namely, the need to apply consistently certain international rules provided for under either state or individual responsibility where these rules are called into question in connection with the other body of international law. For example, there are cases in which the establishment of state and individual responsibility requires the application of the same legal standard. From the standpoint of state responsibility, the ICJ has recently made clear that the conviction of state organs is not a pre-requisite for holding a state responsible for international crimes.[24] Therefore, it is less likely that an international court dealing with state responsibility may need to apply the standards of international criminal law. This does not imply that, if an international court relies on international criminal law notions, it should not try to apply such

---

[23] *See* supra Chapter 8.

[24] *See* ICJ, *Genocide* case, supra the Introduction, note 1, paras. 180–182 ("State responsibility can arise under the Convention for genocide and complicity, without an individual being convicted of the crime or an associated one", para. 182). However, the judgment of the ICJ has been criticized for applying categories of international criminal law to the different issue of state responsibility for genocide. *See* A. Cassese, 'On the Use of Criminal Law Notions in Determining State Responsibility for Genocide', 5 *JICJ* (2007), pp. 875–887. In particular, P. Gaeta, 'Génocide d'Etat et responsabilité pénale individuelle', 111 *RGDIP* (2007), p. 276, holds that: "*La responsabilité pénale individuelle pour génocide, dans les différentes modalités prévues par la Convention, devient ainsi simplement la condition préalable de la responsabilité internationale de l'Etat. La Cour internationale de Justice se charge elle-même de constater cette responsabilité personnelle en déclarant vouloir appliquer les critères élevés d'établissement de la preuve normalement requis lorsqu'on a affaire à des accusations d'une telle gravité*". However, these two issues should be examined separately. With respect to the second issue concerning the standard of proof, it is true that the judgment of the ICJ is not entirely clear. The Court first adopted as general standard of proof a "fully conclusive" standard (para. 209), but then it applied to a typical question of state responsibility (*i.e., de facto* agency determination) the much more demanding "beyond reasonable doubt" standard (para. 422), which is typical of criminal law proceedings. On this specific issue, *see* A. Gattini, 'Evidentiary Issues in the ICJ's *Genocide* Judgment', 5 *JICJ* (2007), pp. 889–904.

notions consistently.[25] However, it is from the standpoint of international criminal law that international practice shows the most interesting cases in which the rules pertaining to the law of state responsibility have been called into question. Similar cases generally concern the application of rules of state responsibility to preliminary questions that are essential to establish the existence of a breach amounting to an international crime. Accordingly, it seems logical that the same rules should be applied in a consistent manner, independently of the specific field of international law in which they may be at stake.[26] For example, the rules on state agency determination must be consistently applied under the law of state responsibility and, if necessary, by international criminal tribunals having to decide the nature of an armed conflict.

Finally, the described theoretical framework for the relationship between state and individual responsibility for international crimes covers the different degrees of this relationship. Indeed, the relationship between state and individual responsibility can vary according to the different features of international crimes.

It is certainly true that there are crimes defined in terms of pure individual conduct. With respect to such individual crimes, there may nonetheless be a link between individual criminal liability and ordinary state responsibility, because for example defences must be co-ordinated or because the punishment of state organs can be seen as a form of satisfaction for the injured state. Or there may be a relationship between individual criminal liability and aggravated state responsibility if the same legal standards are applicable, as in the case of official torture and the need to apply the rules on state agency determination.

At the other end of the spectrum, it is possible to identify a few crimes rigorously defined in terms of state conduct, such as the crime of aggression. With respect to these crimes, there is certainly a much closer relationship between individual criminal liability and aggravated state responsibility. For example, with respect to aggression, a preliminary determination of the state act of aggression is necessary to proceed with the prosecution of state leaders. The determination of state aggression can be seen as one of the elements of the establishment of state leaders' criminal liability. Moreover, the relationship between state and individual responsibility for this category of crimes can concern other elements of crime, as for example defences.

In the middle lies the most critical category of international crimes, those addressing prohibited conduct that can only be carried out at the collective level. These

---

[25] On this specific issue, *see* A. Cassese, supra note 24, pp. 875–887. More generally, on the need to avoid the fragmentation of international law in the identification of the rules applicable to cases in which there is a limited jurisdiction of the ICJ, *see* E. Cannizzaro and B.I. Bonafè, 'Fragmenting International Law through Compromissory Clauses? Some Remarks on the Decision of the ICJ in the *Oil Platforms* Case', 16 *EJIL* (2005), pp. 481–497.

[26] *See* supra Chapter 7.

crimes proved to be a real challenge from the standpoint of international criminal law. With respect to collective crimes, no direct link exists between the regime of aggravated state responsibility and international criminal law. However, there is a clear trend in international practice pointing to a substantial similarity in the establishment of the facts entailing state and individual responsibility for collective crimes.[27] This is mainly due to the growing reliance on the elements of the general criminal context in the establishment of individual criminal liability and the development of specific modes of liability to address collective forms of participation in the commission of international crimes. Thus, international criminal tribunals have increasingly focused on collective criminality. The methodology used to establish the commission of international crimes has been widely discussed above. Generally, it is first established that international crimes have been perpetrated at the collective level, and then individual criminal liability is ascribed to the offenders that have contributed to a much broader criminal conduct. Increasingly, international criminal tribunals rely on modes of collective liability. Accordingly, they no longer evaluate the elements of international crimes with respect to the personal conduct of single perpetrators, but they establish that the material element has been carried out by a plurality of perpetrators and that they share the required psychological element. As illustrated above, the possibility to apply joint criminal enterprise to large-scale cases can lead to a substantial equivalence between the establishment of aggravated state responsibility and the establishment of state leaders' criminal liability. This is not to say that today international criminal tribunals engage in a previous establishment of aggravated state responsibility for the relevant crimes. What is certain is that they increasingly focus on the same conduct that can also trigger aggravated state responsibility.

At any rate, it is worth stressing that this classification of international crimes into individual, collective, and state crimes, is purely descriptive and in no way intends to be normative. The definition of international crimes may vary over time, and the relationship between state and individual responsibility may change accordingly.

3. *Towards a Dual Responsibility Paradigm?*

It remains to be seen, on the basis of how customary international law develops, whether the general conceptual scheme proposed here to appraise the relationship between state and individual responsibility for international crimes can be understood as an emerging dual responsibility paradigm. This study has tried to address

[27] *See* in particular Chapters 3, 4 and 5.

the various connections between these regimes that are so often disregarded. It seems undeniable that most international crimes give rise to two different forms of international responsibility, neither of which can exhaust the other. These two different forms of international responsibility need to be established in a consistent manner because they originate from the breach of the same primary norms and they accordingly focus on the same material conduct. These are two different regimes between which a relationship is nonetheless established by the fact that they both belong to the same international legal order.

This study has led to the conclusion that there is indeed a relationship between these regimes, and has proposed a theoretical framework which has been applied above to explain the various degrees of relationship between state and individual responsibility for international crimes. It must be added that this is at the same time a flexible framework that can take into account further developments of international law. For example, the degrees of relationship can change over time. Indeed, the relationship between state and individual responsibility essentially depends on the definitions of international crimes, that is, primary norms. If, in the future, international law undergoes a radical change and broadens the scope of self-defence to include the use of armed force against private individuals, the crime of aggression would be defined in totally different terms and private individuals could be charged with aggression. Inevitably, the degree of relationship between state and individual responsibility would change accordingly. To give another example, if the international community one day reaches an agreement on the definition of terrorism, this definition will necessarily entail a particular degree of relationship between state and individual responsibility,[28] and this relationship will vary according to the elements describe above.

The main result of this analysis is that aggravated state responsibility and individual criminal liability are to be seen under a unitary legal framework. State and individual responsibility for international crimes could have been conceived of in (almost) perfect isolation at a time when international criminal law was applied episodically under exceptional circumstances. But the rapid development of international criminal law and its increasing focus on mass atrocities and state leaders' liability have significantly brought to the surface the problems connected to the overlap between state and individual responsibility for the same crimes. Currently, it seems impossible to see them as perfectly isolated fields of international law.

[28] P.-M. Dupuy, 'States Sponsor of Terrorism: Issues of International Responsibility', in A. Bianchi (ed.), *Enforcing International Law Norms Against Terrorism* (Oxford, Hart Publishing, 2004), p. 3. For the view according to which a customary rule on the crime of international terrorism has already evolved in the world community, *see* A. Cassese, *International Criminal Law* (2nd edn, Oxford, Oxford University Press, 2008), pp. 162–178.

Finally, the conceptual scheme proposed here to describe the complementarity between state and individual responsibility for international crimes can be useful to explain a general trend emerging from international practice that raises concern among international law scholars, namely, the increasing individualization of international responsibility for international crimes.[29] Compliance with the prohibition of international crimes has taken two completely different paths as regards, on the one hand, the repression of individual crimes and, on the other, the reaction against states' most serious wrongful acts. Prosecutions for international crimes have been promoted both at the international and the domestic level, while international rules on the international community's means of reacting against international crimes committed by states are still at an embryonic level or, more precisely, at the level of progressive development. International law scholars have highlighted the risk that aggravated state responsibility could be reduced to an exceptional or secondary mechanism of reaction against the most serious breaches of community obligations.[30] From this perspective, attention is rather to be given to the unity of state and individual responsibility for international crimes and their complementary application that can be a useful tool in fostering respect with the most important obligations owed to the international community as a whole.

In light of these general trends, the limited relationship due to the identity of primary norms prohibiting core crimes shows all its importance. It can facilitate the assessment of aggravated state responsibility, even though it cannot eliminate the risk that individual criminal liability will become, in practice, a sort of substitute for state responsibility. International law scholars point out that individual criminal liability cannot be regarded as the *panacea* to international crimes, nor can it constitute an effective substitute for aggravated state responsibility.[31] In a recent case the ICTR has stressed the fact that international law today certainly has the potential to apply to individuals, but that international law remains a body of law

[29] *See* M.D. Evans, 'International Wrongs and National Jurisdiction', in M.D. Evans (ed.), *Remedies in International Law: The Institutional Dilemma* (Oxford, Hart Publishing, 1998), p. 175; A. Nollkaemper, supra note 6, p. 615; M. Wladimiroff, 'The Individual within International Law', in R. Thakur and P. Malcontent (eds.), *From Sovereign Impunity to International Accountability: The Search for Justice in a World of States* (Tokyo, New York, Paris, United Nations University Press, 2004), p. 111.

[30] According to Rao, "the very concept of State crimes was opposed as non-existent, undesirable, impractical and certainly not in conformity with the well-advanced and accepted trend in favour of individual criminal responsibility" (P.S. Rao, 'International Crimes and State Responsibility', in M. Ragazzi (ed.), *International Responsibility Today: Essays in Memory of Oscar Schachter* (Leiden, Boston, M. Nijhoff, 2005), p. 67).

[31] *See* supra Chapter 7, note 85 and accompanying text.

primarily made for states.[32] In an imperfect world, complicated by the co-existence of (among other actors) both states and individuals, the relationship between state and individual responsibility for international crimes cannot be avoided, and – as the ICJ has recently pointed out – the "duality of responsibility continues to be a constant feature of international law".[33]

[32] ICTR, *Prosecutor v. Muvunyi*, 12 September 2006, TJ, para. 459 ("The principle of individual responsibility for serious violations of international law is one of the key indicators of a paradigm shift from a view of international law as law exclusively made for and by States, to a body of rules with potential application to individuals"). *See* also the more general views expressed by E. McWhinney, 'Shifting Paradigms of International Law and World Order in an Era of Historical Transition', in S. Yee and W. Tieya (eds.), *International Law in the Post-Cold War World: Essay in Memory of Li Haopei* (London, New York, Routledge, 2001), p. 17.

[33] ICJ, *Genocide* case, supra the Introduction, note 1, para. 173.

Bibliography

Abellán Honrubia, V. 'La responsabilité internationale de l'individu', 280 *RCADI* (1999), pp. 135–428.

Abi-Saab, G. 'De la sanction en droit international. Essai de clarification', J. Makarczyk (ed.), *Theory of International Law at the Threshold of the 21st Century. Essays in Honour of K. Skubiszewski* (The Hague, Kluwer Law International, 1996), pp. 61–77.

Abi-Saab, G. and Abi-Saab, R.-M. 'Les crimes de guerre', in H. Ascensio *et al.* (eds.), *Droit international pénal* (Paris, Pedone, 2000), pp. 265–291.

Abi-Saab, G. 'The Uses of Article 19', 10 *EJIL* (1999), pp. 339–351.

Acquaviva, G. 'Unlawful Transfer, Unlawful Labour, Plunder, and Persecution: The State of the Law in *Prosecutor v. Naletilic and Martinovic*', 3 *The Global Community Yearbook of International Law & Jurisprudence* (2003), pp. 145–167.

——. 'Verso una responsabilità delle multinazionali per gravi violazioni dei diritti umani? Note in margine a *Doe v. Unocal*', 57 *Comunità Internaz.* (2002), pp. 593–611.

Ago, R. 'La colpa nell'illecito internazionale', in *Scritti giuridici in onore di Santi Romano*, vol. III (Padova, Cedam, 1940), pp. 177–206.

——. 'Le délit international', 68 *RCADI* (1939), pp. 415–554.

——. 'Obligations *Erga Omnes* and the International Community', in J.H.H. Weiler *et al.* (eds.), *International Crimes of State. A Critical Analysis of the ILC's Draft Article 19 on State Responsibility* (Berlin, De Gruyter, 1989), pp. 237–239.

Alfaro, R.J. 'La question de la définition de l'agression', 29 *RDISDP* (1951), pp. 367–381.

Alland, D. 'Countermeasures of General Interest', 13 *EJIL* (2002), pp. 1221–1239.

——. *Justice privée et ordre juridique international. Etude théorique des contre-mesures en droit international public* (Paris, Pedone, 1994).

Allott, P. *Eunomia. New Order for a New World* (Oxford, Oxford University Press, 1990).

Alston, P. and Steiner, H.J. *Human Rights in Context. Law, Politics, Morals. Text and Materials* (Oxford, Clarendon Press, 1996).

Ambos, K. 'Article 25', in Triffterer O. (ed.), *Commentary on the Rome Statute of the International Criminal Court* (Baden-Baden, Nomos, 1999), pp. 475–492.

——. 'Individual Criminal Responsibility in International Criminal Law: A Jurisprudential Analysis – From Nuremberg to The Hague', in G. Kirk McDonald and O. Swaak-Goldman (eds.), *Substantive and Procedural Aspects of International Criminal Law*, vol. I (The Hague, Kluwer Law International, 2000), pp. 1–31.

——. 'Joint Criminal Enterprise and Command Responsibility', 5 *JICJ* (2007), pp. 159–183.

——. 'Superior Responsibility', in A. Cassese *et al.* (eds.), *The Rome Statute of the International Criminal Court. A Commentary*, vol. I (Oxford, Oxford University Press, 2002), pp. 823–872.

Annacker, C. 'The Legal Régime of *Erga Omnes* Obligations in International Law', 46 *AJPIL* (1994), pp. 131–166.

Anzilotti, D. *Corso di diritto internazionale* (Roma, Athenaeum, 1923).

——. *Teoria generale della responsabilità dello Stato nel diritto internazionale* (Firenze, Lumachi, 1902).

Arangio-Ruiz, G. 'Fine prematura del ruolo preminente di studiosi italiani nel progetto di codificazione della responsabilità degli Stati: specie a proposito di crimini internazionali e dei poteri del Consiglio di sicurezza', 81 *Riv. Dir. Int.* (1998), pp. 110–129.

——. 'On the Security Council's "Law-Making"', 83 *Riv. Dir. Int.* (2000), pp. 609–725.
——. 'State Fault and the Forms and Degrees of International Responsibility: Questions of Attribution and Relevance', in *Mélanges Michel Virally. Le droit international au service de la paix de la justice et du développement* (Paris, Pedone, 1991), pp. 25–42.
——. 'The Establishment of the International Criminal Tribunal for the Former Territory of Yugoslavia and the Doctrine of Implied Powers of the United Nations', in F. Lattanzi and E. Sciso (eds.), *Dai Tribunali penali internazionali ad hoc a una Corte permanente* (Napoli, Editoriale Scientifica, 1996), pp. 31–45.
——. *Diritto internazionale e personalità giuridica* (Bologna, Cooperativa libraria universitaria, 1972).
Arbour, L. and Bergsmo, M. 'Conspicuous Absence of Jurisdictional Overreach', in A.M. Von Hebel *et al.* (eds.), *Reflections on the International Criminal Court. Essays in Honour of Adrian Bos* (The Hague, TMS Asser Press, 1999), pp. 129–140.
Arsanjani, M.H. 'Reflections on the Jurisdiction and Trigger Mechanism of the International Criminal Court', in A.M. Von Hebel *et al.* (eds.), *Reflections on the International Criminal Court. Essays in Honour of Adrian Bos* (The Hague, TMS Asser Press, 1999), pp. 57–76.
Ascensio, H. 'La responsabilité selon la Cour internationale de Justice dans l'affaire du génocide bosniaque', 111 *RGDIP* (2007), pp. 285–304.
—— *et al.* (eds.), *Droit international pénal* (Paris, Pedone, 2000).
Barberis, J.A. 'Nouvelles questions concernant la personnalité juridique internationale', 179 *RCADI* (1983), pp. 145–304.
Barboza, J. 'International Criminal Law', 278 *RCADI* (1999), pp. 9–199.
Bassiouni, M.C. (ed.), *Commentaries on the International Law Commission's 1991 Draft Code of Crimes against the Peace and Security of Mankind* (Erès, Paris, 1993).
—— (ed.), *International Criminal Law* (Ardsley, Transnational Publishers, 1999).
——. 'The Normative Framework of International Humanitarian Law: Overlaps, Gaps and Ambiguities', in M.C. Bassiouni (ed.), *International Criminal Law*, vol. I (Ardsley, Transnational Publishers, 1999), pp. 617–642.
——. 'The Sources and Content of International Criminal Law: A Theoretical Framework', in M.C. Bassiouni (ed.), *International Criminal Law*, vol. I (Ardsley, Transnational Publishers, 1999), pp. 3–125.
——. 'Universal Jurisdiction for International Crimes: Historical Perspectives and Contemporary Practice', 42 *Va. J. Int'l L.* (2001–2002), pp. 81–162.
——. *Crimes against Humanity in International Criminal Law* (The Hague, Kluwer Law International, 1999).
——. *Crimes against Humanity in International Criminal Law* (Dordrecht, M. Nijhoff, 1992).
Bassiouni, M.C. and Ferencz, B.B. 'The Crime Against Peace', in M.C. Bassiouni (ed.), *International Criminal Law*, vol. I (Ardsley, Transnational Publishers, 1999), pp. 313–347.
Bassiouni, M.C. *Le fonti e il contenuto del diritto penale internazionale. Un quadro teorico* (Milano, Giuffré, 1999).
Bassiouni, M.C. and Nanda, V.P. (eds.), *A Treatise on International Criminal Law* (Springfield, Thomas, 1973).
Bergsmo, M. 'Occasional Remarks on Certain State Concerns about the Jurisdictional Reach of the International Criminal Court, and Their Possible Implications for the Relationship between the Court and the Security Council', 69 *Nord. J. Int'l L.* (2000), pp. 87–113.
Berman, F. 'The Relationship between the International Criminal Court and the Security Council', in A.M. Von Hebel *et al.* (eds.), *Reflections on the International Criminal Court. Essays in Honour of Adrian Bos* (The Hague, TMS Asser Press, 1999), pp. 173–180.
Bernardini, A. 'Il Tribunale penale internazionale per la (ex) Iugoslavia: considerazioni giuridiche', 4 *I diritti dell'uomo, cronache e battaglie* (1993), pp. 15–25.

Bettati, M. 'Le crime contre l'humanité', in H. Ascensio *et al.* (eds.), *Droit international pénal* (Paris, Pedone, 2000), pp. 293–317.

Bierzanek, R. 'Reprisals as a Means of Enforcing the Laws of Warfare: The Old and the New Law', in A. Cassese (ed.), *The New Humanitarian Law of Armed Conflict* (Napoli, Editoriale Scientifica, 1980), pp. 232–257.

Blakesley, C.L. 'Jurisdiction, Definition of Crimes, and Triggering Mechanisms', 25 *Den. J. Int'l L. & Pol'y* (1996–7), pp. 233–280.

Bonafè, B.I. 'Finding a Proper Role for Command Responsibility', 5 *JICJ* (2007), pp. 599–618.

——. 'Imputazione all'individuo di crimini internazionali e immunità dell'organo', 87 *Riv. Dir. Int.* (2004), pp. 393–426.

——. 'Responsabilità dello Stato per fatti illeciti particolarmente gravi e responsabilità penale dell'individuo: due approcci a confronto', in M. Spinedi *et al.* (eds.), *La codificazione della responsabilità degli Stati alla prova dei fatti* (Milano, Giuffrè, 2006), pp. 501–517.

Boot, M. *Genocide, Crimes against Humanity, War Crimes: Nullum Crimen Sine Lege and the Subject Matter Jurisdiction of the International Criminal Court* (Antwerpen, Oxford, New York, Intersentia, 2002).

Bos, A. 'Crimes of State: In Need of Legal Rules?', in G. Kreijen (ed.), *State, Sovereignty, and International Governance* (Oxford, Oxford University Press, 2002), pp. 221–237.

Bouiffror, S. and Derycke, C. 'Les organisations criminelles', in H. Ascensio *et al.* (eds.), *Droit international pénal* (Paris, Pedone, 2000), pp. 167–179.

Boustany, K. and Dormoy, D. (eds.), *Génocide(s)* (Bruxelles, Bruylant, 1999).

Briggs, H.W. (ed.), *The Law of Nations: Cases, Documents and Notes* (New York, Appleton-Century-Crofts, 1952).

Broms, B. 'The Definition of Aggression', 154 *RCADI* (1977), pp. 299–400.

Brownlie, I. *International Law and the Use of Force by States* (Oxford, Clarendon Press, 1963).

——. *Principles of Public International Law* (6th edn, Oxford, Oxford University Press, 2003).

Burgers, J.H. and Danelius, H. *The United Nations Convention against Torture* (Dordrecht, M. Nijhoff, 1988).

Byers, M. 'Conceptualising the Relationship between *Jus Cogens* and *Erga Omnes* Obligations', 66 *Nord. J. Int'l L.* (1997), pp. 211–239.

Cameron, I. 'UN Targeted Sanctions, Legal Safeguards and the European Convention on Human Rights', 72 *Nord. J. Int'l L.* (2003), pp. 159–214.

Cançado Trinidade, A.A. 'Complementarity between State Responsibility and Individual Responsibility for Grave Violations of Human Rights: The Crime of State Revisited', in M. Ragazzi (ed.), *International Responsibility Today: Essays in Memory of Oscar Schachter* (Leiden, Boston, M. Nijhoff, 2005), pp. 253–270.

Cannizzaro, E. 'Entités non-étatiques et régime international de l'emploi de la force. Une étude sur le cas de la réaction israélienne au Liban', 111 *RGDIP* (2007), pp. 331–352.

——. 'Interconnecting International Jurisdictions: A Contribution from the Genocide Decision of the ICJ', 1 *European Journal of Legal Studies* (2007), <www.ejls.eu>.

——. 'Le operazioni aeree della NATO contro la Repubblica federale di Iugoslavia e il diritto umanitario', 84 *Riv. Dir. Int.* (2001), pp. 133–135.

Cannizzaro, E. and Bonafè, B.I. 'Fragmenting International Law through Compromissory Clauses? Some Remarks on the Decision of the ICJ in the *Oil Platforms* Case', 16 *EJIL* (2005), pp. 481–497.

Cannizzaro, E. *Il principio della proporzionalità nell'ordinamento internazionale* (Milano, Giuffrè, 2000).

Caracciolo, I. *Dal diritto penale internazionale al diritto internazionale penale* (Napoli, Editoriale Scientifica, 2000).

Carella, G. 'I *punitive damages* e la riparazione del danno morale in diritto internazionale', 67 *Riv. Dir. Int.* (1984), pp. 751–766.

——. 'Il Tribunale penale internazionale per la ex Iugoslavia', in P. Picone (ed.), *Interventi delle Nazioni Unite e diritto internazionale* (Padova, Cedam, 1995), pp. 463–517.

——. *La responsabilità dello stato per crimini internazionali* (Napoli, Jovene, 1985).

Carlebach, A. *Le problème de la faute et sa place dans la norme du droit international* (Paris, LGDJ, 1962).

Caron, D. 'State Crimes: Looking at Municipal Experience with Organizational Crime', in M. Ragazzi (ed.), *International Responsibility Today: Essays in Memory of Oscar Schachter* (Leiden, Boston, M. Nijhoff, 2005), pp. 23–30.

——. 'The Legitimacy of the Collective Authority of the Security Council', 87 *AJIL* (1993), pp. 552–588.

Carpenter, A.C. 'The International Criminal Court and the Crime of Aggression', 64 *Nord. J. Int'l L.* (1995), pp. 223–242.

Cassese, A. (ed.), *The New Humanitarian Law of Armed Conflict* (Napoli, Editoriale Scientifica, 1980).

——. 'Crimes against Humanity', in A. Cassese *et al.* (eds.), *The Rome Statute of the International Criminal Court. A Commentary*, vol. I (Oxford, Oxford University Press, 2002), pp. 353–378.

——. 'Genocide', in A. Cassese *et al.* (eds.), *The Rome Statute of the International Criminal Court. A Commentary*, vol. I (Oxford, Oxford University Press, 2002), pp. 335–351.

——. 'La communauté internationale et le génocide', in *Mélanges Michel Virally. Le droit international au service de la paix de la justice et du développement* (Paris, Pedone, 1991), pp. 183–194.

——. 'On the Use of Criminal Law Notions in Determining State Responsibility for Genocide', 5 *JICJ* (2007), pp. 875–887.

——. 'The *Nicaragua* and *Tadić* Tests Revisited in Light of the ICJ Judgment on Genocide in Bosnia', 18 *EJIL* (2007), pp. 649–668.

——. 'The Proper Limits of Individual Responsibility under the Doctrine of Joint Criminal Enterprise', 5 *JICJ* (2007), pp. 109–133.

——. 'When May Senior State Officials Be Tried for International Crimes? Some Comments on the *Congo v. Belgium* Case', 13 *EJIL* (2002), pp. 853–875.

—— *et al.* (eds.), *Problemi attuali della giustizia penale internazionale* (Torino, Giappichelli, 2005).

Cassese, A. and Delmas-Marty, M. (eds.), *Crimes internationaux et juridictions internationales* (Paris, PUF, 2002).

—— (eds.), *Juridictions nationales et crimes internationaux* (Paris, PUF, 2002).

Cassese, A. *Diritto internazionale* (Bologna, Il Mulino, 2006).

—— *et al.* (eds.), *The Rome Statute of the International Criminal Court. A Commentary* (Oxford, Oxford University Press, 2002).

——. *International Criminal Law* (Oxford, Oxford University Press, 2003).

——. *International Criminal Law* (2nd edn. Oxford, Oxford University Press, 2008).

——. *International Law* (Oxford, Oxford University Press, 2001).

Cavicchioli, L. 'Sull'elemento soggettivo nei crimini contro la pace e la sicurezza dell'umanità', 76 *Riv. Dir. Int.* (1993), pp. 1047–1097.

Charney, J.I. 'Third States Remedies in International Law', 10 *Mich. J. Int'l L.* (1989), pp. 57–101.

Christakis, T. *L'ONU, le Chapitre VII et la crise Yougoslave* (Paris, Montchrestien, 1996).

Clark, R.S. 'Crimes against Humanity', in G. Ginsburg and V.N. Kudriavtsev (eds.), *The Nuremberg Trial and International Law* (Dordrecht, M. Nijhoff, 1990), pp. 177–199.

Clark, R.S. and Sann, M. (eds.), *The Prosecution of International Crimes* (New Brunswick, London, Transaction Publishers, 1996).

Combacau, J. and Alland, D. 'Primary and Secondary Rules in the Law of State Responsibility: Categorising International Obligations', 16 *NYIL* (1985), pp. 81–109.

Condorelli, L. 'Conclusions Générales', in M. Politi and G. Nesi (eds.), *The International Criminal Court and the Crime of Aggression* (Aldershot, Ashgate, 2004), pp. 151–164.

——. 'Legalità, legittimità, sfera di competenza dei Tribunali penali *ad hoc* creati dal Consiglio di sicurezza delle Nazioni Unite', in F. Lattanti and E. Sciso (eds.), *Dai Tribunali penali internazionali ad hoc a una Corte permanente* (Napoli, Editoriale Scientifica, 1996), pp. 47–63.

——. 'Measures Available to Third States Reacting to Crimes of State', in J.H.H. Weiler *et al.* (eds.), *International Crimes of State. A Critical Analysis of the ILC's Draft Article 19 on State Responsibility* (Berlin, De Gruyter, 1989), pp. 264–266.

——. 'Responsabilité Etatique et Responsabilité Individuelle pour Violations Graves du Droit International Humanitaire', in L.C. Vohrah *et al.* (eds.), *Man's Inhumanity to Man. Essays on International Law in Honour of Antonio Cassese* (The Hague, M. Nijhoff, 2003), pp. 211–219.

——. 'The Continuity between Certain Principles of Humanitarian Law and the Concept of Crimes of States', in J.H.H. Weiler *et al.* (eds.), *International Crimes of State. A Critical Analysis of the ILC's Draft Article 19 on State Responsibility* (Berlin, De Gruyter, 1989), pp. 233–237.

Conforti, B. *Diritto internazionale* (7th edn, Napoli, Editoriale Scientifica, 2006).

——. *International Law and the Role of Domestic Legal Systems* (Dordrecht, M. Nijhoff, 1993).

——. *Le Nazioni unite* (7th edn, Padova, Cedam, 2005).

Crawford, J. *et al.*, 'The ILC's Articles on Responsibility of States for Internationally Wrongful Acts: Completion of the Second Reading', 12 *EJIL* (2001), pp. 963–991.

Cremer, H.-J. *et al.* (eds.), *Tradition und Weltoffenheit des Rechts. Festschriff für Helmut Steinberger* (Berlin, Springer, 2002).

Danner, A.M. and Martinez, J.S. 'Guilty Associations: Joint Criminal Enterprise, Command Responsibility, and the Development of International Criminal Law', 93 *Calif. L. Rev.* (2005), pp. 75–169.

Darcy, S. *Collective Responsibility and Accountability under International Law* (Leiden, Koninklijke Brill NV, 2007).

Daví, A. *Comunità europee e sanzioni economiche* (Napoli, Jovene, 1993).

De Hoogh, A. *Obligations* Erga Omnes *and International Crimes. A Theoretical Inquiry into the Implementation and Enforcement of the International Responsibility of States* (The Hague, Kluwer, 1996).

De Sena, P. 'Condotta di singoli organi e condotta dell'apparato statale in tema di colpa nell'illecito internazionale', 71 *Riv. Dir. Int.* (1988), pp. 525–553.

——. 'Immunità dell'individuo-organo dalla giurisdizione e responsabilità dello Stato: rapporti e problemi di coordinamento', in M. Spinedi *et al.* (eds.), *La codificazione della responsabilità degli Stati alla prova dei fatti* (Milano, Giuffré, 2006), pp. 467–499.

——. *Diritto internazionale e immunità funzionale degli organi statali* (Milano, Giuffré, 1996).

Degan, V.D. 'Responsibility of States and Individuals for International Crimes', in S. Yee and W. Tieya (eds.), *International Law in the Post-Cold War World: Essay in Memory of Li Haopei* (London, New York, Routledge, 2001), pp. 202–223.

Del Ponte, C. 'Prosecuting the Individuals Bearing the Highest Level of Responsibility', 2 *JICJ* (2004), pp. 516–519.

Delaplace, E. 'Torture', in H. Ascensio *et al.* (eds.), *Droit international pénal* (Paris, Pedone, 2000), pp. 369–376.

Delbrück, J. (ed.), *The Future of International Law Enforcement. New Scenarios – New Law?* (Berlin, Duncker & Humblot, 1993).

Derby, D.H. 'Torture', in M.C. Bassiouni (ed.), *International Criminal Law*, vol. I (Ardsley, Transnational Publishers, 1999), pp. 705–749.

Destexhe, A. and Foret, M. (eds.), *Justice internationale. De Nuremberg à La Haye et Arusha* (Bruxelles, Bruylant, 1997).

Dinstein, Y. 'Crimes against Humanity', in J. Makarczyk (ed.), *Theory of International Law at the Threshold of the 21st Century. Essays in Honour of K. Skubiszewski* (The Hague, Kluwer Law International, 1996), pp. 891–908.

Dinstein, Y. 'The Distinctions between War Crimes and Crimes against Peace', in Y. Dinstein and M. Tabory (eds.), *War Crimes in International Law* (The Hague, M. Nijhoff, 1996), pp. 1–18.

Dinstein, Y. and Tabory, M. (eds.), *War Crimes in International Law* (The Hague, M. Nijhoff, 1996).

——. (eds.), *International Law at a Time of Perplexity. Essays in Honour of Shabtai Rosenne* (Dordrecht, M. Nijhoff, 1989).

Dinstein, Y. *War, Aggression and Self-Defence* (2d edn. Cambridge, Cambridge University Press, 1994).

Dixon, R. 'Article 7 – Chapeau', in O. Triffterer (ed.), *Commentary on the Rome Statute of the International Criminal Court* (Baden-Baden, Nomos, 1999), pp. 122–129.

Dominicé, C. 'La question de la double responsabilité de l'Etat et de son agent', in E. Yakpo and T. Boumedra (eds.), *Liber Amicorum Judge Mohammed Bedjaoui* (The Hague, Kluwer Law International, 1999), pp. 143–157.

——. *L'ordre juridique international entre tradition et innovation. Recueil d'études* (Paris, PUF, 1997).

Donnedieu de Vabres, H. 'La théorie des délits de droit des gens en droit pénal interétatique', 28 *RDISDP* (1950), pp. 21–29, and pp. 159–172.

——. 'Le procès de Nuremberg devant les principes modernes du droit pénal international', 70 *RCADI* (1947), pp. 477–582.

——. *Les principes modernes du droit pénal international* (Paris, Recueil Sirey, 1928).

Dopagne, F. 'La responsabilité de l'Etat du fait des particuliers: les causes d'imputation revisitées par les Articles sur la responsabilité de l'Etat pour fait internationalement illicite', 34 *RBDI* (2001), pp. 492–525.

Drost, P.N. *Humanicide. International Governmental Crime Against Individual Human Rights* (Leiden, Sythoff, 1959).

——. *The Crime of State. Genocide* (Leiden, Sythoff, 1959).

Dugard, J. 'L'apartheid', in H. Ascensio *et al.* (eds.), *Droit international pénal* (Paris, Pedone, 2000), pp. 349–360.

Dumée, M. 'Le crime d'agression', in H. Ascensio *et al.* (eds.), *Droit international pénal* (Paris, Pedone, 2000), pp. 251–264.

Dupuy, P.-M. 'A General Stocktaking of the Connections between the Multilateral Dimension of Obligations and Codification of the Law of Responsibility', 13 *EJIL* (2002), pp. 1053–1081.

——. 'Crimes et immunités, ou dans quelle mesure la nature des premiers empêche l'exercice des secondes', 103 *RGDIP* (1999), pp. 289–295.

——. 'Faute de l'Etat et "fait internationalement illicite"', 5 *Droits* (1987), pp. 51–63.

——. 'International Criminal Responsibility of the Individual and International Responsibility of the State', in A. Cassese *et al.* (eds.), *The Rome Statute of the International Criminal Court. A Commentary*, vol. II (Oxford, Oxford University Press, 2002), pp. 1085–1099.

——. 'L'unité de l'ordre juridique international', 297 *RCADI* (2002), pp. 9–489.

——. 'Le fait générateur de la responsabilité internationale des Etats', 188 *RCADI* (1984), pp. 9–183.

——. 'Observations sur la pratique récente des 'sanctions' de l'illicite', 87 *RGDIP* (1983), pp. 505–548.

——. 'Quarante ans de codification de la responsabilité internationale des Etats. Un bilan', 107 *RGDIP* (2003), pp. 305–348.

——. 'States Sponsor of Terrorism: Issues of International Responsibility', in A. Bianchi (ed.), *Enforcing International Law Norms Against Terrorism* (Oxford, Hart Publishing, 2004), pp. 3–16.

——. *Droit international public* (7th edn, Paris, Dalloz, 2004).

Eagleton, C. 'Faut-il proscrire seulement les guerres d'agression ou toutes les guerres?', 36 *RGDIP* (1932), pp. 498–511.

Escudero Espinosa, J.F. *La Corte penal internacional y el Consejo de seguridad* (Madrid, Dilex, 2004).

Eser, A. 'Individual Criminal Responsibility', in A. Cassese *et al.* (eds.), *The Rome Statute of the International Criminal Court. A Commentary*, vol. I (Oxford, Oxford University Press, 2002), pp. 767–822.

Eustathiades, C.T. 'Les sujets du droit international et la responsabilité internationale. Nouvelles tendances', 84 *RCADI* (1953), pp. 397–633.

Evans, M.D. 'International Wrongs and National Jurisdiction, in M.D. Evans (ed.), *Remedies in International Law: The Institutional Dilemma* (Oxford, Hart Publishing, 1998), pp. 173–190.

Ferencz, B.B. 'The Crime of Aggression', in G. Kirk McDonald and O. Swaak-Goldman (eds.), *Substantive and Procedural Aspects of International Criminal Law*, vol. I (The Hague, Kluwer Law International, 2000), pp. 33–62.

——. *Defining International Aggression. The Search for World Peace. A Documentary History and Analysis* (Dobbs Ferry N.Y. Oceana Publications, 1975).

Finch, G.A. 'The Nuremberg Trial and International Law', 41 *AJIL* (1947), pp. 20–37.

Fischer, H. 'Grave Breaches of the 1949 Geneva Conventions', in G. Kirk McDonald and O. Swaak-Goldman (eds.), *Substantive and Procedural Aspects of International Criminal Law*, vol. I (The Hague, Kluwer Law International, 2000), pp. 63–93.

—— *et al.* (eds.), *International and National Prosecution of Crimes under International Law: Current Developments* (Berlin, Spitz, 2001).

Fletcher, G.P. *Basic Concepts of Criminal Law* (New York-Oxford, Oxford University Press, 1998).

Fletcher, G.P. and Ohlin, J.D. *Defending Humanity. When Force is Justified and Why* (Oxford, New York, Oxford University Press, 2008).

——. 'Reclaiming Fundamental Principles of Criminal Law in the Darfur Case', 3 *JICJ* (2005), pp. 539–561.

Focarelli, C. *Le contromisure nel diritto internazionale* (Milano Giuffré, 1994).

Fois, P. 'Sul rapporto tra i crimini internazionali dello Stato e i crimini internazionali dell'individuo', 87 *Riv. Dir. Int.* (2004), pp. 929–954.

Forlati Picchio, M.L. *La sanzione nel diritto internazionale* (Padova, Cedam, 1974).

Foucault, M. *Surveiller et punir. Naissance de la prison* (Paris, Gallimard, 1975).

Frowein, J.A. 'Reactions by Not Directly Affected States to Breaches of Public International Law', 248 *RCADI* (1994), pp. 345–437.

Frulli, M. *Immunità e crimini internazionali* (Torino, Giappichelli, 2007).

Gaeta, P. 'Génocide d'Etat et responsabilité pénale individuelle', 111 *RGDIP* (2007), pp. 272–284.

——. 'Il diritto internazionale e la competenza giurisdizionale degli Stati per crimini internazionali', in A. Cassese *et al.* (eds.), *Problemi attuali della giustizia penale internazionale* (Torino, Giappichelli, 2005), pp. 497–511.

——. 'On What Conditions Can a State Be Held Responsible for Genocide?', 18 *EJIL* (2007), pp. 631–648.

——. 'War Crimes Trials Before Italian Criminal Courts: New Trends', in H. Fischer *et al.* (eds.), *International and National Prosecution of Crimes under International Law: Current Developments* (Berlin, Spitz, 2001), pp. 751–768.

Gaja, G. 'Immunità squilibrate dalla giurisdizione penale in relazione all'intervento armato in Liberia', 86 *Riv. Dir. Int.* (2003), pp. 762–4.

——. 'The Long Journey towards Repressing Aggression', in A. Cassese *et al.* (eds.), *The Rome Statute of the International Criminal Court. A Commentary*, vol. I (Oxford, Oxford University Press, 2002), pp. 427–441.

——. 'The Respective Roles of the ICC and the Security Council in Determining the Existence of an Aggression', in M. Politi and G. Nesi (eds.), *The International Criminal Court and the Crime of Aggression* (Aldershot, Ashgate, 2004), pp. 121–124.

Gargiulo, P. 'The Controversial Relationship between the International Criminal Court and the Security Council', in F. Lattanzi and W.A. Schabas (eds.), *Essays on the Rome Statute of the International Criminal Court* (Ripa di Fagnano Alto, Il Sirente, 1999), pp. 67–103.

Garner, J.W. 'Punishment of Offenders against the Laws and Customs of War', 14 *AJIL* (1920), pp. 70–94.

Gattini, A. 'A Return Ticket to 'Communitarisme', Please', 13 *EJIL* (2002), pp. 1181–1199.

——. 'La notion de la faute à la lumière du projet de convention de la Commission du droit international sur la responsabilité internationale', 3 *EJIL* (1992), pp. 253–284.

——. 'Smoking/No Smoking: Some Remarks on the Current Place of Fault in the ILC Draft Articles on State Responsibility', 10 *EJIL* (1999), pp. 397–404.

——. *Le riparazioni di guerra nel diritto internazionale* (Padova, Cedam, 2003).

——. 'Evidentiary Issues in the ICJ's *Genocide* Judgment', 5 *JICJ* (2007), pp. 889–904.

Ginsburg, G. and Kudriavtsev, V.N. (eds.), *The Nuremberg Trial and International Law* (Dordrecht, M. Nijhoff, 1990).

Glaser, S. 'Culpabilité en droit international pénal', 99 *RCADI* (1960), pp. 467–593.

——. *Introduction à l'étude du droit international pénal* (Bruxelles, Bruylant, 1954).

Glueck, S. *The Nuremberg Trial and Aggressive War* (New York, Knopf, 1946).

Gowlland-Debbas, V. (ed.), *United Nations Sanctions and International Law* (The Hague, Kluwer Law International, 2001).

——. 'The Relationship between the Security Council and the Projected International Criminal Court', 3 *JACL* (1998), pp. 97–119.

Graefrath, B. 'Iraqi Reparations and the Security Council', 55 *ZaöRV* (1995), pp. 1–68.

——. 'Universal Criminal Jurisdiction and an International Criminal Court', 1 *EJIL* (1990), pp. 67–88.

Graven, J. 'Les crimes contre l'humanité', 76 *RCADI* (1950), pp. 433–607.

——. 'Principes fondamentaux d'un code répressif des crimes contre la paix et la sécurité de l'humanité', 28 *RDISDP* (1950), pp. 173–204, and 361–392.

Gray, C.D. *Judicial Remedies in International Law* (Oxford, Clarendon Press, 1987).

Green, L.C. 'International Crimes and the Legal Process', 20 *ICLQ* (1980), pp. 567–584.

Greenawalt, A.K.A. 'Rethinking Genocidal Intent: The Case for a Knowledge-Based Interpretation', 99 *Colum. L. Rev.* (1999), pp. 2259–2294.

Greenwood, C. 'The Twilight of the Law of Belligerent Reprisals', 20 *NYIL* (1989), pp. 35–69.

Gros Espiell, H. 'International Responsibility of the State and Individual Criminal Responsibility in the International Protection of Human Rights', in M. Ragazzi (ed.), *International Responsibility Today: Essays in Memory of Oscar Schachter* (Leiden, Boston, M. Nijhoff, 2005), pp. 151–160.

Gustafson, K. 'The Requirement of an 'Express Agreement' for Joint Criminal Enterprise', 5 *JICJ* (2007), pp. 134–158.

Hailbronner, K. 'Sanctions and Third Parties and the Concept of International Public Order', 30 *AVR* (1992), pp. 2–15.

Haquani, Z. 'La Convention des Nations Unies contre la torture', 90 *RGDIP* (1986), pp. 127–170.

Hart, H.L.A. *The Concept of Law* (Oxford, Clarendon Press, 1994) (originally published in 1961).

Henzelin, M. *Le principe de l'universalité en droit pénal international. Droit et obligation pour les Etats de poursuivre et juger selon le principe de l'universalité* (Bâle, Genève, Munich, Helbing & Lichtenhahn, 2000).

Higgins, R. 'The Relationship between the International Criminal Court and the International Court of Justice', in A.M. Von Hebel *et al.* (eds.), *Reflections on the International Criminal Court. Essays in Honour of Adrian Bos* (The Hague, TMS Asser Press, 1999), pp. 163–172.

Hogan-Doran, J. and Van Ginkel, B.T. 'Aggression as a Crime under International Law and the Prosecution of Individuals by the Proposed International Criminal Court', 43 *NILR* (1996), pp. 321–351.

Iovane, M. *La riparazione nella teoria e nella prassi dell'illecito internazionale* (Milano, Giuffré, 1990).

——. *La tutela dei valori fondamentali nel diritto internazionale* (Napoli, Editoriale scientifica, 2000).

Jones, J.R.W.D. 'Whose Intent is it Anyway?', in L.C. Vohrah *et al.* (eds.), *Man's Inhumanity to Man. Essays on International Law in Honour of Antonio Cassese* (The Hague, M. Nijhoff, 2003), pp. 467–480.

Jørgensen, N.H.B. 'A Reappraisal of Punitive Damages in International Law', 68 *BYIL* (1997), pp. 247–266.

——. *The Responsibility of States for International Crimes* (Oxford, Oxford University Press, 2000).

Jurovics, Y. *Réflexions sur la spécificité du crime contre l'humanité* (Paris, LGDJ, 2002).

Kalshoven, F. 'Belligerent Reprisals Revisited', 21 *NYIL* (1990), pp. 43–80.

——. 'Reprisals and the Protection of Civilians: Two Recent Decisions of the Yugoslavia Tribunal', in L.C. Vohrah *et al.* (eds.), *Man's Inhumanity to Man. Essays on International Law in Honour of Antonio Cassese* (The Hague, M. Nijhoff, 2003), pp. 481–509.

——. *Belligerent Reprisals* (Leiden, M. Nijhoff, 1971).

Kamto, M. 'Responsabilité de l'Etat et responsabilité de l'individu pour crime de génocide. Quels mécanismes de mise en œuvre?', in K. Boustany and D. Dormoy (eds.), *Génocide(s)* (Bruxelles, Bruylant, 1999), pp. 487–511.

Kaul, H.P. 'Towards a Permanent International Criminal Court. Some Observations of a Negotiator', 18 *HRLJ* (1997), pp. 169–174.

Kirgis, F.L. 'The Security Council's First Fifty Years', 89 *AJIL* (1995), pp. 506–539.

Kirk McDonald, G. and Swaak-Goldman, O. (eds.), *Substantive and Procedural Aspects of International Criminal Law* (The Hague, Kluwer Law International, 2000).

Kittichaisaree, K. *International Criminal Law* (Oxford, Oxford University Press, 2001).

Knoops, G.-J. *Defenses in Contemporary International Law* (Ardsley, Transnational Publishers, 2001).

Kress, C. 'L'organe *de facto* en droit international public. Réflexions sur l'imputation à l'Etat de l'acte d'un particulier à la lumière des développements récents', 105 *RGDIP* (2001), pp. 93–144.

——. 'The Darfur Report and Genocidal Intent', 3 *JICJ* (2005), pp. 562–578.

——. 'The Iraqi Special Tribunal and the Crime of Aggression', 2 *JICJ* (2004), pp. 347–352.

Lamb, S. '*Nullum crimen, nulla poena sine lege* in International Criminal Law', in A. Cassese *et al.* (eds.), *The Rome Statute of the International Criminal Court. A Commentary*, vol. I (Oxford, Oxford University Press, 2002), pp. 733–766.

Lattanzi, F. 'Riflessioni sulla competenza di una Corte penale internazionale', 76 *Riv. Dir. Int.* (1993), pp. 661–697.

——. *Garanzie dei diritti dell'uomo nel diritto internazionale generale* (Milano, Giuffré, 1983).

Lattanti, F. and Schabas, W.A. (eds.), *Essays on the Rome Statute of the International Criminal Court* (Ripa di Fagnano Alto, Il Sirente, 1999).

Lauterpacht, H. (ed.), *Oppenheim's International Law* (London, Longmans, 1940).

——. 'The Law of Nations and the Punishment of War Crimes', 21 *BYIL* (1944), pp. 58–95.

Lee, R.S. (ed.), *The International Criminal Court. Elements of Crimes and Rules of Procedure and Evidence* (Ardsley, Transnational Publishers, 2001).

——. *The International Criminal Court. The Making of the Rome Statute. Issues, Negotiations, Results* (The Hague, Kluwer, 1999).

Lehto, M. 'The ICC and the Security Council: About the Argument of Politicization', in M. Politi and G. Nesi (eds.), *The International Criminal Court and the Crime of Aggression* (Aldershot, Ashgate, 2004), pp. 145–150.

Lemkin, R. *Axis Rule in Occupied Europe* (Washington, Carnegie Endowment for International Peace, 1944).

Levy, A.G.D. 'Criminal Responsibility of Individuals and International Law', 12 *The University of Chicago Law Review* (1945), pp. 313–332.

Lippman, M. 'Genocide', in M.C. Bassiouni (ed.), *International Criminal Law*, vol. I (Ardsley, Transnational Publishers, 1999), pp. 589–613.

——. 'The History, Development, and Decline of Crimes Against Peace', 36 *The George Washington International Law Review* (2004), pp. 957–1055.

Loewenstein, A.B. and Kostas, S.A. 'Divergent Approaches to Determining Responsibility for Genocide', 5 *JICJ* (2007), pp. 839–857.

Lombois, C. 'La culpabilité en droit international', 24 *Annales de l'Université des sciences sociales de Toulouse* (1976), pp. 137–149.

Luzzatto, R. 'Responsabilità e colpa in diritto internazionale', 51 *Riv. Dir. Int.* (1968), pp. 53–107.

Macdonald, R.St.J. 'International Prohibitions Against Torture and Other Forms of Similar Treatment or Punishment', in Y. Dinstein and M. Tabory (eds.), *International Law at a Time of Perplexity. Essays in Honour of Shabtai Rosenne* (Dordrecht, M. Nijhoff, 1989), pp. 385–406.

Maison, R. 'Le crime de génocide dans les premiers jugements du Tribunal Pénal international pour le Rwanda', 103 *RGDIP* (1999), pp. 129–145.

——. 'Les poursuites pénales internationales comme modalité de réparation du crime d'Etat', in *Studi di diritto internazionale in onore di Gaetano Arangio-Ruiz*, vol. I (Napoli, Editoriale Scientifica, 2004), pp. 807–826.

——. *La responsabilité individuelle pour crime de l'Etat en droit international public* (Bruxelles, Bruylant, 2004).

Makarczyk, J. (ed.), *Theory of International Law at the Threshold of the 21st Century. Essays in Honour of K. Skubiszewski* (The Hague, Kluwer Law International, 1996).

Malekian, F. 'International Criminal Responsibility', in M.C. Bassiouni (ed.), *International Criminal Law*, vol. I (Ardsley, Transnational Publishers, 1999), pp. 153–221.

Mansfield, L. 'Crimes against Humanity: Reflections on the Fiftieth Anniversary of Nuremberg and a Forgotten Legacy', 64 *Nord. J. Int'l L.* (1995), pp. 293–341.

May, L. *Crimes Against Humanity: A Normative Account* (Cambridge, Cambridge University Press, 2005).

McCaffrey, S.C. 'Article 5: Responsibility of States', in M.C. Bassiouni (ed.), *Commentaries on the International Law Commission's 1991 Draft Code of Crimes against the Peace and Security of Mankind* (Erès, Paris, 1993), pp. 129–131.

McCormack, T.L.H. and Simpson, G.J. (eds.), *The Law of War Crimes: National and International Approaches* (The Hague, Kluwer Law International, 1997).

——. 'A New International Criminal Law Regime?', 42 *NILR* (1995), pp. 177–206.

McWhinney, E. 'Shifting Paradigms of International Law and World Order in an Era of Historical Transition', in S. Yee and W. Tieya (eds.), *International Law in the Post-Cold War World: Essay in Memory of Li Haopei* (London, New York, Routledge, 2001), pp. 3–17.

Meron, T. 'Classification of Armed Conflict in the Former Yugoslavia: *Nicaragua's* Fallout', 92 *AJIL* (1998), pp. 236–242.

——. '*Lex Lata*: Is there already a Differentiated Regime of State Responsibility in the Geneva Conventions?', in J.H.H. Weiler *et al.* (eds.), *International Crimes of State. A Critical Analysis of the ILC's Draft Article 19 on State Responsibility* (Berlin, De Gruyter, 1989), pp. 225–231.

Meyrowitz, H. *La répression des crimes contre l'humanité par les tribunaux allemands en application de la loi n.10 du Conseil de Contrôle Allié* (Paris, LGDJ, 1960).

Morelli, G. *Nozioni di diritto internazionale* (edn, Padova, Cedam, 1967).

Morris, V. and Scharf, M.P. *The International Criminal Tribunal for Rwanda* (Irvington-on-Hudson, Transnational Publishers, 1998).

Nollkaemper, A. 'Concurrence between Individual Responsibility and State Responsibility in International Law', 52 *ICLQ* (2003), pp. 615–640.

Nolte, G. 'From Dionisio Anzilotti to Roberto Ago: The Classical International Law of State Responsibility and the Traditional Primacy of a Bilateral Conception of Inter-state Relations', 13 *EJIL* (2002), pp. 1083–1098.

Ntanda Nsereko, D.D. 'Genocide: A Crime against Mankind', in G. Kirk McDonald and O. Swaak-Goldman (eds.), *Substantive and Procedural Aspects of International Criminal Law*, vol. I (The Hague, Kluwer Law International, 2000), pp. 113–140.

Nyiri, N.A. *The United Nations' Search for a Definition of Aggression* (New York, Peter Lang, 1989).

O'Keefe, R. 'Universal Jurisdiction. Clarifying Basic Concepts', 2 *JICJ* (2004), pp. 735–760.

Ohlin, J.D. 'Three Conceptual Problems with the Doctrine of Joint Criminal Enterprise', 5 *JICJ* (2007), pp. 69–90.

Oosterveld, V. 'The Elements of Genocide – The Context of Genocide', in R.S. Lee (ed.), *The International Criminal Court. Elements of Crimes and Rules of Procedure and Evidence* (Ardsley, Transnational Publishers, 2001), pp. 41–49.

Oosthuizen, G.H. 'Some Preliminary Remarks on the Relationship between the Envisaged International Criminal Court and the UN Security Council', 46 *NILR* (1999), pp. 313–342.

Palchetti, P. 'Il potere del Consiglio di sicurezza di istituire tribunali penali internazionali', 79 *Riv. Dir. Int.* (1996), pp. 413–438.

——. *L'organo di fatto dello Stato nell'illecito internazionale* (Milano, Giuffré, 2007).

Palmisano, G. 'Les causes d'aggravation de la responsabilité des Etats et la distinction entre 'crimes' et 'délits' internationaux', 98 *RGDIP* (1994), pp. 629–674.

——. 'Les garanties de non-répétition entre codification et réalisation juridictionnelle du droit: à propos de l'affaire LaGrand', 106 *RGDIP* (2002), pp. 753–790.

——. *'Colpa dello Stato e colpa dell'organo nella responsabilità internazionale: spunti critici di teoria e di prassi'*, 19–20 *Comun. e Stud.* (1992), pp. 623–755.

Pella, V.V. *La criminalité collective des Etats et le droit pénal de l'avenir* (Bucharest, State Printing Office, 1926).

——. *La guerre-crime et les criminels de guerre* (Neuchâtel, La Baconnière, 1964).

Pellet, A. 'Can a State Commit a Crime? Definitely, Yes!', 10 *EJIL* (1999), pp. 425–434.

——. 'La responsabilité des dirigeants pour crime international de l'Etat. Quelques remarques sommaires au point de vue du droit international', G. Doucet (ed.), Terrorisme, victimes et responsabilité pénale internationale (Paris, Calmann-Lévy, 2003), pp. 195–209.

——. 'La responsabilité pénale individuelle, alternative aux sanctions collectives?', in V. Gowlland-Debbas (ed.), *United Nations Sanctions and International Law* (The Hague, Kluwer Law International, 2001), pp. 105–116.

——. 'Le Tribunal criminel international pour l'ex Yougoslavie', 98 *RGDIP* (1994), pp. 7–60.

——. 'Présentation de la Ière Partie', in H. Ascensio *et al.* (eds.), *Droit international pénal* (Paris, Pedone, 2000), pp. 83–89.

——. 'Vive le crime! Remarques sur les degrés de l'illicite en droit international', in *Le droit international à l'aube du XXIème siècle – Réflexions de codificateurs* (New York, United Nations, 1997), pp. 287–315.

Perrin, G. 'La détermination de l'Etat lésé. Les régimes dissociables et les régimes indissociables', in J. Makarczyk (ed.), *Theory of International Law at the Threshold of the 21st Century. Essays in Honour of K. Skubiszewski* (The Hague, Kluwer Law International, 1996), pp. 243–247.

Piacente, N. 'Importance of the Joint Criminal Enterprise Doctrine for the ICTY Prosecutorial Policy', 2 *JICJ* (2004), pp. 446–454.

Picone, P. (ed.), *Interventi delle Nazioni Unite e diritto internazionale* (Padova, Cedam, 1995).

——. 'Interventi delle Nazioni Unite e obblighi *erga omnes*', in P. Picone (ed.), *Interventi delle Nazioni Unite e diritto internazionale* (Padova, Cedam, 1995), pp. 517–578.

——. 'La distinzione tra norme internazionali di *jus cogens* e norme che producono obblighi *erga omnes*', 91 *Riv. Dir. Int.* (2008), pp. 5–38.

——. 'Obblighi *erga omnes* e codificazione della responsabilità degli Stati', 88 *Riv. Dir. Int.* (2005), pp. 893–954.

——. 'Obblighi reciproci ed obblighi *erga omnes* nel campo della protezione internazionale dell'ambiente marino dall'inquinamento', in V. Starace (ed.), *Diritto internazionale e protezione dell'ambiente marino* (Milano, Giuffré, 1983), pp. 15–135.

——. 'Sul fondamento giuridico del Tribunale penale internazionale per la ex Iugoslavia', 51 *Comunità Internaz.* (1996), pp. 3–24.

——. *Comunità internazionale e obblighi erga omnes: studi critici di diritto internazionale* (Napoli, Jovene, 2006).

Plawski, S. *Etude des principes fondamentaux du droit international pénal* (Paris, LGDJ, 1972).

Politi, M. and Nesi, G. (eds.), *The International Criminal Court and the Crime of Aggression* (Aldershot, Ashgate, 2004).

Raab, D. 'Evaluating the ICTY and its Completion Strategy', 3 *JICJ* (2005), pp. 82–102.

Ragazzi, M. (ed.), *International Responsibility Today: Essays in Memory of Oscar Schachter* (Leiden, Boston, M. Nijhoff, 2005).

——. *The Concept of International Obligations Erga Omnes* (Oxford, Oxford University Press, 1997).

Randall, K.C. 'Universal Jurisdiction Under International Law', 66 *Texas Law Review* (1987–1988), pp. 785–841.

Rao, P.S. 'International Crimes and State Responsibility', in M. Ragazzi (ed.), *International Responsibility Today: Essays in Memory of Oscar Schachter* (Leiden, Boston, M. Nijhoff, 2005), pp. 63–80.

Ratner, S.R. 'The Relationship between the International Criminal Court and the Security Council: An Appraisal of the United States Position', in S.I.D.I. *Cooperazione fra Stati e giustizia penale internazionale. III Convegno. Siena 12 e 13 giugno 1998* (Napoli, Editoriale Scientifica, 1999), pp. 237–243.

Ratner, S.R. and Abrams, J.S. *Accountability for Human Rights Atrocities in International Law* (Oxford, Oxford University Press, 2001).

Reid, N.L. 'Bridging the Conceptual Chasm: Superior Responsibility as the Missing Link between State and Individual Responsibility under International Law', 18 *Leiden Journal of International Law* (2005), pp. 795–828.

Reydams, L. *Universal Jurisdiction. International and Municipal Legal Perspectives* (Oxford, Oxford University Press, 2003).

Rifaat, A.M. *International Aggression. A Study of the Legal Concept: Its Development and Definition in International Law* (Stockholm, Almqvist & Wiksell International, 1979).

Robinson, D. 'Defining 'Crimes against Humanity' at the Rome Conference', 93 *AJIL* (1999), pp. 43–57.

——. 'The Context of Crimes against Humanity', in R.S. Lee (ed.), *The International Criminal Court. Elements of Crimes and Rules of Procedure and Evidence* (Ardsley, Transnational Publishers, 2001), pp. 57–92.

Röling, B.V.A. 'Aspects of the Criminal Responsibility for Violations of the Laws of War', in A. Cassese (ed.), *The New Humanitarian Law of Armed Conflict* (Napoli, Editoriale Scientifica, 1980), pp. 199–231.

——. 'International Law and the Maintenance of Peace', 4 *NYIL* (1973), pp. 1–103.

——. 'The Significance of the Laws of War', in A. Cassese (ed.), *Current Problems of International Law* (Milano, Giuffré, 1975), pp. 133–155.

——. *The Tokyo Trial and Beyond. Reflections of a Peacemonger* (Cambridge MA, Polity Press, 1993).

Romano, C.P. *et al.* (eds.), *Internationalized Criminal Courts: Sierra Leone, East Timor, Kosovo, and Cambodia* (Oxford, Oxford University Press, 2004).

Rosenne, S. 'State Responsibility and International Crimes: Further Reflections on Article 19 of the Draft Articles on State Responsibility', 30 *NYU J. Int'l L. Pol.* (1997–1998), pp. 145–166.

——. 'War Crimes and State Responsibility', in Y. Dinstein and M. Tabory (eds.), *War Crimes in International Law* (The Hague, M. Nijhoff, 1996), pp. 65–106.

Rousseau, J.-J. *Du contrat social* (Paris, Gallimard, 1993) (originally published in 1762).

S.I.D.I. *Cooperazione fra Stati e giustizia penale internazionale. III Convegno. Siena 12 e 13 giugno 1998* (Napoli, Editoriale Scientifica, 1999).

Saland, P. 'International Criminal Law Principles', in R.S. Lee (ed.), *The International Criminal Court. The Making of the Rome Statute. Issues, Negotiations, Results* (The Hague, Kluwer, 1999), pp. 189–216.

Saldaña, Q. 'La justice pénale internationale', 10 *RCADI* (1925), pp. 223–429.

Salmon, J. 'L'intention en matière de responsabilité internationale', in *Mélanges Michel Virally. Le droit international au service de la paix de la justice et du développement* (Paris, Pedone, 1991), pp. 413–422.

Satchivi, F.A. *Les sujets de droit. Contribution à l'étude de la reconnaissance de l'individu comme sujet direct du droit international* (Paris-Montréal, L'Harmattan, 1999).

Schabas, W.A. 'Article 6', in O. Triffterer (ed.), *Commentary on the Rome Statute of the International Criminal Court* (Baden-Baden, Nomos, 1999), pp. 107–116.

——. 'International Sentencing: From Leipzig (1923) to Arusha (1996)', in M.C. Bassiouni (ed.), *International Criminal Law*, vol. III (Ardsley, Transnational Publishers, 1999), pp. 171–193.

——. 'Le génocide', in H. Ascensio *et al.* (eds.), *Droit international pénal* (Paris, Pedone, 2000), pp. 319–332.

——. *Genocide in International Law. The Crime of Crimes* (Cambridge, Cambridge University Press, 2000).

Scharf, M.P. 'Results of the Rome Conference for an International Criminal Court', *ASIL Insights*, August 1998, <www.asil.org>.

——. 'Trial and Error: An Assessment of the First Judgment of the Yugoslavia War Crimes Tribunal', 30 *NYU J. Int'l L. Pol.* (1998), pp. 167–200.

Schwarzenberger, G. *International Law as Applied by International Courts and Tribunals* (London, Stevens & Sons Limited, 1968).

Schwelb, E. 'Crimes against Humanity', 23 *BYIL* (1946), pp. 178–226.

Sciso, E. 'I rapporti fra Consiglio di sicurezza e Corte penale internazionale', in S.I.D.I. *Cooperazione fra Stati e giustizia penale internazionale. III Convegno. Siena 12 e 13 giugno 1998* (Napoli, Editoriale Scientifica, 1999), pp. 245–264.

Scobbie, I. 'The Invocation of Responsibility for the Breach of 'Obligations under Peremptory Norms of General International Law'', 13 *EJIL* (2002), pp. 1201–1220.

Scovazzi, T. *Corso di diritto internazionale, Parte I*, (Milano, Giuffré, 2000).

Shany, Y. *The Competing Jurisdictions of International Courts and Tribunals* (Oxford, Oxford University Press, 2003).

Shaw, M.N. 'Genocide and International Law', in Y. Dinstein and M. Tabory (eds.), *International Law at a Time of Perplexity. Essays in Honour of Shabtai Rosenne* (Dordrecht, M. Nijhoff, 1989), pp. 797–820.

Shraga, D. 'The Second Generation UN-Based Tribunals: A Diversity of Mixed Jurisdictions', in E. Skaar *et al.* (eds.), *Roads to Reconciliation* (Lanham, Lexington Books, 2005), pp. 55–79.

Shraga, D. and Zacklin, R. 'The International Criminal Tribunal for Rwanda', 7 *EJIL* (1996), pp. 501–518.

Sicilianos, L.-A. 'The Classification of Obligations and the Multilateral Dimension of the Relations of International Responsibility', 13 *EJIL* (2002), pp. 1127–1145.

——. *Les réactions décentralisées à l'illicite. Des contre-mesures à la légitime défense* (Paris, LGDJ, 1990).

Simma, B. 'From Bilateralism to Community Interest in International Law', 250 *RCADI* (1994), pp. 217–384.

Skaar, E. *et al.* (eds.), *Roads to Reconciliation* (Lanham, Lexington Books, 2005).

Solera, S. *Defining the Crime of Aggression* (London, Cameron May, 2007).

Sperduti, G. 'Sull'esenzione degli Stati stranieri dalla giurisdizione', 27 *Giurisprudenza completa della Corte suprema di cassazione. Sezioni civili* (1948), pp. 591–597.

——. 'Sulla colpa in diritto internazionale', 3 *Comun. e Stud.* (1950), pp. 79–104.

——. *L'individuo nel diritto internazionale* (Milano, Giuffré, 1950).

Spinedi, M. 'From One Codification to Another: Bilateralism and Multilateralism in the Genesis of the Codification of the Law of Treaties and the Law of State Responsibility', 13 *EJIL* (2002), pp. 1099–1125.

——. 'International Crimes of State. The Legislative History', in J.H.H. Weiler *et al.* (eds.), *International Crimes of State. A Critical Analysis of the ILC's Draft Article 19 on State Responsibility* (Berlin, De Gruyter, 1989), pp. 7–138.

——. 'La responsabilité de l'État pour 'crime': une responsabilité pénale?', in H. Ascensio *et al.* (eds.), *Droit international pénal* (Paris, Pedone, 2000), pp. 93–114.

——. 'On the Non-Attribution of the Bosnian Serbs' Conduct to Serbia', 5 *JICJ* (2007), pp. 829–838.

—— *et al.* (eds.), *La codificazione della responsabilità degli Stati alla prova dei fatti* (Milano, Giuffré, 2006).

Steinberg, M. 'Le génocide au XXe siècle: lecture juridique ou historique?', in A. Destexhe and M. Foret (eds.), *Justice internationale. De Nuremberg à La Haye et Arusha* (Bruxelles, Bruylant, 1997), pp. 49–64.

Stern, B. 'La compétence universelle en France: les cas des crimes commis en ex-Yougoslavie et au Rwanda', 40 *GYIL* (1997), pp. 280–299.

Stone, J. *Aggression and World Order* (London, Stevens & Sons Limited, 1958).

——. *Conflict through Consensus* (Baltimore, Johns Hopkins University Press, 1977).

Sunga, L.S. *Individual Responsibility in International Law for Serious Human Rights Violations* (Dordrecht, M. Nijhoff, 1992).

——. *The Emerging System of International Criminal Law* (The Hague, Kluwer Law International, 1997).

Swaak-Goldman, O. 'Crimes against Humanity', in G. Kirk McDonald and O. Swaak-Goldman (eds.), *Substantive and Procedural Aspects of International Criminal Law*, vol. I (The Hague, Kluwer Law International, 2000), pp. 141–168.

Szurek, S. 'Historique. La formation du droit international pénal', in H. Ascensio *et al.* (eds.), *Droit international pénal* (Paris, Pedone, 2000), pp. 7–22.

Tams, C.J. 'All's Well That Ends Well. Comments on the ILC's Articles on State Responsibility', 62 *ZaöRV* (2002), pp. 759–808.

——. 'Do Serious Breaches Give Rise to Any Specific Obligations of the Responsible State?', 13 *EJIL* (2002), pp. 1161–1180.

——. *Enforcing Obligations* Erga Omnes *in International Law* (Cambridge, Cambridge University Press, 2005).

Taylor, T. *The Anatomy of the Nuremberg Trials* (New York, Knopf, 1992).

Thakur, R. and Malcontent, P. (eds.), *From Sovereign Impunity to International Accountability: The Search for Justice in a World of States* (Tokyo, New York, Paris, United Nations University Press, 2004).

Tomuschat, C. 'Ein internationales Strafgerichtshof als Element einer Weltfriedensordnunng', 49 *Europa Archiv* (1994), pp. 61–70.

——. 'International Law: Ensuring the Survival of Mankind on the Eve of a New Century', 281 *RCADI* (1999), pp. 9–438.

——. 'Reparation in Cases of Genocide', 5 *JICJ* (2007), pp. 905–912.

——. 'The Duty to Prosecute International Crimes Committed by Individuals', in H.-J. Cremer *et al.* (eds.), *Tradition und Weltoffenheit des Rechts. Festschriff für Helmut Steinberger* (Berlin, Springer, 2002), pp. 315–350.

Tornaritis, C.G. 'The Individual as a Subject of International Law and International Criminal Responsibility', in M.C. Bassiouni and V.P. Nanda (eds.), *A Treatise on International Criminal Law* (Springfield, Thomas, 1973), pp. 103–121.

Triffterer, O. (ed.), *Commentary on the Rome Statute of the International Criminal Court* (Baden-Baden, Nomos, 1999).

UNWCC, *History of the United Nations War Crimes Commission and the Development of the Laws of War* (London, H.M. Stationery Office, 1948).

Van Der Wilt, H. 'Genocide, Complicity in Genocide and International v. Domestic Jurisdiction', 4 *JICJ* (2006), pp. 239–257.

——. 'Joint Criminal Enterprise: Possibilities and Limitations', 5 *JICJ* (2007), pp. 91–108.

Van Sliedregt, E. 'Joint Criminal Enterprise as a Pathway to Convicting Individuals for Genocide', 5 *JICJ* (2007), pp. 184–207.

——. *The Criminal Responsibility of Individuals for Violations of International Humanitarian Law* (The Hague, TMC Asser Press, 2003).

Vandermeersch, D. 'La compétence universelle', in A. Cassese and M. Delmas-Marty (eds.), *Juridictions nationales et crimes internationaux* (Paris, PUF, 2002), pp. 589–611.

Verhoeven, J. 'La spécificité du crime de génocide', in A. Destexhe and M. Foret (eds.), *Justice internationale. De Nuremberg à La Haye et Arusha* (Bruxelles, Bruylant, 1997), pp. 39–47.

——. 'Le crime de génocide. Originalité et ambiguïté', 24 *RBDI* (1991), pp. 5–26.

Villalpando, S. *L'émergence de la communauté internationale dans la responsabilité des Etats* (Paris, PUF, 2005).

Vitucci, M.C. *Il Tribunale ad hoc per la ex Iugoslavia e il consenso degli Stati* (Milano, Giuffré, 1998).

Viviani, A. *Crimini internazionali e responsabilità dei* leader *politici e militari* (Milano, Giuffré, 2005).

Vohrah, L.C. *et al.* (eds.), *Man's Inhumanity to Man. Essays on International Law in Honour of Antonio Cassese* (The Hague, M. Nijhoff, 2003).

Von Hebel, A.M. *et al.* (eds.), *Reflections on the International Criminal Court. Essays in Honour of Adrian Bos* (The Hague, TMS Asser Press, 1999).

Weil, P. 'Towards Relative Normativity in International Law', 77 *AJIL* (1983), pp. 413–442.
Weiler, J.H.H. *et al.* (eds.), *International Crimes of State. A Critical Analysis of the ILC's Draft Article 19 on State Responsibility* (Berlin, De Gruyter, 1989).
Weiss, F. 'Time Limits for the Prosecution of Crimes against International Law', 53 *BYIL* (1982), pp. 163–196.
Wengler, W. 'Public International Law. Paradoxes of a Legal Order', 158 *RCADI* (1977), pp. 9–86.
Werle, G. *Principles of International Criminal Law* (The Hague, TMC Asser Press, 2005).
Wladimiroff, M. 'The Individual within International Law', in R. Thakur and P. Malcontent (eds.), *From Sovereign Impunity to International Accountability: The Search for Justice in a World of States* (Tokyo, New York, Paris, United Nations University Press, 2004), pp. 103–115.
Wyler, E. 'From "State Crime" to Responsibility for "Serious Breaches of Obligations under Peremptory Norms of General International Law"', 13 *EJIL* (2002), pp. 1147–1160.
Yakpo, E. and Boumedra, T. (eds.), *Liber Amicorum Judge Mohammed Bedjaoui* (The Hague, Kluwer Law International, 1999).
Yarnold, B.M. 'The Doctrinal Basis for the International Criminalization Process', in M.C. Bassiouni (ed.), *International Criminal Law*, vol. I (Ardsley, Transnational Publishers, 1999), pp. 127–152.
Yee, L. 'The International Criminal Court and the Security Council: Articles 13(b) and 16', in R.S. Lee (ed.), *The International Criminal Court. The Making of the Rome Statute. Issues, Negotiations, Results* (The Hague, Kluwer, 1999), pp. 143–152.
Yee, S. 'A Proposal to Reformulate Article 23 of the ILC Draft Statute for an International Criminal Court', 19 *Hastings Int'l & Comp. L. Rev.* (1995–6), pp. 529–538.
Yee, S. and Tieya, W. (eds.), *International Law in the Post-Cold War World: Essay in Memory of Li Haopei* (London, New York, Routledge, 2001).
Yengejeh, S.M. 'Reflections on the Role of the Security Council in Determining an Act of Aggression', in M. Politi and G. Nesi (eds.), *The International Criminal Court and the Crime of Aggression* (Aldershot, Ashgate, 2004), pp. 125–132.
Zappalà, S. 'L'universalità della giurisdizione e la Corte penale internazionale', in A. Cassese *et al.* (eds.), *Problemi attuali della giustizia penale internazionale* (Torino, Giappichelli, 2005), pp. 549–559.
Zegveld, L. *The Accountability of Armed Opposition Groups in International Law* (Cambridge, Cambridge University Press, 2002).
Zimmermann, A. 'The Creation of a Permanent International Criminal Court', 2 *Max Planck Y. UN L.* (1998), pp. 169–237.
Zoller, E. 'La définition des crimes contre l'humanité', *JDI* (1993), pp. 549–568.
Zourek, J. 'Enfin une définition de l'agression', 20 *AFDI* (1974), pp. 9–30.

List of Cases

International Court of Justice

Case Concerning the Application of the Convention on the Prevention and Punishment of the Crime of Genocide (Bosnia and Herzegovina v. Serbia and Montenegro), *Merits*, Judgment, 26 February 2007, <www.icj-cij.org>.

Case Concerning Armed Activities on the Territory of the Congo (Democratic Republic of the Congo v. Uganda), Judgment, 19 December 2005, <www.icj-cij.org>.

Case Concerning Avena and other Mexican Nationals (Mexico v. USA), Judgment, 31 March 2004, *ICJ Reports* 2004, p. 12 et seq.

Case Concerning Legality of Use of Force (Serbia and Montenegro v. Belgium), *Preliminary Objections*, Judgment, 15 December 2004, *ICJ Reports* 2004, p. 279 et seq.

Case Concerning Legality of Use of Force (Serbia and Montenegro v. Canada), *Preliminary Objections*, Judgment, 15 December 2004, *ICJ Reports* 2004, p. 429 et seq.

Case Concerning Legality of Use of Force (Serbia and Montenegro v. France), *Preliminary Objections*, Judgment, 15 December 2004, *ICJ Reports* 2004, p. 575 et seq.

Case Concerning Legality of Use of Force (Serbia and Montenegro v. Germany), *Preliminary Objections*, Judgment, 15 December 2004, *ICJ Reports* 2004, p. 720 et seq.

Case Concerning Legality of Use of Force (Serbia and Montenegro v. Italy), *Preliminary Objections*, Judgment, 15 December 2004, *ICJ Reports* 2004, p. 865 et seq.

Case Concerning Legality of Use of Force (Serbia and Montenegro v. Netherlands), *Preliminary Objections*, Judgment, 15 December 2004, *ICJ Reports* 2004, p. 1101 et seq.

Case Concerning Legality of Use of Force (Serbia and Montenegro v. Portugal), *Preliminary Objections*, Judgment, 15 December 2004, *ICJ Reports* 2004, p. 1160 et seq.

Case Concerning Legality of Use of Force (Serbia and Montenegro v. United Kingdom), *Preliminary Objections*, Judgment, 15 December 2004, *ICJ Reports* 2004, p. 1307 et seq.

Legal Consequences of the Construction of a Wall in the Occupied Palestinian Territory, Advisory Opinion, 9 July 2004, in *ICJ Reports* 2004, p. 136 et seq.

Case Concerning Oil Platforms (Islamic Republic of Iran v. United States of America), Judgment, 6 November 2003, in *ICJ Reports* 2003, p. 161 et seq.

Application for the Revision of the Judgment of 11 July 1996 in the Case Concerning the Application of the Convention on the Prevention and Punishment of the Crime of Genocide (Yugoslavia v. Bosnia and Herzegovina), *Preliminary Objections*, Judgment, 3 February 2003, *ICJ Reports* 2003, p. 7 et seq.

LaGrand Case (Germany v. United States of America), *Merits*, Judgment, 27 June 2001, *ICJ Reports* 2001, p. 466 et seq.

Case Concerning Legality of Use of Force (Yugoslavia v. Belgium), Request for the Indication of Provisional Measures, Order, 2 June 1999, *ICJ Reports* 1999, p. 124 et seq.

Case Concerning Legality of Use of Force (Yugoslavia v. Spain), Request for the Indication of Provisional Measures, Order, 2 June 1999, *ICJ Reports* 1999, p. 761 et seq.

Case Concerning Legality of Use of Force (Yugoslavia v. United States of America), Request for the Indication of Provisional Measures, Order, 2 June 1999, *ICJ Reports* 1999, p. 916 et seq.

Case Concerning the Application of the Convention on the Prevention and Punishment of the Crime of Genocide (Bosnia and Herzegovina v. Yugoslavia), *Preliminary Objections*, Judgment, 11 July 1996, *ICJ Reports* 1996, p. 595 et seq.

Legality of the Threat or Use of Nuclear Weapons, Advisory Opinion, 8 July 1996, ICJ *Reports* 1996, p. 226 et seq.

Case concerning East Timor (Portugal v. Australia), Judgment, 30 June 1995, *ICJ Reports* 1995, p. 102 et seq.

Case Concerning Military and Paramilitary Activities in and against Nicaragua (Nicaragua v. United States of America), *Merits*, Judgment, 27 June 1986, *ICJ Reports* 1986, p. 14 et seq.

Case Concerning United States Diplomatic and Consular Staff in Teheran (United States of America v. Iran), Judgment, 24 May 1980, *ICJ Reports* 1980, p. 3 et seq.

International Military Tribunal

International Military Tribunal, *Nuremberg* Judgment, 1 October 1946, 41 *AJIL* (1947), pp. 172–333.

International Criminal Tribunal for Former Yugoslavia

ICTY, "Final Report to the Prosecutor by the Committee Established to Review the NATO Bombing Campaign Against the Federal Republic of Yugoslavia", <www.un.org/icty/pressreal/nato061300.htm>.

ICTY, *Prosecutor v. Aleksovski*, IT-95-14/1, AC, Judgment, 24 March 2000, <www.un.org/icty>.

ICTY, *Prosecutor v. Aleksovski*, IT-95-14/1, TC, Judgment, 25 June 1999, <www.un.org/icty>.

ICTY, *Prosecutor v. Blagojević and Jokić*, IT-02-60, TC, Judgment, 17 January 2005, <www.un.org/icty>.

ICTY, *Prosecutor v. Blaškić*, IT-95-14, AC, Judgment on the Request of the Republic of Croatia for Review of the Decision of Trial Chamber II of 18 July 1997, 29 October 1997, <www.un.org/icty>.

ICTY, *Prosecutor v. Blaškić*, IT-95-14, AC, Judgment, 29 July 2004, <www.un.org/icty>.

ICTY, *Prosecutor v. Blaškić*, IT-95-14, TC, Judgment, 3 March 2000, <www.un.org/icty>.

ICTY, *Prosecutor v. Brđanin*, IT-99-36, AC, Judgment, 3 April 2007, <www.un.org/icty>.

ICTY, *Prosecutor v. Brđanin*, IT-99-36, TC, Judgment, 1 September 2004, <www.un.org/icty>.

ICTY, *Prosecutor v. Brđanin and Talić*, IT-99-36, TC, Decision on Form of Further Amended Indictment and Prosecution Application to Amend, 26 June 2001, <www.un.org/icty>.

ICTY, *Prosecutor v. Delalić et al.*, IT-96-21, AC, Judgment, 20 February 2001, <www.un.org/icty>.

ICTY, *Prosecutor v. Delalić et al.*, IT-96-21, TC, Judgment, 16 November 1998, <www.un.org/icty>.

ICTY, *Prosecutor v. Erdemović*, IT-96-22, AC, Judgment, 7 October 1997, <www.un.org/icty>.

ICTY, *Prosecutor v. Erdemović*, IT-96-22, TC, Judgment, 29 November 1996, <www.un.org/icty>.

ICTY, *Prosecutor v. Furundžija*, IT-95-17/1, TC, Judgment, 10 December 1998, <www.un.org/icty>.

ICTY, *Prosecutor v. Galić*, IT-98-29, AC, Judgment, 30 November 2006, <www.un.org/icty>.

ICTY, *Prosecutor v. Galić*, IT-98-29, TC, Judgment, 5 December 2003, <www.un.org/icty>.

ICTY, *Prosecutor v. Jelisić*, IT-95-10, AC, Judgment, 5 July 2001, <www.un.org/icty>.

ICTY, *Prosecutor v. Jelisić*, IT-95-10, TC, Judgment, 14 December 1999, <www.un.org/icty>.

ICTY, *Prosecutor v. Karadžić and Mladić*, IT-95-5/18, TC, Review of the Indictments pursuant to Rule 61 of the Rules of Procedure and Evidence, 11 July 1996, <www.un.org/icty>.

ICTY, *Prosecutor v. Kordić and Čerkez*, IT-95-14/2, AC, Judgment, 17 December 2004, <www.un.org/icty>.

ICTY, *Prosecutor v. Kordić and Čerkez*, IT-95-14/2, TC, Judgment, 26 February 2001, <www.un.org/icty>.

ICTY, *Prosecutor v. Krajišnik*, IT-00-39/40, TC, Decision on Prosecution Motions for Judicial Notice of Adjudicated Facts and for Admission of Written Statements of Witnesses pursuant to Rule 92*bis*, 28 February 2003, <www.un.org/icty>.

ICTY, *Prosecutor v. Krajišnik*, IT-00-39/40, TC, Judgment, 27 September 2006, <www.un.org/icty>.

ICTY, *Prosecutor v. Krnojelac*, IT-97-25, AC, Judgment, 17 September 2003, <www.un.org/icty>.

ICTY, *Prosecutor v. Krnojelac*, IT-97-25, TC, Judgment, 15 March 2002, <www.un.org/icty>.

ICTY, *Prosecutor v. Krstić*, IT-98-33, AC, Judgment, 19 April 2004, <www.un.org/icty>.

ICTY, *Prosecutor v. Krstić*, IT-98-33, TC, Judgment, 2 August 2001, <www.un.org/icty>.

ICTY, *Prosecutor v. Kunarac et al.*, IT-96-23&23/1, AC, Judgment, 12 June 2002, <www.un.org/icty>.

ICTY, *Prosecutor v. Kunarac et al.*, IT-96-23&23/1, TC, Judgment, 22 February 2001, <www.un.org/icty>.

ICTY, *Prosecutor v. Kupreškić et al.*, IT-95-16, TC, Judgment, 14 January 2000, <www.un.org/icty>.

ICTY, *Prosecutor v. Kvočka et al.*, IT-98-30/1, AC, Judgment, 28 February 2005, <www.un.org/icty>.

ICTY, *Prosecutor v. Kvočka et al.*, IT-98-30/1, TC, Judgment, 2 November 2001, <www.un.org/icty>.

ICTY, *Prosecutor v. Limaj*, IT-03-66, TC, Judgment, 30 November 2005, <www.un.org/icty>.

ICTY, *Prosecutor v. Martić*, IT-95-11, TC, Judgment, 12 June 2007, <www.un.org/icty>.

ICTY, *Prosecutor v. Martić*, IT-95-11, TC, Review of the Indictment pursuant to Rule 61 of the Rules of Procedure and Evidence, 8 March 1996, <www.un.org/icty>.

ICTY, *Prosecutor v. Milošević*, IT-98-29/1, TC, Judgment, 12 December 2007, <www.un.org/icty>.

ICTY, *Prosecutor v. Milutinović et al.*, IT-99-37, AC, Decision on Ojdanić's Motion challenging Jurisdiction – Joint Criminal Enterprise, 21 May 2003, <www.un.org/icty>.

ICTY, *Prosecutor v. Mrkšić*, IT-95-13, TC, Review of the Indictment pursuant to Rule 61 of the Rules of Procedure and Evidence, 3 April 1996, <www.un.org/icty>.

ICTY, *Prosecutor v. Naletilić and Martinović*, IT-98-34, TC, Judgment, 31 March 2003, <www.un.org/icty>.

ICTY, *Prosecutor v. Orić*, IT-03-68, TC, Judgment, 30 June 2006, <www.un.org/icty>.

ICTY, *Prosecutor v. Orić*, IT-03-68, AC, Judgment, 3 July 2008, <www.un.org/icty>.

ICTY, *Prosecutor v. Simić et al.*, IT-95-9, TC, Judgment, 17 October 2003, <www.un.org/icty>.

ICTY, *Prosecutor v. Stakić*, IT-97-24, AC, Judgment, 22 March 2006, <www.un.org/icty>.

ICTY, *Prosecutor v. Stakić*, IT-97-24, TC, Judgment, 31 July 2003, <www.un.org/icty>.

ICTY, *Prosecutor v. Strugar*, IT-01-42, AC, Judgment, 17 July 2008, <www.un.org/icty>.

ICTY, *Prosecutor v. Strugar*, IT-01-42, TC, Judgment, 31 January 2005, <www.un.org/icty>.

ICTY, *Prosecutor v. Tadić*, IT-94-1, AC, Decision on the Defence Motion for Interlocutory Appeal on Jurisdiction, 2 October 1995, <www.un.org/icty>.

ICTY, *Prosecutor v. Tadić*, IT-94-1, AC, Judgment, 15 July 1999, <www.un.org/icty>.

ICTY, *Prosecutor v. Tadić*, IT-94-1, TC, Judgment, 7 May 1997, <www.un.org/icty>.

ICTY, *Prosecutor v. Todorović*, IT-, 95-9/1TC, Judgment, 31 July 2001, <www.un.org/icty>.

ICTY, *Prosecutor v. Vasiljević*, IT-98-32, AC, Judgment, 25 February 2004, <www.un.org/icty>.
ICTY, *Prosecutor v. Vasiljević*, IT-98-32, TC, Judgment, 29 November 2002, <www.un.org/icty>.

International Criminal Tribunal for Rwanda

ICTR, *Prosecutor v. Akayesu*, ICTR-96-4, TC, Judgment, 2 September 1998, <www.ictr.org>.
ICTR, *Prosecutor v. Bagilishema*, ICTR-95-1A, TC, Judgment, 7 June 2001, <www.ictr.org>.
ICTR, *Prosecutor v. Elizaphan and Gerard Ntakirutimana*, ICTR-96-10 & ICTR-96-17, TC, Judgment, 21 February 2003, <www.ictr.org>.
ICTR, *Prosecutor v. Gacumbtsi*, ICTR-01-64, TC, Judgment, 17 June 2004, <www.ictr.org>.
ICTR, *Prosecutor v. Kajelijeli*, ICTR-98-44A, TC, Judgment, 1 December 2003, <www.ictr.org>.
ICTR, *Prosecutor v. Kamuhanda*, ICTR-99-54A, AC, Judgment, 19 September 2005, <www.ictr.org>.
ICTR, *Prosecutor v. Kamuhanda*, ICTR-99-54A, TC, Judgment, 22 January 2004, <www.ictr.org>.
ICTR, *Prosecutor v. Kanyabashi*, ICTR-96-15, TC, Decision on the Defence Motion on Jurisdiction, 18 June 1997, <www.ictr.org>.
ICTR, *Prosecutor v. Karemera et al.*, ICTR-98-44-AR73, AC, Decision on Prosecutor's Interlocutory Appeal of Decision on Judicial Notice, 16 June 2006, <www.ictr.org>.
ICTR, *Prosecutor v. Karemera et al.*, ICTR-98-44-AR72, AC, Decision on Jurisdictional Appeals: Joint criminal enterprise, 12 April 2006, <www.ictr.org>.
ICTR, *Prosecutor v. Kayishema and Ruzindana*, ICTR-95-1, AC, Judgment, 1 June 2001, <www.ictr.org>.
ICTR, *Prosecutor v. Kayishema and Ruzindana*, ICTR-95-1, TC, Judgment, 21 May 1999, <www.ictr.org>.
ICTR, *Prosecutor v. Muhimana*, ICTR-95-1B, TC, Judgment, 28 April 2005, <www.ictr.org>.
ICTR, *Prosecutor v. Musema*, ICTR-96-13A, TC, Judgment, 27 January 2000, <www.ictr.org>.
ICTR, *Prosecutor v. Muvunyi*, ICTR-00-55A, TC, Judgment, 12 September 2006, <www.ictr.org>.
ICTR, *Prosecutor v. Nahimana et al.*, ICTR-99-52, TC, Judgment, 3 December 2003, <www.ictr.org>.
ICTR, *Prosecutor v. Ndindabahizi*, ICTR-01-71, TC, Judgment, 15 July 2004, <www.ictr.org>.
ICTR, *Prosecutor v. Niyitegeka*, ICTR-96-14, TC, Judgment, 16 May 2003, <www.ictr.org>.
ICTR, *Prosecutor v. Ntagerura et al.*, ICTR-99-46, AC, Judgment, 7 July 2006, <www.ictr.org>.
ICTR, *Prosecutor v. Ntagerura et al.*, ICTR-99-46, TC, Judgment, 25 February 2004, <www.ictr.org>.
ICTR, *Prosecutor v. Rutaganda*, ICTR-96-03, AC, Judgment, 26 May 2003, <www.ictr.org>.
ICTR, *Prosecutor v. Rutaganda*, ICTR-96-03, TC, Judgment, 6 December 1999, <www.ictr.org>.
ICTR, *Prosecutor v. Rwamakuba*, ICTR-98-44C, AC, Decision on Interlocutory Appeal Regarding Application of Joint Criminal Enterprise to the Crime of Genocide, 22 October 2004, <www.ictr.org>.
ICTR, *Prosecutor v. Semanza*, ICTR-97-20, TC, Judgment, 15 May 2003, <www.ictr.org>.
ICTR, *Prosecutor v. Simba*, ICTR-01-76, AC, Judgment, 27 November 2007, <www.ictr.org>.
ICTR, *Prosecutor v. Simba*, ICTR-01-76, TC, Judgment, 13 December 2005, <www.ictr.org>.

Inter-American Court for Human Rights

IACHR, *Case of the Plan de Sánchez Massacre v. Guatemala*, Judgment of 29 April 2004, *Annual Report of the Inter-American Court of Human Rights*, Series C, No. 105 (2004).

IACHR, *Myrna Mack Chang* Case, Judgment, 25 November 2003, *Annual Report of the Inter-American Court of Human Rights*, Series C, No. 101 (2003).

IACHR, *Godinez case*, Compensatory damages, Judgment, 21 July 1989, *Annual Report of the Inter-American Court of Human Rights*, Ser. C, No. 8 (1990).

IACHR, *Velásquez Rodriguez case*, Compensatory damages, Judgment, 21 July 1989, *Annual Report of the Inter-American Court of Human Rights*, Ser. C, No. 7 (1990).

IACHR, *Godinez Cruz*, Judgment, 20 January 1989, *Annual Report of the Inter-American Court of Human Rights*, Ser. C, No. 5 (1989).

IACHR, *Velásquez Rodriguez* Case, Judgment, 29 July 1988, *Annual Report of the Inter-American Court of Human Rights*, Series C, No. 4 (1988).

International Criminal Court

ICC, *Prosecutor v. Ahmad Harun and Ali Kushayb*, Pre-Trial Chamber, Decision on the Prosecution Application under Article 58(7) of the Statute, 27 April 2007, <www.icc-cpi.int>.

ICC, Paper on Some Policy Issues before the Office of the Prosecutor (ICC Policy Paper), September 2003, <www.icc-cpi.int>.

ICC, Summary of the Case: Prosecutor's Application for Warrant of Arrest under Article 58 Against Omar Hassan Ahmad Al Bashir, 14 July 2008, <www.icc-cpi.int>.

National Case Law

Belgian Assize Court of Bruxelles, *Butare Four* case, verdict of 8 June 2001, <www.asf.be>.

German Federal Supreme Court, *Sokolovic case*, 21 February 2001, BGHSt. 46, 292.

House of Lords, *Jones case*, Judgment of 29 March 2006, <www.publications.parliament.uk/pa/ld200506/ldjudgmt/jd060329/jones.pdf>.

House of Lords, *Regina v. Bartle and the Commissioner of Police for the Metropolis and others EX Parte Pinochet* (*Pinochet I*), 25 November 1998, 19 *HRLJ* (1998), p. 419 et seq.

House of Lords, *Regina v. Bartle and the Commissioner of Police for the Metropolis and others EX Parte Pinochet* (*Pinochet II*), 24 March 1999, 20 *HRLJ*, (1999), p. 61 et seq.

Israeli District Court, *Enigster Case*, 4 January 1952, 18 *ILR* (1951), p. 542 et seq.

Israeli Supreme Court, *Eichmann case*, 29 May 1962, 36 *ILR* (1968), p. 277 et seq.

Spanish Audiencia Nacional, *Cavallo case*, Decision of 12 September 2000, and Mexico Supreme Court, decision of 11 June 2003, <www.derechos.org>.

Spanish Audiencia Nacional, *Scilingo case*, Decisions of 25 March 1998, 11 May 1998, 4 November 1998, and 27 June 2003, and judgment of 19 April 2005, <www.derechos.org>.

Spanish Supreme Court, *Guatemala Generals* Case, Decision of 25 February 2003, <www.derechos.org>.

US Court of Appeals, Second Circuit, *Kadić v. Karadžić*, Decision on Subject Matter Jurisdiction, 13 October 1995, 70 F.3d 232.

US Court of Appeals, Sixth Circuit, *Demjanjuk case*, 31 October 1985, 776 F.2d 571.

US District Court, *Doe I v. Unocal Corp.*, 25 March 1997, 963 F. Supp. 880.

US District Court, *Tachiona v. Mugabe*, 30 October 2001, 169 F. Supp. 2d 259.

US Nuremberg Military Tribunal, *Flick and Others*, 22 December 1947, 14 *ILR* (1947), at 266.
US Nuremberg Military Tribunal, *Krauch and Others*, 29 July 1948, 15 *ILR* (1948), at 678.
US Nuremberg Military Tribunal, *Krupp and Others*, 30 June 1948, 15 *ILR* (1948), at 627.
US Nuremberg Military Tribunal, *Ohlendorf et al.*, 10 April 1948, 15 *ILR* (1948), at 656.
US Nuremberg Military Tribunal, *Von Weizsäcker et al.*, 14 April 1949, 16 *ILR* (1949), at 344.

Index

www.ingramcontent.com/pod-product-compliance
Lightning Source LLC
LaVergne TN
LVHW102103300926
849161LV00001B/13